BUILDING SMALL BOATS

BUILDING
SMALL BOATS

by Greg Rössel

A WoodenBoat Book

Second printing 2000

Cover Design: Olga Lange
Book Design: Lindy Gifford
Printed in the U.S.A.

Published by WoodenBoat Publications
P.O. Box 78, Naskeag Road
Brooklin, Maine 04616 USA

ISBN 0-937822-50-7

Library of Congress Cataloging-in-Publication Data
Rössel, Greg, 1951–
Building Small Boats / written and illustrated by Greg Rössel.
     p.   cm.
   Includes bibliographical references.
   ISBN 0-937822-50-7 (alk. paper)
     1. Wooden boats—Design and construction.
     2. Boatbuilding
     I. Title.
VM321.R68 1998   98-41593
623.8'44—dc21   CIP

Many thanks to all those good friends who freely offered kind advice, suggestions, debuggings, and encouragement:

Will Ansel, Jenny Bennett, Bret Blanchard, John Brooks, Harry Bryan, Jerry Cumbo, Eric Dow, Jennifer Elliott, Dean Pike, Chris Kulczycki, Rich Hilsinger, Matt (P.) Murphy, Matt (G.) Murphy, Mike O'Brien, Carolyn Page, Bernice Palumbo, Ric Pomilia, Ford Reid, Peter Spectre, Charley Tosi, and Roy Zarucci.

And especially to my wife Norma whose support was always there, whose patience (and humor) never flagged, and who graciously endured a year in a house immersed in a collapsed mineshaft of maritime research detritus.

INTRODUCTION

Since shortly after the end of World War II the demise of traditional wooden boat building has been predicted with monotonous regularity. Industry pundits have declared over and over that the public no longer has the temperament to deal with wood—at least not when they can go downtown and purchase the latest homogenized metalflaked muscle marvel exactly like their neighbor's. Who could ask for more?

Yet the wooden boat survives, and part of the reason why is that many do ask for more. Wood construction, easily customized without extensive retooling, offers unparalleled options. No other boatbuilding medium allows such easy design changes at low cost or is as versitile as wood. The raw materials are renewable, and the construction technology is simple and accessible.

For one-off construction, there is no competion. If you wish a fuel-efficient launch designed by William Hand, or an elegant pulling boat of the Rangeley style, or any other type, wood is the way to get it.

For repairability, wood is also a practical choice. Why? Wooden boats are built of individual pieces that can be replaced with relatively easily available materials.

For sheer beauty, wood has no competition.

Manufacturers of fiberglass boats know this. Witness their attempts to simulate wooden construction by casting plank lines into hulls and their extensive use of wood trim.

For an investment, wooden boats, properly maintained, can hold their own. Many have lasted for generations. Compare their track record with that of other big-ticket items, such as automobiles.

And for home construction, the wooden boat is ideal.

There are, however, a few matters that should be kept in mind by anyone who wishes to take up wooden boat building in a serious manner. Building a wooden boat isn't rocket science. It isn't black magic, either. You do not need a magic wand and a conical hat with stars and moons on it to create a good product. What you do need is patience.

Wooden boat building differs somewhat from house carpentry, in that there is a definite progression of steps. A wooden boat is an interlocked matrix, where the quality of the whole is dependent on the quality of the independent pieces comprising the whole.

There is a good reason for taking the time to do the job right. In the long run, it is easier and cheaper. Since the structure is interlocked, if you cheat on a piece in one step, you will pay for it in another—in time and material.

Our society is so used to "production" work that we sometimes forget that complex joinery takes longer than simple carpentry. It's tempting to take shortcuts, to jump past a step here and a step there, to leave off a dab here and neglect a time-consuming detail there.

"Get with the program! No slow-dancin'! After all, there's a job to be done, right?"

'T ain't so, pilgrim. There are good reasons why the principal adage of the competent boatbuilder is "measure twice and cut once."

The secret to success in this business is to think the project through before going into it. That's the "measure twice" part. If you have never done a particular task before, such as spiling a plank, write a checklist of all the necessary steps, then take your time working your way through it. That's the "cut once" part. The first plank will be slow; it always is. But don't worry, you will pick up speed with the next, and the next.

And now for an insurance pitch. Power tools, such as the bandsaw, are truly wonderful devices to have around the boatshop, cutting everything from graceful sweeps to stock-car-track tight turns, quickly and with great accuracy. That accuracy, however, can be a siren's call to disaster (or at least disappointment), as it encourages the user to cut "right-to-the-line." One miscue and the whole job can be botched.

Get in the habit of leaving a little extra as insurance. It's a lot easier to plane out that extra by hand than it is to add it—or worse, to have to make a new piece because adding won't work. Safer, too.

And don't look for perfection. We're not building a Steinway piano. The goal is just good old-fashioned clean workmanship—a job that fits well and looks good.

'Nuf said.

C. Greg Rössel
Boatbuilder
Troy, Maine

1 • A Boat and a Shop to Build It In

One of the great advantages of building in wood is the extraordinary variety and range of style in the designs available to the builder. A multitude of plans are out there, obtainable from designers, mail-order houses, and museums. The greatest challenge is selecting the right boat for you.

Selecting a Design

No design does everything well. The qualities that make for a slick pulling boat may not make for the best sailing vessel. If clamming is your forte, perhaps that svelte yacht tender you saw at the boat show may not be the answer. On the other hand, if your notion is to load up the family for a picnic on an island, that tender may be just what the doctor ordered.

Performance can sometimes come at the cost of stability, which is something to consider if young children are to be out in the boat alone.

If powerboating fits your bill, why not take a look at some of the designs from the 1920s and '30s? Designers of this period created swift and elegant craft suited for low-horsepower engines (not a bad alternative to the pernicious Cigarette boat).

How about one of the many versions of the dories and semi-dories that worked the New England coast? Seaworthy, easy to build, and as salty looking as can be, many of these hulls retain much of the qualities of a round-bottom boat at a fraction of the cost.

Keep in mind that bigger isn't always better. Indeed, some say there is an inverse ratio or at least a size-maintenance-use matrix that indicates the larger the boat is, the less it is used.

Which to choose? Although you can narrow down your choices by reading and talking to owners, the best way to choose is, if possible, to borrow, rent, or at least beg a ride in the boat in the waters in which you intend to use it. Perhaps that deep-draft daysailer may not be the best choice for the shallow bay near home after all. If the owner blanches at the sight of Ralph, your noble (and constant) Newfoundland canine companion, this may be an indication that this boat is a trifle too fancy for your anticipated use. How does the craft feel to you; how does it handle? Does it feel solid? Will it carry the expected payload safely?

Your next job, after tentatively selecting the design, is to consider the construction time and costs for the project, and the shop space required. Depending on the complexity of the design, your investment may be relatively modest to something quite grand in scale. For a first project, many home builders will select a classic hull with all the trimmings—a complex hull shape, with a complicated construction jig, ballast keel, and lots of varnish—in other words, the works. And a beautiful thing such a vessel is, but fast building, or cheap, it is not. Working part time and on weekends, in competition with the exigencies of home repair, auto payments, spousal commentary, and so on, this could turn into an extended project, indeed. Or worse, this noble vessel, unfinished, could be relegated to the back end of the shop awaiting its day as just another item at a tag sale.

To avoid such a grim fate, do a little research. Investigate and find someone who has built the boat you are considering and see what goes into building it. Will you need to hire help (or at least be able to dragoon that neighbor who is likely to be hanging around, gumming up the works, anyway) for the tough jobs? Where did the builder get the hardware and lumber? Will you need to buy extra tools? (Well, you probably did need them....) And most importantly, how long did the job take? The answers will help clarify the wisdom of your choice.

If your preferred design seems too grandiose, perhaps a bit smaller version might do the trick. Or maybe a simpler design will get you out on the water faster, instead of causing you to spend too much time in the shop.

After all these nettlesome problems have been solved, or at least you have figured a way around them, then it's time to buy those plans and start building!

☞ Don't Be Deterred by the Need to Loft

Many builders tend to limit their choice of plans to those that come with full-size patterns and templates. This is unfortunate. While the plans that are so endowed are usually quite good, their numbers are few. Lofting is not a difficult skill to learn (okay, there are a few tricks to it, but they are covered in detail in Chapter 7), and the learning time invested is worth it. After you have lofting under your belt, the available spectrum of plans suddenly opens from a mere handful to virtually thousands.

SETTING UP THE SHOP

Many a fine boat has been built under the spreading chestnut or coconut palm. And for many, such informality is the only alternative. But alfresco boatbuilding does have its down side—primarily the weather. Blizzards, Ark-launching rains, and blistering sun can all put a crimp into even the most productive builder's time schedule. If possible, appropriate shelter for your construction is the way to go.

A proper boatshop doesn't have to be large, swanky, or expensive—just effective. As it is axiomatic that no matter how large your shop is, it is still likely to seem too small, extra space can be obtained with properly laid out temporary structures.

Plan your shop by drawing out a floor plan. Boats are bulky affairs, and a shop that seemed spacious for cabinetry will suddenly seem rather claustrophobic after the addition of 18 feet of boat. A graphic approach is to make your drawing of the shop to scale, with scale cardboard cutouts of your bench, stationary milling machinery, storage racks, and the largest boat you expect to fit within. Much can be revealed in this intellectual exercise. For example, are those doors really large enough to allow the removal of the boat from the shop? (Yes, a boat too big for the shop doors really does exist.) Will you have enough room to swing and mill a plank? Planning ahead can save you time and money.

One way some builders deal with milling long stock in a short shop is to set up their equipment so they can run a plank through the table saw by going in one door and out another door, a window, or even a "doggie door." The same technique can be used when surfacing lumber with a power planer.

The workbench

One essential tool in any boatshop is a good, stout workbench for getting out planks and making spars. Make it as long as possible, and outfit it with at least two woodworking vises.

Yes, you can get by with sawhorses, but they are rarely satisfactory. Sawhorses usually must be anchored down to avoid energy-wasting movement, and usually they are difficult to clamp to.

You will need sawhorses, however, if not for a workbench. Make up a few substantial sets, as they will see yeoman service for a multitude of operations, such as sawing, clamping, painting, and as a convenient perch when answering the telephone or partaking restorative beverages.

Storage

Storage is always problematic in the boatshop. Lumber and hand tools take up a lot of room, and if they are not well organized, you can waste a tremendous amount of time searching for them.

Work out a plan for lumber storage. Will it be inside, outside, or overhead? Will you have inside racks for lumber you will be using immediately? If you store lumber outside, will you be able to get at it under five feet of snow? Wood is expensive. Can you afford not to have protected storage? Perhaps there is a local barn or warehouse in which you can lease inexpensive space.

While you're at it, figure out what you will be doing

with the wooden boat builder's blessing and bane—the vast, inevitable quantities of scrap wood.

You will need a safe place for paints, glues, and solvents. Consider a fireproof, lockable, metal cabinet.

Then there is the matter of fastenings. You'll be using a lot of them, in a multitude of sizes. Wall-mounted bins make a convenient place for storage and easy access. The same goes for sandpaper, metal rod, and miscellaneous hardware.

Small tool storage is yet another consideration. Both hand and electric tools must have a regular place, so you can find them when you need them. Tool chests work well for hand planes, as do wall racks for chisels, mallets, levels, and squares. Some builders prefer the convenience of under-bench stowage of electric tools, while others prefer a cabinet.

Lighting

Boatbuilding demands high-quality joinery, and having adequate light will make getting it a lot easier. The ubiquitous fluorescent "shop" lamps are inexpensive and easy to install. Adding the more pricey "natural" tubes will avoid the shop being bathed in a eerie, bluish cast. Natural light is great. If designing your shop from scratch, consider a row of windows on the sunny side.

Electrical power

Now is the time to make sure you have adequate electrical outlets, extension cords, and service for both 110 volts and 220 volts. Check your local electrical codes and/or electrician. Having enough well-grounded outlets nearby is significantly handier—and safer—than having extension cords snaking all over the shop floor like so many serpents waiting to trip you up. Drop cords from the ceiling allow for easy access to power while keeping cords from underfoot.

Be sure to include ground fault interruption (GFI) receptacles on every circuit that will be used outside or under damp conditions. A GFI is a supplementary circuit breaker that trips when it detects current differences too small to trip a conventional breaker but large enough to cause harm.

The Casablanca look

For ventilation, consider installing one or two of those old-fashioned ceiling fans. Boatshops are notorious for being difficult to heat in the winter, but they make up for it by being hot in the summer. Ceiling fans are great for distributing heat in the cold months, and they will provide cooling zephyrs when the weather is hot. All for pennies of electricity. What a deal!

Dealing with dust

Wooden boat building generates a lot of wood dust and shavings—enough on productive days to cover the floor like snow drifts. This aromatic detritus can become a real hazard underfoot and must be removed at regular intervals. Plan on outside storage in bins or barrels pending disposal. Better yet, install a dust-collection system that not only keeps the stuff off the floor but out of the air as well.

Safety

Finally, a few words on boatshop safety are in order here. A boatshop can be a hazardous place! Potential problems can come from a variety of sources, including fire from an overheated woodstove, a steam box, or a heat gun; spontaneous combustion from oil-soaked rags; and no end of problems from flammable liquids and boiling lead.

Put on your green plastic visor and survey the joint as though you were the agent for the Acme Pinch-Penny Insurance Company. How's that woodstove setup look to you now? That pile of shavings may be a little too close to the steam box, perhaps? How about that pile of rags you've been meaning to take out? Or maybe that thinner can with the rag stuffed in the spout where the lost cap would go? Isn't that nothing more than a good old-fashioned Molotov cocktail?

Take the time to go through the place and set it right. Check out the fire extinguisher or maybe get a new one. Take a peek in the first aid box and make sure it's topped up. (When was the last time you looked in there anyway?) Make sure there is more than a half-empty box of adhesive bandages.

When you are done, not only will the place be safer but also more pleasant and easier to work in.

2 • TOOLS

Few of the tools necessary for boatbuilding are what could be described as truly specialty items. Indeed, most can be found in a well-appointed multipurpose home workshop. Granted, "having the right tool for the right job" can make a job easier, but it doesn't guarantee perfection. Sometimes it seems as if having too many tools can be as problematic as having too few.

Tool acquisition can be habit forming. Siren-like woodworking catalogs are replete with glossy color photos of must-have whiz-bang implements and gizmos of every size and fashion that are, at best, of limited utility and, at worst, a waste of hard-earned cash. On the other hand, it is difficult to beat a tool kit containing a few reliable tools of decent quality for greasing the ways to the proper job. To that end, let's look at some tools and a few of their uses in the boatshop.

EDGE TOOLS

Low-angle (12 degrees) block plane

Probably the most useful plane in the shop, the low-angle block plane is the tool to use on end or cross-grain, or squirrelly-grained hardwoods. Not to be confused with its clunkier 20-degree cousin, the low-angle block is the sports car of planes—it is nimble, fast, and corners superbly. It is equally at home tuning up mating surfaces of joints, working a compound bevel into a plank, chamfering or relieving the edges of frames, and fairing and smoothing up a half model.

Jack plane

Fourteen inches in length, the jack is the workhorse of planes, used for general stock removal and fairing.

Fore plane

Eighteen inches in length, the fore plane is lighter to use than the longer jointer but still offers much the same benefits. It can be used for truing up mating pieces for transoms, rudders, and centerboards. It is also handy when used in a jig to cut scarf joints for planking (see Chapter 14).

Rabbet plane

A rabbet, also known as a rebate, is a cut or groove along or near the edge of a piece of wood that allows another piece to fit into it to form a joint. The rabbet plane will

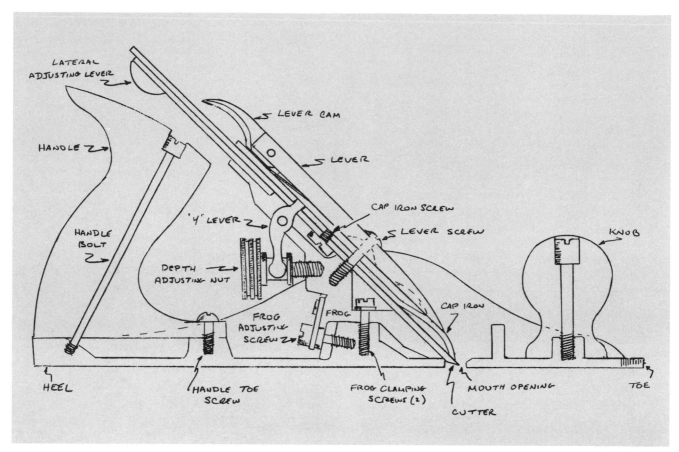

2-1: The anatomy of a Stanley No. 4 1/2 plane.

2-2: A well-used jack plane, the workhorse of the boatshop.

clean up that hand-cut rabbet in the stem, cut the gains for your lapstrake planking, make up shiplap staving, and perform a multitude of other operations that power tool manufacturers claim can only be done with a pricey router or dado cutter.

Spokeshave

The spokeshave is an old-timey, two-handed tool, sometimes confused with a drawknife, that will quickly shape, shave, and fine-tune all sorts of work, such as knees, breasthooks, rails, thwart chamfers, posts, oar looms, and half models.

Long-handled chisels

Do not be tempted by the short, run-of-the-mill, plastic-handled chisels—a.k.a., butt chisels—that inhabit the discount-chain hardware store bins. The "shorties" simply don't provide leverage or afford control when cutting

rabbets, inlaying patches, or paring off plugs or bungs. Also, garden-variety chisels often have short irons that can impede progress and be difficult to sharpen.

Get a decent set of chisels. This isn't a command to spend a fortune. The super-hardened Japanese chisels with brass ferrules and zebra wood handles don't really cut that much better than the less-fancy type, and they are considerably more heartbreaking when bashed into a hidden iron bolt—which you will be doing sooner or later if you are like any other boatbuilder I've known. All you need are moderately priced chisels that can be hit with authority. A selection of four (¼ inch, ½ inch, ¾ inch, 1 inch) should do the trick.

Wooden mallet

A good, solid mallet will save your tool handles and provide greater control over your work than a hammer will. The shape of the mallet head is a matter of personal preference; many boatbuilders opt for a flat-sided model, as it allows a good swing in tight quarters.

2-3: A small rabbet plane.

Sharpening stones

A coarse and a fine stone are all that are needed to keep most edge tools sharp. Traditional choices include stones of either natural or synthetic materials, used with either oil or water as a lubricant. Or you might consider the new monocrystalline diamond-embedded whetstones.

A handy rig to keep at hand as you work is a diminutive diamond whetstone with a folding handle that protects the stone when it is not in use. Small enough to fit in a tool apron pocket, the handy size and shape of this stone encourages you to use it often.

☞ Sharpening Edge Tools

It is axiomatic that a cheap, sharp chisel will cut better than an expensive, dull one. A sharp tool is akin to a scalpel and a joy to use. A dull one is akin to a stone ax. To do its job properly, an edge tool must start keen and be rehoned frequently.

There are many schools of thought concerning the business of sharpening. There are those who believe that only slow-speed motorized water-cooled grindstones provide the best edge. True, these units are the safest, as the water keeps the iron cool, eliminating any chance of burning the iron, and they produce a fine edge. But they are also expensive and, well, slow. Alternately, with a bit of care, a perfectly acceptable edge, quickly achieved, will come from a standard all-purpose bench grinder and a whetstone.

A couple of cautions

Always, without exception, wear a face shield when using a high-speed grinder! The wheel can produce a veritable cascade of metal flakes that can easily get in your eyes even if you are wearing glasses.

Always beware of overheating the steel while grinding, as it can spoil the cutting edge. This is easy to do by using a heavy hand to remove stock rapidly. This mani-fests itself as a gunmetal-blue color, usually starting at the edges of the tool. The way to avoid this is to keep the edge moving quickly across the stone; it is better to make more light passes than a few heavy ones. Keep a tin of water handy to quench the steel frequently, even after each pass.

While all edge tools have their own sharpening peculiarities, a plane iron is representative, so let's run through the steps for one of those.

Grinding a plane iron

When grinding an iron, you are looking for a hollow bevel; i.e., the curve of the face of the stone grinds equally across the face of the bevel. This technique eliminates "crown" on the bevel; the hollow that is produced creates a very small edge that only needs to have a "micro" bevel honed into it. As you work, it is but a simple matter to touch up that micro bevel and keep the edge sharp.

For practice, let's grind the bevel on an old plane iron. The chances are good that the current bevel is either flat or crowned.

Begin by setting the adjustable rest on the grinder to approximately 25 degrees. Without the wheel running, lay the iron on the rest with the center of the bevel touching the wheel. This is the position you will want to hold when you are actually grinding-in your bevel.

Some grinder rests have a clamp-like affair that runs in a track to hold the iron in the proper position. These are a rarity, however. To obtain the same result, a handy trick is to hold the iron tightly between your thumb and forefinger. Your forefinger will run along the bottom edge of the rest and act as a guide, always keeping the iron the same distance from the stone and the edge parallel to the axis of the stone.

Turn on the grinder and run the iron across the stone, lightly and quickly. Quench the iron in water at the end of the pass. After a few passes you will see a hollow begin to develop in the face of the bevel. (To check for this hollow and to be sure that no flatness or convexity is produced, roll the iron back and forth in the light.) Continue grinding and quenching until the hollow gets quite close to the edge of the iron. Remember to quench the iron often at this point for if it is ever to burn, this is the time.

Grinding creates a burr, or "wire" edge, and this must be removed by rubbing the back side of the iron against a whetstone. After you have knocked off the burr, hold the iron to a bright light and watch for reflections off the edge. If the edge reflects light, more grinding and quenching are called for. When there is no reflection, grinding will be finished and it will be time to hone the edge.

What about those nicks?

Alas, you will get nicks in your plane irons and chisels—it comes with the territory. This is especially true if you find yourself in the restoration business. Also, if you have been buying used tools at fleamarkets, you will surely have to deal with a nick or two. Before you hollow-grind the bevel, these imperfections must be ground out by drawing the iron square across the rotating stone in a manner similar to the above. Watch for burning, quench as you go, and check the edge often with a square.

Honing stones

There are a number of choices for honing stones, or whetstones. Which is best is totally a matter of personal preference. The old favorites are the natural or Arkansas stones, which are available in a variety of grits, from coarse to fine. These are lubricated with oil to prevent

2-4: A sharpening guide holds the tool at a precise, constant bevel against the surface of the stone.

the stone from clogging or glazing in use.

Synthetic whetstones, made by Norton and others, are used in the same way as the natural stones. The most common of this type is the combination stone: coarse on one side and fine on the other.

Another choice is the Japanese waterstone, which uses water instead of oil to prevent clogging. Waterstones tend to be softer than their Western counterparts, allowing a sharp surface to be continually exposed in use.

Finally, there are the diamond whetstones, a relatively new product wherein diamond dust is embedded in a plastic and metal "stone." Fast cutting, these stones come in a variety of grits and are lubricated with water.

A most useful variation on the diamond whetstone is a pocket diamond stone, in which the case folds out to become a handle. Used in a manner similar to an old-fashioned scythe stone, this handy rig allows (and encourages) you to sharpen your irons quickly and often at the bench or work site without having to go over to the sharpening table and break out the old whetstones.

When using any of the above stones, always wipe the surface free of any metal residue after use.

Honing the micro-bevel

To use a whetstone, lay the ground edge of your iron on the stone with the bevel edge down, then rock it up slightly so only the forward edge touches. This is the angle at which to hold the iron. Some woodworkers like to hold the iron with two hands and lock their elbows to their sides to hold the proper angle. Others will hold the iron in one hand and apply pressure on the end with the other hand. However you prefer to hold it, the edge of the iron should be honed on the stone with a random or figure-eight pattern to prevent wearing a trough in the stone over time.

The micro-bevel honed into a plane iron only has to be ¹⁄₁₆ to ³⁄₃₂ inch wide. Again, to check your work, study the edge for reflection under a bright light.

As with grinding, honing produces a little wire edge on the back side of the bevel. Remove it by lying the iron backside down on the whetstone and "wiping" against the stone. Alternately, strop the wire edge off on a piece of leather. Eyeball the edge one more time for reflected light; if there is none, you are in business.

Sharpening guides

If you are looking for extreme accuracy in honing a bevel at the exact angle desired and square to the edge, you might want to consider using one of the many mechanical sharpening guides now available. Although varying in appearance, all the guides work basically in the same manner. They use a frame on a roller with a clamping device to hold the iron in place with a certain amount of projection. The amount of projection determines the angle of the bevel.

To use a guide, install the cutting iron in the frame with the correct amount extending and push the bevel against the stone. As with the by-hand method, hone in a small micro-bevel, strop off the wire edge, and check for reflected light.

CUTTING TOOLS

Backsaw

For trimming, quick cutoffs, and general joinery. With many builders, however, it has been superseded by the Japanese Ryoba.

Crosscut saw, 8 or 10 point

For general cutting and making long wood short.

Japanese two-sided Ryoba saw

The Ryoba is a curious and extremely useful tool, a piranha-on-a-stick that slices through stock with little effort. With its centrally mounted handle, it closely resembles a pancake spatula. The blade has two sets of cutting teeth—one for ripping, the other for crosscutting. Like all Japanese saws, it cuts on the pull stroke, and is fast and extremely sharp. The thin blade allows it to make a very fine kerf and to bend for neatly cutting off bungs flush with a surface.

Hacksaw

Handy for slicing up round stock for bolts and drifts, as well as flat bronze and steel stock.

DRILLING TOOLS

Jobbers twist bits in a drill index

For all-purpose drilling in wood, metal, or plastic.

Speedbores or Forstner bits

For cutting large-caliber holes (such as counterbores for bolts). Speedbores are cheaper; Forstners do a better job.

Fuller bits

A Fuller bit is a combination tool composed of a tapered bit combined with an adjustable cutter that countersinks and counterbores for bungs (plugs). Available in various sizes, the Fuller is a good alternative to multi-drill boring for screw fastenings. Also available are plug cutters to match the counterbored holes.

Bell-hanger bits

Also known as installer's or electrician's bits, these extra-long bits are stock hardware-store items, are relatively inexpensive, are available in a good range of sizes, and are just the ticket for boring long bolt holes in the stem, keel, and deadwood, as well as holes for drifts in rudders and centerboards.

Tap and die set

For making all those homemade bolts, and repairing threads.

MEASURING DEVICES

25-foot tape measure

For all-purpose measuring.

Framing square

For lofting of lines, setup of the construction jig, and much more.

Combination square

The carpenter's combination square is a standard hardware store item. The handle, or head, of the tool has 90- and 45-degree faces; the blade slides in and out of the handle and can be locked in place. The combination square is a most handy tool, used for all those hard-to-square situations; it can also serve as a depth gauge, a marking gauge, and more. Most combination squares also have a scriber and level vial in the handle.

Wing dividers

For lofting, spiling planks, and laying out the locations for fastenings.

Pencil compass

Indispensable for drawing circles and arcs. Use a high-quality compass designed for carpentry, not a cheap grammar-school model from the five-and-ten.

Trammel points

Trammel points are used like a large-scale divider or compass for lofting lines, squaring, and scribing circles. They are available in pairs from quality tool suppliers and are mounted on a wooden beam supplied by the builder. The size of the arc to be drawn with the points is limited only by the length of the beam along which the points are slid.

Bubble level, 4-feet long

For setting up molds, leveling transoms, and plumbing stems, and as a handy straightedge.

Plumb bob

An all-around tool for determining a plumb line and truing up molds and other vertical members.

Sliding bevel gauge

For general layout, transferring angles on planking, fitting breasthooks and knees, and more. The standard house-carpenter's version is of limited utility in boatbuilding, however, as the chunky handle and locking screw always seem to get in the way. The best bevel gauges are made in the shop of two pieces of thin, flat metal stock held together with a rivet. (See how to make your own in Chapter 3.)

MISCELLANEOUS TOOLS

Hammer

A good quality 20-ounce hammer is the best all-around size for boatbuilding. It will be used constantly, from lofting to launching.

Light ball-peen hammer

For peening the cut end of a rivet over a rove.

Screwdrivers

Get a quality set. Cheapie ribbed-plastic handles can't compare to quality oval handles for a comfortable grip and significant leverage. Many stock drivers for slot-head screws have flared ends that can damage the edges of counterbored screw holes. These should be modified with a grinder to eliminate the flare.

Brace and bit

This tool will quickly spin in larger caliber screws as well as provide extra leverage in setting or removing reluctant fasteners. The ratchet action allows the user to "sneak-up" on

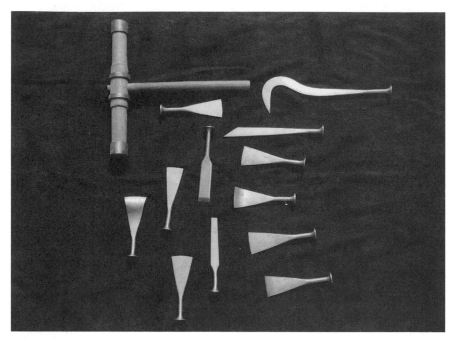

2-5: A selection of caulking tools, including several irons of special shapes, a reefing hook (top right), and a caulking mallet.

a fastener, drawing it in slowly, click-by-click, lessening the danger that the fastener will snap off.

Ice pick

The ice pick is a multifarious tool. Use it for lofting, scribing, poking holes in caulking tubes and the lips of paint cans, lining up holes, starting holes for small fastenings, etc.

Chalkline and chalk

Used for laying out straight lines when lofting and setting up the strongback and jig assembly.

End-cutting nippers

Used for cutting off the ends of rivets, snipping wires, and shortening fasteners.

"Four-in-one" hand rasp

A standard hardware store item, it combines a wood rasp and a file in one tool. One side is flat, the other curved. Useful for shaping, carving, and rounding stock without splitting it.

VISE-GRIPS–type pliers

VISE-GRIPS are a save-the-day tool. Useful for locking a spinning bolt long enough to get a nut on it, grabbing and pulling out a broken drill bit, twist-tightening a wire tie, and emergency clamping.

Crescent-type adjustable wrench

A.k.a., the boatbuilder's socket wrench set. Well, not quite that, but very handy for quick adjustments, provisional tightening, and such. However, steer clear of bargain-bin wonders.

Hex-key wrench set

Hex-keys are inexpensive, ubiquitous, and necessary for adjusting a plethora of tools, ranging from Fuller bits to bandsaws.

Putty knife

For spreading putty and bedding compound, scraping, prying the lids off cans, and all the rest.

Pocket knife

For whittling plugs, roughing out stopwaters, cutting in index bevels, sharpening pencils, opening the mail, and more.

Gloves

Rubber gloves for working with glues and solvents; leather work gloves for handling rough lumber.

EXOTICA

Drawknife

This two-handed tool is great for removing a lot of stock in a hurry. It is preferred for roughing in bevels on dory planking.

Slick

The boatbuilder's slick is a big, heavy, industrial-strength broad chisel used for fast stock removal and smoothing.

Caulking iron

This is a chisel-like tool used in conjunction with a mallet to drive caulking into plank and deck seams.

Caulking wheel or roller

Looking somewhat like a seam roller used for hanging wallpaper, this tool is an alternative to the caulking iron for small craft. It is used to roll or press caulking into a seam. Although formerly an "off-the-shelf" item, it now must be user made. (See how to do that in Chapter 3.)

Yankee screwdriver

The Yankee is an old favorite—a quick-return spiral ratchet-drive screwdriver—and still has its place in this era of the cordless screw gun. It is handy for speedily setting screws in planking. The tool has fallen out of favor with some boatbuilders, as close attention must be paid when using the tool to keep the bit from jumping out of the screw slot. This shortcoming is outweighed by the nature of the Yankee's manual action, which allows the mechanic to judge how the screw is doing as it moves through the wood and to vary driving pressure accordingly to avoid breaking off the fastening.

Backing iron and rivet set

These tools are essential for riveting. They are available commercially, but can also be made easily in the shop (see how in Chapter 3).

Clenching iron

This is a curved hand-held iron used to turn copper cut nails back on themselves (i.e., clench), so they become staple-like fastenings. The standard item is available by mail order, but a garden-variety auto-body repair iron also works well.

Backing-out plane

This is a round-bottomed plane fitted with a radiused iron. It is used to hollow out the inside of carvel (smooth-seam) planks so they lie firmly against the frames, and as a scrub plane to remove a lot of softwood stock in a hurry. Though occasionally found in antique stores, the backing-out plane is usually homemade by modifying the sole of a wooden-bodied plane and regrinding the iron.

Barefoot auger

The barefoot auger, a long drill bit, is similar to the conventional carpenter's auger, but without the lead screw and the cutting spurs. Available in various sizes, this is the bit of choice for boring long holes. (The lack of a lead screw prevents the auger from wandering off the line.)

Clamps

It would be difficult to have too many clamps. They are used for planking, backbone assembly, putting together a transom, fastening a centerboard case, all sorts of joinery, and just about every other operation on the vessel. What type of clamp? A short list would include: C-clamps (with as deep a throat as possible), ¾-inch pipe clamps, sliding bar clamps, and spring clamps. Again, get a good grade of all types. But remember this: a passion for clamps is no vise, so get a decent one for your workbench. You'll be glad you did.

HAND-HELD POWER TOOLS

While working with hand tools can be a pleasure, there is much to be said for the speed of production afforded by a well-designed power tool. A router with the proper cutter will make short work of milling a piece of cross-grained oak, while the same job with the old Stanley Multiplane would be an exercise in tedium that just might yield a product of lesser grade. And few will pine for the romance of fairing a hull totally by hand after doing the job in a fraction of the time using a disc sander with a foam pad. On the other hand, some manufacturers would lead one to believe that life as we know it did not exist before the introduction of their particular power product—usually a plunge router. 'T ain't the case. The truth is, hand and power tools complement one another.

Variable-speed ⅜-inch drill

This tool will be used all the time, so get a good one. If the choice has to be between a plug-in or a cordless, opt for the plug-in. The cordless variety is extremely handy and versatile, but most lack the punch, speed, or battery capacity to be a primary tool.

7¼-inch circular saw

For general crosscutting and ripping; in moments of exigency, it can even be used to rip out planks.

Disc sander with foam pad

Not to be confused with a disc grinder, this low-RPM machine can make fairing a hull a tolerable or even an enjoyable experience.

Hand-held planer

For fast stock removal, fairing heavy hardwood stock, and mass production of plank scarves.

Power block sander

The quarter-sheet model is one of the best for getting dreary, fine- sanding jobs out of the way.

☞ Notes on Buying Used Tools

For the savvy and thrifty boatbuilders who know their tools, antique stores and flea markets can be a treasure trove for specialty implements that are either no longer made or, if new, have prices per ounce equal to gold. Many older tools are of better quality than those sold new today. But keep in mind that because a tool is old is not a warranty that it is better that its brand-new counterpart, only that it is old. Be on the lookout, for example, for warp in the sole of a plane; to check, turn the plane over and sight down its length. Beware of cracks in castings. Distrust brazing and welds.

Unfortunately, tools have become yet another "collectible," and prices have become quite high on some items. Before you go used-tool hunting, check the catalog prices for comparable new tools. It is not unusual to find a secondhand plane priced higher than the list price of a new tool, of equal quality, with a new iron.

All that being said, there are some bargains available on the used market. Chisels can be a real find. High-quality tools with small chips in the cutting edge or with broken or smashed handles are often snubbed by collectors and are available at a fraction of their real value.

Chips are easily ground out and handles readily replaced.

Another prize is the short wooden plane. Usually affordable, one of these units can readily be converted into a backing-out plane in short order.

Flea markets are a prime source for long twist bits. Few collectors display drill bits over their mantels, so the street value of these items is usually low. Yet with quick sharpening you're in business. (Be sure that the shank of the bit is straight.)

Other used tools to watch for include spokeshaves, backing-out planes, slicks, shipwright's adzes, drawknives, barefoot augers, Yankee screwdrivers, saws that can be resharpened, long smoothing planes—Stanley and Bailey are names to look for—dividers, rabbet planes, and mallets. Used squares are suspect—you don't know where they've been.

A caveat: Beware of used hand-held power tools. That funky art-deco hand drill that looks as if it might have been used to build Buck Rogers's spaceship might have been produced before electrical grounding became popular. In other words, using it could be shocking. Far better to stick with the new stuff.

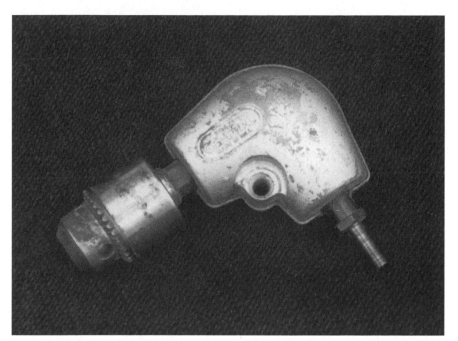

2-7: A right-angle drive for an electric drill—an accessory that you won't need very often, but it's indispensable when you do.

Router

Although not the universal panacea the manufacturers make it out to be, this very useful tool is great for shaping, beading, trimming, inlaying, and manufacturing concave/convex strip planking. Mounted in a router table it makes a first-rate pocket shaper.

Reciprocating saw, or sabersaw

For plunge cutting, scroll cutting, and making large, curved cuts that would be impractical for the bandsaw.

A FEW GOOD STATIONARY POWER TOOLS

Stationary power tools, also known as bench tools, are the most expensive investment for any shop. They also require maintenance and take up floor space.

Here is the place to go for quality over quantity. The better tool will give years of reliable service. The El Cheap-O-Matic brand will provide years of dyspepsia caused by bad bearings, lousy castings, and mismatched parts.

Fortunately, unlike the production cabinet shop, the small boatshop needs relatively few bench tools. The jobs performed by the jointer, shaper, drill press, and radial-arm saw can be done well by small hand or power tools without tying up significant capital and space. The tools that do see regular use—the bandsaw, table saw, and thickness planer—are worth the investment if one is planning to do a number of projects of any size.

It is possible to purchase good tools secondhand or at auctions, but research and discretion is required! Many of those charmingly ornate, three-phase, belt-driven, babbitt-bearinged wonders are time bombs waiting to get you when you least expect it. These malevolent marvels were built in a time when safety of the worker had very low priority for the captains of industry. Tool guards are nonexistent and bearings can be worn; some machines have been known to throw blades right off the machine at the most inconvenient of times. At best, these tools will need extensive tuning and refitting. For many, the best route is to buy new from a reputable outfit.

Bandsaw

This is the number-one saw for the boatshop, as it is able to make those long, continuous curves that are found in planking, stems, transoms, molds, and so on. Most saws are equipped with a tilting table, which allows the builder to make a bevel cut. The most popular bandsaw size for the small boat shop is the 14-incher; Delta seems to be the favorite brand.

☞ Words of Caution

Bench power tools pack a punch—they have to if they are to slice up heavy hardwood timbers. When used with respect they can do a lot of work for you. But they are never, ever your friend. These machines are not particular about what they "eat." To be blunt, they are as jolly as a rattlesnake with ulcers after eating a plate of hot chili peppers, and they are just waiting for you to become a hotshot cowboy, familiar and complacent. So, caution is a requirement when using these devices.

- Read the manual. All of it! If you haven't used the machine before, get checked out on it.
- Take your time and think through the operation before ever turning on the machine.
- Know how the fences and guards work, and use them.
- Use a roller or "deadman" to support your work, or get help.
- Don't ask the machine to do more than it was designed to do.
- Keep in mind that all machines are like loaded cannon, ready to launch a projectile: stand to one side out of the line of fire when operating.
- If you are on medication or are prone to having beer with your lunch, don't use the machine.
- And always wear that safety equipment!

Table saw

For repetitive and accurate straight cuts. For ripping frame, rail, and thwart stock, and transom blanks: this machine will do it.

Thickness planer

For making fat wood thin and turning rough stock into finished. When getting out carvel planking, this machine is a boon.

Bench grinder

Useful for making tools, producing custom hardware, and sharpening edge tools.

Safety equipment

Power tools demand safety equipment. Without a doubt, these tools are the most important in your kit. Get, and use, eye protection (either protective glasses, goggles, or better yet, a full face shield), ear protection (earphones or plugs), and dust masks (canister respirator for heavy dust, NIOSH/MSHA-approved paper mask for general use). All these items are like lifejackets; they won't work if you don't wear them.

3 • HOMEMADE TOOLS

Boatbuilding is a curious enterprise. Just as soon as the builder entertains a notion that the situation is well in hand, yet another never-before-seen dilemma rears its ugly head. The positive side of these moments of exigency is that they provide the opportunity to add yet another handy gadget to the toolbox: grit your teeth, cheerfully mutter "Goodness, how unusual!" and invent your way out of the predicament. Few of these practical contrivances are really new or fancy. In many cases, they are merely modifications of something seen in action or stumbled upon in some dusty periodical.

The first half of this century were halcyon days for boating magazines such as *The Rudder, Fore An' Aft,* and *Motor Boating.* Back then, the boating public was a hands-on fraternity of tinkerers, nautical shade-tree mechanics, and amateur naval architects. To satisfy this eclectic crowd, the editors always included a nicely illustrated column chock-filled with ingenious tips and ideas on retrofitting your naphtha launch, making a lead pipe stuffing box, or even building a 50-cent planimeter. Alas, somewhere along the way (I believe it was in the enlarged automobile tailfin and lava-lamp era) the smart money crowd declared the boating public had miraculously evolved into idle, passive consumers who had little interest in repairing or, much less, building a boat. What was needed was more advertising! And those wonderful columns gradually vanished into history and/or the family attic to await rediscovery.

There are certain winter days, when the temperature is hovering somewhere about -10 degrees F, the wind is careening out of the northeast, and the snow has turned the shop into an igloo, that will inspire a soul to take some time out for serious professional research. At such reflective moments, I retreat to the kitchen, put a fresh pot of coffee on the woodstove, drag those crates of antique nautical periodicals and memorabilia out of the garret, and get down to the business of prospecting for buried nuggets of wisdom. From the past, those sages of the pre-composite era once again reveal their tricks of the trade—inviting you to save a little time here and a little money there, and suggesting that you probably have better things to do than to reinvent the wheel. It is from this virtual encyclopedia of supplements, and from a few other reputable sources, that I offer a few gleanings that I and others have found to be quite useful.

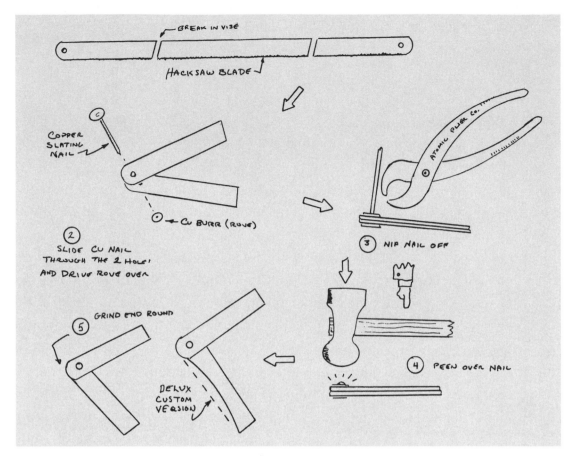

Hacksaw Planking Bevel Gauge

When building a boat, no tool gets greater use than the humble bevel gauge. Whether for spotting bevels on a plank, fitting a knee, or setting the bandsaw for that perfect cut, this is the tool to use. But where do you get one? Better hardware stores and fancy tool catalogs offer the ubiquitous brass-bound rosewood-handled house carpenter's bevel. It's a lovely thing to have in the toolbox, but its large size limits its utility in constructing small craft.

On the other end of the size scale, some speciality outfits carry expensive little brass bevels. These highly polished little gems are wonderful to behold and generally are misplaced within hours of acquisition. What to do? Build yourself a hacksaw bevel gauge. (See Figure 3-1.)

To start, find one of those dull, used hacksaw blades that you have been saving. Insert about three inches of the blade in the vise and, after donning safety glasses, give the blade a quick bend, which will snap it off right off at the line of the vise's jaws. Release the vise, invert the remaining section of the blade, insert a length equal to the first into the vise, and break that off as well. You will now have two pieces of flat metal with holes in them.

Line up the two holes in the two pieces of blade and insert a soft copper wire nail. Drive a rove (burr) down onto the nail, nip off the excess shank of the nail with the nippers, and peen the nipped end of the nail over the burr, thus turning the nail into a rivet. And voila! There you have a bevel gauge for planking! Well, almost.

Take the newly assembled bevel gauge back to the bench for a little cosmetic pruning and tuning. The first thing that you'll want to do is dull the probably still-sharp piranha-like teeth on the legs of the gauge, otherwise they will sooner or later end up perforating your hand. This can easily be done by clamping each leg into a vise and attacking the edge with a flat file. Next, round the riveted end of the gauge. Just filing a little more radius in the end will improve the performance of the tool.

That's all there is to it. Total assembly time: maybe five minutes.

Curve Capture Device

At the turn of the bilge and other sections with tight turns on a shapely hull, cold bending or even steaming a carvel plank won't be enough to allow the plank to take the curve and land flush on the frame. In this case, it will be necessary to hollow or back out the inside face of the plank with a round-nosed plane. The question is, How much hollow will be required? One possible way to determine this is to make a template to be used at strategic locations, which is effective albeit time consuming. But what if you had a gauge that you could simply place

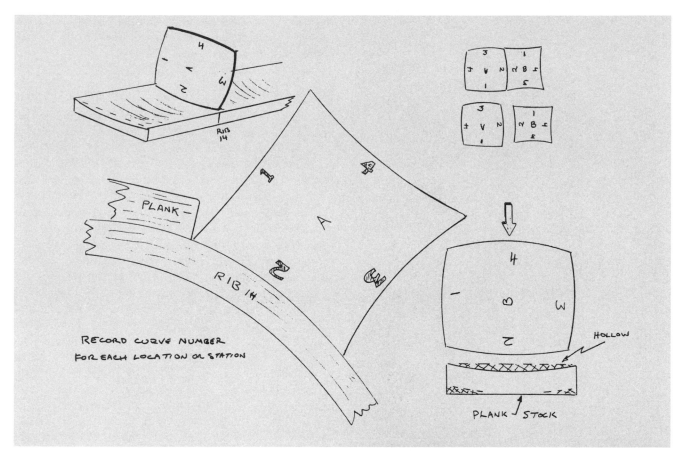

RIB 14

PLANK

RIB 14

RECORD CURVE NUMBER
FOR EACH LOCATION OR STATION

HOLLOW

PLANK STOCK

3-2: The curve capture device.

against a rib or mold to record the shape as a reference number in a notebook? Such a gauge is the Curve Capture Device.

The Curve Capture Device is actually a pair of four-sided ¼-inch plywood templates that have different complementary curves cut into each side. One of the pair consists of a series of concave shapes; the other, convex. Concave curve "A" nests into Convex curve "B", "C" into "D" and so on. (See Figure 3-2.) To employ this miracle of engineering, match the curve of the hull with one of the concave curves on template "A", and record the number and location. (See Figure 3-3.) When you get ready to back out the inside of the new plank, just break out template "B" and use the selected convex curve as a depth gauge. When the plank fits the gauge, you're there. (See Figure 3-4.)

And where do the curves come from? Although it is possible to mathematically generate them, it is much easier to use standard boatbuilding curves—that is, the top of a 5-gallon can, an oil drum, a dustbin, and so on. Just trace the curves onto ¼-inch plywood (even thinner aircraft plywood works better), cut out the curves with a bandsaw, label the gauges, and you're ready to go.

Though I am getting ahead of myself here, I might mention that

3-2: The curve capture device.

3-3: Using the concave device to capture the curve of a frame.

when the plans for a carvel boat provide plank thickness, the dimension means the finished thickness, after the plank has been backed out.

BLIND REACH-AROUND MARKING DEVICE

There are many occasions when the builder is called upon to do what could best be called "blind sawing." A good example of this is when the planks that overrun the transom must be trimmed off. As you will be sawing from the outside of the planking where you can't really see where to start the cut, there are lots of opportunities for the cut to go awry. You could, for example, saw at an incorrect angle or worse, saw into the transom.

This problem can be solved by using the plank scriber, a.k.a., the blind reach-around marking device, a handy and elegant rig whose design graced the pages of *The Rudder* magazine in February of 1950. (See Figure 3-5.) The concept of the tool is simple: it carries the plane of the transom over the plank ends to the outside of the plank where the pencil can mark it. To use the rig, ride the bottom edge of the plywood scriber along the flat of the transom while holding the point of the pencil to the planking. Then cut to the outside of the lines with a handsaw, and you're in business.

A more prosaic version of this tool can be quickly whipped up on the spot by cutting a circular aperture into

3-4: Testing a backed-out plank with the convex curve capture device.

3-5: The plank scriber, or blind reach-around marking device, as described in *The Rudder* magazine, February 1950.

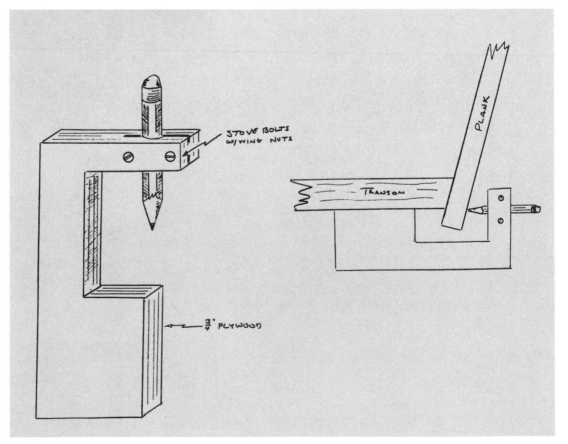

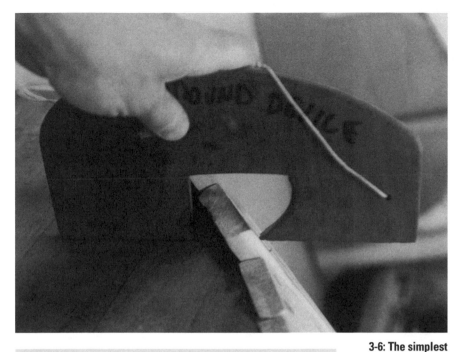

a piece of scrap wood with a straight edge. (See Figure 3-6.) The end of the circular cut acts as a pointer on the outside of the plank. Mark the position of the pointer with a pencil. (See Figure 3-7.)

PIZZA-CUTTER CAULKING WHEEL

What with all the available modern flexible adhesives, caulks, sealants, and other feats of chemical legerdemain, the notion of keeping King Neptune at bay by driving cotton between planks might seem to be a trifle archaic. Such is not the case, however. Driven caulking not only excludes water but also tightens and stiffens a vessel, joining the edges of the planking like splines in a panel. Caulking exclusively with elastic compounds, without driven cotton, is akin to linking your planks with rubber bands.

3-6: The simplest type of blind reach-around marking device in use.

For many builders, the weapons of choice for driving cotton are the caulking iron and mallet. On large vessels, this is the only way to go. But for small craft there is a faster, and quieter alternative: rolling in the cotton with a caulking wheel.

There are basically two versions of the caulking wheel—the straight-handled "roller-on-a-stick" model and the pistol-grip type. (See Figure 3-8.) The former used to be a stock item and can still occasionally be purchased at ship chandleries; more likely it will be discovered

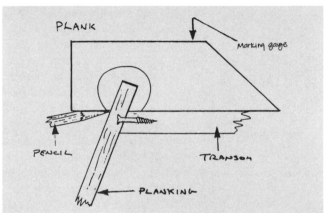

3-7: Make your mark with a pencil where the pointer hits the plank.

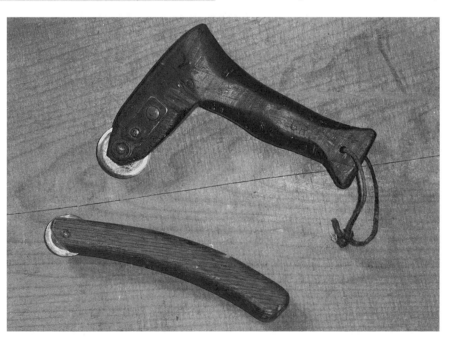

3-8: The caulking wheel, two types: easiest to use (top), easiest to make (bottom). You can cut pizza with either.

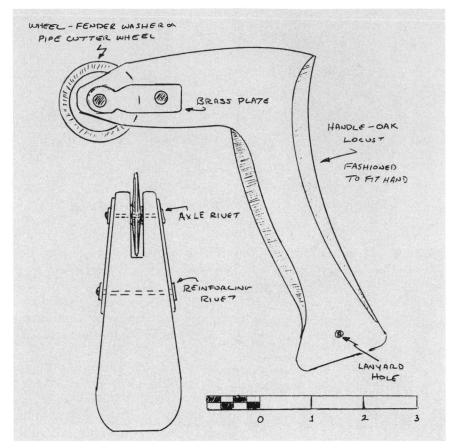

WHEEL - FENDER WASHER or PIPE CUTTER WHEEL

BRASS PLATE

HANDLE - OAK LOCUST

FASHIONED TO FIT HAND

AXLE RIVET

REINFORCING RIVET

LANYARD HOLE

0   1   2   3

3-9: Pistol-grip caulking wheel.

in a curio shop. The latter, a dandy version of which appeared in Royal Lowell's 1977 book *Boatbuilding Down East*, you must build yourself. (See Figure 3-9.)

Of the two, the pistol-grip type is the better, as it allows you to grasp the handle in a more natural or ergonomic manner. The shape also seems to encourage the user to follow the seam, while allowing the downward pressure of the arm to be most effective in setting the cotton. Either style sports a tapered wheel that not only presses the cotton into place but also opens tight seams, producing a uniform wedge-shaped opening.

Start making your wheel by sketching a shape that will approximately fit your hand onto a piece of light plywood pattern stock. Saw it out, then whittle a little here and shave a little there until you have something that feels just about right. Then take the pattern to a likely piece of rugged hardwood—oak works well. After aligning the pattern to take advantage of the grain, trace the shape and rough it out with a bandsaw. While the wood is still square-sided and therefore easy to hold, cut the slot for the wheel.

What to use for a wheel? Some have good luck using a wheel from a pipe cutter, although a suitable one is sometimes difficult to locate. A fender washer—a large metal disk with a small center hole—makes a good alternative. A small taper can be ground on the edges of the washer if desired. Small washers glued on either side of the fender

washer will act as bushings and keep the wheel running free and true.

Drill a hole in the handle for the rivet that will act as the axle for the wheel. Line up the wheel, insert the rivet, and check out the alignment. Pretty good? Then peen the rivet. All that is left to do is to rasp the handle to shape, sand it smooth, and anoint it with oil or varnish to seal it, and you are ready to roll.

ROVE SET

Another tool that is difficult to find is a rove set, a simple but necessary device for driving and setting the burr, or rove, onto a rivet with a hammer. If you are lucky and do find one for sale, the price will likely be pretty dear for what is basically a piece of metal with a long hole in it. What to do? Make one yourself!

One easy fix is to use a piece of ¾-inch metal rod (bronze works well). How long should it be? Grab a length of the rod and decide how close you want the hammer to come to your hand. Cut it there. Clamp the piece in a vise and, using your sharpest bit, slowly bore a 2-inch-long hole into the end of the rod. For a touch of elegance and comfort, wrap the rod with a few turns of duct tape.

SQUARING BRIDGE

Whether you are indexing the keel to the stations, checking that the keel is at the proper height above the base, or simply recording the rabbet lines on the stem, having pre-drawn reference lines on the backbone assembly can be most helpful. The easiest time to record this information is when you can lay the assemblage right atop the drawn pieces on the lofting board. One way to bring the information up from the board is to use a square to carefully square up the lines onto each (vertical) side of the piece and connect those lines across the upper (horizontal) face with a pencil. Or you can use a squaring bridge.

A bridge is a homemade squaring tool made from a piece of straight and true stock, roughly 2 inches thick, with a square notch, much like a tunnel, removed from the wide face. (See Figure 3-10.) The cutout is large enough to allow a stem, keel, or other backbone member to slide under it with about ¹⁄₁₆ inch to spare. The notch allows the device to "bridge" the backbone member while the two "legs" stand on the lofting board.

A bridge can be used like a square to transfer waterlines, stations, and other reference lines onto the stock. To use, simply drop the device over the stem or keel and align the legs with a waterline or station. That line is automatically transferred to the raised backbone face. Simply trace the line in pencil and label it. Then proceed to the next reference line.

BENT-TANG SEAM CLEANER

One of the more tedious chores when preparing to recaulk a hull or replace a plank is the removal or "reefing out" of the old caulking cotton from the seams. The old stuff can be petrified, ossified, and thoroughly resistant to extraction. But, as with every job, having the right tool can make all the difference.

The right tool in this situation is a hooked implement sometimes called a reef hook, a rake hook, or just "that reefing tool." This unit is just the ticket to get under the offending caulking fiber and other detritus and give it the old heave-ho. The problem is, if you don't already have such a tool, where do you get one? It is yet another item not likely to be on the shelves of your local hardware emporium.

What to do? Invent one, of course. (See Figure 3-11.)

The first step is to get that worn-out mill file from under the workbench and clamp it in a vise. Next, using a portable propane torch, heat the tang (the tapered end that fits into the handle) to soften the steel. While the steel is still hot, grab the tang of the file with VISE-GRIPS pliers about ½ inch back. Bend the tang to make a 90-degree hook. Take the file to the grinder wear—safety spectacles for this operation, as the sparks will fly—and machine it to a chisel-plough shape. You now have your basic seam-reefing device.

For a deluxe model retemper the tip of the bent-over tang. Heat the tang over a blue flame (the kitchen stove gas flame will do) until the shiny surface glows with a straw yellow color, then immediately quench the tip by dipping it in water.

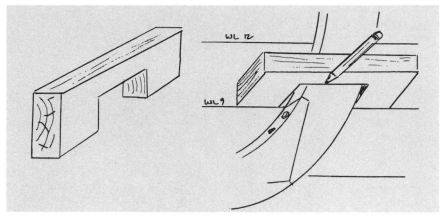

3-10: A bridge device, used to carry a line from one side of a timber to the other.

HOMEMADE LAPSTRAKE CLAMPS

Tight clamping of lapped joints is critical for successful fastening of lapstrake and dorylap planking. But coming up with enough deep-throated clamps to do the job can be a problem for the home builder. These specialty tools are available from mail-order supply houses, but you have to wait for them to be shipped from Timbuktu or someplace equally unhandy. Chances are not good that you'll find what you want at your local "ClampMart," but it's edifying to know that there is an easy homespun solution to this problem.

There are a number of different lapstrake clamp styles, from "clothespin" to adjustable handscrew. The theory behind all of them is the same: depth of throat will provide what you need to squeeze the lap tightly. For most situations, 8 inches seems to work well. The jaws can be made from any hardwood scraps that are kicking around the shop.

By far, the "clothespin and wedge" (see Figure 3-12) is the easiest type of clamp to make, but for elegance and ease of use, it's difficult to beat the curved-jaw adjustable type (see Figure 3-13)—they are easy to set and less likely to come lose and fall off at embarrassing moments.

So, what's needed? Some handy items to have in your deep-throat clamp kit might include the following:

- An assortment of carriage bolts: different lengths, different diameters.
- An assortment of "all thread" rod: ⅜ inch, ⁷⁄₁₆ inch, ½ inch.
- Some large washers for the carriage bolts and threaded rod.
- Bolt rod nuts. These look a little like an old-time cast-iron stove lid lifter welded onto a threaded nut. They come in ⅜-inch, ⁷⁄₁₆-inch, and ½-inch sizes, and are available at good old-fashioned hardware stores or by mail order (see Appendix B, Sources).
- A few long "low-angle" wooden wedges.
- Inexpensive butt hinges for use with the curved-jaw adjustable-style clamp.

3-11: A simple seam cleaner made from an old file.

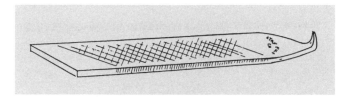

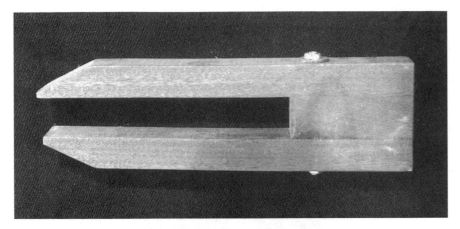

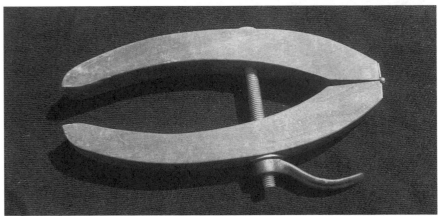

3-13: A curved-jaw, hinged-back adjustable clamp.

3-14: A variation on the clothespin-type clamp. The maximum spread of the jaws is controlled by the width of the block.

BENT PIPE CLAMP

One of the limiting factors with either a bar or pipe clamp is that these tools are designed to pull (or compress) in a linear fashion. They excel in operations such as drawing together the pieces that make up a centerboard or gluing up a panel. However, when used in a situation involving curves, such as when edge-setting planking on a round-bottomed hull, they are nearly useless. Initially bar and pipe clamps are helpful in setting the planks closest the keel. But as the hull begins to develop some shape, the clamp will shoot right off the hull on a tangent. What to do?

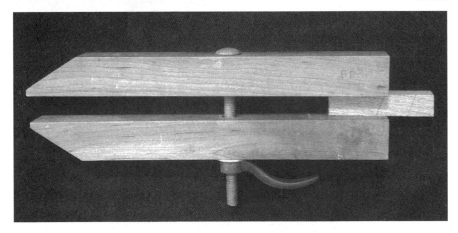

Well, there is not much to be done with a bar clamp—it is irreconcilably bullheaded in its straight-arrow habit. A pipe clamp, on the other hand, you can do business with.

Iron pipe, especially the ½-inch size, bends with relatively little effort. Special tools are not necessary. Just place the clamp's pipe in a vise, and slide a larger pipe "cheater" over the smaller. Then, gently, little-by-little, pull an arc into the smaller pipe that is roughly similar to the shape of the hull. You now have a scimitar-shaped

pipe clamp ready for action.

Although unsophisticated in appearance, this modified marvel will outperform any of its fancier, factory-made colleagues when applied to a round hull. Simply hook one jaw over a (relatively) immovable object, such as the keel, and slide the other end up to the plank that needs to be moved. Give the handle a twist or two, and the plank will edgeset home.

One caveat though: Use caution when clamping to a lightweight keel, such as that of a Whitehall. Overenthusiastic pressure can torque the keel into pretzel-like contortions.

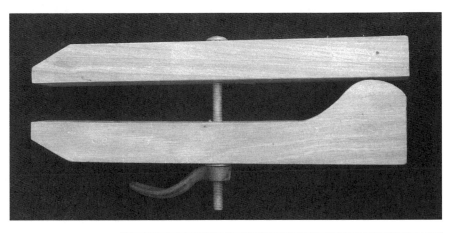

THE TWELVE-AND-A-HALF-CENT SOLUTION

Handy as they are for quick-and-dirty repairs and assemblies, spring clamps have their shortcomings: (1) the depth of throat is limited, and (2) you never seem to have enough of them. The solution for this conundrum is 3-inch and 4-inch plastic Schedule 40 sewer pipe, the very same product that is favored for the construction of potato guns. It is inexpensive and available wherever quality drain pipe is sold—usually at your local hardware store.

Making sewer-pipe spring clamps is easy. Simply slice the pipe crosswise into 1-inch sections to produce a selection of plastic rings. Then lay each ring on its side and split it with one cut of a bandsaw. That's all there is to it. With their natural deep throats, these babies are just the ticket for gluing an outwale in place, aligning strip planking, or even holding a chart down on a thwart while underway. And, for about 15 bucks, a ten-foot section of pipe will give you 120 clamps at about 12½ cents apiece.

HACKSAW BLADE WATERLINE SCRIBER

There is something about a sharp, crisp waterline that gives a boat a certain salty air. Springing a batten around the hull and tacking it in place will indicate the waterline, but now what? Draw the line with a pencil? That's okay for this season, but what about next when the line has been covered up with paint or has been sanded off? The only really reliable way to capture and maintain that line is to scribe it in.

The question then is, what tool to use? You could employ your trusty awl or icepick, which can do an adequate job—at least until the point not surprisingly starts to veer as it follows the grain of the wood. How about using the aforementioned seam cleaner? Not too bad, providing it's mighty sharp and care is exercised so that it, too, doesn't run off course. The best solution is to use another of those old hacksaw blades.

The last tooth on a hacksaw blade (always sharp, it seems) acts as a micro-rabbet plane. For a good grip, wrap the rest of the blade with tape (or make a wooden handle), then guide the end of the blade along the batten. That last tooth will turn up a nice curl as it slices along the wood, leaving the right-size trough in its wake. And there you have it, a perfectly scribed waterline.

☞ Oddball Tools

Wooden boat construction requires a coterie of unusual implements not usually available at your local hardware store or even from the tonier woodworking catalogs. While often the only recourse is to build the tool yourself, many times just the right tool is available at an "off-the-beaten track" supply house. Some specialty catalogs to explore for tools useful in boatbuilding are:

Aviation

Actually such a source should not be unexpected, as aircraft construction is a related industry to boatbuilding. This is a source for industrial heat guns, Aerolite glue, extremely low-angle drill attachments, air hammer and riveting sets, bucking bars, and ratchet wire twister and cutoff pliers, which are handy when temporarily fastening steam-bent ribs.

Homesteading and "nonelectric" hardware

Just the place to look for blacksmithing tools, lead-melting pots and ladles, end-cutting nippers, spokeshaves, and nuts with handles for making wooden clamps.

Greenhouse supply

Here you will find greenhouse polyethylene sheeting, which is a superior product for covering temporary buildings as it has greater ultraviolet resistance than standard plastic and is extraordinarily elastic in subfreezing temperatures.

Drafting supply

A sure source for ship curves, flexible splines, drafting ducks, proportional dividers, vellum, and Mylar.

Automotive

Among other items, you will find body work irons, which are merely backing irons in disguise for clench nailing

4 • WOOD FOR BOATBUILDING

Deciding what wood to use in your boatbuilding project will require a little detective work. Seek out a local builder or the staff of the boatshop in a marine museum and ask them what wood they would use and why. Inquire about alternatives. Builders are generally quite open with this type of information. Check out the technology section of your local library. Consult the nearest university or government natural resource department. These can be treasure-troves of information. Make up your shopping list of first choices and substitutes. You'll be needing this when you meet with your friendly purveyor of wood.

WHICH WOOD TO USE?

Any final selection of boatbuilding wood involves a number of factors and variables. They include:

Practicality

In other words, utility, applicability, and regional availability. Will the wood you have selected do the job you ask of it? That massive chunk of white oak that you squirreled away in the garage next to the DeSoto back in '57 might make a dandy keel, but it shouldn't be your first choice for the mast. The plans might specify Maine white cedar for the planking, but that could be a difficult commodity to find if you are building, say, in Utah. Practicality suggests that when choosing wood, it is good to have a fall-back position.

Philosophical conundrums

Such as, in the long run, is it wise to use an endangered species simply for its beauty, economy, or current availability at your local lumber emporium? Might not an alternative wood serve as well? This vexatious question is not merely one that pits environmental rhetoric versus the notion of aesthetics, convenience, and "anyway, there's still plenty of trees." Perhaps it's time to consider the true cost of utilizing those lovely exotic species and the advantages of alternatives.

Most boatbuilders will acknowledge that the days of easy access to cheap, long, clear, old-growth timber are over. The trees are simply not there. The reasons for this are many and well known. They include over-cutting, governmental prohibitions, and a thriving (some might say profligate) export market for raw logs. Fortunately, this is occurring at a time when new adhesives and preservatives have appeared on the market that allow the builder to efficiently employ species that were impractical before. These alternative solutions also open the door to new designs and techniques while retaining high quality in the old. Conserving limited resources has always been good business.

Tradition!

Wooden boat building is the quintessential traditional industry. Over time, regional builders have found that certain woods have proven track records of success (and others, failure). What works in Newfoundland might prove to be a disaster in Miami. Builders have always been reluctant to incorporate inappropriate woods into their work that might bring customers back bearing torches and pitchforks.

PURCHASING THE WOOD

Locating sources for wood can prove to be an interesting challenge. You'll find no "Boat Lumber Depot" down at the mall to serve all your boatbuilding needs. Nor will access to a yard catering to woodworkers guarantee success. Most often these businesses will stock kiln-dried woods in dimensions inappropriate for boat construction. More sleuthing will be required.

Begin by looking locally. Check the classified pages of the hometown newspaper and the "lumber for sale" entries in Uncle Louie's Swap and Sell. The small mills listed usually sell air-dried lumber in unusual lengths, and generally at a fair price. If given a reasonable amount of lead time, local sawyers are able to do custom work and are more likely to let you select your own lumber (as long as you restack the piles neatly).

Next, peruse the ads in marine publications. There you will find merchants who are used to dealing with the idiosyncrasies of the boatbuilder. You may end up paying a little more per board foot than you would locally, and there is the cost of shipping to be figured in, but generally the quality is quite good and you will have saved all that time restacking all those lumber piles. Many of the mail-order yards do custom milling at a reasonable price; indeed, when buying imported lumber, there are times when it is cheaper to buy milled stock by mail than it is to purchase raw stock locally.

WHAT TO AVOID

Acquisition of boatbuilding lumber will probably require a bit of change from the "cut and dried" approach generally used when purchasing wood for cabinet making or even for conventional carpentry. The "cut" may be totally different, and you may not want the wood to be dried at all. Kiln-dried, quartersawn, square-sided boards

that are straight as a die might be just the ticket for building a Chippendale-style home entertainment center, but they are likely to be less than useful when planking a clamming skiff.

Even if you are purchasing lumber from a knowledgeable merchant who caters to the trade, it is helpful to know some of the peculiarities of nonstandard lumber in general and boat lumber in particular when selecting construction stock. After all, selecting lumber is a bit like electing politicians. There are very few "perfect" choices. Some are crooked, some cracked, and some are twisted, but some are better than others.

Warps

Your eye is the best tool for sorting out the warped lumber. First, sight down the length of your candidate and look for crook, cup, bow, or twist.

A crook is a deviation from a straight line of a flat and level board, somewhat like a bend in the road.

Cup refers to curling up at the edges, almost as if the plank were trying to be a gutter.

A bow is a bend on the flat—the same sort of bend a plank will take when it is wrapped around a hull.

Twist is a spiraling or corkscrewing of a plank.

A piece of wood with crook or cup can be dealt with if necessary, although it will cost you some time and stock as you cut and plane the piece down to a usable condition. If, however, the piece is twisted or bowed, discard it.

Cracks and splits

Watch out for all cracks, splits, checks, and shakes. Checks are cracks that usually occur at the ends and affect the last few inches of the board. Shakes are a separation along the grain in the interior of the plank. Often difficult to spot, shakes can weaken bent pieces, such as planks.

Decay

Generally speaking, all wood with rot should be avoided. In its early stages rot may just appear as a mottled discoloration; in its later stages the wood fiber disintegrates. In any stage, you don't need it, no matter how nice the rest of the board looks.

Knots

Due to the continued presence of branches on trees, knots are to be expected in lumber. Small, sound (free of decay) knots are of little concern when contained within a plank. The ones to look out for are black knots (a dead branch has been overgrown by new wood), rotten knots, or spike knots (those with a long cross-section). Planks with a reasonable number of small knots can be satisfactorily patched if care is taken.

Don't automatically give an otherwise sound plank the heave-ho just because it has a few jumbo knots. Such an often discounted plank with its gloriously whorled grain curling around the knot might be just what you need for making some dandy thwart or stern knees.

Unwanted guests

Sometimes the best wood is found in the field, or the woods next to it. Before milling rough lumber, check out your stock for deleterious imperfections acquired in the wild, such as embedded gravel, barbed wire, and bullets.

Sapwood

Beware of sapwood, which comes from the "live" part of the tree closest to the bark and which carries nutrients. Sapwood generally is lighter in color than heartwood, which is found farther into the log. It also is much more prone to decay than heartwood. Planks cut closer to the edge of the log will contain more sapwood than those cut closer to the center.

A FEW MORE DEFINITIONS

Quartersawn lumber

Sometimes called edge- or vertical-grain lumber, this has been sawn so the grain runs at right angles to the flat side of the board. Wood cut in this way is considered top-notch, as it shrinks and swells less in width, and is resistant to twisting and cupping. Expect to pay a premium for quartersawn lumber, if you can find it. It is more likely that you will find plainsawn—also known as flat-grained or through-sawn—lumber at small sawmills. For most applications on a boat, either quartersawn or plainsawn will do just fine.

Board foot

A unit of volumetric measurement for wood. One board foot equals a piece 1 inch thick, 12 inches wide, and 12 inches long. A piece of wood 8 feet long, 6 inches wide, and 1 inch thick would equal 4 board feet.

Air dried

Wood that has been dried or seasoned naturally, with air circulating around the boards on all sides.

Kiln dried

Wood that has been artificially dried in a forced-draft oven to a lower moisture content than that possible by air drying. Kiln drying is thought by boatbuilders to take the "life" out of the wood.

"Green" lumber

Wood that has been recently cut and therefore is unseasoned. This is the best lumber to use for steam-bending.

Rough vs. dressed lumber

Rough lumber is of the full thickness stated when sawed. Dressed lumber has been machine planed, so a 1-inch board that has been dressed will be closer to $\frac{3}{4}$ inch in thickness. Dressed lumber is usually sold trimmed and square edged.

Quarters

A method of stating the thickness of lumber; e.g. $\frac{4}{4}$ is the same as 1 inch thick; $\frac{5}{4}$ is $1\frac{1}{4}$ inched thick. "Ya want six quarter?" That means the questioner wants to know if you are looking for lumber that is $1\frac{1}{2}$ inches thick.

BOATBUILDING WOODS, AN ANNOTATED LIST

White ash

Straight grained, steam-bends well (think snowshoes), available in long, clear lengths, quite strong for its weight. Sailboat tillers, rails, and oars are good applications. Drawback is its affinity for rot. White ash keels, stems, and frames can turn to black mush over time. Use only where good ventilation and dry conditions prevail.

White oak

A top-notch boatbuilding wood. Heavy, rugged, takes fastenings well, and is exceptionally good for steam-bending (buy it "green" or unseasoned and straight-grained for this purpose). For all other purposes white oak should be well seasoned, as it shrinks a good deal in the drying process. Air drying is preferred over kiln drying, as it seems to damage the wood less.

White oak has a closed cell structure that inhibits the intrusion of rot-promoting fresh water. It does not glue particularly well, especially with epoxy. A good choice for backbone members: stem, keel, and deadwood. Great for steam-bent ribs. It also makes a fine small-boat transom or a bright-finished sheerstrake.

Red oak

A close runner-up to white oak, as it has many of the same qualities. In addition, it is easier to get in long, clear lengths. The greatest drawback is its open cell structure, which will wick water up into the wood like a bundle of pipette tubes. Not a particularly endearing quality, although it will probably draw up liquid preservatives as well.

The cedars

Almost all cedars have long been the preferred wood for planking small craft. As a rule, the various species are light, are quite rot resistant, bend well, and have low shrinkage. Each species does have its own characteristics to consider.

Eastern white cedars

Northern white (a.k.a., eastern arborvitae) and Atlantic white. Both are usually available as "flitch" or "live-edge" sawn. This means the lumber is flat on only on two sides—the top and the bottom—sawn through-and-through with the natural curve of the tree. This type of lumber is a boon to the conventional builder, as it allows the builder to utilize the tree's natural curve to full advantage in planking. Northern white cedar is surprisingly strong and quite forgiving, but expect to find knots, as there is little clear stock left to be cut. Dealing with this slight aggravation is a small price to pay for all the positive qualities of this wood.

Port Orford cedar

Indigenous to the Pacific Northwest of the United States. This spicy-smelling wood tends to be available in clear, straight-grained lengths. Heartwood is very resistant to decay and is relatively stable and strong.

Western red cedar

This wood is quite resistant to decay; available in advantageous widths and lengths for planking. It is, however, quite brittle and low in strength, oftentimes breaking right across the grain. It can be used with success as strip planking on canoes and other light craft, and also as veneers for cold-molded construction.

Eastern (or Northern) white pine

Available in good lengths and widths for planking. Light in weight but, unfortunately, soft, low in strength, and low in shock resistance. Do not be surprised to find hidden structural flaws and cracks that only show up after milling. The wood can be used with success on small workboats and dories.

Longleaf or yellow pine

Grows in southern United States. Strong, resinous, and durable. Quite heavy. Yellow pine is used in structural components, such as clamps, keel, deadwood, and occasionally planking if the curve is not too great.

Cyprus

This wood is strong, and the heartwood is very resistant to decay, but quality lumber is getting difficult to find. Be aware that cyprus planks absorb a lot of water and will therefore make the boat heavy in use.

Sitka spruce

The Cadillac of the spruces. Grows on the Pacific Coast in a band stretching from northern California to Alaska. It is lightweight and relatively strong and stiff. Resists taking a "set" when bent. Available in long, defect-free, clear lengths with tight (closely spaced), straight grain. A top choice for the aircraft industry and for boatbuilding:

spars, oars, rails, and lofting and fairing battens. It laminates well if care is taken to properly prepare and saturate the gluing surfaces. It does, however, have low resistance to decay and should not be installed anywhere in constant contact with rot-promoting fresh water or damp earth. For this reason it should be varnished rather than painted, so it can be inspected on a regular basis. The demand for this limited species is great, and the domestic price is therefore quite high.

Eastern spruce, white and red

These woods have most of the same qualities of the Sitka spruce at a much lower price. As the trees are smaller, expect to find more knots and wider spacing of the grain. Because this wood is commonly used as construction lumber on the east coast (2 by 4s, 2 by 6s, etc.), it is readily available at the local lumberyard. If your yard man lets you pick through the piles, you are likely to find stock suitable for making spars mixed in with the lesser grades. Another source for usable spruce might be a roof truss manufacturer, as they are looking for the same characteristics in their wood as a boatbuilder is.

Douglas fir

This is a Pacific Northwest wood. It is essentially clear and straight grained. The wood is quite strong and moderately decay resistant, and it holds fastenings well. Douglas fir can be used for spars when weight is not of the utmost importance. On the west coast it is used in many of the structural applications not requiring steam that oak would be used for, such as keels, floors, clamps, and deck beams.

The mahoganies

Harvested in Central America and Africa. A relatively hard and strong wood. It glues and holds fastenings well. Mahogany is versatile and can be used for backbones, transoms, and interior joinery. Might make a good alternative choice if no suitable domestic wood is available.

Philippine "mahogany"

Not a true mahogany, Philippine "mahogany" is the marketing term for red luan and tangile woods grown primarily in the Philippine islands. The wood is stiff, rot resistant, and holds fastenings well (though not as well as true mahogany). It glues well and is available in long, clear lengths. It is often used for planking and as a stand-in for true mahogany.

OTHER GOOD WOODS TO KNOW
Hackmatack, tamarack, Eastern larch

Lots of names, same tree. Found from Maine to Minnesota. A rugged, underutilized wood. Although the lumber can be used for planking, the roots are the boatbuilding focus: prized for use as stems on small craft and knees for vessels of all sizes. For a softwood, it has good fastening-holding qualities and decent resistance to decay. Hackmatack is a bit of a specialty lumber, and you will probably find yourself working through local wood-cutters and sawyers to get it. Also check classified ads, as a renewed interest in hackmatack knees has inspired a small mail-order cottage industry.

Apple

The crooks of the branches from the apple tree are sometimes used for knees and breasthooks in traditional small craft. Knees when made from fully dried apple crooks are strong, moderately rot resistant, and elegant when varnished. For a source, inquire at a local orchard for sound branches pruned from their trees. Also, many orchards are replacing their old standard-size trees with easier-to-pick dwarf varieties, and the wood is often available at cordwood prices.

Black locust

A good, and often neglected, alternative to white oak, this wood is heavy, close grained, stiff, and strong, and the heartwood is quite resistant to rot. The crooks of the branches offer opportunities for knees and small-boat stems. The wood itself is handsome when finished bright; some wags have even tagged it "American teak." Locust can also be used to make small deck hardware, such as cleats.

Plywood

When the plans simply specify plywood for construction, it is akin to specifying automobiles for transportation—the range is from Yugo to Mercedes. The grade of plywood to use depends on the quality of the boat, what the boat will be used for, and how much money you have.

If you are building a quick-and-dirty work skiff, domestic exterior grade Douglas-fir plywood might suit the bill. On the other hand, if you are looking for longevity and a fine finish, one of the more expensive imported brands would be the appropriate choice. What makes the difference between these two options? Quality of materials and standards of manufacture.

American plywood tends to be made of Douglas fir or Western larch, while the imported sheets are usually made of tropical hardwoods. American plywood standards allow for more gaps or voids and for repairs to the plies; they also generally allow thicker (and fewer) plies per sheet than their British cousins. When purchasing American marine plywood look for the stamp of the American Plywood Association. And whenever shopping for any marine plywood, buy from a reputable dealer who is familiar with the product.

☞ Approximate Weights Per Cubic Foot of Some Selected Woods in Pounds

Species	Oven Dry	Green
Ash, White	40	50
Cedar, Atlantic White	21	
Cedar, Western Red	21	31
Cedar, Port Orford	28	37
Cedar, Northern White	19	41
Cedar, Spanish	35	42
Cedar, Alaska	29	35
Bald Cypress	29	58
Douglas Fir	32	40
Hackmatack, Eastern Larch	28	36
Locust, Black	46	66
Lauan, Red	28	
Mahogany, West Indies	30	
Mahogany, "Philippine," Tangile	38	
Mahogany, "African" Khaya	29	
Oak, White	46	62
Oak, Northern Red	40	63
Pine, Eastern White	23	39
Pine, Yellow	44	47
Spruce, White (Eastern)	27	38
Spruce, Sitka	26	33
Teak	39	

SOURCE: *WOOD: A MANUAL FOR ITS USE AS A SHIPBUILDING MATERIAL*—BUREAU OF SHIPS, U.S. DEPARTMENT OF THE NAVY

A FEW OTHER NOTES

Any way you cut it, wood for boats is expensive, and always has been. To get the most for your money while conserving resources, get in the habit of using patterns. To some, the making of patterns before the finished piece is felt to be a waste of time.

"No time for sissy patterns," cries our cranky colleague. "Get on with it!"

Baloney. Patterns save time. They enable you to make the right cut, the first time, with no waste. They also allow you to lay out all your pieces at once, maximizing the utility of each piece of wood and utilizing natural grain patterns for greatest strength.

Also, try using recycled (pre-owned?) lumber. There are a number of businesses that specialize in stocking lumber resurrected from old mills, salvaged from the bottom of rivers, and such. The quality of the lumber can be quite high, as the trees it came from were likely as not old growth.

For a list of certified sources of "good wood" and recycled lumber, contact the Certified Forest Products Council, 14780 S.W. Osprey Dr., #285, Beaverton, OR 97007, tel. 503–590–6600, fax 503–590–6655.

☞ Avoiding Decay

Decay is the hobgoblin of the boatbuilder. It can wreak havoc on a vessel, attacking the keel, frames, transom, and deck. The culprit in this tale of rot and degradation is growth and proliferation of fungi, which attack and weaken wood by breaking down the cell walls that provide strength. To make matters worse, the fungi produce spores that are easily dispersed and can spread further decay.

Rot is not inevitable in a wooden boat, and with a bit of planning it can be avoided entirely. The fungi that are responsible for decay need quite specific conditions to thrive:

- The moisture content must be over 25 percent of the dry weight of wood for rot to take place; anything less cannot sustain wood-attacking fungi. (Waterlogged wood, however, cannot sustain decay fungi either.)
- Decay fungi prefer fresh water to salt.
- Warm, dead air—roughly 75 to 90 degrees Fahrenheit—will provide the proper greenhouse conditions for promoting growth of decay fungi.

If the boatbuilder can remove or change one or more of the above prerequisites, the fungus has much less chance of surviving.

Ventilation

The easiest route to the discouragement of decay is to ensure that there will be continuous circulation and supply of fresh air. Be sure to include vents to all enclosed areas including bulkheads, compartments, and lockers. Be sure you have removable panels and floorboards to encourage the circulation of drying air, prevent condensation, and allow easy inspection. If the boat has a ceiling (interior planking), include an air course (a gap in the ceiling planking) near the top to allow air to freely circulate between the frames and for moist air to be drawn up and out somewhat like a chimney.

Drainage

Get rid of any opportunity for fresh water to linger in the boat and to aid and abet the fungi. Be sure there are plenty of limbers (drains) in the floors, between the butt blocks and the frames, in maststeps, and in often overlooked areas, such the sawn frames at the notches for the chine and the bottom edges of cabin windows. Bevel the tops of butt blocks and the top edges of chines. Be sure that the deck, whether laid or covered, is tight, including the joint between the deck and the hull. All wood-to-wood joints should be painted before assembly and well bedded. Bed all fittings as well. Install garboard drains at the lowest areas.

Selecting wood

Some wood species have far more natural decay resistance than others; hence, use the most rot-resistant woods available. This is especially true for boats used in freshwater lakes and streams. White oak should be selected over red. White cedar over pine. Ash is considered nondurable and should be avoided for keels and frames.

Woods with nonresistant qualities but with other endearing qualities, such as spruce for spars, should always be well varnished and placed in dry and well-ventilated situations.

Determining which woods are best for your region will require a bit of research and reliance on local knowledge. Local conditions and availability will dictate the species to select. Use only the heartwood of the resistant species; avoid sapwood, as its resistance to rot is very low. Inspect all stock for signs of infection, discoloration, insect damage, or punkiness indicating actual early decay.

What about preservatives?

Time was—and it was not that long ago—when you talked preservatives, you meant coal-tar creosote, lead, pentachlorophenal, or copper naphthanate. Vile and efficacious, for the most part, these potions were lavishly applied by boatbuilders with the same zealotry as the farmer once spread DDT. But that was before laboratory and medical research on the toxicity of these products to mammals (not to mention, mandates of governmental regulatory agencies) changed the landscape. In some regions, wood preservatives have become highly restricted commodities, and in some communities their use has been banned outright.

A possible effective alternative to the old standbys is borate wood preservatives. Borate treatment has been in use for many years in Australia, New Zealand, and Europe to deter fungi and insects in wood. The most basic borate preservative is simple boric acid. Other, more refined formulations have been developed to address particular needs, such as enhanced stability and improved penetration of wood.

One of the most positive aspects of borate preservatives is their ease and safety of application. A borate solution is easy to mix: simply add the recommended weight of powder to a gallon of hot tap water and stir. It can be brushed, sprayed, dipped, or rolled onto the wood. As the product is water soluble, any wood so treated that is exposed to running water must be sealed with paint or varnish.

Finally

The best defenses against decay are good building and good maintenance techniques. Approaching the construction of the boat as building for the ages will go a long way toward making it last for ages. Taking the time to do the job right will pay dividends for years to come.

5 • FASTENINGS

Selecting and determining the correct use of fastenings is more important than often realized. For example, when considering the task to be done—say, attaching a plank to a frame—the builder must first consider a number of factors:

What type of fastener? Rivet, screw, or nail?

The fastener should be properly sized for the job. Too small, and the structure will be weak. Too large, and the frame can be split.

What metal shall you use? Metals like copper and bronze carry a high price tag. (But, remember that it is the stingy builder who pays the highest price.)

Mixing the wrong metals can turn your boat into a battery and ruin the fastenings. (More on this later.)

Before selecting which fastening to use, it's useful to think of the fasteners simply as tools to hold what you have in place rather than a bunch of baby clamps to be used to pull things together. Occasionally, fasteners can serve for the latter use, but success is more serendipitous than by design.

Before choosing a type of fastening, dust off your crystal ball and contemplate whether repairs will ever be needed to the structure. There can be a price to be paid down the line for using those easy-to-install but oh-so-inextractable ring nails.

Beware of over-fastening. If two screws will do the job, four is definitely not better. Indeed, doubling the fastenings will probably weaken the assembly.

A LOOK AT THE METALS

Galvanized "iron"

"Iron" fastenings today are likely to be nondurable mild steel. Beware of so-called "galvanized" fittings from the hardware store that are merely electroplated—that is, zinc flavored. If galvanized fastenings and fittings are used, demand only the genuine hot-dipped variety.

Silicon bronze

This metal is the top choice when seeking a combination of strength, durability, and price. The holding power of bronze screws is superior to galvanized, as the threads are sharper.

Copper

Perhaps the most ancient and reliable of fastening metals. However the metal is so soft that it is really only appropriate for rivets and clench nails.

Stainless steel

Fastenings made from stainless steel should be viewed with suspicion. A number of different alloys are marketed as stainless steel, and it is difficult to tell what you are getting or how much resistance to corrosion the fastening will have. Caution suggests using stainless steel only in above-water situations.

Brass

Brass is a poor choice for a marine fastening, as it contains a large amount of zinc; galvanic action will erode the zinc and reduce the fastening to a pink amalgamous mush.

Monel

This nickel-copper alloy is unsurpassed for strength and corrosion resistance. It's difficult to beat for high price, too: hardly any fastening costs more.

GALVANIC ACTION

Sometimes referred to as electrolysis, galvanic action occurs when two dissimilar metals are immersed in salt water. Each metal has a different tendency, or electrical potential, to ionize. When the two metals are brought in contact with each other by an electrolyte (the salt water), a battery-like action occurs, creating an electrical current between the metals, causing one of them to waste away. The metal that wastes away is known as the least noble or anodic. The other metal is called the most noble or cathodic. The greater the differences in electrical potential between the metals, the greater the problem.

The table at top right is a partial galvanic series. It lists metals and alloys relative to their nobility. The closer the metals are to each other on the table the less difference in electrical potential there is between them.

Ideally, it would be best to use just one kind of metal throughout the construction of the hull and avoid the problem of galvanic action altogether, but this is not always practical. The next best thing is to utilize metals that are galvanically compatible relative to the series. An example of this might be using copper rivets and silicon-bronze screws.

A LOOK AT THE FASTENINGS

Copper rivet

The copper rivet is in many ways the ideal fastening, as copper is very corrosion resistant and the rivet itself is a very simple concept. The rivet is a nail that is driven through a hole drilled through two boards clamped

☞ Galvanic Series

Most Noble or Cathodic
- Titanium
- Stainless Steel (passive)
- Monel
- Nickel
- Silicon Bronze
- Copper
- Brass
- Lead
- Stainless Steel (active)
- Cast Iron
- Wrought Iron
- Mild Steel
- Aluminum
- Galvanized Steel or Iron
- Zinc

Least Noble or Cathodic

together. A rove or burr is driven over the nail, and the excess of the nail is cut off with nippers. The stub of the nail is then peened against the rove with a hammer while the head of the rivet is backed up by a heavy iron.

And there you have it. The materials—the nail and the rove—are relatively cheap, the hole does minimal damage to the materials being fastened, and a damaged rivet is easily replaced. The one big disadvantage is that riveting generally takes two people, one to back up the head and another to peen over the end, and that takes time and money.

Wood screw

The development of the screw fastening was a major advance for the production boatbuilder. While fastening a plank to a frame with rivets generally requires two mechanics to do the job, fastening with screws requires only one. As the screws don't protrude through the frame, boats can be more easily built upside down over a production jig. Hardware can be fastened from one side, and the screws can be quickly and easily removed for repairs.

Clench nail

A clench nail is a small, square-cut copper nail. It is used in light construction, such as fastening plank laps between frames. It is driven though a pre-drilled hole and turned back on itself (clenched) by holding a heavy curved iron on the inside of the plank.

Carriage bolt

A carriage bolt is a screw bolt with a round head. A square section beneath the head locks into the wood and prevents the bolt from spinning. The carriage bolt is the fastening of choice for putting together heavy-duty assemblies, such as the stem and the keel.

Drift

In many ways, the drift—also known as drift pin, or drift bolt—can be categorized as a homemade spike. It is generally made from rounded bronze or iron rod, slightly pointed or chamfered by pounding on one end. The other end will usually have a ring placed over it and the end will be peened over. A drift can be used to great advantage in "blind" fastening to large timber assemblies. Examples might be when fastening floor timbers to the keel, attaching the sternpost to the deadwood, or edge fastening one centerboard plank to the next.

Annular, or ring nail

The ring nail is sometimes referred to by the trade name "Anchorfast." It is driven into a slightly undersized pilot hole. The ring barbs force the wood fibers apart as the nail is driven, "locking" the nail into the wood, thus preventing it from backing out. The ring nail should be viewed as a permanent or nonrepairable fastening, as it is very difficult to extract.

Hot-dipped galvanized boat nail

The galvanized boat nail is a close relation to the old-fashioned iron cut nail. Although ancient in appearance, the boat nail has exceptional holding power. Used primarily for heavier workboat construction, this distinctive fastening is identified by its square-cut shank, blunt point, and distinctive, chunky, rosette-like head. It is used mostly to fasten planks to heavy frames. To avoid splitting the stock, an undersized hole should be drilled for the nail. When installed, the head should be set below the surface. Care should be taken to avoid chipping the galvanized protective surface.

Machine screw

Silicon-bronze machine screws with nuts and washers are sometimes used as a replacement for rivets in both new construction and repairs.

DEPARTMENT OF TEMPORARY FASTENINGS

Sheetrock or drywall screws

Boats were built before the invention of these bugle-headed prodigies, but it is difficult to imagine how. Their uses are many: constructing a strongback, building molds, building up patterns, fastening bracing, and any number of temporary tasks. These handy little rascals are available from any hardware store in either black or galvanized form. Made of hardened steel, and very sharp, they do their best work in softwood, where they can be quickly driven with a screw gun, without need of predrilling a pilot hole. Their performance is less stellar

in hardwood, where the screw's brittleness allows the shank to snap off easily the first time the going gets tough.

Do not use drywall screws as permanent fastenings in the boat, as they will swiftly turn to rust. If using these screws to anchor freshly glued assemblies, remember to coat them with a release agent, such as wax, for easy removal.

Duplex or staging nails

Staging nails are manufactured with two heads on the shank of the nail, one below the other. When hammering in such a nail, drive it until the first head makes contact with the surface of the wood. The second head, set a bit further up at the end of the nail, allows easy removal of the nail with a small crowbar. A pound or two of these specialty fasteners are mighty handy to have around the shop for quick emergency jobs, such as anchoring bracing when setting up molds or erecting a temporary shelter.

Staples

Staples have many assorted uses around the shop. To avoid unsightly rust stains from them, use staples of either bronze, stainless steel, monel, or one of the new plastics.

Hot-melt glue

The ever-popular hot-melt glue gun, although better known for its yeoman duty in the manufacture of an uncounted myriad of Styrofoam Christmas ornaments, has found a niche in boatbuilding as well, especially in the construction of patterns and strip-planked canoes. Even though standard hot-melt glue is not particularly tenacious, its quick setting quality is a boon when putting together temporary assemblies. Patterns that are not predicted to take hard use can be quickly held together by strategically placed blobs of the hot stuff. Light cedar strips can be provisionally "spot welded" together with short beads of clear glue, rather than staples or nails that will have to be dealt with later. You can even hang up your blueprints with hot-melt glue.

A CLOSER LOOK AT WOOD SCREWS

For most small craft, silicon-bronze screws are the fastening of choice. Durable, highly resistant to ordinary corrosion, and relatively reasonably priced, these little jewels are without peer. But for the builder unfamiliar with the habits of the metal or who is a devotee of the high-speed screw-gun, the installation of bronze screws can be an exercise in frustration. One can encounter wrung-off shanks, torn-out slots, "unwound" threads, and worse.

Part of the difficulty is in the metal itself. Although considerably stronger than traditional yellow brass, bronze fastenings can seem brittle when compared to steel fastenings. However, much of the difficulty with screw installation comes not from the fastening itself, but rather from a misunderstanding of how a wood screw should actually be installed. Perhaps this phenomenon is due to the now-ubiquitous drywall screw, which can be blasted into almost any softwood, often without a pilot hole or the use of clamps to hold the pieces together. Try that with a standard bronze wood screw, in oak, and the results can prove ruinous. For sure, a more circumspect approach is required here.

A little philosophy

There is one thing screws and rivets have in common. They are both designed to fasten together pieces of wood that have already been drawn into place. They are not intended to pull together the pieces of wood as if they were mini C-clamps. That's not to say you can't get away with that sort of legerdemain occasionally, but it's best not to count on it.

To understand better how a screw works, let's take a quick look at how it compares to a rivet. A rivet is simply a nail fixed into a tightfitting drilled hole. A snug washer (burr, or rove) is driven down over the end of the nail until it contacts the wood. The excess nail is clipped off, and the remaining stub of the nail is peened over the washer. That's all there is to it. The rivet cares little what kind of wood it passes through as long as its hole is the right size. The actual holding power comes from the end rings—the nail head and the rove—that keep the pieces of wood together.

Screws employ a different technology to hold things together. Instead of the external rings of the rivet, the screw gets its holding power from its threads, which are tapped into the wood. Here the type of wood being fastened does make a difference. Harder woods will hold screw fastenings better than soft woods.

Now hold a typical wood screw up to inspection and you'll see that it is a rather complex creation. There is a conical head with a slot, or other driving configuration, a stout shank, cut threads, and a center "root" to which the threads are attached. For the fastening to gain maximum holding power and not break, the screw hole has to be drilled just right. Drilling a single hole with a twist bit will just about guarantee a broken screw. So what to do?

Drilling the hole

One route is to break out your drill index and select one bit for the countersink, another for the shank to slide through, and still another for the "root"—roughly, the caliber of the root in hardwood—of the screw. It's a bit of a chore, but at least you know you'll have a proper screw hole.

But, you say, you don't have 50 years to build this boat. Isn't there another way?

Aye, Mate, there is: The patent countersink-counterbore with tapered bits, the most popular model of which is made by Fuller. This fully adjustable unit automatically counterbores and sinks a hole for the head; the tapered bit bores a hole that approximates the shape of the shank and root.

Does the Fuller-type combination bit produce a product as good as that from multiple bits? Probably not. It is a compromise, but one that works fairly well. But whatever system you use, be sure to drill deep enough! Short holes are yet another cause of heartbreaking screw failure.

Screw lubrication

So, you have your hole drilled to perfection, and you're ready to go, right? Well, maybe not. Yet another cause of breakage is when a screw binds up in the hole and our unsuspecting builder merrily continues to advance the screwdriver until the fastening twists off, leaving an embedded stump. This is quite bothersome, especially when it is so easily avoided with a little lubrication.

There are a number of different types of slippery stuff that will work. Old-timers favored paint, such as red lead. Others prefer soap, tallow, or grease (although, some express doubt at the wisdom of introducing stearic acid or other deleterious chemicals found in grease into the structure). Boatyard bedding compound, albeit a bit messy, is a good option, as it hangs right onto the screw and is chemically benign.

Perhaps the best choice of all is a product obtained from your local plumbing house. I refer to, of course, the trusty wax toilet bowl seal. This permanently softened wax has the perfect consistency for sticking to the threads of a screw, is readily available, and, best of all, is cheap. Just jab a handful of screws into the ring, and you're ready to go.

Just one more thing

Whatever screw-driving tool you use—brace-and-bit, Yankee screwdriver, or power driver—once you start installing that screw, keep right on going. For some reason or another, if you stop midway for coffee, chances are good the fastening will fetch up in mid-hole. Then when driving is recommenced, the screw will snap, causing unnecessary consternation. So just go all the way for the screw, then go for the coffee.

And if you're using that macho power driver, keep it in first gear, and do the final tightening of the screw by hand.

A Closer Look at Rivets

The rivet has been in use in boat construction since at least 800 A.D.. In the United States, a rivet is usually a copper common nail—flat head, smooth shank, and a diamond point—combined with a flat copper burr. A European rivet is square in cross section, with either a flat, or proud rosette head, and a dished copper rove.

For the sake of this discussion, a burr is a roove is a

☞ The Screw Gun

The battery-powered screw gun has proliferated over the last few years. And a handy rig it is, too. For building patterns, assembling molds, and putting up drywall, this powerful unit is unsurpassed. With a screw gun it is possible to shoot vast quantities of fastenings into a job in very short order. But when it comes to using such a tool on boats, the enthusiasm for this technological wonder should be tempered with caution.

The problem with a screw gun is that it is primarily designed to install steel fasteners into materials of uniform density. In boat construction, a builder often needs to secure woods of unequal densities, such as a soft cedar to hard oak. It takes little effort for a screw gun to drive a screw right through the cedar and to even split the oak behind. It also is quite easy for it to wring off a brittle bronze fastening that has become seized in the oak. Before tackling a project, it is prudent to run a few instructive trials in a couple of pieces of scrap stock. And always remember to pre-lubricate the screws with wax.

---

rove (by any other name would smell as sweet). Whatever you call this copper washer, it should be slightly undersized so it can be driven onto the nail without falling off.

Riveting tools

The tools necessary to do the job are as few as they are simple. Although they can be purchased right of the shelf (usually through catalogs), most of the required implements are also easily manufactured in the boatshop.

End-cutting nippers

These are a bit more difficult to find than side-cutting wire-snipping pliers, but they are definitely available (although your hardware merchant may have to special order them for you). Get good-quality nippers, and if you have a choice, get the pair with the longer handles. You'll appreciate the extra leverage.

Ball-peen hammer

We're not talking locomotive size here. Good results can be obtained with a hammer in the 4- to 8-ounce range.

Standard carpenter's hammer

For driving the rivets (nails) into place. 12- to 16-ounce is fine.

Holding iron or dolly

The holding iron is a cylinder of metal similar to the head of a large hammer. A common commercial size is 6 pounds. The mass of the iron is important, so that when you are backing the rivet head the iron will stay put rather than bounce in response to the blows of the ball-peen hammer. The best holding irons have a stud or tip protruding from one end for backing countersunk and counterbored nail heads.

The holding iron can be a shop-built item: a sledge-hammer head, a turned piece of propeller shaft, or even a large bolt. A hole can be drilled and tapped in one end to let in a piece of threaded rod to act as a stud.

Rove iron or rivet set

This is similar to a heavy nail set with a hole drilled in one end and is used to drive the rove over the pointed end of the rivet after it has been driven. This can be as simple as a piece of heavy rod with a hole drilled into one end. Some deluxe models are knurled on a lathe for a better grip for the mechanic.

Drill index and electric drill

For boring the pilot holes.

Hearing protection

Peening rivets is a noisy business.

The technique

Let's assume that we're riveting planks to frames. (Rivets can be used to rivet the laps in lapstrake planking, which is what is being shown in Figure 5-2.) The job begins by

5-1: The tools of the riveter, including a light hammer, end-cutting nippers, and homemade holding devices.

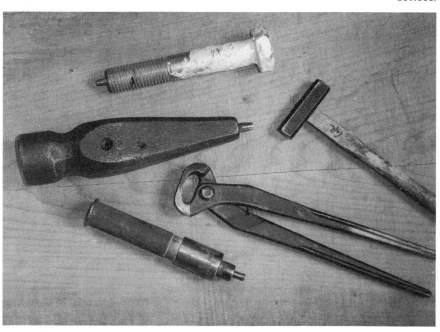

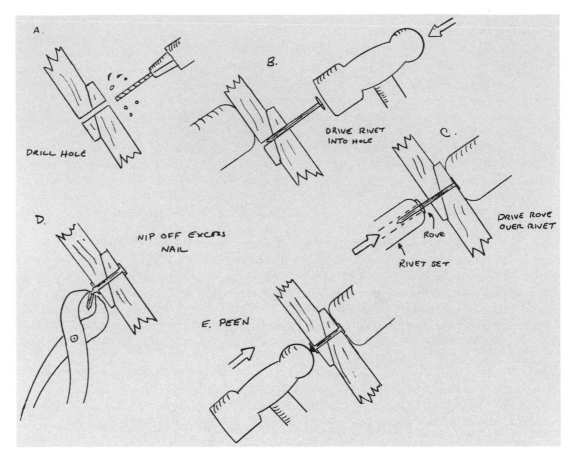

A. DRILL HOLE

B. DRIVE RIVET INTO HOLE

C. DRIVE ROVE OVER RIVET — ROVE — RIVET SET

D. NIP OFF EXCESS NAIL

E. PEEN

clamping tightly the pieces to be riveted, as the rivets are not intended to draw the wood together, only to hold what you have. Use deep-throated clamps to ensure the farther edge of the plank is indeed pulled in tightly, and be sure to wedge the plank tightly next to the previous one.

Next, bore a pilot hole for the rivet. Drill a slightly undersized hole, so the nail will grip the wood that it is going through. This will keep the plank from backing away from the frame after the clamps are removed, as well as allow you to install all of the rivets without having to stop to set the roves and peen on each rivet as you go along.

By the way, to break up the tedium of riveting, some builders prefer to set and peen the rivets on each plank as it is hung, rather than have to deal with a virtual iron maiden of a hull bristling with spikes. If, however, the boat is being built upside down over a construction jig, the builder may have no other choice than to wait until the boat is off the jig and right-side up to do the riveting.

Drive the nail through the pilot hole with a standard weight hammer. Holding an iron to the inside of the frame next to the drilled pilot hole will make your hammer blows more efficient.

The rove can be set using the rivet set and hammer to drive the rove down over the nail while the head of the nail is backed up with the holding iron. If the nail is to be set flush with the surface of the plank, the flat of the holding iron can just be pressed against the head of the nail. If, on the other hand, it is to be set in a counterbored hole, the blunt point or stud of the iron must be pressed against the head in the counterbored hole.

Nip off the excess stock, leaving $1/8$ inch or so (roughly, the diameter of the nail) beyond the rove. Some builders prefer to grip the shank of the nail first with the end nippers and "rock" the rounded end of the plier against the rove to further set the rivet. They will then take a second bite and nip the excess off.

The rivet can now be finished off. Hit the nipped end with the flat end of the hammer to slightly flare the metal, then finish it off with light taps from the ball end, mushrooming the rivet. As soon as the rivet has been rounded, your job is done; further beating will only serve to harden the metal, causing the peened end to crack.

A caveat: When peening, watch your aim with the hammer, as inattention will make the wood surrounding the rivet look as though it had been, well, mugged by a ball-peen hammer.

Power play

If you are doing production work, the novelty of peening thousands of rivets can soon wear off. An answer to this is the pneumatic rivet gun, a.k.a. air hammer. This handy item can be purchased through aviation supply houses. The gun will accept a number of different rivet sets that will give the desired round to the end of the rivet.

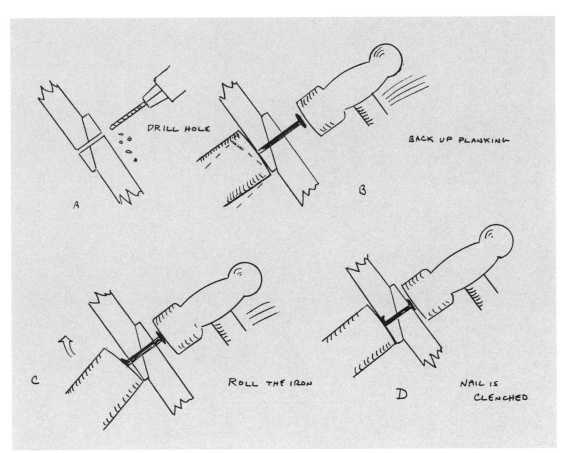

Practice with this tool is essential, as the trigger is most sensitive; pulling it is akin to using a mini machine gun.

A CLOSER LOOK AT COPPER CLENCH NAILS

A copper clench nail is a cut nail with the sharp, beveled point of a tack. When installed, it perhaps can best be described as a one-legged staple. Instead of peening the end of the nail over a rove, the nail is turned back on itself as soon as it emerges from the wood.

Clench nails can be used just about anywhere a rivet can be used, and although they are probably not quite as good a fastening as the rivet, they certainly are adequate for light construction. They have the added bonus of being faster to install than rivets, and they can be driven single-handedly. Clench nails have particular value in fastening the laps between the frames in lapstrake and dory-lap construction.

Clenching tools

Light hammer—for driving the nails.

Drill and a slightly undersized bit—for boring pilot holes.

Holding iron—this can be a large hammer head or even an automotive body work iron (the mushroom-shaped type works well).

The technique

As with riveting, clench nailing requires practice for proficiency, but the rewards are well worth the time. Begin by clamping your stock tightly together. Next, drill a sightly undersized pilot hole for the nail. There are occasions where you can get away by driving the nail directly, but you stand a much greater chance of splitting out the wood.

When clenching planks, builders like to pre-mark the nail locations equally by "walking" them out with dividers. Generally speaking, two nails between frames will do the job.

Next, while holding the backing iron to the inside of the pilot hole, drive in the nail. When the beveled point contacts the face of the iron, roll the iron ever so slightly to turn the point back on itself. (The nail should be rolled from the beveled side of the point and turned inward toward the middle of the plank.)

Although it might be a mite faster to work with two people—one outside nailing, one inside backing—a fine clenching job can be done by one person working alone, and there is a lot to be said for that.

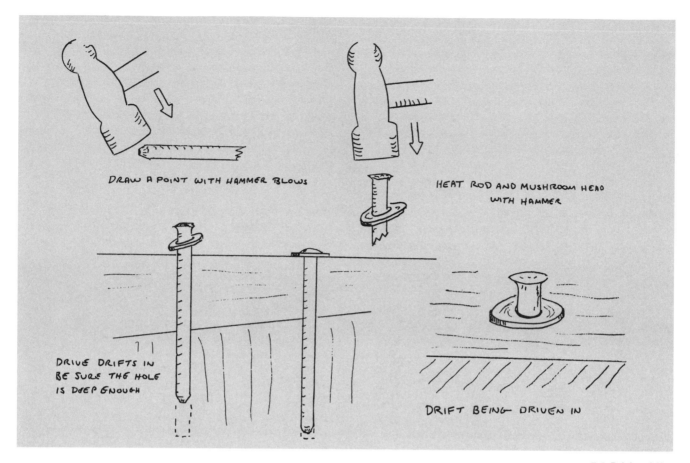

DRAW A POINT WITH HAMMER BLOWS

HEAT ROD AND MUSHROOM HEAD WITH HAMMER

DRIVE DRIFTS IN BE SURE THE HOLE IS DEEP ENOUGH

DRIFT BEING DRIVEN IN

5-4: Driving drifts, step by step.

A Closer Look at Drifts and Long Bolts

Many will be the occasion when the builder is faced with a lack of off-the-shelf fasteners, because they are either too expensive or unavailable. He must make them himself. Actually, homemade fasteners are common fare in small craft. After all, what is the rivet but a homemade fastener (a nail and a washer)? Two prime candidates for quick manufacture are drift pins and extra-long bolts.

Drifts

Drifts are most commonly made of either bronze or galvanized rod cut to length as needed. The "head" is formed by a washer or clinch ring that has been slid over the rod, and the end of the rod is mushroomed or peened over the washer.

Perhaps the easiest way to get a good job of peening is to first clamp the rod vertically in a vise. Then, after heating the end with a propane torch to anneal the metal and prevent work hardening and cracking, beat the top of the rod until it flares enough to secure the ring from sliding off. The other end of the drift can be slightly pointed as an aid to driving. Some builders nick the sides of the rod with a cold chisel to increase holding power; the effect is similar to that of a ring nail.

Even though the drift can be considered a close cousin of the spike, there are important differences, such as the necessity of pre-drilling for the drift with a bit of just the right size. And unlike threaded bolts (another close cousin), once the drift is driven, it is there for good. You won't have a second chance to get it right. Hence, drilling for and driving drifts requires a little preparation.

A hole for a drift must be drilled just slightly undersize to provide a "driving" or driven fit. If the hole is oversize, the pin won't hold at all; if it is too much undersize, the pin will bind up partway in and may buckle in the hole or even split the timber, either one of which is most undesirable. Take the time to run a few experimental holes in scrap stock to make sure you are using the right size bit for the job.

Lay out the locations of your drifts on the side of stock to be joined. Be sure that you won't be running into any other bolts or stopwaters. Many builders like to install their drifts in an offset pattern; that is, the drifts are driven so they are not parallel to each other. The thought here is that if the joined timbers try to back off, they will be immediately locked up on the opposing pins, much like the action of those old-fashioned "Chinese Finger-Snapper" toys: the harder you pull, the tighter the lock becomes.

Check that the timbers to be joined are tightly clamped together for drilling and driving. If there is a gap between the pieces when the drift is driven, it will be ever thus. No amount of pounding will bring them together. And before starting to drive that drift home, plumb the bored hole with a piece of wire to make sure it is slightly longer than the drift. Better to find out now that the hole is too short than later. Then after checking one more time, and after adding any bedding compounds or adhesives required by the situation in the joint, drive that baby home.

Long bolts

Extra-long homemade bolts are a straightforward alternative to the store-bought, and expensive, carriage bolt. All that is necessary to make one up is a length of rod, a couple of washers, a nut sized to the rod, and a thread-cutting die.

Begin by laying out the location for the bolt on the side of your stock. Measure and cut the rod to size. Then, in the same fashion as the drift bolt, slide on the ring and peen over one end of the rod. Then, flip the rod over in the vise. Select a thread-cutting die that matches the threads of the nut (probably an NC thread). Cut just enough threads into the rod to allow the nut to firmly tighten the rod, and you are in business! Use this fastening like any other carriage bolt.

Concerned that the bolt might rotate as you tighten the nut and you'll have no way to hold it? Try this:

Instead of peening one end to keep the washer in place, cut just enough threads (plus a little more) on that end. Twist on a nut until it tightens against the end of the threads. Then, peen the extra threads to lock the nut in place. Now, you'll be able to easily tighten the other nut by putting a socket wrench on each end.

6 • GLUES, PAINTS, AND POTIONS

Years ago when wood was plentiful and glues were unreliable and made from the feet of dead horses, boatbuilders could eschew the use of adhesives. Who wanted them? Who needed them?

Alas, times changed. No longer were the great timbers available. Wood needed to be looked at in a different light: more as an engineering material that could be cut up and reassembled in a myriad of ways, maximizing its strengths and minimizing its weaknesses. But the first water-resistant synthetic resin adhesive wasn't developed until the early part of this century; only then could wood be reliably glued for marine use.

WATERPROOF GLUE

Truly "waterproof" glues did not arrive on the scene until World War II. Today, there are basically three time-tested types: plastic resin, resorcinol resin, and the ubiquitous epoxies.

Plastic resin

This urea resin adhesive is commonly known by its trade name Weldwood and is readily identified by its familiar plastic tub sitting on the glue aisle at your local hardware store. A dry powder mixed with water, it is not truly waterproof; rather, it is classified as "water resistant." This old war horse enjoys considerable popularity, as it is inexpensive, readily available, easy to use, and reliable. When cured, Weldwood is relatively strong and durable, although somewhat brittle. Some devotees of this product will use nothing else, but for boat work its less-than-completely-waterproof classification makes total reliance on it a poor policy.

Resorcinol resin

Rugged, truly waterproof, and somewhat pricey, this glue is packaged in two parts—one a powder and the other a deep-purple liquid. It is a good choice when working with oak (epoxy has a history of failures with that species). The joints joined by resorcinol are stronger than the wood itself. The glue can be somewhat temperamental to use, however. As it does not fill gaps well, resorcinol demands tightfitting joints that should be tightly clamped during assembly. Workplace temperatures can be finicky as well, as the glue wants roughly 70 degrees F to cure properly. Yet raising the temperature too much can cause the glue to set up too quickly. A drawback if the wood being joined is to be finished bright is the stunning purple color that resorcinol imparts to wood.

Epoxy

Epoxy glues, long known for their high strength, gap-filling qualities, and their low clamping pressure requirements, are an excellent choice for a boatbuilding adhesive. Epoxies are a bit different from the run-of-the-mill glues that can simply be whipped up by a standard recipe, spread on, and clamped. Indeed, the term "epoxy," is really a catchall for various and sundry products based on epoxy resin. The resin and companion hardeners are modified (by the outfits that manufacture the product) to address different needs, properties, and applications, and also "to build a better mousetrap."

What this means is that all epoxies are not the same. Some are formulated to be more elastic, or less; some to have lower viscosity for greater substrate penetration; some to allow a quicker cure or perhaps to cure at a lower temperature. Some are mixed in different ratios of resin to hardener, such as 5:1, 2:1, and 1:1. Some are formulated to be safer to use—that's good. Some aren't even waterproof—that's not so good.

Epoxies have been highly promoted (perhaps too much). The terms "easy-to-use," "panacea," "elixir," and "a gift to mankind" come to mind. Yes, the stuff does a pretty decent job of sticking things together, but it is only as good as the techniques used by the builder who applies it. The product is fairly sophisticated, and much of the grumbling over failed projects—"That blasted *$@!!*#%@! no good epoxy!"—can be traced back to operator error.

Close attention must be paid to the properties of the product and the recipe that makes it do its job. Take the time to do a little research about the application you're going to use epoxy on. The companies that sell the stuff want you to succeed, and they have technical staff and support literature available to help you get the job done right the first time.

There are a few health risks associated with epoxy, primarily skin sensitization from prolonged and repeated contact with the product. This condition can sneak up on you, as it appears that the condition is cumulative. Hence, it is imperative to always work safely and cleanly.

Wear disposable gloves or barrier cream when working with epoxy. Don't smoke while working, or use the glue-up station as your lunch table, with the resin as a condiment. Be sure that there is adequate ventilation. And always wear an effective dust mask when sanding cured epoxy.

Don't even think of using solvents to remove epoxy from your skin. The solvents will drive the chemicals right into your body. Instead, use a waterless handcleaner for the job. For cleaning up tools, try vinegar; it's cheap and effective.

FILLERS, COMPOUNDS, AND PUTTIES

Most boatbuilders agree that some sort of water-excluding goop should be placed between any two pieces of wood being fastened together, but there is little consensus about what type. Nearly every boatbuilder has a favorite elixir he believes is just the substance to use. The choices range from concoctions of pine tar, linseed oil, and bee's wax to the same industrial adhesives used to hold the space shuttle together. The conundrum of which is best to use seems to have as many philosophical considerations as there are practical. Making a choice involves a lively mix of utility, romance, tradition, faith healing, and the proper amount of juju. Let's examine a few applications and options.

Old-time planking seam compounds

After the boat has been caulked (or recaulked), the next step is to fill the seams with a flexible compound. Old-timers like Pete Culler, who wrote extensively on the subject, favored home remedies, such as a white lead and whiting paste for above-the-waterline use. Apparently this mix was highly durable, lasting for years. Underwater, a mixture of pine tar and whiting was the preferred filling. For an old, tired boat, Mr. Culler recommended tallow and slaked lime, as it was cheap and easy to reef out when the time came to recaulk. As concerns over health have made white lead difficult or impossible to come by, some traditionalists have opted for roofing tar. This works well and certainly is economical, as long as your plans include painting the boat black to camouflage bleeding tar.

A more practical off-the-shelf solution is prepared seam compound in a can. Available in white for topsides work and brown for underwater, these products work on the principle of a binder system that allows the surface skin to dry. Beneath the skin, the product remains flexible, allowing the planks to work, while still staying in place. Intended to be used for caulked and paint-primed seams, this product is easily applied with a putty knife.

The stuff in the tube

Visit your local chandlery and you'll see a plethora of synthetic products in a tube that can be suitable, or even great, for use as seam compound or bedding, and new ones are being introduced all the time. One caveat, however: just because it comes in a tube doesn't mean it's all the same stuff. Not only are the materials different between brands—thiokol-based polysulfides are not the same as polyurethanes, for example—their formulated qualities are different as well. Rates of adhesion, resistance to solvents, flexibility, speed of cure, and available colors can vary widely, even among products of a single manufacturer. Some are formulated to be a flexible adhesive; others to be a sealant with adhesive qualities.

A few of the polyurethane formulas, such as Sikaflex's

240 and 3M's 5200, are tremendous adhesives; tougher than an old truck tire yet flexible like a motor mount. They'll stick to just about anything insistently and tenaciously as long as the surface is clean. These might make a good choice for bedding a stem assembly. Other products, such as Boatlife's Lifecaulk, are formulated specifically as a sealant and have been used with great success for years. Curiously, Lifecaulk uses moisture to cure, which means it can even be gunned underwater in an emergency.

Silicone caulks are generally not recommended for marine use.

None of these products are intended to replace driven or rolled cotton caulking in plank seams. Cotton caulking not only excludes water but also mechanically stiffens the hull, locking one plank to another as if they were splined.

Paying deck seams

For paying, or filling, deck seams, incurable traditionalists are partial to hot-melted marine glue, such as Ferdico or Jefferies. Quite durable, this time-tested product is probably the best choice for historic restorations. It is not, however, user friendly. It must be melted and poured when hot, and can cause very nasty burns if it gets on your skin.

For the rest of us, the synthetic products, such as LifeCaulk or Sikaflex, may be the way to go. These products are difficult to beat for weather, UV, and chemical resistance. This is not to say that they are any bed of roses to apply, either. Requirements include proper priming of the seam, laying a bond-breaking tape in the bottom of the seam, masking the edges of the seam, and maintaining the patience, endurance, and tranquility of a monk. There is much to be said, therefore, for canvas or plywood decks.

By-the-by, if you are casting about for an implement to tool paying compound into a neat, concave seam, you need look no farther than the humble teaspoon. Just the right shape for the job, a spoon steers easily and allows the application of finger pressure right where you need it. Remember to clean the spoon before the compound cures, and your spouse will never know.

General bedding compound

Before spreading gasket compound between two pieces of wood or between a fitting (cleat, chock, etc.) and the surface it will be mounted on, first ask yourself this question: "Will I have to take this assembly apart ever again?"

As mentioned previously, some of the new bedding adhesives have extraordinarily persistent holding power, almost like a flexible epoxy. This might be exactly what the doctor ordered for some backbone members or that otherwise chronically leaking centerboard trunk. On the other hand, this may not be the best product for bedding the planking or portlights. Perhaps a more circumspect approach might be in order.

While old-fashioned leaded pastes will do the trick, boatyard bedding compound offers much of the same qualities without the potential health risks of lead. Versions of this product are offered by most of the marine paint companies. It is basically a nonadhesive linseed-oil-based product with the look and consistency of peanut butter. But it's just these low-tech qualities that give standard bedding compound its charm. It is inexpensive, efficacious, and above all, repairable. What it lacks in everlasting tenacity is more than made up by allowing easy disassembly of components. No need of a 7-foot pry bar to remove the toerail. No blasting powder necessary to loosen that plank. Just take out the fastenings and off it comes.

If you opt for the modern chemical solution, check the manufacturers' spec sheets. For example, LifeCaulk should not be used on polycarbonate plastics, such as Lexan or ABS, and most silicone caulks cannot be painted over. Surprises like these, no one needs.

Filling checks in wood

There are a number of approaches when dealing with weather checks in backbone members. The jury is still out on what is best. Roofing tar is often mentioned. One yard in Connecticut used to use a grease gun to pump a vile mixture of tallow and white lead into checks. (It was believed that the lead would keep the rats from eating the tallow.)

As for filling checks in masts and spars, it's questionable as to whether it really is necessary. Using fillers may be more a balm and panacea than anything else. Options range from adding fragrant emulsions of bee's wax, linseed oil, and rosin, working in wads of thickened epoxy, pouring in molten sulfur, and troweling in cement, to simply doing nothing at all. Which way to go is probably dictated by local conditions and customs.

PAINTS AND POTIONS

How to finish the boat? Before you pull out a can from under the cellar steps, the paint left over from the job you did on Uncle Wally's garage, let's consider the smorgasbord of choices. They range from the perennial time-tested favorites—linseed-oil-based paint, varnish, or oil—all the way to those miracle bulletproof modified neo-polyelastomorph finishes based on synthesized betel nuts and latex. And then there's Uncle Wally's garage paint....

Topside

What about house paint? With all due respect to the devotees of this product, house paint on a boat is generally a bad idea. Why? The tip-off is in the name. House paint is formulated to stand up on, well, houses. The worst that houses usually have to deal with is sunlight and weather.

Boats live in a far more hostile environment that includes abrasion by seawater, bumping into docks, and flexing of the hull. Marine finishes have been formulated to offer a more durable finish, better gloss retention, and longevity under these less-than-ideal conditions. That doesn't mean you need to run out and spend $100 a quart for a toxic concoction better suited for jet fighters. A good old-fashioned alkyd marine enamel will do for most jobs. But if you insist on using "El Cheapo" brand, remember, you gets what you pays for.

Perhaps the most important consideration in getting a quality finish is not how much you spend for the paint, but how much you take care in applying it. Painting has always been an under-appreciated art by the uninitiated, and today's sophisticated paints demand even greater attention to detail. Selection of the brush (or roller), surface preparation, proper use of thinners and brushing liquids, temperature, and time of day of application must all be considered before the job is begun.

And—free spirits and libertarians take note—read the instructions on the label. Better yet, follow them. Still stumped? Most paint manufacturers have helpful customer-service people, complete with "800" telephone numbers, who can walk you through your project.

Painting over epoxies

Many epoxies are cured with amines that produce a "blush" that will come to the surface as the epoxy cures. If untreated, this blush will react with the paint's driers and inhibit the drying of the paint. What to do? Allow the final coat of epoxy to cure thoroughly, up to a week. As amines are water soluble, wash the surface with soap and water and flush with fresh water. Then sand, clean off the residue, and paint normally.

NOTE: Washing is the key; sanding alone will not do the trick. When in doubt, make up an experimental panel with an epoxy coating to test what your paint will do.

Bottom paint

Bottom paints are formulated to discourage marine growth, grasses, and shell creatures from making a home on and in the bottom of your boat. They work by either releasing a biocide or by the sloughing off (washing away) of the outer layers of the paint.

Who needs bottom paint? If your boat spends its life in the water at a dock or a mooring, and if the temperature of that water is greater than 48 degrees F, you need it.

What kind to buy? This will involve some investigation. Rely on local knowledge. What works in your area? Give the manufacturer's technical staff a call. Tell them what you'll be using the boat for and where you'll be using it. Select the least toxic variety of paint that is effective in your operating area. There's no use in buying the industrial strength Caribbean brand if you never venture far from the coast of Maine.

Bottom coatings are toxic—that's why they work. Use proper protection when applying and removing bottom paint.

Bottom paints have their effect on the environment as well, in the water and out. Many of the more egregious formulations have been phased out. Legislation has prompted development of more "environmentally friendly" paints. Request them from your dealer. Follow the application instructions on the label and pay close attention to launching times; i.e., how long must the paint cure before the boat is put in the water. This will vary from paint to paint.

Bright finishes

Few coatings will enhance the beauty of wood as well as will varnish. A highly finished Chris-Craft or custom yacht can take your breath away. That bright finish can also take away a lot of your free time as well, as varnish is persnickety to apply and demands a blemish-free surface. Furthermore, after varnish has been applied, maintenance is the name of the game.

Before choosing a bright finish, consider how you will be using the boat. Do your cruising plans involve large dogs or small children. Will you be visiting clam flats often? Do you like boating better than varnishing? If your answer is yes to any of the above, perhaps a painted finish is what you really need. A practical compromise could be varnishing only trim or accent areas, such as rails, thwarts, transom, etc., and painting the rest.

If you find varnish's siren call impossible to resist, at least select one that is UV (ultraviolet light) resistant for improved durability.

Some alternatives to varnish

One practical alternative to varnish is a traditional oil finish. Whipped up at home from a mixture of pine tar, boiled linseed oil, and turpentine, this coating can be just the ticket for the interior of a workboat. When applied to new wood it looks great and is very easy to maintain: just brush on more oil when the surface needs it. Drawbacks? Few, as long as you like a black (or charcoal gray) interior, as this is the color the wood will eventually take after it has been exposed to the elements.

Another possibility for the incurable bright finisher is one of the relatively new wood finishes that fall somewhere in between varnish and oil. These products promise much of the appearance of varnish with (almost) the ease of application of oil, with much easier maintenance. A couple of trade names for these potions are Sikkens Cetol and Deks Olje.

☞ A Recipe for Spar and Deck Oil

1 quart boiled linseed oil
1 quart turpentine
½ pint pine tar
½ pint Japan driers.

Season to taste. More pine tar—darker color and longer drying time.

Achtung! Caution! Oily rags can burn down your shop! Never let them pile up. Do not toss in the garbage. Dispose of them safely outside.

SOURCE: THE HAMILTON MARINE CATALOG, SEARSPORT, MAINE

WATER-BASED PAINTS AND VARNISHES

U.S. federal and state governmental concerns about the ozone-producing effects of organic solvents in paints, varnishes, and preservatives (as well as in other products), have led to legislation limiting or eliminating the use of volatile solvent-based chemicals. These regulations have motived industry to develop new water-based products to meet the challenge.

How good are they? The results are mixed. Varnishes seem to be quite adequate, especially in interior applications. Topside paints have been received with less enthusiasm due to some concerns over adhesion to bare wood. In the bottom-paint department, the results have been good, the paints offering moderate protection and respectable durability. Are these products up to the standards of their more volatile cousins? Probably not, yet. But give these products a try; it will encourage manufacturers to excel and might even give us a cleaner environment.

7 • LOFTING DEMYSTIFIED

Lofting could be called series of full-size topographical mappings of the shape of the hull that allows the builder to acurately fashion all the molds, patterns, parts, and pieces to build the boat. The technique of "laying down the lines" as it is done today is relatively unchanged from practices in the mid-17th century. Prior to the introduction of lofting, vessels were built by "eye," often from half models. Depending on the creativity of the builder, it was not unusual for the finished vessel to vary considerably from the original design. The introduction of lofting was a boon to designers, as plans could be easily followed by shipyard personnel and accurate representations of the plans built.

The term lofting as it was originally used seems to have had less to do with the activity itself and more with where it occurred. The practice of drawing out the vessel's lines (and laying out the fabric for her sails) requires a goodly amount of hard-to-find dust-free and protected floor space. In the old shipyards, this space could often be economically obtained by building a floor in the loft under the rafters of one of the yard buildings. Over time, the word loft became synonymous with the activity—laying down the lines—that took place there.

Despite acceptance of lofting in shipyards, the technique has often been viewed with scepticism by the small builder and considered a waste of valuble construction time. A number of years ago, I visited a boatbuilder in Down East Maine. His family had been building a boat of the same model for years, and it had become a local classic. Partway through our conversation, I asked where he lofted his boats. He stopped in mid-plane stroke, and politely informed me that you didn't need to loft to build a boat—and that was that.

And, of course, he was absolutely right. All he needed was a keel with a transom and stem attached, a 'midship mold that could be temporarily secured with C-clamps, and lots of battens. He could set up the mold and spring the battens around it from stem to transom. By loosening up the C-clamps, he could move the mold forward or aft until the shape pleased the eye. The mold could then be fixed in place and the battens nailed to the transom, station, and stem. Then it was just a matter of making the rest of the station molds. Their dimensions would be determined by fitting to the shape developed by the sprung battens. After testing, shaving, testing, and shaving again, he was ready to fasten in his station molds. He had to remember to bevel the transom and cut the rabbet in place—more testing and fitting, shaving, and chiseling, But there you are, ready to go, and with no lofting!

Or did he end up lofting anyway—replacing pencil and eraser with a spokeshave and shims? After all, what is lofting but bending battens around known points and changing them if they are unfair? Why, it could be said that he was lofting in 3D.

What about this business of lofting? Is it really necessary to do when just building a small boat or not? We have computer-aided lofting, which can fine-tune a design and produce a set of full-sized lines on Mylar in a (relative) twinkling of an eye. Besides, many small-boat plans come with full-sized templates. Perhaps old-time lofting is but an outdated bastion for the fuzzyheaded, technopbobic, neo-Luddite nerds among us. Maybe.

Consider, however, the matter of understanding. One can intellectually get the idea of what a topographic map means without ever climbing a mountain, but the lines on that map gain enhanced meaning and purpose after you have climbed the mountain. After developing the lines yourself, you will know that they are correct—something you can't be 100 percent sure of with someone else's product, even if it was drawn by the all-knowing computer.

And there is more to be gained from a lofted set of lines than merely the station molds. That's just the beginning. You want the inside and outside faces of the transom? No problem. How about the layout of the rabbet? Easy as you please. Patterns for your stem? Layout of the stopwaters? Length of the keelbolts? Just sharpen your pencil. How about bevels on your floors or the shape of a bulkhead or how much to deduct for plank thickness? Only a few more minutes at the lofting board, and you have it.

The best part of lofting is the independence it gives you. Once you have lofted one round-bottomed boat, you pretty much have the key to lofting any boat—everything else is but a variation on a theme. Give lofting a try. It won't change the world as we know it, but you might just end up looking at boatbuilding in a whole new light.

MAKING SENSE OF THE LINES

Take the time to study your plans. Too often, this simple (and educational) step is ignored in the rush to get started. Slow down, put on the coffee pot, and roll out the sheets.

Looking at the plans

Our working plans for this exercise are for a small open boat, the Catspaw Dinghy (see Figure 7-1), but for a moment let's talk about the generic lines plan. The level of detail provided by the designer varies from extreme to minimalistic, but all plans basically follow the same architectural conventions.

Usually on one sheet, the designer will supply the lines plan, a table of offsets, and other information pertinent to the lofting of the lines. The lines plan is essentially a topographic map of your boat; it's nothing more exotic than that. In the same way that planes slicing through a mountain at regular intervals on a topographic map document and illustrate the mountain's shape, so, too, do the lines on your plan provide you with the shape of the hull. The only difference is that we have a more complete mapping of the boat than we do of the mountain. This is achieved by slicing and mapping the hull in more than one direction. All of the views (or maps) are interdependent; this means that if you change a line in one view, it will affect elements of the other views. Imagine a fishing net stretched over the outside of a salad bowl. Tug at a corner of the net, and you'll see what I mean.

Let's move on to the table of offsets. This contains reference points used in the same manner as parallels of latitude and meridians of longitude are used on maps. Offsets are your coordinates for finding specific locations on your map of the hull. The offsets are generally given in feet, inches, and eighths (although some small-craft plans, including those for the Catspaw, offer sixteenths rather than eighths). Hence, a reading of 2-3-4 in the table of offsets would be two feet, three inches, and four eighths of an inch; in other words, 2 feet 3½ inches.

By the by, although the offsets provided on plans are generally accurate, they are not infallible. The possibility that the draftsman will transpose a number here and there, or make some other faux pas when generating a table such as this, is great. Random errors like this are no big deal, as the lofting process identifies the bogus numbers and allows you to root them out.

The offsets for the stem face, the stem rabbet, the rake of the transom, etc., will generally not be in the table of offsets but will be found on the drawing itself. Also, do not assume that all the offset information is restricted to a single sheet. If your plans have multiple sheets, the data could be spread over a number of pages. You'll do well to review the entire set of plans before getting started.

Check the plans for waterline, buttock, and station spacing. Check the regularity of the spacing; for example, some of the stations on the Catspaw are spaced at 16½ inches, while others are at 19¹³⁄₁₆ inches. Also note the coordinates for the locations of the diagonals on the body plan. Sometimes the reference is given numerically; for example, Diag B—24½ inches up on CL, 19¹³⁄₁₆ inches out on WL 11 inches. Other times, you need only to look at the body plan itself, and the reference will be obvious (probably).

Check for the notation "offsets to inside of plank" or "to outside of plank." This means exactly what it says, and what it says determines how you draw the rabbet,

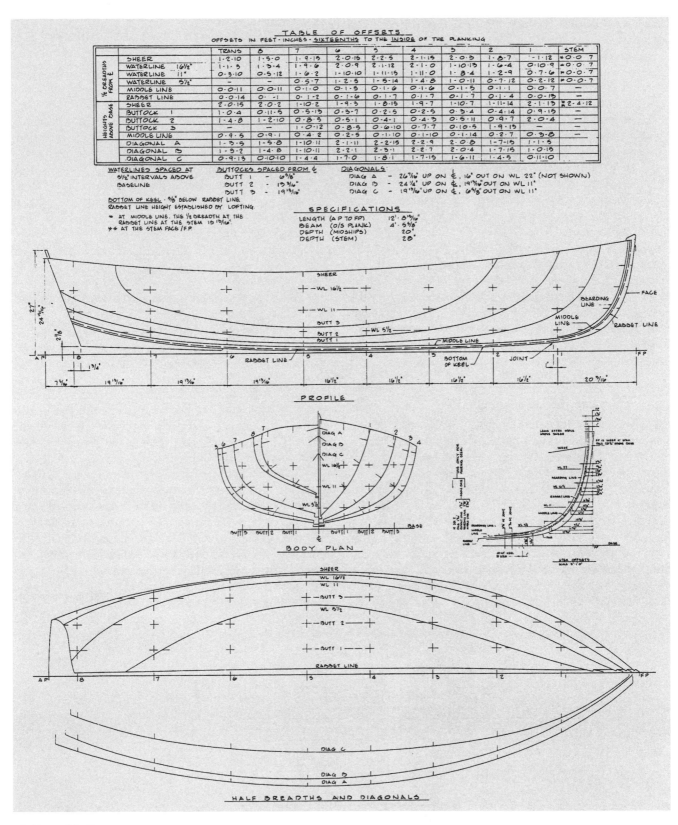

7-1: Lines and off-sets for the 12'8" Catspaw dinghy, the example used in this chapter.

whether or not you deduct planking thickness for your molds, etc.

Look for the scale, or ratio of inches to feet, the designer used in drawing the plans. Check this on every sheet: the designer could very well have changed scale from sheet to sheet, especially if he were trying to illustrate details in a larger size. Also, look for the notation "N.T.S.," which means "not to scale." This indicates that the drawing is an illustration of how something is done, but it hasn't been measured exactly.

Use caution in measuring directly from the plans. The print might have been distorted as it passed through the copying machine, or the paper might have stretched due to weather conditions. Given this caveat, measuring from the plans can be useful in debunking a bum offset.

Sometimes, after a long and thorough search, the information you seek is nowhere to be found on the plans. The reason is probably that it wasn't there in the first place. Although inconvenient, this is no real problem. The magic of lofting will provide the information.

☞ Common Lofting Abbreviations

CL = Centerline
WL = Waterline
LWL = Load waterline
DWL = Design waterline
Butt = Buttock
Sta = Station
LOA = Length overall
LWL = Length at load waterline
FP = Forward perpendicular
AP = After perpendicular
Diag = Diagonal
Base = Baseline

Reviewing the views

Let's take a moment to discuss the definitions of the different views:

The profile: A longitudinal view that shows the sheer of the deck, the shape of the boat at the centerline as viewed from the side, the buttock lines (which are the

☞ What Is This Thing?

Although not included on the Catspaw plans, many plans contain a variation of this illustration. This is a mechanical scale rule that can be used to take measurements off the plans. Here is how it works:

The "V" in the first box mechanically divides the lines into 12 segments that are equal to scale inches. Record the desired measurement onto a tick strip and hold it to the scale. Align one end of the marked strip with the farthest whole-inch line that still allows the other end of the marked strip to fall in the "V" portion of the scale. Slide the marked strip up the scale horizontally until the mark on the tick strip intersects a "V" crossed

line (see illustration). Count the number of inches shown on the "V" scale and add the inches. And there you have your measurement.

So, why bother? You can always use a scale rule, right? True. But, suppose you wish to replicate the rudder on your classic boat, and the only available plan is one that has been reduced for publication. The printed notification of scale will no longer be valid, but the mechanical scale would have been reduced at the same rate as the rest of the drawing. Using the mechanical scale and tick strip can provide you with a quick and surprisingly accurate check on the drawing.

Using the graphic scale rule.

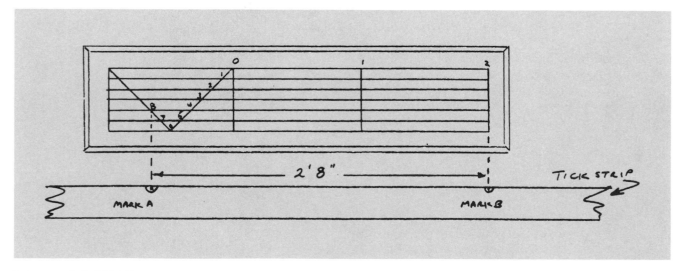

slices through the hull at intervals parallel to the center-line plane), and the rabbet line—and perhaps the middle line and bearding line as well. Stations appear as vertical lines. Waterlines run parallel to the baseline.

The half-breadths: A plan view, best understood as a topographic map of the boat hull with the keel up. It shows half of the hull, split at the centerline. The horizontal planes, called waterlines (analogous to lines of elevation on a topographic map), are curved. Also illustrated are the half-breadths of the keel. Buttocks appear as straight, vertical lines parallel to the centerline.

The body plan: This shows the form of the hull at transverse vertical planes, called sections or stations. If you think of a slice of bread as a transverse vertical plane, the hull is like the loaf. (How about a toasted transverse vertical plane with marmalade?) Anyway, the sections show up here as curves.

The diagonals: Arbitrary slices through the hull, running fore and aft, cutting across the majority of the sections at a good angle. The diagonals are designed to provide information on areas, primarily at the turn of the bilge, not well served by either the buttocks or waterlines.

BEFORE BEGINNING, A FEW CONSIDERATIONS

When lofting, it is quite handy to work in pairs—one person on the floor (or at the table), the other reading numbers from the table of offsets. The advantages are speed and accuracy. The person on the floor need only record the offsets on the grid without getting up, while the one with the offsets need only read the numbers aloud. The person on the floor should repeat the offset out loud; this double-checking can eliminate embarrassing transpositions of numbers (for example, it can help prevent 1-1-2 from mysteriously turning into 1-2-1).

Wear knee pads when lofting on a floor. They make the work much more enjoyable.

When using a steel tape measure, make it a practice to do all your measuring from the 10- or 12-inch marks. That little grabber hook on the end of most tapes tends to get worn and sloppy—leading to inaccuracies—and prevents the tape from lying flat.

When making marks on your grid, take the time to circle and label them. This will help prevent confusion when you are confronted with a plethora of mysterious dots.

If a line isn't fair when you bend a batten around the points, check the offsets for accuracy. It isn't unusual for the offset table to contain a few errors. This is where a good batten, a sharp eye, and your judgment will make the difference.

Inasmuch as the views on the lines plan are interdependent, each offset measurement is used only once. For example, if you use the offset number 2-3-4 to obtain the height of the sheer at Station 6 in the profile view, you

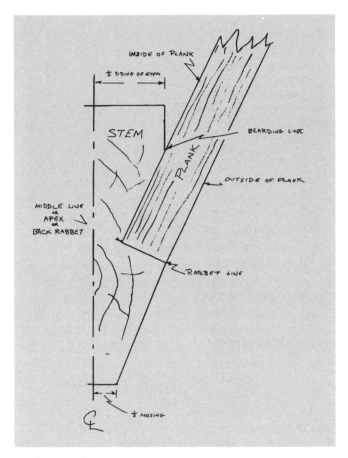

7-2: Anatomy of a rabbet.

would not again use your tape measure to obtain the height 2-3-4 for the sheer at Station 6 in the body plan view. Instead, you would mark that distance on a recording device—either on a long strip of paper, cardboard, or wood, or with trammel points—to transfer that height from the profile to the body plan. Using the offsets just once and transferring the information to other views ensures that you will produce a truly interdependent system of views. This system will also help to check the offsets.

Don't be confused by the words apex, back rabbet, and middle line. They all refer to the same line, even though for some time there has been great debate over what is the proper name for this line. (See Figure 7-2.) The significance of this debate is about the same as the question of how many angels can dance on the head of a pin.

SETTING THE STAGE

Lofting is, essentially, drafting full scale, so you will need a full-scale drawing board. Although, traditionally, the "board" is a painted floor in the shipyard's mold loft, for most small craft a combination of plywood sheets is a better choice than a floor. Quarter-inch plywood with at least one "A" face works just fine, as it has a generally consistent surface and is light enough to be easily transported and stored.

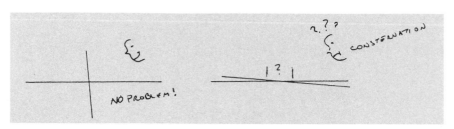
Three sheets of plywood are required to loft the Catspaw dinghy. At least two of these sheets should be screwed down to a surface; if that surface happens to be a newly refinished maple floor, you might want to consider another arrangement. A better arrangement anyway is to build a rough table frame that can sit atop sawhorses and hold the lofting above the floor; this will save your back and knees. We're talking about a unit measuring 4 feet by 16 feet for the Catspaw dinghy, and it should be fairly rugged in construction.

There is nothing wrong with lofting on the floor; indeed, there really is no alternative when the design calls for a large drawing. Just remember to wear your

kneepads, and it's "socks only" for your feet. (Shoes will make a lofting surface look like the floor of a bus terminal long before you're finished.)

Whatever the lofting surface, paint it before drawing your lines, preferably with a roller. A satin or flat paint, white in color, works well. A good choice is shellac-based, white-pigmented primer, as it does a decent job of covering, is tough, and is fast drying.

Now round up some battens. Battens are long, straight strips of straight-grained wood used for fairing and drawing curved lines. I prefer spruce or Philippine mahogany, as these woods are flexible yet retain enough stiffness to provide a fair curve. A batten that is too lim-

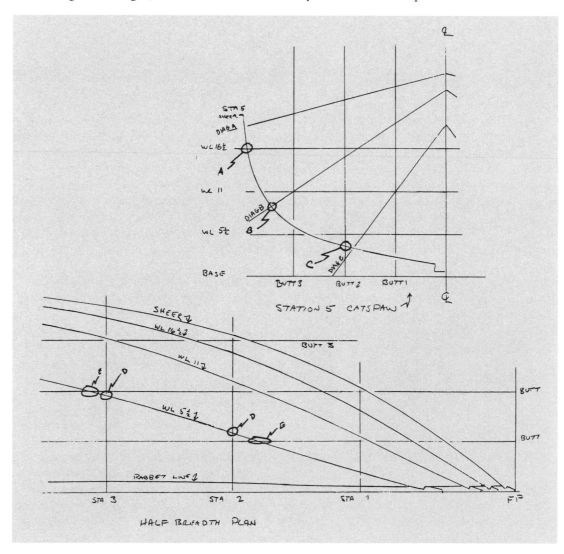

7-4: At point A the waterline provides the most accurate measurement. At point B the diagonal probably is most accurate. At point C the buttock is likely to be most accurate. Points D are more likely to be correct than points E.

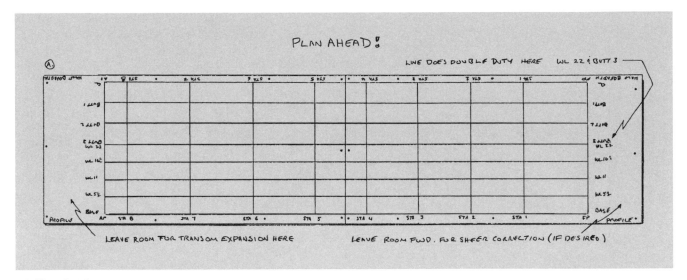

7-5: Plan ahead when laying out the grid. There is nothing more aggravating than not having enough room to do the job properly.

ber is a floppy affair, and it is untrustworthy. A good batten should be rectangular in section and totally without knots. It may be necessary to scarf your batten (at least a 12:1 glued scarf) out of two pieces to gain the desired length.

Make up a selection of battens of varying cross-sectional dimension. Use lighter battens for tight curves, such as those found in the body plan, and heavier ones for long, gentle sweeps, such as the line of the sheer. Paint all the battens black so they will make a sharp contrast with the white of the lofting surface.

Ducks and splines, which are available from drafting-supply shops, are not absolutely necessary, but on a small craft with tight curves, you'll be glad to have them. Splines are small plastic battens. I prefer a spline with a groove that runs its length, into which the grabber hook of the duck (a.k.a., "whale" or "spline weight") can fit. A duck is cast of lead and has felt glued to the bottom. A brass hook sticks out of one end and acts as a little hand to hold the curve in the batten while you draw the line. (Note: One of these babies weighs in at about 4 pounds, so avoid dropping it on your foot.)

Proper lofting etiquette dictates releasing your battens and splines after use. If left in place for any length of time, they can, and probably will, take a set, and you'll have a batten with a permanent wave in it. A good way to store a plastic spline is to hang it from one end, using a clothespin, so it dangles straight down. Even a crinkled spline will sometimes straighten out when hung in this manner.

Other items you'll find useful for lofting include: a framing square; dividers; a set of beam trammel points; a pound of three-penny "box" nails, or lots of ice picks (the battens will be bent around these); a 16-ounce claw hammer; a roll of tick-strip tape (calculator tape, or genuine ticker tape if you can find it) on which to record measurements; a long, true straightedge (a reasonably good

one can be made by ripping a 6-inch strip from an 8-foot piece of plywood and working to the mill-cut edge); good lighting; hard pencils and a pencil sharpener; a felt marking pen; and patience.

A QUESTION OF CREDIBILITY, OR, WHICH INTERSECTION DO YOU BELIEVE?

As the lofting develops, a great number of line intersections will be generated. A typical station line in the body plan will intersect several waterlines, usually a few buttock lines, and some diagonals. The points through which the station was drawn either would have come from offsets or would have been brought over from another view.

The question is, do all intersections have the same degree of accuracy? The answer is, generally speaking, they do not. Lines that cross at or near right angles tend to be more accurate than those that cross at acute angles. (See Figure 7-3.)

LAYING OUT THE GRID

It is now time to lay out the grid. This is perhaps the least exciting part of the lofting process. It is persnickety, and probably even the good Messrs. Ptolemy and Mercator found it a bit of a yawn. But take the time to do the job right. Accuracy in establishing your grid is essential. Cheat here, and you will definitely pay for it later—probably about halfway through the drawing. So, who needs problems?

By the way, neatness counts.

For a small boat, I like to have the profile and the half-breadth plans on one board and the body plan on another. These are called scrive boards.

One method that works well is to draw the profile and half-breadths on opposite sides of the board. (See Figure 7-5.) Both views utilize the same station lines.

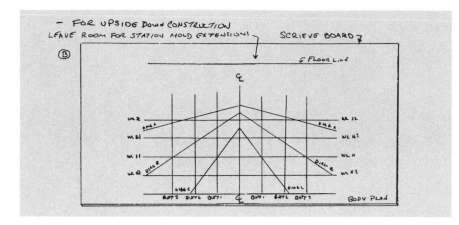

Each view works from the edge of the board toward the center. For the Catspaw, WL 22 and Butt 3 can share a line, thus eliminating an extra reference line. Setting up the board in this way has two benefits—the sheers of the two views tend to nest in each other, which reduces the number of overlapping lines; and, because you are working from each edge of the board, the labeling of the other view is upside down (as shown in the drawings here), which reduces confusion.

Leave room for the transom expansion. This true-size expansion is usually developed off the transom at a right angle in the profile view. Measure the widest transom dimension in the body plan, and leave that much extra behind the transom in profile for space to draw the expansion.

Let's move to the layout of the body plan. (See Figure 7-6.) If your boat is to be built upside down (and many boats are), it is good to leave room at the top of your plan for the "legs"—extensions of the station molds past the sheer—to reach a common line. This is some-

times called a floor line or construction baseline. (See Figure 7-7.) The exact location of this floor line depends on the height at which it is most convenient for you to work, but generally it falls above the sheer at the stem, plus a few inches. This will allow for easier planking.

Striking the baseline

Drawing the baseline is simply a matter of stretching out the chalkline and snapping it, right? Not a good idea. Chalklines tend to bounce quite a bit, giving you several lines to choose from; also, any ripple or defect on the board can grab the string and give you an inaccurate reading. When using a chalkline, it is much safer to stretch the string over blocks, which will elevate the string above the board. (See Figure 7-8.) The string wants to be humming tight. (For large vessels, piano wire and a turnbuckle are just the ticket.) Mark a series of points directly below the string and connect them with a straightedge. Now you will have a truly straight baseline.

Avoiding unsightly cumulative error

Cumulative error occurs when an incorrect measurement is repeatedly used in laying out specific points on a line; for example, when establishing stations on a baseline. Incorrect measuring technique can cause each succeeding point to be farther out of whack. Try to make it a practice to mark all your points from the same

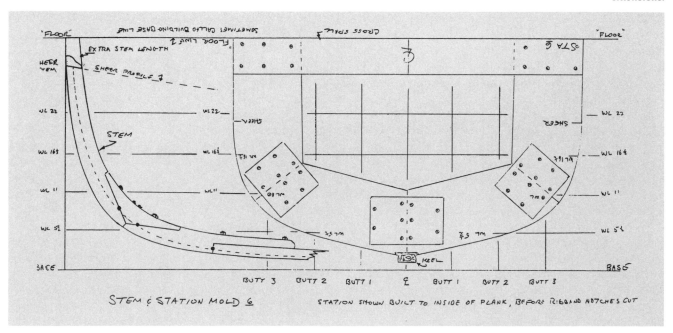

STEM & STATION MOLD 6   STATION SHOWN BUILT TO INSIDE OF PLANK, BEFORE RIBBAND NOTCHES CUT

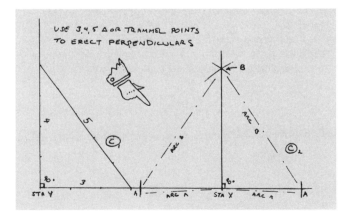

D FOR BASE & q : MARK A SERIES OF POINTS DIRECTLY UNDER TIGHTLY STRETCHED STRING - CONNECT WITH STRAIGHTEDGE   COX 91

starting point, using an extended stationary rule. This is preferable to measuring from point "A" to point "B," then sliding your rule to point "B" and measuring to point "C," and so on, a method loaded with potential for error.

As an example of correct procedure: If your boat were exactly 10 feet long and the plans called for 2-foot spacing, the stations would fall at 2 feet, 4 feet, 6 feet, and 8 feet, and the AP, or endpoint, would be at 10 feet. Extend your tape rule to approximately 12 feet in length. Line up the 1-foot mark on the starting point (the FP). Then make a mark every 2 feet—on your rule, at 3 feet, 5 feet, 7 feet, 9 feet, and 11 feet, the latter being at the AP, or the endpoint. This method almost eliminates any potential for cumulative error.

Usually the station spacing on a plan is in whole numbers, and the distances between the stations are all the same. Occasionally you will come across a set of plans in which the station spacing varies and the distance between any two stations is a number that sounds as if it could be a hat size. The Catspaw is one of those plans. This is no problem. It just involves converting the fractions into numbers that we can use and that can be added quickly. For example, the distance from FP to Station 1 is 20³⁄₁₆ inches, or 20.1875 inches. The distance from Station 1 to Station 2 is 16½ inches, or 16.5 inches. Hence, the distance from FP to Station 2 is 20.1875 inches plus 16.5 inches, which equals 36.6875 inches, or 36¹¹⁄₁₆ inches. (The rest of the other station locations can be figured in this way.)

Is all this arithmetic worth the trouble? Yes and no. It does take a moment to make the conversions. But, on the other hand, once you have developed your table of conversions, you can move right along, free of the angst caused by the possibility of cumulative error.

Erecting the perpendiculars

After establishing our station locations, it's time to erect the perpendiculars, which are to be at true right angles to the baseline. This is critical, as working with a rhombus when you thought it was a square can lead to disappointing, albeit interesting results.

There are a number of ways to achieve a true perpendicular. You can build a very large square, then nail a batten along the baseline and run the square along the batten, marking your perpendicular station lines as you go. You can use the 3, 4, 5 triangle method (see Figure 7-9) or you can use trammel points. Whatever method you use, don't forget to check for squareness.

And then the horizontals

Establish the waterlines, buttock lines, and centerline. Check and make sure that they are parallel to the baseline. It's a good idea to label them. Labels really do make the whole business easier.

The body plan

The grid for the body plan is drawn using the same technology as for the profile and half-breadth plans—the only difference is the addition of diagonals. Take care in drawing these, as they are not at all difficult to get in the wrong places. Their placement is determined by running a straight line through two intersections, starting at the centerline. On the Catspaw plans, the locations of these intersections are given just below the table of offsets. So, to draw Diag. A, measure up 26³⁄₁₆ inches from the baseline and make a mark. Then find WL 22, measure out

7-8: To run a baseline or a centerline, mark a series of points directly under a tightly stretched string and then connect the points with a straightedge.

7-9: Use a 3,4,5 triangle or two equal-radius arcs struck with trammel points on a beam to erect perpendiculars.

☞ Catspaw Dinghy Station Schedule from FP to Station

To Sta #1	20.1875"	20³⁄₁₆"
2	36.6875"	36¹¹⁄₁₆"
3	53.1875"	53³⁄₁₆"
4	69.6875"	69¹¹⁄₁₆"
5	86.1875"	86³⁄₁₆"
6	106.0000"	106"
7	125.8125"	125¹³⁄₁₆"
8	145.6250"	145¹⁰⁄₁₆"
AP	152.9375"	152¹⁵⁄₁₆"

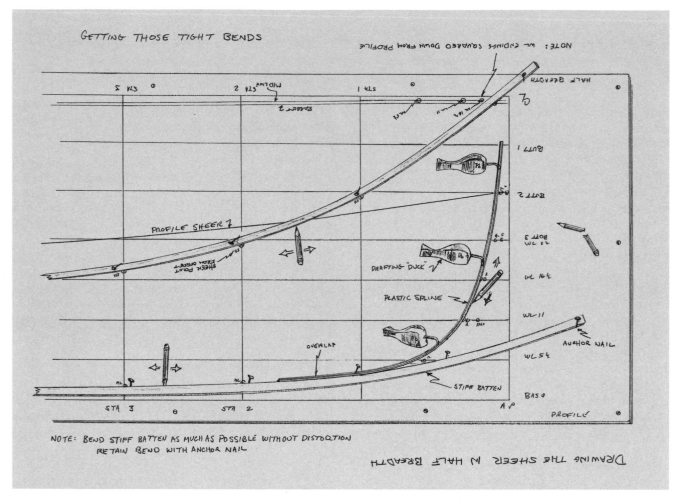

7-10: For the middle line in profile:
- Set up your heavy batten on the outer (baseline) side of the middle-line offsets along the keel, getting as much bend out of the batten as you can without distortion.
- Set up your plastic batten (spline) and ducks on the middle line of offsets on the stem, starting at the sheer. Run the batten on the inside of the offsets.
- Somewhere around the turn of the stem, the battens will meet and overlap, one running on one side of the offsets, the other batten on the opposite side. As much overlap as possible is desirable. (This overlap business requires resetting some nails to accommodate both battens.)
- Sight along the combined battens for fairness, using the usual technique.
- Draw the first part of the line—probably the stem section—and then draw the second portion. The lines should match perfectly in one continuous run from the sheer at the stem to the transom.

from the centerline 16 inches in both directions and make a mark. Draw a straight line through both marks—on each side of the centerline—and there you have Diag. A. Use the same method for Diags. B and C. Recheck the body plan, and you are done—or, really, you're done with the grid and you're ready to start on the lofting.

But first, some theory.

WHAT IS A FAIR LINE?, OR, THE PHILOSOPHY AND PRACTICAL USE OF THE BATTEN

Just what is a fair line? An example could be the sheer on a particularly elegant yacht. It is a smooth, flowing curve with no bumps, kinks, or flat spots in it. A fair line should not only be mechanically correct but also pleasing to the eye. It is, indeed, the product of a partnership between your eye and a quality batten.

In using a batten, the intent is not to follow slavishly every single point, or offset. Yes, the offsets are a neat guide to establishing your curve, and you will end up running your batten through the vast majority of them. But remember, some bummers probably lurk in every table of offsets. Your eye and batten will sort these out in short order. Also remember, you will only use these offsets once; from then on, you will be transferring points from one view to another.

When drawing a typical curve—say, a sheer in profile view—first mark your points, or offsets. Then, circle and label them. Using small wire nails (or ice picks) as benchmarks, we will begin bending our batten. It is good practice to use the outside of the curved batten to draw the line. This seems to provide a smoother line and keeps

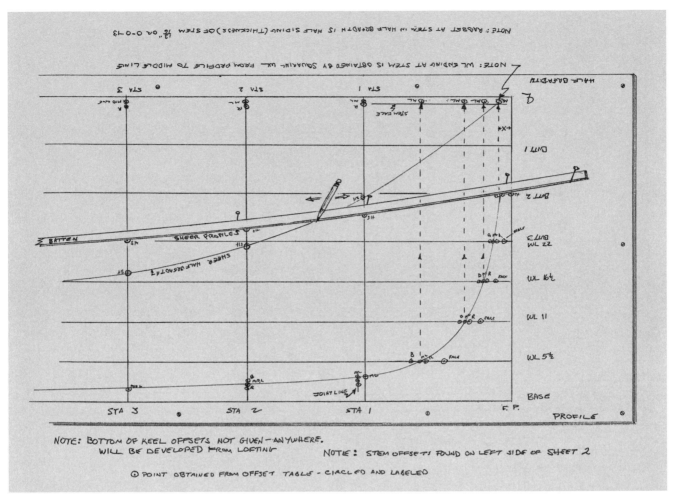

NOTE: RABBET AT STEM IS HALF BREADTH (THICKNESS) OF STEM ½" OR 0-0-13

NOTE: WL ENDING AT STEM IS OBTAINED BY SQUARING WL FROM PROFILE TO MIDDLE LINE

NOTE: BOTTOM OF KEEL OFFSETS NOT GIVEN – ANYWHERE. WILL BE DEVELOPED FROM LOFTING

NOTE: STEM OFFSETS FOUND ON LEFT SIDE OF SHEET 2

⊙ POINT OBTAINED FROM OFFSET TABLE – CIRCLED AND LABELED

7-11: The sheer profile and the sheer half-breadth at the bow.

the nail holes away from the line (saving your pencil point for higher uses).

So, the first step is to drive a nail at the offset point at the transom. Pushing the batten against that nail, bend the batten to Station 8. Put a nail on the inside of the curve, so that one side of the batten is touching the offset and the other is touching the nail. Next, bend the batten to Station 7, and again drive a nail on the opposite side of the batten. Continue on in this manner until you have reached the stem, where you can then anchor the batten at its offset with a nail placed on the outside of the curve.

Now cast your critical eye along the batten. Is it as smooth and pleasing as you'd like it to be? Try popping (pulling) a nail at a suspect location. Did the batten move? Try pulling every second nail. Does the batten still run through all the points? All but one? Does the curve flow a little bit easier?

When you are establishing fairness in the batten, you are looking for the weight of evidence to give you the proper curve. If you stick with offset "Y", does it pull you off offsets "X" and "Z"? It is probably better to fair past offset "Y" in favor of "X" and "Z".

It is not unusual for one offset to be incorrect by as much as an inch, an error that is easy to spot. It's the close calls that will require your judgment. Trust your eye! And don't worry if you miss one offset by $\frac{1}{16}$ inch. The sun will still come up in the morning.

By the way, establishing fairness does get easier as you go along.

Finally, after you have determined the batten to be fair, and still as close to the original points as possible, mark the line with a pencil and label it.

How do they get that tight turn with the batten?

Some lines, such as the keel-to-stem line and the buttock lines, consist of a length of very gentle curve which then rapidly changes to a very tight curve. To get a reasonably accurate representation of a gentle curve—such as the middle line along the keel—you really need a good, stiff (some might say hefty) batten. But then the line goes through a sharp turn as it heads up the stem. Those heavy-duty battens will only bend so far before they distort or, worse yet, snap. This you want to avoid, as good battens don't grow on trees. (Well, they do, but....) To avoid this, you can employ the trusted two batten technique. (See Figure 7-10.)

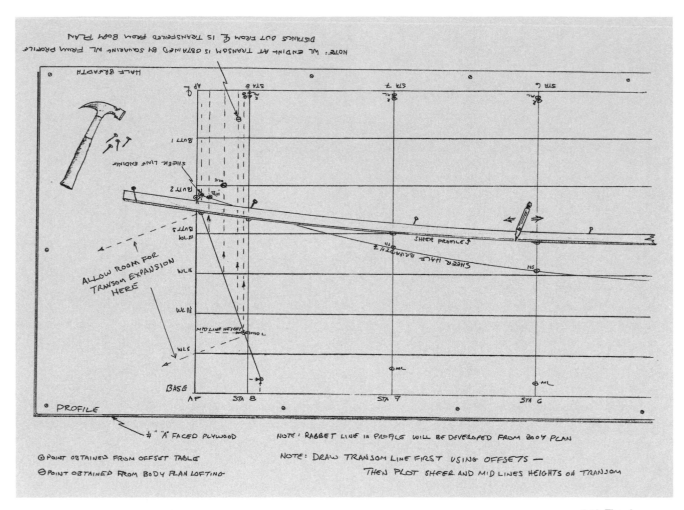

7-12: The sheer profile and the sheer half-breadth at the transom.

RECONCILING THE VIEWS

"I shall try to correct where shown to be errors and I shall adopt my new views as fast as they shall appear to be true views."

—Abraham Lincoln, 1862

If you are a seeker of truth, a distiller of facts, a corrector of errors, then lofting is your game. The whole business is about the winnowing-out of bogus data to achieve an accurate 3-D portrayal of your boat. There is no way to cheat. You cannot simply change a waterline width on the half-breadth plan without affecting the waterline width on the body plan. But, if you change the line in the body plan too radically to accommodate the halfbreadth, you could end up altering a buttock or a diagonal, requiring changes in those views as well. And so on. So, what to do?

As with any skill, the more you use it, the better you get. The eye gets used to seeing relationships. But in the meantime, there are a few rules of thumb that can help you to decide which lines to keep and which to move.

- In the body plan, waterlines tend to be more accurate near the sheer, and the buttocks more accurate near the keel (because of the nearly right-angle intersections of lines).

- Look for clusters of points. An example on the Catspaw drawings is Station 3 on the body plan, where the offsets for WL 11, Butt 3, and Diag. B are so close. This multi-point verification indicates that this line is probably in the right place.

- Look with suspicion at buttock-end information brought down to the profile from the half-breadth plan. The waterlines in the half-breadth plan intersect the buttock lines at an acute low angle, and just a small movement of the waterline in or out will change the point of intersection greatly.

- If necessary, scale from the plans to help you make the right choice.

- If you must change a point, look first for a location that doesn't require you to make changes in two or more other views.

- After you have made your decision, fair and mark your new line and label it "corrected." This will avoid confusion later on.

- Don't fret about discrepancies that amount to the thickness of a pencil line between views. Save your anxieties for the ½-inch discrepancies.

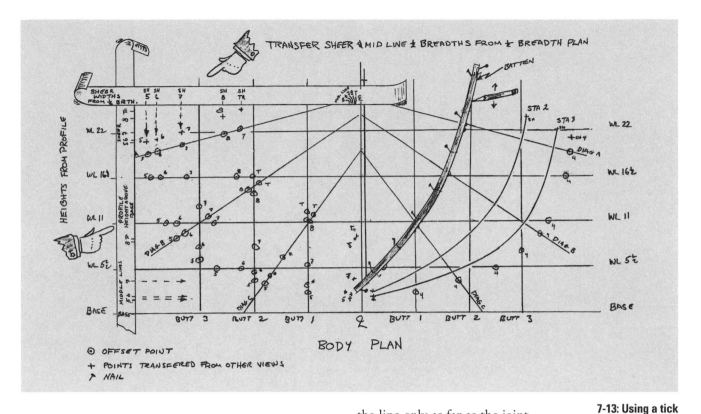

TRANSFER SHEER & MID LINE & BREADTHS FROM & BREADTH PLAN

BODY PLAN

⊙ OFFSET POINT
+ POINTS TRANSFERRED FROM OTHER VIEWS
↗ NAIL

7-13: Using a tick strip to develop the body plan.

STARTING THE DRAWING

The profile view is where we begin. First, draw the after face of the transom. It is a straight line, running from the top of the transom at 27 inches up on the AP to the end of the skeg just forward of Station 8.

Now, plot the offsets for the sheer, measuring up from the baseline along the FP, Stations 1 through 8, and the AP. The transom offset is measured up the AP, then squared over until it hits the transom line.

Spring a batten through the points. Make sure the line is fair. Draw it with a pencil and label it.

Next, plot the points for the middle line along the keel. Note that there are no offsets for the bottom of the keel; don't worry, we'll deal with that later.

Plot the lines defining the stem: the face, the rabbet line, the bearding line, and the middle line. We're lucky in choosing the Catspaw Dinghy for our example. Rare are the plans that give this much detail on the shape of the stem rabbet. Usually you would just get information about the rabbet line or the middle line, and you would have to develop the other lines yourself. (Later, because it is a useful technique, we will develop a rabbet when not all the information is provided.)

Note that the offsets which look as though they fall on Station 1 actually fall on the stem/keel joint 1 inch behind Station 1. Why? Because that's the way the plans were drawn. Another imponderable in life. In addition, if you swing the plans 90 degrees clockwise, you will find fairing points for Station 2. This means that you should bring your batten to these points on Station 2, but draw the line only as far as the joint.

Fair the middle line from the transom through to the sheer at the stem. Fair the other lines from Station 2 through to the sheer at the stem.

It is now time to move to the half-breadth view.

STARTING THE HALF-BREADTHS

First, plot the offsets for the rabbet and the middle line. The lines forward of Station 1 are straight and equidistant from the centerline, because the rabbet line is traveling along the face of the stem and all the middle-line offsets are the same along the stem. Fair with a batten and draw the lines.

Plot the half-breadth offsets for Stations 1 through 8, measuring out from the centerline, and label them.

Remember that the profile view and the half-breadth view are interconnected. This means that if the intersection of the sheerline with the middle line occurs at distance "X" aft of the FP in profile view, then that intersection in the half-breadth view will also occur at "X" distance aft of the FP. (See Figure 7-11.) So, all we need to do to find where the sheer in the half-breadth meets the middle line is to square that distance over from the profile. (Or, with a tick strip, that distance aft of the FP can be recorded and brought over to the half-breadth plan.)

To find the sheerline ending at the transom for the half-breadth, first go to the end of the sheerline in the profile. Bring the distance (forward of the AP) of the point where the sheer meets the transom square over to

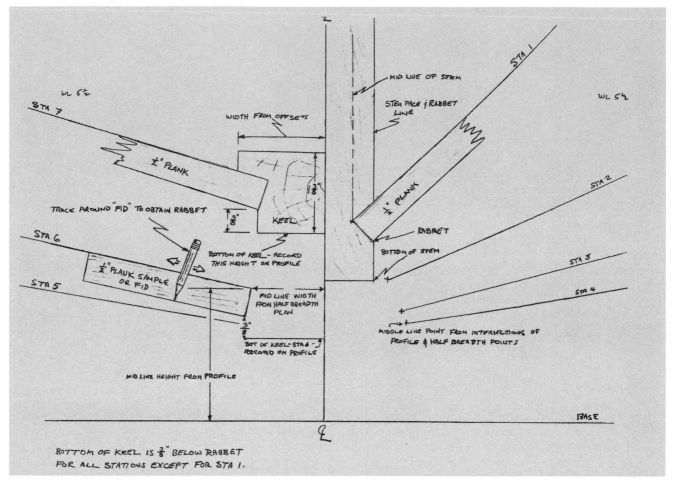

WL 5½

STA 7

MID LINE OF STEM

STEM FACE & RABBET LINE

STA 1

WL 5½

WIDTH FROM OFFSETS

¼" PLANK

KEEL

¾"

TRACE AROUND "FID" TO OBTAIN RABBET

3" ———
—8—

¼" PLANK

STA 2

STA 6

¼"
¼" PLANK SAMPLE OR FID

BOTTOM OF KEEL - RECORD THIS HEIGHT ON PROFILE

RABBET

BOTTOM OF STEM

STA 3

STA 5

MID LINE WIDTH FROM HALF BREADTH PLAN

STA 4

3"
—8—

BOT OF KEEL - STA 6 - RECORD ON PROFILE

MIDDLE LINE POINT FROM INTERSECTIONS OF PROFILE & HALF BREADTH POINTS

MID LINE HEIGHT FROM PROFILE

BASE

℄

BOTTOM OF KEEL IS ⅜" BELOW RABBET FOR ALL STATIONS EXCEPT FOR STA 1.

the centerline in the half-breadth view. (See Figure 7-12.) Using your framing square, measure out your offset for the transom (1-2-10). This is done in exactly the same manner as measuring out on the station lines.

And, voila! You have all your points.

Spring a batten through the points, fair and draw the line in pencil, and label it.

THE BODY PLAN

The body plan is the most trying area of your offsets, so care in lofting here will definitely pay off. Most of the really bad coordinates will be sorted out at this time.

Start the body plan by transferring the heights and breadths of the sheer and middle lines from the profile and half-breadth plans to the body-plan grid. (See Figure 7-13.) This is done with a tick strip. For the heights mark the baseline on the bottom of the strip, align the strip on a station in profile (with the base mark on baseline), and record the height of the middle line and the sheer for that station. Move to the next station and repeat.

On another tick strip, pick up the sheer and middle-line widths from the half-breadth plan. The sheer and middle-line points on the body plan are determined by the intersection of these recorded points.

Next, record the rest of the off-sets (from the table of offsets) onto the body plan grid—waterlines horizontally measured from the center-line, buttocks vertically measured up from the base, and diagonals measured out along the diagonal starting from the centerline. Then, spring a batten through the points.

Here there is a little flexibility to make judgment calls on your points—with the exception of the sheer and middle-line points, which are already locked into the profile and half-breadth views. Look to get a smooth, fair line passing through all points. Frequently check the body plan on your plans to make sure that what you are getting in full scale matches the small-scale drawing.

There might be some points that simply don't work and that cause curious bumps or flats in the batten. Some offsets (probably for a diagonal) will be obviously bogus; others may be more ambiguous. Try your scale rule to check the offset. As mentioned before, using a scale rule on a set of plans can be a dicey procedure at best, but it can be useful in detecting a bum offset.

After making any small adjustments to the batten necessary to get it to follow the overwhelming majority of points and still give you a fair line, draw it (in pencil!).

7-14: Finding the bottom of the keel with a half-inch fid, or plank sample.

☞ A Sheer Correction Technique

Occasionally, a designed sheer in profile, if it is nearly flat or only has a very subtle curve to it on the plans, can develop a downturned or "powderhorn" look up forward after the boat has been built. The more "full" a craft is forward, the greater the chance that this will occur. Of course, this can be corrected after the boat is built by lowering the sheer amidships, but that can be a bother. Then there are times when, even though the designed sheer will work, raising the sheer forward can make the boat just a little more sporty looking.

Raising the sheer mechanically is a very simple technique. It takes little time and is effective, and the fuller the boat is forward, the more sheer the technique will give you.

Begin by wrapping a light batten around the sheer of the half-breadth (as though you were going to redraw the sheer), starting at the stem and going back at least as far as Station 3. On the batten, mark Stations 3, 2, and 1, and the middle line. Label them.

Remove the batten from the half-breadth and bring it down to the profile. Making sure the batten is straight, align it on a waterline (on the Catspaw, WL 16½ works

well.) Line up the Station 3 mark on the batten with Station 3 on the waterline. Notice that Station 2 on the batten is a little ahead of Station 2 on the waterline. Station 1 on the batten is even farther ahead on the waterline, etc.

Mark (from the batten) the locations of Stations 2 and 1, and the middle line on WL 16½ on the profile. The middle line will be ahead of FP, so the sheerline must be extended. Remove the batten from WL 16½.

Bring the batten up to the sheer in the profile as though you were going to remark it. Let the curved batten extend 6 inches or so ahead of FP. Draw in that sheer "extension." Remove the batten.

Using a square, from the new Station 2 and 1, and the middle line points on WL 16½ in profile, square up to the profile sheerline. Mark these intersection points. Now, square these points back to the vertical Stations 2, and 1, and the middle line squared up. Mark these points.

Bring your batten back to the sheer. Follow the station/sheer points 8 through 3, and re-fair through Stations 2 and 1, and middle line. This should increase the sheer by about ¾ inch. Mark the line with a pencil and label it as the "Corrected Sheer."

Correcting the sheer.

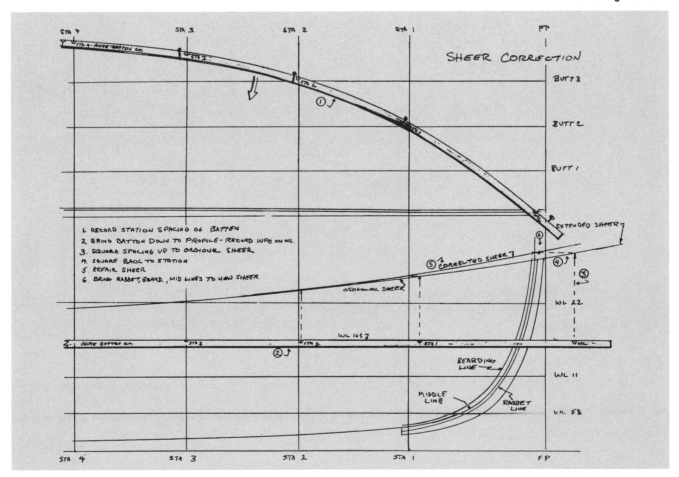

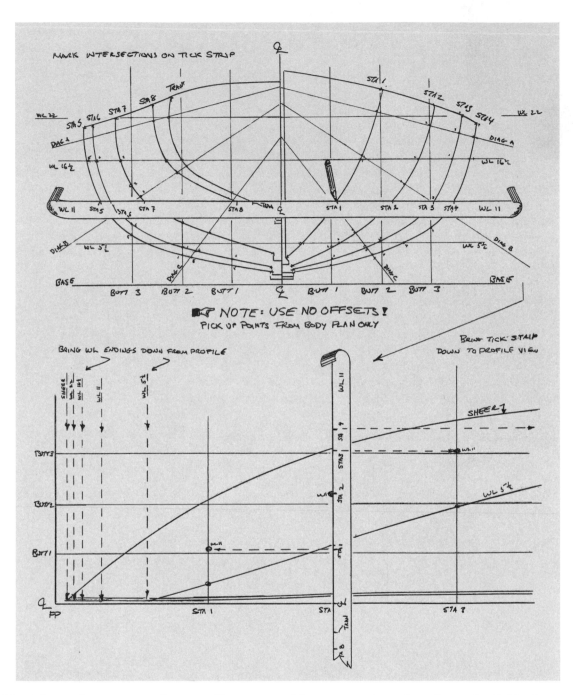

The line is probably right on the money, and any small corrections needed will happen in the course of running the waterline, buttocks, and diagonals.

Draw all the rest of the stations and the transom.

JUST WHERE IS THAT "BOTTOM OF KEEL," ANYWAY?

I have mentioned that no offsets are given for the bottom of the keel. The plans carry only the cryptic statement: "Bottom of keel—³⁄₈ inch below rabbet line. Rabbet line height established by lofting." So, there you are.

Although somewhat inconvenient, this situation pre-

sents a golden opportunity to introduce a fiendishly clever lofting instrument called a "fid," a.k.a., "plank sample." This is nothing more than a piece of wood (in this case, ½ inch thick) that is used to represent how the plank will actually enter the rabbet. What makes it so nifty is that it replaces all those untidy squares, offsets, dividers, and the other conveyances of secondhand information with something real. (By the way, hang onto your fid, as we will be using it later on when doing stem sections; it will also be used when the rabbet is cut into the stem.)

How is the fid used? By now, the body plan has been drawn and faired to the inside of the plank. The station line ends at the middle-line point, which was derived

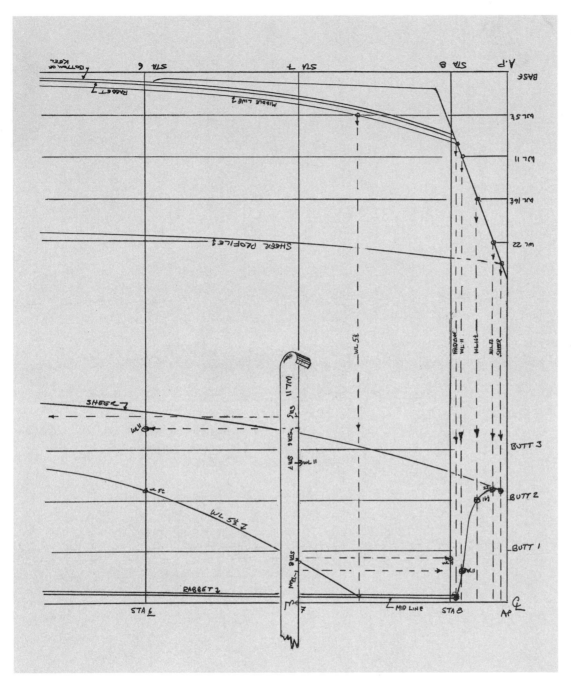

from the intersections of the profile and half-breadth middle-line points. Take the fid and align it on the station line, with one end touching the middle-line point (see Figure 7-14); this is exactly what the plank will do in the boat. Draw around the fid with the pencil. The right-angle point formed ½ inch down from the middle line point is the rabbet.

To find the bottom of the keel, measure plumb down from the rabbet point ³/₈ inch. That will be the bottom of the keel. (Station 1 falls on the stem. The "bottom of keel" there is not ³/₈ inch below the rabbet. The "bottom of stem" offset is given on Sheet 2.) Square back to the centerline. From the bottom of the keel measure up 1³/₈

inches. This will give you the top of the keel.

From the "top of keel" point, square half the keel width given on the plans for that station. Then square down to your original station curve that we started with. You have just drawn a cross section of the keel for that station. You will need that "top of keel" information later when you cut the notch in the station molds, for the keel, in preparation for construction.

Now record the "bottom of keel" and rabbet-line heights for that station on the profile. Repeat the process for all the other stations. Then spring a batten through these points and draw the "bottom of keel" and rabbet in profile.

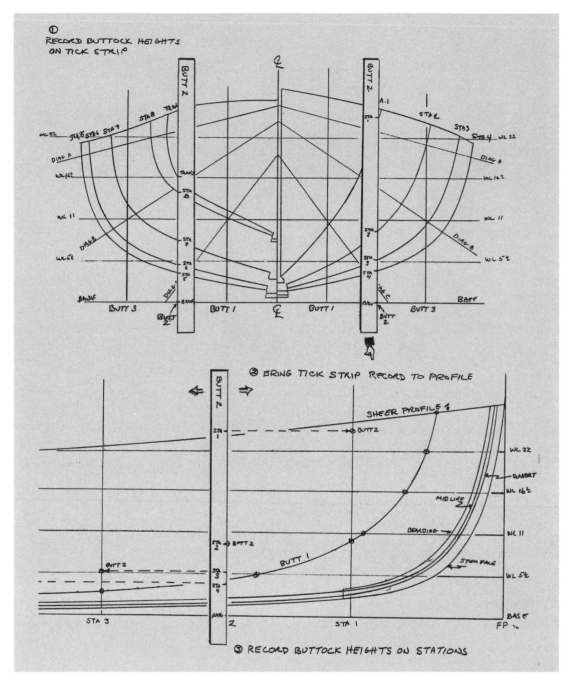

RUNNING THE WATERLINES IN THE HALF-BREADTH VIEW

Now that you have the body plan, it's time for the waterlines, which run parallel to the base in the profile and body plan. They are drawn curved on the half-breadth plan. (They are the contour intervals of the topographic map.)

From now on, we'll only be using information derived from the lofting, instead of offsets, to complete the drawing.

First, take a tick strip of sufficient length and align it along the desired waterline on the body plan. (See Figure 7-15.) Record and label the centerline and the intersections with the stations. Next, move the tick strip to the half-breadth view. Align the tick strip along Station 1, matching the centerline on the strip with that on the board. Record the Station 1 intersection distance out from the centerline and label it. Then, move to the rest of the stations and repeat the exercise.

The next operation is to square down the waterline endings from the profile in the same manner as we brought down the sheerline ending. Measure your tick-strip distance for the transom. (See Figure 7-16.) And that's all there is to establishing the points.

Spring a batten through the points and check for

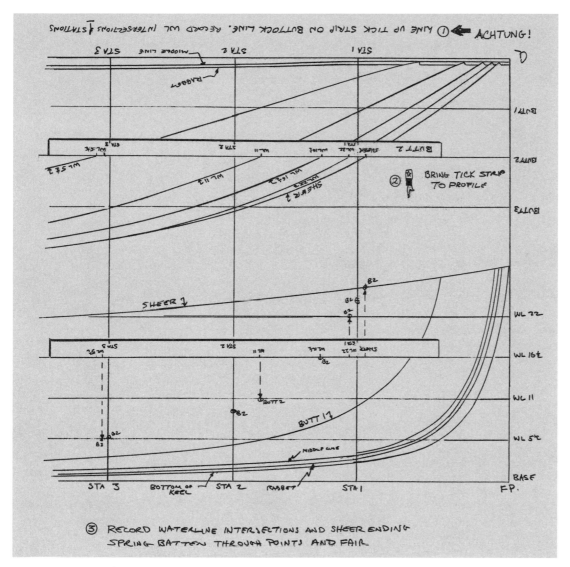

fairness. If the batten is fair, draw the line. If not, turn to the section "Reconciling the Views," above.

Using the same method, draw the rest of the waterlines. The lofting is starting to take shape.

ESTABLISHING THE BUTTOCKS

Now the plot thickens. The buttocks draw on information that has been developed in two other views—the half-breadth plan and the body plan. If there are problems in the lines, they are likely to crop up here. Also, this is the time when any indiscretions in the construction of the grid system will show up.

How to tell which problem is which? Usually if just one or two points are out of whack, but the line looks relatively proper, the chances are that the difficulty comes from one of the other views. Then it's just a matter of working that out. If, on the other hand, the line looks nothing like the one on the plans or doesn't stand a chance of ever being fair, check your grid system.

Not to worry! Just get another cup of coffee and a doughnut, and come back and have another look at it. In all likelihood, the answer will reveal itself.

Remember that the buttock lines are fore-and-aft slices through the hull, running parallel to the centerline plane. They are drawn as curves in the profile view.

The place to begin is the body plan. (See Figure 7-17.) Lay a tick strip along the desired buttock line; in this case, Butt 2. Record the baseline and all the intersections with the stations. After recording the intersections on one side, move to the corresponding buttock line on the other side of the centerline and record those station intersections.

Next, take the tick strip to the profile view and, holding it vertical, lay it on Station 1. Line up the baseline on the tick strip with the baseline of the profile. Where the strip says "Sta 1," make a mark and label it "Butt 2." Proceed to Station 2, and repeat the process. Mark the "Sta 2" point on the line and label it "Butt 2." Continue the process, and mark all the remaining stations and transom.

Now that you have all the buttock heights, it is time

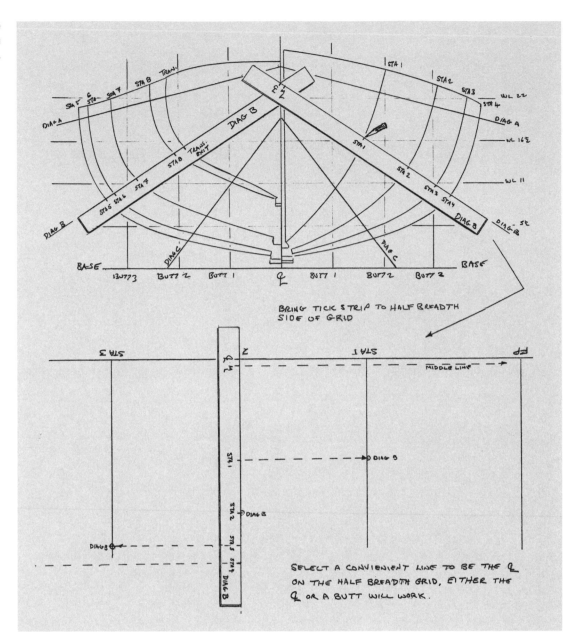

THE DIAGONALS

Despite rumors to the contrary, running the diagonals is more pleasant and easier than having your taxes audited. In fact, diagonals have received bad press for years, and really, the lines are no more difficult to run or understand than the waterlines or buttocks. The main thing to remember is that each diagonal is a freestanding view unto itself and just happens to be cohabiting on the grid with the half-breadths and other diagonals.

First, pick up the widths of the diagonals at the stations, the transom, and the middle line. (See Figure 7-19.) Record this information on a tick strip, measuring out from the centerline.

Select a convenient line to be the diagonal centerline on the half-breadth grid—either the half-breadth center-

to record the buttock ends. (See Figure 7-18.) Take a tick strip to the half-breadth plan. Place the tick strip along the selected buttock and mark at least one station reference (index) point. Next, record each location where a waterline crosses the buttock line.

After recording data from the lines plan, move to the profile view. Line up the strip on a waterline, indexing it with the reference station(s). Mark the intersection point and label it Butt 2. Move to the next waterline and repeat the operation.

Continue this process both forward and aft.

Spring a batten through the points and fair it. Some line adjustments may be necessary to make the waterlines and buttock lines agree.

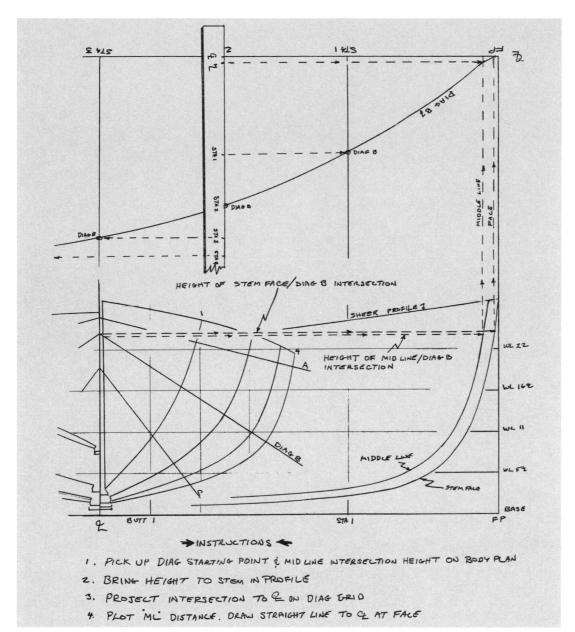

➤ **INSTRUCTIONS** ◀

1. PICK UP DIAG STARTING POINT & MID LINE INTERSECTION HEIGHT ON BODY PLAN
2. BRING HEIGHT TO STEM IN PROFILE
3. PROJECT INTERSECTION TO ℄ ON DIAG GRID
4. PLOT 'ML' DISTANCE. DRAW STRAIGHT LINE TO ℄ AT FACE

line or a buttock line will work. (All you are interested in here is the station spacing. You could, if you wish, select a different line to be the centerline for each diagonal.) In the same way you plotted the waterline half-breadths, mark the diagonals' locations on Stations 1 through 8. Label them.

Now it's time to develop the ends of the diagonals' ends at the bow and the stern.

For the stem:

• Take a new tick strip to the body plan and pick up the height above the base of the diagonal starting point (on the centerline) and also the point where it crosses the middle line.

• Bring that height to the stem in the profile view. (See Figure 7-20.) Mark the intersection with the middle line and the stem face. An easy way to do this is to mea-

sure up the FP and then square across.

• Project those intersections to the centerline on the diagonals grid. Mark these points.

• Square out the middle-line width (from your first tick strip) the same way you plotted the station widths. Draw a straight line from the middle-line point to the stem-face point on the centerline.

For the transom (see Figure 7-21):

• Use your new tick strip to pick up the height of the point where the diagonal crosses the transom—a.k.a., the "transom exit." You already have the centerline height recorded on the strip.

• Bring that height to the transom in profile. Mark the intersection with the transom exit and the transom centerline.

• Project these intersections to the centerline on the

The Diagonals • 69

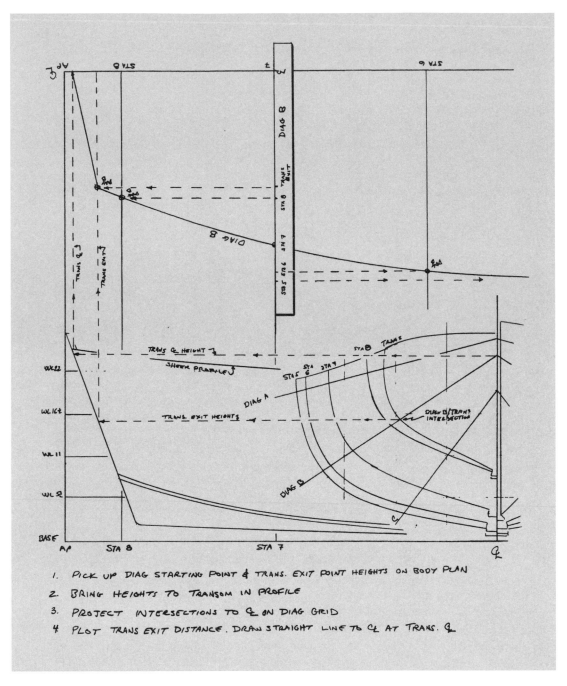

1. PICK UP DIAG STARTING POINT & TRANS. EXIT POINT HEIGHTS ON BODY PLAN

2. BRING HEIGHTS TO TRANSOM IN PROFILE

3. PROJECT INTERSECTIONS TO CL ON DIAG GRID

4. PLOT TRANS EXIT DISTANCE. DRAW STRAIGHT LINE TO CL AT TRANS. CL

diagonal grid. Mark these points.

• Square out the transom exit-point width (from your first tick strip) the same way you plotted the station widths. Draw a straight line from the transom exit point to the transom centerline point on the centerline.

Now you have your points! Spring a batten through all of them: the transom exit, the stations, and the end of the middle line. Fair the batten in the conventional manner, and there you have it. No problem.

Why does it look different on the plans? Two reasons. First, the lines on the plans only represent the diagonal cutting through the curved part of the hull and do not bring the diagonal back to the centerline. Second,

Diag. A was drawn from a nonillustrated centerline approximately 2 inches out from the illustrated centerline. This was done to eliminate confusion.

That does it for the "long lines." Now it's time to expand the transom.

EXPANDING THE TRANSOM

Although the transom is portrayed on the body plan, this view is inaccurate because of the raked angle at which the transom lies. To obtain the proper shape, the transom must be projected, or mechanically drawn, to the correct proportions. The technique is similar to that used in

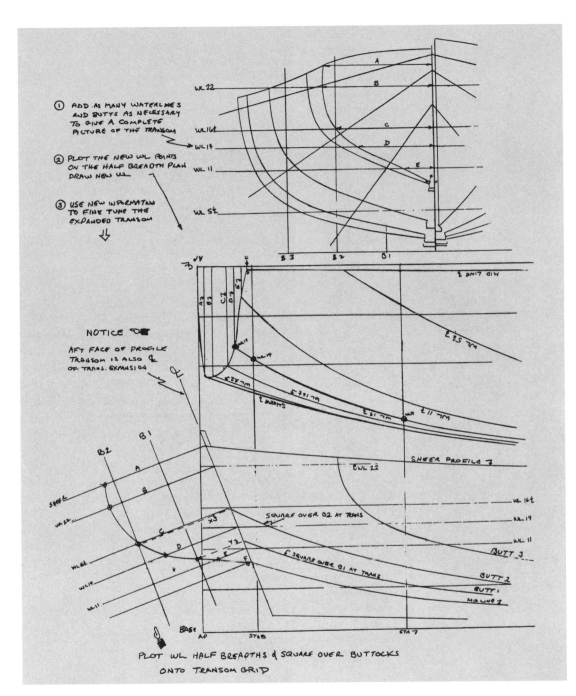

① ADD AS MANY WATERLINES AND BUTTS AS NECESSARY TO GIVE A COMPLETE PICTURE OF THE TRANSOM

② PLOT THE NEW WL POINTS ON THE HALF BREADTH PLAN DRAW NEW WL

③ USE NEW INFORMATION TO FINE TUNE THE EXPANDED TRANSOM

NOTICE ⌐E
AFT FACE OF PROFILE TRANSOM IS ALSO ₵ OF TRANS. EXPANSION

PLOT WL HALF BREADTHS & SQUARE OVER BUTTOCKS ONTO TRANSOM GRID

making the body plan.

The first order of business is to establish a grid. Draw a centerline parallel to the rake of the transom. One convenient method is simply to use the after or outer face of the transom as the centerline. (See Figure 7-22.) Square out the waterlines, sheerline, and middle line from the intersection of these and the after transom line. Lay out the spacing of the buttock lines the same as in the half-breadth and body plans, parallel to the transom line (centerline).

Next, square across the buttock intersection (with the transom centerline) to their corresponding buttock lines on the new grid.

Then, using a tick strip, pick up the half-breadths of the sheer, the waterlines, and the middle line at the transom from the half-breadth plan. Plot these points on the transom grid.

Now, look at the grid. Are there enough points to give you an accurate picture of the transom? Sometimes there is an important change in shape in the transom between two existing waterlines or buttocks. If more information is desirable, it's just a matter of going to the body plan and running another waterline in the half-breadth plan—say, WL 14. (The same could be done with buttock lines.) Add a new reference line to the transom grid, and plot the point.

Expanding the Transom • 71

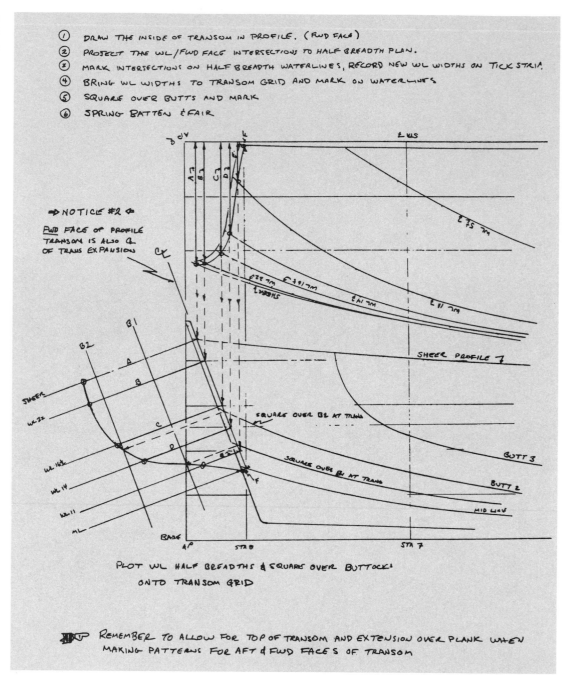

① DRAW THE INSIDE OF TRANSOM IN PROFILE. (FWD FACE)
② PROJECT THE WL/FWD FACE INTERSECTIONS TO HALF BREADTH PLAN.
③ MARK INTERSECTIONS ON HALF BREADTH WATERLINES, RECORD NEW WL WIDTHS ON TICK STRIP.
④ BRING WL WIDTHS TO TRANSOM GRID AND MARK ON WATERLINES
⑤ SQUARE OVER BUTTS AND MARK
⑥ SPRING BATTEN & FAIR

→ NOTICE #2 ←
FWD FACE OF PROFILE TRANSOM IS ALSO ℄ OF TRANS EXPANSION

PLOT WL HALF BREADTHS & SQUARE OVER BUTTOCKS ONTO TRANSOM GRID

☞ REMEMBER TO ALLOW FOR TOP OF TRANSOM AND EXTENSION OVER PLANK WHEN MAKING PATTERNS FOR AFT & FWD FACES OF TRANSOM

After establishing all the points on the grid, spring the batten through the points, and there you have it. Or at least you have the after face, which is the small face. To get the bevels and shape of the inside or forward face, another operation is required.

Although there are different ways to pick up the bevels, one of the easiest ways is to simply expand the forward face in the same manner as the after face. This will provide a pattern for each face.

The method for expanding the forward face is the same as used in expanding the after face. The only difference is that you will be using the forward face of the transom for the centerline of the new grid. (See Figure 7-23.) Establish the grid in the same fashion—square out the waterlines, buttock lines, etc. This can become confusing. Some folks, to sort it all out, use a different-colored pencil or even tape down a piece of cardboard on which to draw their expansion.

On a tick strip, record the new widths of the sheer, waterlines, and middle line from the half-breadth plan and plot them on the new grid. Square over the new buttock intersections to the buttock lines on the grid. Spring the batten through the points, fair it, and there you are!

To make the transom from the lofting, use your patterns to lay out the after (smaller) face on one side of your stock, and the forward (larger) face on the other. Line up

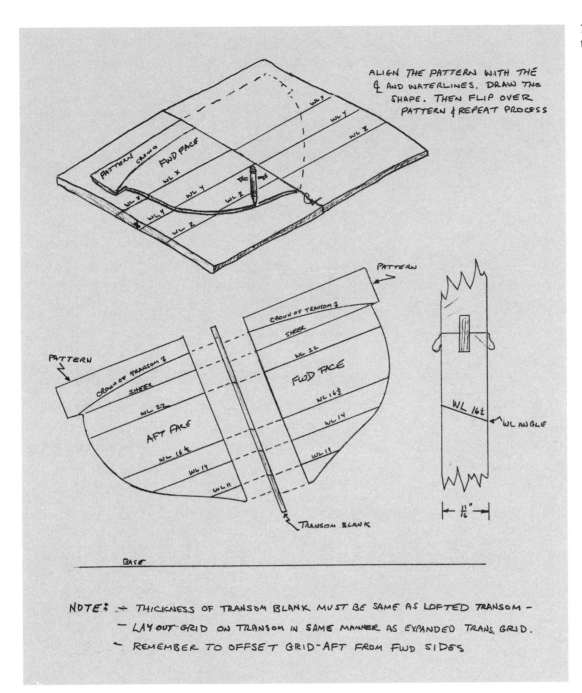

ALIGN THE PATTERN WITH THE ℄ AND WATERLINES. DRAW THE SHAPE. THEN FLIP OVER PATTERN & REPEAT PROCESS

NOTE: — THICKNESS OF TRANSOM BLANK MUST BE SAME AS LOFTED TRANSOM —
— LAY OUT GRID ON TRANSOM IN SAME MANNER AS EXPANDED TRANS. GRID.
— REMEMBER TO OFFSET GRID-AFT FROM FWD SIDES

the pattern on the reference waterlines and the centerline, draw the shape, then flip it to the other side of the centerline and draw it again. This gives you a perfectly symmetrical transom. Then take the stock to the bandsaw and cut to the large side and simply spokeshave to the small. The bevels will automatically take care of themselves.

Easy, yes? Yes and no. Caution must be used to avoid bad mistakes. (See Figure 7-24.)

Note:

• This system works only if your transom is exactly the same thickness as that lofted on the profile. Change the thickness of the stock, and the angle of the bevel will change.

• Remember that the transom is raked. This means that the reference waterlines will be higher on one side (the after face) of the transom stock than on the other. Therefore, although you can square the reference centerline over from one side to the other on the stock, you cannot square the reference waterlines over from one side to the other. Use your bevel gauge to carry over the line offset. Lay out your waterlines, and then take the stock to the lofting board and check it against the transom in profile.

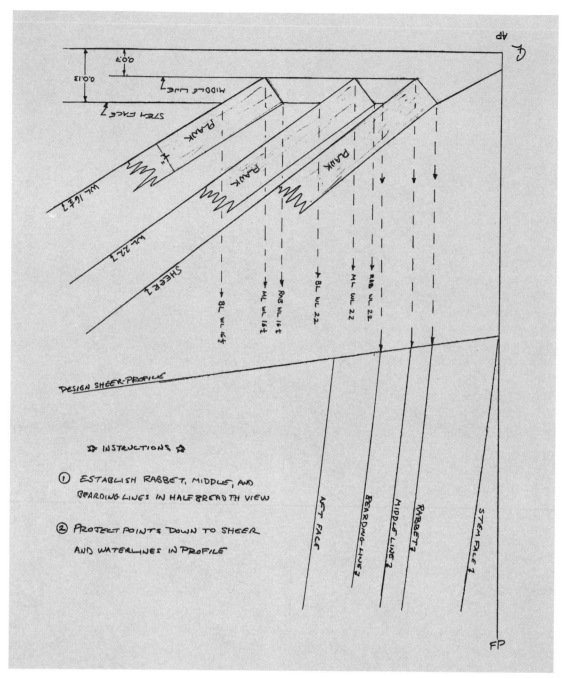

DETERMINING THE STEM RABBET

One of the best aspects of lofting is the opportunity you get to lay out the stem rabbet. This conveniently allows you to cut the rabbet into the stem while it is clamped to the workbench. The Catspaw plans contain offsets for the entire stem rabbet—that is, the rabbet, middle, and bearding lines. The completeness of this information is unusual. Generally, the designer will supply either a rabbet line or a middle line only; the rest of the information must be developed yourself by lofting.

Fortunately, much of the information needed to plot the rabbet on the stem has already been generated on other parts of the drawing, and all that is necessary is to record it on the stem.

For the bottom of the stem, at Station 1, information is taken directly from the body plan. This information should be quite accurate, as it comes from a right-angle slice through the stem.

For the top and near-plumb parts of the stem, information can be projected down from the half-breadth plan. (See Figure 7-25.) The bearding and rabbet lines are generated in the same manner as they were when you developed the bottom of the keel. That is, align the fid (plank sample) on the waterline (e.g., WL 22), with one end touching the middle line. Draw around the fid with

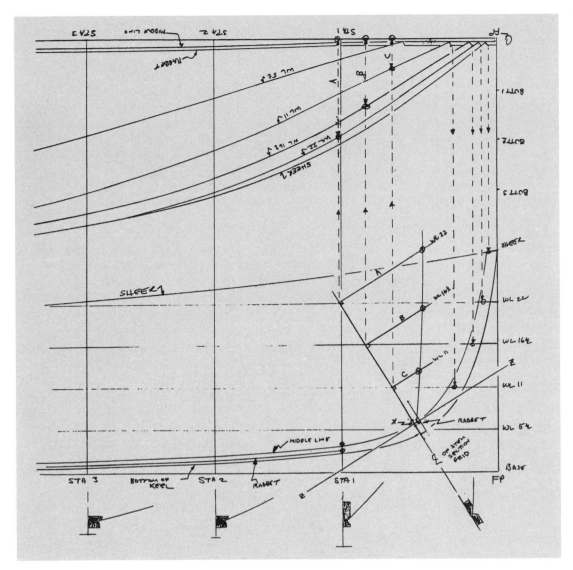

a pencil. The rabbet and bearing lines are developed automatically. Just square that information down to WL 22 in the profile, and you've got it! This method is quite accurate for the top of the stem and the near-plumb portions of the stem, because the waterlines are entering the stem at nearly right angles. But, in the curved portions of the stem, this method is suspect. For the curved parts of the stem (in the forefoot), you must use another method to get an accurate picture.

Essentially, the method involves running a station (a.k.a., "stem section") perpendicularly through the rabbet at the curved part of the stem. (See Figures 7-26 and 7-27.) Basically, everything works the same as for the regular stations you have already lofted. There will be a centerline, a grid to mark half-breadths on, a middle line, and an "outside of stem" face. This stem section is the lofting equivalent of slicing off the bow of the boat with a chainsaw to see what's inside.

To begin, go to your middle line on the stem (or stem face, if it is running fairly parallel to the middle

line). Pick a point (X) on the curve at which you wish to run a station, and draw a straight line (Z-Z) roughly tangent to the curve at that point.

At point "X," erect a line perpendicular to line Z-Z. This will be the centerline of your stem section. Next, measure out from the centerline, one-half the stem thickness (in the Catspaw it is 0-0-13), and draw a short line parallel to the centerline. This represents one side of the stem.

Next, at each profile waterline intersection with the stem section's centerline, square out a line. Now, we have completed the section grid.

Go to the middle-line point (X), and square out and mark the middle-line width (0-0-7).

Our next job is to capture waterline widths from the half-breadth plan and plot them on the grid. First, go to the intersection of the stem section's centerline and WL 11 in the profile. Square a line, from that intersection, up to the centerline of the half-breadth. Measuring along that line, record (on a tick strip) the distance (B) from the

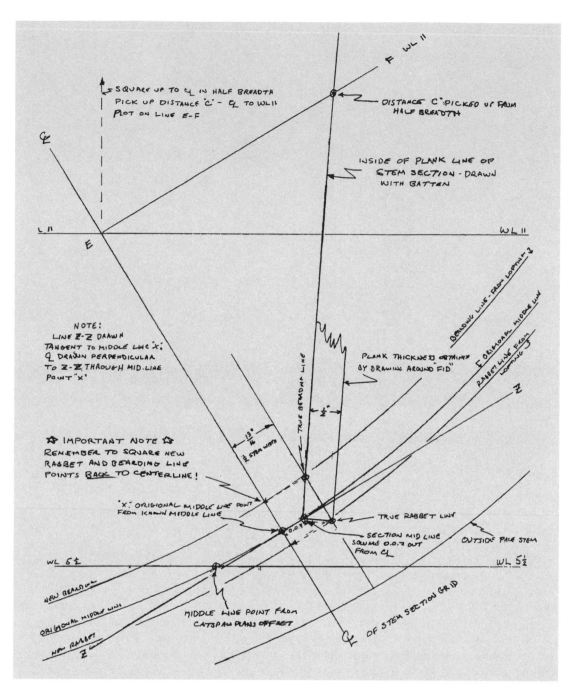

centerline to WL 11. Bring that distance down to the section grid and plot it on WL 11 as B in that view.

Next, go to the intersection of the section centerline and WL 16 in the profile, square up to the half-breadth view, and repeat the process to establish distance C. Then, do it again for WL 22, which yields distance A. Isn't this fun?

We are now ready to spring a batten in the same way as we did on the body plan. Connect the waterline points and the middle-line point (the one that's 0-0-7). Draw the line. Then, take your trusty fid and draw its outline the same as before. All that is left to do is to square those three points back to the section centerline. You now have

an accurate portrayal of how the plank enters the stem at that point. To get a full picture of the rabbet and bearing lines, it would be good to loft one or two more sections. Neatness counts, and be frugal with the pencil lines.

All this seems like a lot of work, but it is the only way to get accurate information for curved stems. On many stems, you may find yourself doing sections along the entire length to locate the rabbet line. Now, there's something to look forward to.

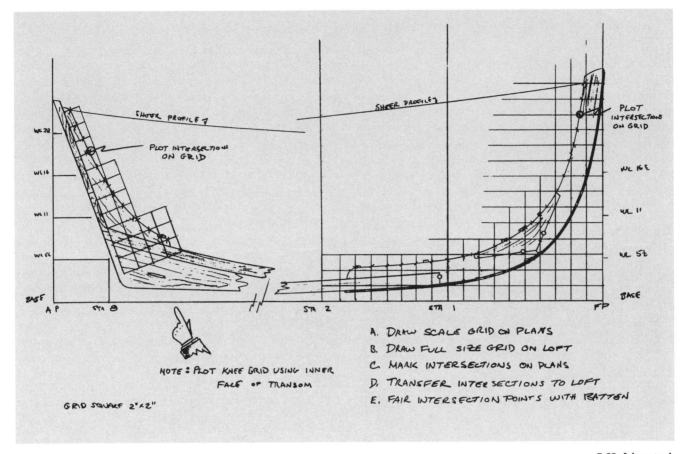

NOTE: PLOT KNEE GRID USING INNER FACE OF TRANSOM

GRID SQUARE 2"×2"

A. DRAW SCALE GRID ON PLANS
B. DRAW FULL SIZE GRID ON LOFT
C. MARK INTERSECTIONS ON PLANS
D. TRANSFER INTERSECTIONS TO LOFT
E. FAIR INTERSECTION POINTS WITH BATTEN

7-28: A low-tech way of establishing the inside face of the stem, the location of the stem knee, and the shape of the stern knee.

Shape Replication, or, How Do You Get the After Face of the Stem?

Offsets for the actual shapes of structural members—stem, knee, gripe, stern knee, etc.—are not provided in the Catspaw plans. In fact, it's a rare plan indeed that offers such information in numerical or offset form. The designer usually leaves that determination to the builder's experience. That's okay, but what do you do if you want to replicate the member exactly as pictured in the plans?

Once again—no problem! There is a low-tech, fun, and easy solution to the question. In a word: grids. Basically, you superimpose a scale grid over the structure from which you want information on the plans and record line intersections on the grid. (See Figure 7-28.) On the lofting board, you establish a full-sized grid in the same location. From there it is just a matter of transferring points from one grid to another. This can usually be done just by eyeball instead of meticulously measuring each point's location. This works because the grid boxes are small enough, giving you lots of points, and the eye is quite good at seeing relationships such as these. Besides, the batten will fair up any kinks.

Finishing Off the Lofting

After establishing the shapes of your structural pieces by using the grid system, what's left to do? Laying out the stopwaters, for one thing. These critical pieces, which prevent water from entering the boat through the joints in the backbone, are often forgotten, which brings much anguish later on. You can also lay out your bolt locations, so the bolts won't cut through the stopwaters. This exercise also tells you the length and number of bolts needed for construction.

With the lofting completed, you're ready to begin making the patterns and building your boat.

☞ A Few Considerations for Lofting to the Outside of Plank

Before you start to build your molds, be sure that you have drawn the stations on the body plan to the inside of plank. This is important, because the outside edge of the molds will be wrapped by the inside of the planks.

Many plans for small craft and most for large craft are drawn to the outside of plank. Why? Basically because it is the most practical way to go. In the same way that the builder who carves a half model fashions the model to reflect the completed boat, the designer renders the drawing of the boat as it will be built.

Occasionally you will find plans drawn to the inside of plank (the Catspaw is one of these), but these are more the exception

Deducting the plank thickness at each mold.

than the rule. How do you know for sure? The key is in the Table of Offsets. There is usually a notation that reads something like "Lines drawn to inside of plank." If there is no notation, the offset table will still reveal its intention. If the lines end at the rabbet line, then the lines are drawn to the outside of plank. On the other hand, if the end point is the apex (middle line, back rabbet) then it is an inside job.

Elementary deduction, Watson

If the lines are drawn to the outside of plank, you must deduct the plank thickness at each mold. For small craft with light planking, you can simply set your pencil compass to the planking thickness and run a series of little arcs

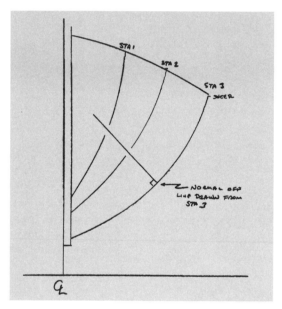

7-A: Draw a line perpendicular to the curve.

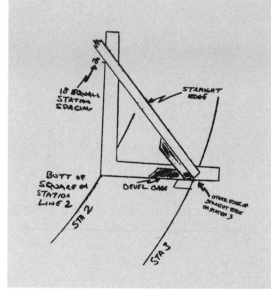

7-B: Stand a framing square on the line.

7-D: Plot the plank thicknesses at A, B, C, etc., on the inside of the original station and bend a batten through the points. The line is the inside of plank.

7-C: Record the bevel on a bevel board.

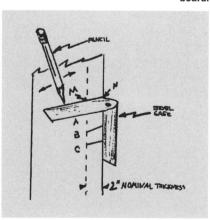

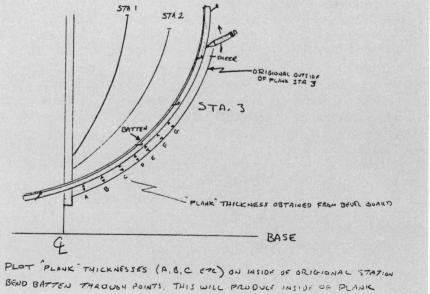

on the inside of the curve of the station, connect them with a batten, and draw the line. There you are—instant inside of plank! Another method is to use a piece of planking as a spacer and run a series of tick marks on the inside of the curve to achieve the same end as the arcs.

Both methods seem easy, but are they accurate? For all practical purposes, yes.

Note for the persnickety builder: With these methods, there is indeed a tiny bit of distortion at the molds at the bow and stern where the planks pass over the station at a steep angle. The molds end up being a tiny bit fuller, but on light-caliber planking, the inaccuracy is probably too insignificant even to notice.

For the big rigs

On vessels with heavy planking, or in situations where it is necessary to deduct the plank thickness and the frame thickness (say, if the design required the frames to be bent directly over the molds), the direct subtraction of plank thickness on the forward and after molds might not provide enough accuracy. To correct this inaccuracy other methods can be used. One such is the Framing Square and Straightedge Technique.

Using the Framing Square and Straightedge Technique

a. Begin by lightly drawing a line perpendicular to the curve of Station 3 on the body plan. (See Diagram 7-A.)

b. Stand a framing square on that line (see Diagram 7-B), with the heel of the square touching Station 2. Be sure that the square stands at 90 degrees to the lofting board.

c. Mark the station spacing distance on the upright edge of the square. (In this case, 18 inches measured up from the surface of the body plan.)

d. Round up a straightedge—a steel rule or yardstick will do. Set the straightedge so that one corner touches Station 3 as shown, and clamp the opposite end of the straightedge at the 18-inch mark directly above Station 2. This will form a right triangle.

e. Pick up the angle formed by the clamped straightedge and the bottom leg of the square with a bevel gauge. Mark and label the location measured on the body plan.

f. Make a bevel board. This can be as simple as a piece of scrap stock with one straight edge. Mark the nominal plank thickness on it by drawing a line parallel to the edge. Hold your bevel gauge (with the angle you have captured) against the straight side of the bevel board, mark the line with your pencil, and label it. (See Diagram 7-C.) The distance traveled by that line, from the straight side of the bevel board to the plank thickness line, will be the "real" plank thickness that must be deducted at that point on the body plan.

g. Continue this method all along the station until you have a series of measurements recorded on your bevel board.

h. Remove the framing square assembly from the body plan. Then, using dividers or a tick strip, plot the "real" plank thicknesses that you have obtained from the bevel board, on the inside or centerline side of the station. Spring a batten through these points (see Diagram 7-D), and there you have your station at the inside of plank. (Don't forget to fair this line to the bearding line on the keel.)

i. Repeat the operation for each of the other stations.

☞ A Lofting Review Checklist for Round-Bottom Boats

1. Check plans for pertinent information: scale, whether lines are drawn to inside or outside of plank, waterline spacing, etc. Highlight if necessary.

2. Establish grid. Separate views as much as possible. Body plan is most handy if drawn on a separate board. Check all perpendiculars with either trammel points or a 3,4,5 triangle. Double-check station, waterline, and buttock spacing for accuracy.

3. Draw the boat's "boundary" lines; i.e., transom, sheer, stem face, keel, and rabbet (or apex) line in profile. Then do the same for the half-breadth. (Line endings for the rabbet and transom are squared down from the profile.)

4. Make any required sheer corrections.

5. Draw the body plan. Sheer and apex intersections come from the profile and half-breadth projections. All other points come from the table of offsets.

6. Run the rest of the waterlines in the half-breadth view, using tick strip to transfer width at each station

from the body plan.

7. Run buttock lines on profile view. Use tick strip to transfer vertical heights from the body plan; horizontal intersections are squared over from the half-breadth plan.

8. Draw the diagonals. Select an uncluttered line to use as your centerline. Station half-breadths come directly from the body plan. Rabbet and transom endings come from vertical measurements on the body plan, brought over to the profile intersection, then squared to the diagonals' centerline.

9. Expand the transom.

10. Loft any necessary sections through the stem to check the rabbet.

11. For boats drawn to the to the outside of plank, deduct planking thickness.

12. Draw in all the parts and pieces for the backbone to prepare for pattern making.

8 • THE STEM

Wood stock for making the stem has changed with the passage of time. In many ways, this change is a chronicle of the evolution of the small-craft industry.

In the early nineteenth century, when construction materials were abundant, the elegantly simple one-piece stem, fashioned from a naturally grown knee, was the way to go. Although the acquisition and selection of the raw material for the one-piece stem is labor intensive, the end result is rugged, stable, and relatively trouble free.

As time went by, production demands and the scarcity and cost of raw materials led to the composition stem, built up of two or more smaller pieces through-fastened with bolts. These machine-cut and mechanically fastened stems depended on quality joinery and bedding compounds to provide a reliable and leakproof component. Built up in pieces like a truss, the stem could be larger; at the same time, the technique allowed the builder to use more commonly available materials.

The development of reliable, high-strength glues after World War II ushered in the era of the laminated stem. When properly executed, the laminated stem is extraordinarily strong for its weight, uses wood efficiently, yet retains many of the desirable characteristics of the nat-

urally grown stem. Better living through chemistry!

But of the three ways of building a wooden stem, which is the best? Considering that all three work well, the answer really lies in the balance of the practical—the time you have to build the stem and the availability of the materials—with the aesthetic: how the stem will look in the boat.

RABBETED OR TWO-PIECE (DORY-TYPE) STEM

After settling on the method of construction, there is one more decision: whether to go with a rabbeted or a two-piece stem. For most heavy or complicated stem assemblies, the rabbeted stem is probably the best bet. But for light or very straightforward construction, there is much to be said for a two-piece stem, as it eliminates the need for cutting a rabbet.

The inner stem of a two-piece stem is beveled at the angle at which the planks will land; for example, typically in dories and sharpies, this bevel runs from the bearding line to the centerline on the face of the inner stem. (See Figure 8-2.) The inner stem is then set up and braced, and the planking is allowed to run by it and is fastened. The plank ends are cut off flush with the face of the inner stem and at a right angle to the centerline of the stem. (It is best to do this as each plank is installed, rather than later when all the planks are on.) The ends of planks can then be primed with a suitable paint, such as red lead. The outer stem, sometimes called a false stem, can then be added. It can be either cut to shape, steambent in a jig (see Figure 8-3), or right on the boat, or it can be laminated in place. Any way you go, the outer stem should be well bedded and fastened with either screws or bolts.

Are there any drawbacks to the two-piece stem? Only a few small ones. The acute angle on the end of the hood ends of the plank may make repairs a little more difficult; an improperly fitted or bedded outer stem can invite rot; and a steam-bent outer stem can break down over time and require replacement. On the other hand, you can take the view that the outer stem is a replaceable item, just like the bumper on your car. If the outer stem becomes worn or beat up, just pop it off and replace it with another.

MAKING THE STEM PATTERN

As with all steps in boatbuilding, the ticket to a successful stem is a good pattern, as it will help you select your stock and lay out the stem. Furthermore the making of the pattern from the lofting will give you a pretty good

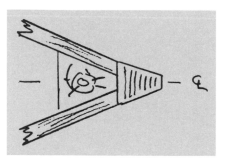

8-1: Cross section of a two-piece stem. The outer or false stem is bent over the forward face of the inner stem after the plank ends have been trimmed.

insight as to what you will be up against when you build the real thing.

The easiest way to transfer the shape of the stem from the lofting to your pattern stock (¼-inch plywood works great for this) is to use nails. Lay the nails on their sides on the lofting, with their heads following the outline of the stem in profile. Carefully lower your pattern stock onto the nails, press down, and bingo! you have a bunch of reference marks on the bottom of your pattern stock. Connect the dots with a batten, draw with pencil, cut out with the bandsaw, and you are in business.

Note: take the time to make a pattern that replicates the shape on the lofting. The dividends accrued are worth it.

THE GROWN STEM

The greatest, and perhaps only, challenge to making a grown stem is foraging the stock. This is not as daunting as it may sound—even for urban dwellers. What you are looking for is the large sweeping crooks and branches of such trees as the oak or black locust. These sometimes can be obtained from small independent logging operations, if the logger is convinced it is worth his time to set them aside for you. Another prospect are highway utility crews; they may be lopping off great branches while opening a path for their wires. Yet another possibility is salvage after storms.

8-2: Beveling the inner stem to take the planking.

Once you have the stock, your next job is to get the wood slabbed out; that is, flattened on two sides. This is not to be undertaken lightly, as there are few things as treacherous to saw out as oddly shaped round stock. You may find someone with a bandsaw mill to do the job, or you can flatten the sides by cutting kerfs with a chainsaw, knocking out the pieces with a chisel and mallet, and finishing off the job with a hand-held power planer.

Another possibility is to purchase a hackmatack crook or knee, which comes from the root of the tree. These are still available and are sold flattened on two sides. No knee stores in your town? Not to worry, knee merchants are used to selling by mail.

However you get the knees, it is important to season them properly. Unseasoned stock will crack, twist, and check.

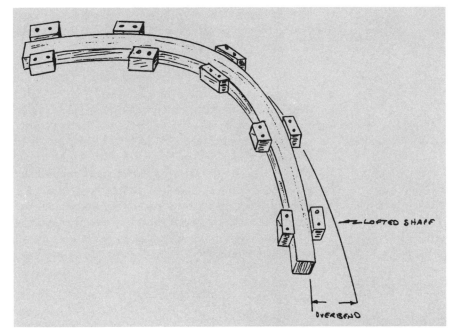

8-3: An outer or false stem steam-bent into a jig whose parts are screwed to the shop floor. Note the over-bend to account for springback.

8-4: A slabbed-out natural crook or knee (bottom) and a stem sawn from a similar crook.

After obtaining seasoned stock you are ready to go. All you need is to plane it to the proper thickness, lay your pattern atop, and mark it. (See Figure 8-5.) Avoid sapwood when laying your pattern on the stem stock. It is tempting to incorporate it in the stem, but to do so is asking for problems down the road.

Cut out the stem on the bandsaw and shape it with your edge tools. Check the finished stem against the lofting, especially where the stem joins the keel. An error here, at this critical joint, even a little one, will be multiplied greatly at the sheer.

Now mark and cut the rabbet. On the face of the stem, mark the parallel lines for fairing (beveling) the cutwater, but don't bevel it yet. Anoint the stem with preservative and set it aside to be joined with the keel later.

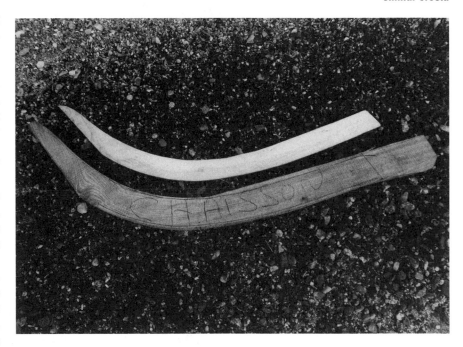

THE BUILT-UP STEM

One of the strongest arguments for the built-up stem is the availability of stock for building it. All you have to do is go down to the lumberyard and order it. Although flitch-sawn lumber (bark on both edges) isn't necessary, it is advantageous, as such stock allows you more wood to work with than that which is four-sided. Keep in mind that if your plans call for six-quarter (1½-inch) stock, unless your wood already has been dressed (planed) to ⁶⁄₄, you will need to order heavier stock than ⁶⁄₄ to allow you

to plane it to size.

When constructing a built-up stem, it is essential that you have accurate patterns for each piece. Making the necessary tight joints is difficult enough without incorporating inconsistencies from a funky pattern. For greatest strength, lay out the patterns on the stock for the maximum amount of long grain that will come as close as possible to paralleling the curve of the stem. "Short" grain, which often shows up at the turn at the bottom of the stem, is weak and can lead to premature failure. Try to incorporate as much curving grain as possible in the knee. Sometimes working the pattern around a large knot can give you just enough swooping grain for the job.

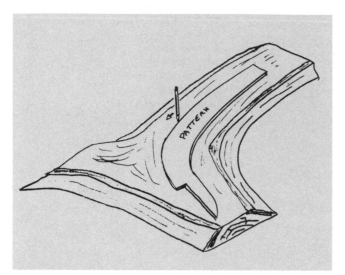

A built-up stem is a synthesis of a number of pieces joined together, and each of the joints is a potential problem. The cut of a joint needs to be off only a bit to throw the entire assembly out of kilter. It is, therefore, good practice to initially leave extra "meat" on the negotiable non-joining surfaces, such as the stem face, the inside of the stem, and, especially, the curved inside face of the knee; this insurance wood will allow you to make any necessary adjustments later. If you trim all the pieces of the knee down to their nicely drawn curved lines right from the git-go, by the time you are done fitting all the joints the knee could very well be too small.

Instead, begin by fitting the joints between all the pieces, and the joint between the stem assembly and the keel. Use the lofting as an assembly jig, screw down blocks to butt against and to hold your pieces in place.

8-5: Using a pattern to lay out a stem on a hackmatack knee. The pattern should be placed to follow the grain of the wood and to avoid sapwood.

8-6: The construction of a typical built-up stem.

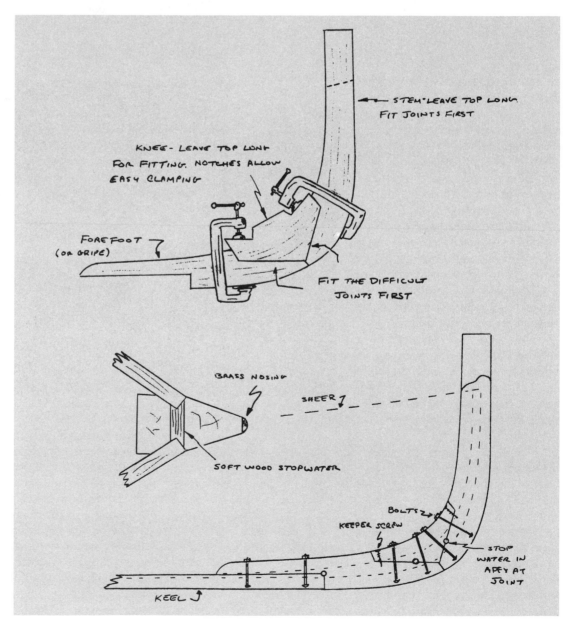

Check that your fits are cut square. Stem joints can look tight on the side facing you, yet can be open on the bottom side.

Watch for "crown" (a slight rise in the center) on the face of mating joints. This phenomenon can drive you nuts when you are trying to get a good fit. Brushing a little carpenter's chalk on one mating surface of the joint and rubbing both surfaces of the joint together can help pinpoint the problem; the chalk on the first surface will transfer to the high points on the opposing one. Sometimes introducing just a hint of concavity in one of the surfaces will allow the joints to close up properly.

After you have a good fit, clamp the joint together tightly and immobilize it in place on the lofting board, making sure the bottom of the stem fits the keel properly. (See Figure 8-7.) You can then replace your patterns on top of the stem and redraw the lines if necessary. Trim up your pieces on the bandsaw and finish up with hand tools. The stem should fit your lofting exactly! Now it's time to drill for the bolts.

8-7: Clamp the parts of the built-up stem directly on the lofting to be certain they match the lines.

Drilling for the bolts

Drilling for the through carriage bolts that will hold the pieces of the stem together should be a straightforward deal. Just mark the bolt locations, clamp everything tightly, and drill. When the bolts are inserted and the nuts are tightened, all the joints should be snug and flush. Most of the time they are, but occasionally, when the assembly is removed from the clamps and the bolts are tightened, the joints will open up. It may be difficult to tell what causes this—perhaps those long, smooth mating surfaces slipped when you bored for the bolts, or maybe the vibration of the drill caused slippage—but whatever it is, a joint that opens instead of closes can be quite disconcerting. What to do?

One tactic is to solve the problem before it arises by laying out your bolt locations in such a way that when the bolts are tightened they will tend to draw the pieces together. This must be done on the lofting board to make sure you avoid the stopwaters.

Another tactic that works well is, while the stem is tightly clamped up, to drive a screw at each end of the piece where they run into the adjoin-

8-8: Grind the sides off the head of a stem bolt.

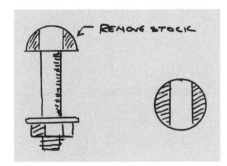

ing pieces. Then drill for your bolt holes. The screws will act like a key or a parking brake to keep the assembly from sliding while the holes are drilled. (See also the section on drilling long holes in Chapter 9, The Keel.)

You can now counterbore for the plugs. For the stem and the other parts of the backbone assembly you can simply use a Forstner or Speedbore bit to drill a round hole for a round plug. You can't do this on the forward face of the stem, however, because this face must be faired (beveled) into a cutwater. If round holes are drilled, the act of fairing will cut into the sides of the holes, producing little half moons on either side of the stem. To prevent this from happening, cut box-shaped "counterbores" into the face of the stem with a chisel, then flatten two sides of your bolt heads: either beat them with a hammer or grind them with a grinder. (See Figure 8-8.) Make up some matching plugs, and you are ready to bolt. Almost.

Bedding and bolting

Before the pieces of the stem are bolted together, the joints must be smeared with bedding compound. If you opt for good old-fashioned oil-based boatyard bedding compound, your joints should first be primed with a durable oil-based paint, such as red lead, to prevent the wood from sucking the oil out of the compound. After the paint is dry, lay on the bedding compound. A heavy layer isn't required; the toothed side of a coarse hacksaw blade makes an excellent "notched" trowel for the job.

If you use a synthetic compound, such as Sikaflex 240 or 3M 5200, no priming is really necessary. In fact, bedding for the stem is a good application for these exceptionally durable adhesive/caulks, as they make a great gasket and are flexible; furthermore, the adhesive quality of the compound will augment the power of the bolts. While synthetic compound makes a virtually permanent bond, the chances are good that you won't need to take apart the stem in the future.

You can now give the bolt holes a dollop of wood preservative, slide in the bolts, and tighten them up. Wipe up any squeezed-out bedding compound and mark the rabbet, then drill and install your stopwaters where the apex of the rabbet crosses the joints.

Cut the rabbet, mark the stem face for fairing, and anoint the stem with preservatives or oil. Then set aside the stem to await the keel.

☞ Stopwaters

For the first-time builder, boatbuilding terminology and jargon must seem to be a conspiracy contrived to confound. Floors not underfoot, transoms not over doors, and a ceiling decidedly not overhead. But then occasionally you find those nautical nouns that are so descriptive as to be almost poetic (or at least German.) Such is the case with the humble stopwater. Stopwaters are softwood dowels inserted into the stem and keel assembly whose sole reason for being is to—stop water.

One often hears of (or has owned) a boat that is a "chronic leaker." The owner tries everything to solve the problem: reefing the seams and driving in new cotton, pumping in countless tubes of high-priced synthetic caulk, even painting the bottom with gelatinous plastic goop that is warranted to stop any leak. All to no avail. That is because the problem is not with the planking at all. It is in the backbone.

Most wooden boats have a built-up stem and keel assembly: joined, bedded, and fastened. But no matter how well joined these pieces were when built, over time they will loosen up. When this happens the now close, but not tight-fitting pieces can allow water to sneak past the planking and on up into the boat. What to do? Install a stopwater.

The stopwater's function is to prevent water from finding a way through the joint. These softwood dowels, usually cedar or pine, are snugly set, without glue, in a hole drilled from side to side through the underwater joint, where it crosses the apex (middle line) of the rabbet. While the joint remains tight, the stopwater has little to do, sitting around like an unused insurance policy. Come the day when the joint opens up, however, the stopwater will spring into action as the softwood swells like a bung in a barrel, heading the leak off at the pass.

Softwood dowels, however, can be a bit of a rarity at the local hardware mart. Likely only maple and birch will be found, and then only in stock sizes. If you need an oddball dimension, chances are good that you'll be out of luck. Probably the best route is to just make them with a homemade stopwater die.

Begin by checking the plans for the caliber of the dowel. Generally they range from ¼ inch to ½ inch. Select the size drill bit to be used for boring the stopwater hole in the keel. Using that bit, make the die by boring a hole in a piece of scrap hardwood. Next, rough out a square-sectioned piece of pine or cedar for the stopwater. For example, for a ½-inch dowel, saw out a slip ½ inch by ½ inch. Then whittle it to a near-round shape with a penknife. Insert one end into the drilled hole in the hardwood and drive it through with a mallet. (See drawing.) The die will round and size the stopwater perfectly, and will compress the wood slightly (all the better for swelling when wet).

That's all there is to it. Bore the stopwater holes (with the same bit used to make the hardwood die), press in your newly minted stopwater, and trim off the excess.

A paleolithic stopwater maker.

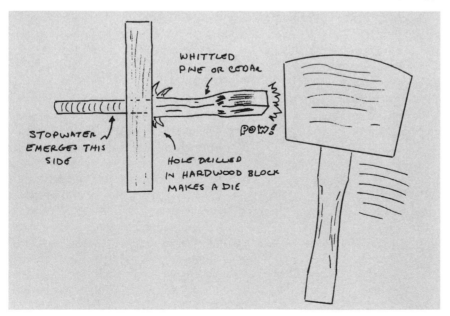

WHITTLED PINE OR CEDAR

POW!

STOPWATER EMERGES THIS SIDE

HOLE DRILLED IN HARDWOOD BLOCK MAKES A DIE

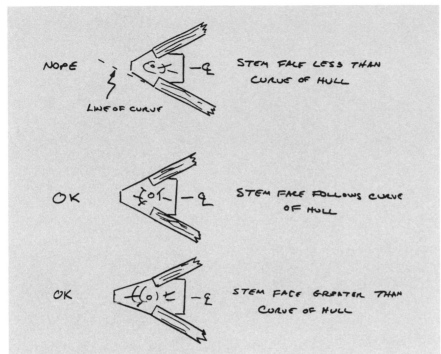

8-9: Fairing the cutwater.

A few thoughts on the cutwater

Along with the line of the sheer, the cutwater—the bevel on the side of the stem that runs from the rabbet to the narrow flat on the forward face—defines the look of your boat. To look right in plan view (half-breadth) the cutwater should either continue the curve of the sheer right out to the end of the stem or, even better, extend out at a slightly optimistic tangent from the curve. (This requires a bit more distance from the rabbet to the stem face.) Cutwaters that jog inward toward the centerline from the curve of the sheer will give the boat an inelegant, snubnosed mien.

You might consider holding off planing in the bevel of the cutwater until after the boat has been planked. The face of the stem can take a beating during the planking process—clamps are affixed to it, screwdrivers can slip, and so on. Waiting until planking has been finished will give you a clean, unblemished face to the cutwater. As an additional bonus, the square sides of the stem will provide a good surface to lay a level against to check for plumbness when setting up the boat.

Adding an apron

Occasionally, if the cut rabbet seems to be particularly short because the plank ends enter the rabbet at a sharp angle, a piece of wood, called an apron, wider than the rest of the stem, is added to the after side of the

8-10: An apron can be fitted to the after face of the stem to provide more landing surface for the planking.

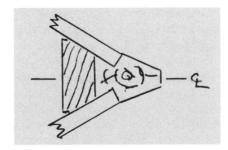

stem. This added width allows the back side of the rabbet to be extended, affording greater landing for the planks on the stem.

THE EPOXY LAMINATED STEM

A laminated stem offers the promise of a synthesis of the strength, dearth of leak-prone joints, and simplicity (at least after it has been glued up) of the grown stem. It also offers the same versatility of commonly available stock provided by the built-up stem. On the flip side, it offers, if one isn't careful, delamination, springback, and not a few anxious moments. But if you are up for messing with epoxy glue, the laminated stem is definitely something to consider.

Before starting

Like most boatbuilding operations, the secret to success in laminating is organization, planning ahead, and having a good idea of what you are getting into before starting the job. A checklist:

1. Have you worked with epoxy before? If so, with this brand? The builder needs to be thoroughly versed in the working qualities of the glue—everything from mixing ratios (they vary from glue manufacturer to glue manufacturer), to pot life and health considerations. Laminating requires a lot of glue that has to be worked very rapidly. Few things are quite as vexatious as being partway through the lay up of a lamination only to find your glue pot smoking and roiling as the contents turn to a murky, crystalline block of plastic. Before you begin, call the manufacturer, get its instruction manual, and run some tests.

2. What species of wood will be used? Some woods, like mahogany, glue quite well. Others, like oak, have a somewhat checkered reputation in combination with epoxy and are better glued with resorcinol. Other factors that can affect proper bonding are moisture content, contamination, porosity of the lumber, and temperature. These are all important matters that must be worked out with your humble adhesive purveyor.

3. Do you have enough tools—especially clamps? You don't want to find yourself with everything ready to go only to discover your brother-in-law Marty has borrowed all

your clamps to hold together the exhaust system on his Studebaker.

Building the jig

You will be needing a jig or form to hold your glued laminates in place. The handiest location to build it is right on top of where you've already drawn the stem—on the lofting floor. Begin by laying a piece of heavy, clear plastic over the work area and shoot in a few staples at the perimeter to keep it from wrinkling or shifting.

Next, saw out a batch of triangular or L-shaped brackets. The design of these should be such that, when a bracket is upright, one leg will be at least as tall as the stem needs to be wide. Pre-drill the "floor" leg for screws. While you are at it, cut out a nest of spacers or shims that are all the same thickness. These will be used to keep the stem laminations off

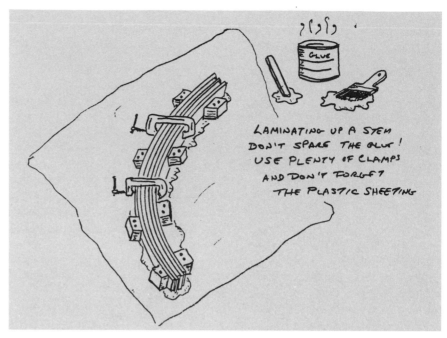

8-11: Laminating a stem.

the floor and make clamping easier. Also make up some clamping pads (plywood is good for this) to spread the pressure of the clamps. And lastly, mill up a series of narrow wedges. These will come in handy when tightening up the glued laminates.

You can now fasten some of your brackets to the outside perimeter of the drawn outer face of the stem with drywall screws. (The brackets will be roughly perpendicular to the curve.) How many brackets are enough? Generally, the tighter the curve, the more brackets that will be necessary. Next, fasten the second series of brackets opposite, and equidistant, from the first, far enough apart to allow the insertion of your laminates and one of those narrow wedges. Then, place your spacers railroad-tie fashion between the paired brackets. This completes your gluing jig.

Springback

Any bent stock, whether it has been steamed or laminated, will have "memory;" that is, it will want to straighten out to some extent when it is released from the clamps. The amount the piece straightens is called springback. Some builders try to compensate for this phenomenon by building in a little extra curve in their bending jig. Others compensate by making the lamination a little heavier; the extra stock allows the piece to be machined to the correct shape after the glue has cured and the piece has sprung back as much as it ever will.

Milling the stock

First determine the thickness of your laminations. This is a trial-and-error proposition. Start milling out a few sample pieces with the table saw and try bending them into

the jig. The laminations should bend easily into place. While there are no hard-and-fast rules dictating dimensions, there are general guides:

a. Cut your laminations from select stock without knots, rot, sapwood, and other imperfections. Look for tight and straight grain.

b. While thinner laminates are easier to bend than thicker ones and will have greater resistance to springback, excessively thin slices gain you little if anything in strength and cost you time and glue in the laminating process.

c. Misalignment and slippage are almost inevitable when gluing up, so cut your stock a bit longer and wider than the finished stem will be to allow for shaping after the lamination has cured.

d. Strive to get your laminations as uniform in thickness as possible. Gaps caused by inconsistent stock thickness will have to be filled with glue (not a good thing); if not, you will be left with structure-weakening voids.

A dry-run

Now is the time to test, practice, and debug your gluing technique. The last thing you need is a surprise when you have your strips slathered up like greased eels.

Dry bend your strips into the jig. Do your have enough room to get them all in, plus some polyethylene film, plus a wedge inserted on the after face of the stem?

Now fit your clamps (quick-gripping bar clamps are best) and pads strategically. Do you have enough of each to draw in the entire laminate tightly? If you place all of your clamps on one side, will you build a twist into the stem?

When you have everything where you want it, mark your clamp locations and disassemble. Keep the pads and clamps handy and ready to go. Lay a sheet of plastic in the jig to insulate the brackets, clamps, and pads from glue.

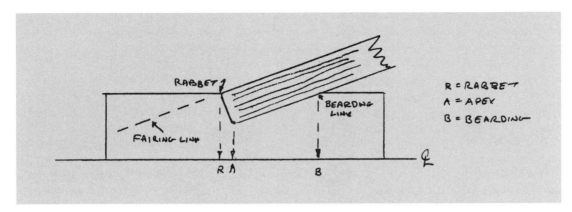

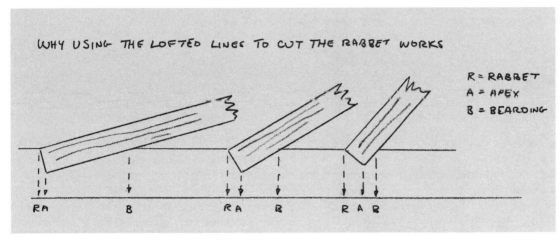

Gluing the stock

Keep in mind that achieving success in laminating is like producing a Broadway show—you must be prepared, you must have the right props, and most of all you must know the strengths and qualities of your actors and what makes them tick. The prima donna in this production is the epoxy. Drop the ball on the glue, buddy, and it's back to vaudeville.

Let's quickly review the conditions that epoxy requires to work. The glue, no matter what brand, is exacting in its demands for mixing and preparation. The builder must be scrupulous in following the manufacturer's recommendations for mixing ratios and time spent blending the resin and hardener. The wood must be free of contamination, and the shop temperature must be within the specified range.

Epoxy is formulated so it will be thin enough to saturate the surface of the wood to produce a good anchor for the bond. The bond itself requires plenty of mixed resin between the pieces being joined to be successful. Without that layer of glue, the joint will be starved and the glue will fail. Unfortunately, the water-like nature of the epoxy will allow it to run out of the joint before the glue has a chance to cure. Ergo, the stuff must be thickened.

Gougeon Brothers, manufacturer of WEST SYSTEM epoxy, recommends microfibers, available from your glue supplier, as a thickening agent. Pre-mixed epoxy should be thickened with microfibers to a heavy syrup or gruel-like consistency that will still be thin enough to be applied with a roller. The epoxy will be able to penetrate but will stay where you want it long enough to fill any voids and not run out of the joints in the laminate.

Begin by laying out your laminates on a plastic sheet. Get out a roller tray and foam roller that is designed for epoxy. (The common gray foam paint rollers act like sponges and will fall apart in short order.) In a separate container mix your epoxy to the specifications outlined by the manufacturer. Remember to wear protective gloves at all times and any other gear necessary to keep the stuff from contacting your skin. Pour your epoxy into the roller tray, and you are ready to apply the epoxy to the lamination.

Note: While some builders feel that a single application of thickened epoxy on the mating surfaces of the laminates is sufficient, others prefer to pre-coat all the surfaces with unthickened epoxy to ensure penetration and then to overcoat with the thickened epoxy. Which technique is better? If the wood is especially porous, go with the two-pronged attack. Otherwise, a single application should do the trick. At any rate, be sure to coat all of the mating surfaces.

After applying the glue, the laminations can be bent into the laminating jig. Check that no plastic gets caught between any of the laminates. Insert wedges (between the

The Epoxy Laminated Stem • 89

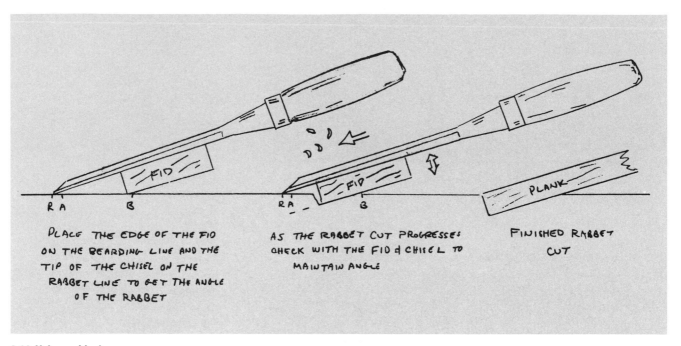

PLACE THE EDGE OF THE FID
ON THE BEARDING LINE AND THE
TIP OF THE CHISEL ON THE
RABBET LINE TO GET THE ANGLE
OF THE RABBET

AS THE RABBET CUT PROGRESSES
CHECK WITH THE FID & CHISEL TO
MAINTAIN ANGLE

FINISHED RABBET
CUT

8-14: Using a chisel and a fid to cut the rabbet.

plastic and the brackets) to prevent the laminations from moving. Then fit the clamps and pads—on the outside of the plastic—and begin to tighten. You will be working against considerable hydraulic pressure as you tighten, so you will probably have to retighten the clamps and wedges a few times until you get the proper amount of "squeeze."

Try not to overtighten the clamps. You need to have that glue in the joints. Simply good, solid pressure on the clamps will do the job. (For more on gluing, see the material on scarfing in Chapter 14, Planking Stock.)

Finishing the job

After the glue has cured properly, you can remove the stem from the jig and begin shaping it. Beware of epoxy cuts on your hand when removing the stem! The leading edge of epoxy that has squeezed out onto plastic and has cured can be as sharp as a razor.

Place your stem pattern on top of the laminated piece and check the fit. With luck there won't have been too much springback. (If there was, you can always add on another laminate.) Trace the shape of the pattern on the piece, cut out the stem with a bandsaw, and shape it. C'est tout!

THE RABBET

The rabbet is the recessed notch cut into the side of the stem to receive the ends of the planks. (See Figure 8-12.) The angle at which this notch is cut will change along its length and depends on the angle at which the planks enter the stem. This can be readily seen when the stem is viewed from the side. The lower the angle the planks

enter the stem, the wider the rabbet (or the distance from the rabbet line to the bearding line) will be; the higher the angle of entrance, the narrower the rabbet will be.

Prior to the introduction of lofting, the only way for the builder to cut a rabbet was to do it on the setup boat. First, a "guesstimation" of the rabbet line was drawn on the stem. Then a batten of the same caliber as the planking was wrapped around the molds or frames. The shipwright would set to work, chipping away at the wood behind the rabbet line until the batten fit along the entire length of the stem.

While this historic method is still effective and certainly is an option for confirmed lofting-o-phobes, there are drawbacks to it. One is a matter of timing. The planking, and to some degree the final fairing of the molds, is held up until the rabbet can be cut. Another is a matter of efficiency. Cutting a bevel in heavy stock while twisted sideways on a vertical surface with a stiff batten springing out at you is not the most comfortable of working positions. Furthermore, unless the stem is well secured, a small portion of the energy from every blow to the chisel is absorbed by movement of the stem.

One of the great benefits of lofting the rabbet and transferring it to the stem is that it allows the rabbet to be cut while the stem is clamped flat on the workbench. Not only does the solidity of the bench guarantee that no effort is lost while chiseling, but also, ergonomically speaking, it's a much better deal. In my book any situation that allows you to work with a mug of steaming coffee right at hand has to be a good one.

Of course, the question that always arises is, "How can you be sure that it works?" After all, when you are working with a batten, mallet, and chisel on the setup boat, you know that what you see is what you get. But,

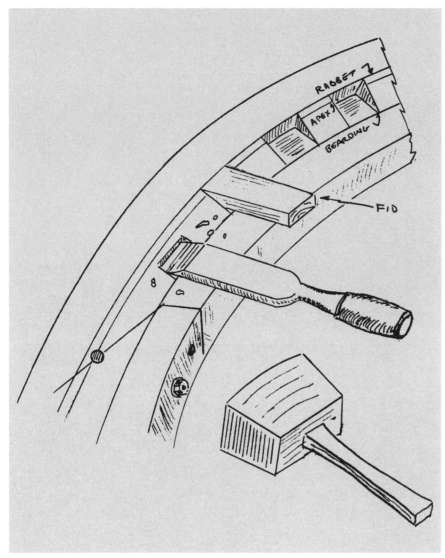

RABBET

Apex

BEARDING

FID

8-15: Notching the stem with a chisel and mallet—the first step in cutting the stem rabbet.

one end and finish at the other. Instead, cut spot notches slightly wider than your fid a few inches apart, then remove the waste between the notches to connect them and finish the rabbet fair.

This connect-the-notch approach allows you to easily correct for errors. If your angle or approach was wrong in one notch, you will probably catch it in the next and will have a lot less to repair. This method is fairly quick as well, as it takes little effort to chip out the waste between the established notches. While there are a number of techniques for cutting the notches, the following is one of the more foolproof approaches:

Start by roughly determining the angle of the cut. Firmly clamp the stem to the bench so you are facing the inside (after face) of the curve. Holding the fid in your hand, place it so the bottom edge is on the bearding line and its rectangular body is at 90 degrees to the curve and pointing at you. Next, hold the chisel to the top side of the fid and, rocking the far end of the fid up and down, slide the chisel forward (or back) until the bottom side of the chisel contacts the rabbet line. That, pilgrim, is the angle of plank entrance for that location. Capture it with your bevel gauge.

Next, starting at the bearding line, begin to cut your notch. Working toward the rabbet line, cut one-third of the way. Slip your fid into the sloping cut and once again place the chisel on the top side of the fid and slide it forward. If the tip of the chisel strikes the rabbet line, you are right on the money and can keep on going. If the tip strikes forward of the rabbet line, your angle is too shallow and you need to shave off a bit more. On the other hand, if the chisel tip hits before the rabbet line, your angle of the notch is too deep—but at least you caught the error in time and can correct it.

Keep right on cutting until the upper edge of the fid hits the rabbet, at which time you will have your first spot notch. You can now move over to the next spot and repeat the process. After all the notches have been cut, they can be joined into one continuously curving rabbet.

when you think about it, part of what you are doing when bending in that batten and chopping away with the chisel is generating a rabbet, an apex, and a bearding line. This is exactly what happens on the lofting board—you have just substituted pencil and eraser for mallet and chisel. So go forth with confidence!

CUTTING THE RABBET

The tools necessary for the job are few. A sharp chisel (one with a long iron; not one of those short, bargain-basement butt chisels), a wooden mallet, and a fid. We met the fid—a small block of wood the same thickness as the planking—when we were lofting; it should be rectangular in shape and square at either end.

Begin by transferring the rabbet and bearding lines from the lofting to the stem. (See sidebar, "Transferring the Rabbet to the Stem.") After the rabbet has been established, you can begin to cut it. While it may seem counterintuitive, the best technique is not to start cutting at

A note of caution

It is easy to cut the rabbet too deep. If you have any doubts about your bearding line, temporarily leave the rabbet a bit shallow. The rabbet can be tuned up in short order with a chisel and a batten after the boat has been set up. The forefoot (gripe) region, where the stem is bolted to the keel, is especially prone to going awry, as there is a considerable amount of action going on, with the angle of the entering planks changing quickly over a short distance of rabbet. Prudence calls for holding off cutting the rabbet (or at least leaving it cut shallow) until the stem has been bolted to the keel and set up.

Can you use a router?

Yes and No. A router can certainly speed the cutting of the rabbet if you have a proper jig to control the constantly changing angle of the tool. The difficulty is that a proper jig can take longer to build than it would take to cut the rabbet by hand. So, unless you are planning mass production of the same boat, the chisel and the mallet are still the way to go.

☞ Transferring the Rabbet to the Stem

Here are a number of options to accurately establish the reference lines for the stem rabbet:

Method A

Place a piece of Mylar over the lofting and trace the outline of the outside of the stem. Then establish the rabbet line, bearding line, apex (middle line), sheerline, and waterlines on the sheet. The Mylar can then be lifted from the lofting floor and draped over the stem, aligned, and anchored in place with thumbtacks. The lines can then be transferred to the wood by using a serrated dressmaker's pattern wheel. The sawtooth edges of the wheel will puncture the Mylar and leave a trail of dents on the stem. (For extra-dark marks, insert a piece of carbon paper between the Mylar and the wood.)

Next, the Mylar can be brought to the other side of the stem and the operation repeated.

The curve can then be cleaned up and faired by springing a flexible batten through the embossed marks. Draw in the curve with a pencil, mark the sheer and the waterlines, and you are in business.

Method B

This method, favored by builders who appreciate durable hard copy and anticipate constructing further copies of the boat, is to utilize the same patterns made for laying out the stem. Using the same system for originally making the patterns, lay out an array of three-penny nails, with the heads lined up along the sheer, the rabbet, the apex, and the bearding lines.

After carefully aligning the pattern over its place on the lofting board, press it into the recumbent nails. Remove whatever nails stick to the pattern and connect the dents with a flexible batten. Then, using a small-caliber bit in a hand drill or a drill press, bore a series of holes every inch or so along the length of each line.

Place the pattern on the side of the stem and hold it in place with brads or a small clamp. An ice pick or an awl can then be poked through each one of the holes, into the wood. This will leave you with a series of points that can then be connected with a flexible batten. Draw the lines with a pencil.

The pattern can then be placed on the other side of the stem and the operation repeated.

Method C

This last, and perhaps the most accurate, technique is begun by placing the completed stem back on top of the lofted stem. Temporarily anchor the stem against movement by tacking a few nails alongside the piece.

Note: Chances are good that your stem will be slightly different in shape from the stem drawn on the lofting floor. If that is the case, align it as closely as you can, making sure the keel-to-stem joint is right. (Trim up the joint if necessary.)

Trace around the stem with a pencil or a pen in a contrasting color to the lofted lines. (Red is tasteful.) Square your waterlines, sheerline, and station lines up the forward and after edges of the stem. Connect the lines across the top face of the stem with a straightedge and a pencil, and label them. Release the stem from its bondage, flip it over, and connect the lines on the opposite face.

With dividers or, better yet, a tick strip, record the rabbet, apex, and bearding lines from each reference line on the lofted stem, using the red traced line to reflect the actual forward and after faces of the stem. The strip should have five marks—the forward face, the rabbet line, the apex, the bearding line, and the after face. Label the strip.

Place the strip on the appropriate reference line, taking care to align the forward and after faces. Transfer the marks to the stem. When done, connect the points with a flexible batten.

The lines will be exactly as drawn on the stem lofting. Got to be!

9 • THE KEEL

The keel is the foundation for the rest of the boat. The approach to its construction varies with the style of the boat and the preference of the designer and the builder. Some keels are simple bent boards. Others are complex, built-up affairs. There are even regional differences among acceptable modes of construction. A common thread running through all the styles, however, is that, like a house foundation, the keel must be built well of the best available materials.

A NOTE ON CONSTRUCTION PLANS

The level of construction detail on boat plans can vary from extraordinarily complete to ambiguous, nebulous, and generally vague. As a rule, the newer plans for small craft tend to offer more detail; older plans are likely to be more sketchy.

In many cases the configuration of the backbone will be left to the builder's discretion. For example, the construction plan for John Alden's North Haven Dinghy illustrates two options for stern construction—one with a sternpost, the other with a large transom knee. The choice whether to use one configuration over another is many times not so much based on one technique being better than another (though it may be), but rather on more mundane matters, such as builder's preference and availability of materials.

Sometimes one type of construction stock must be substituted for that recommended in the plans, which is fine as long as it is of equal or better quality. Some plans drawn in the nineteenth century might specify iron keel bolts for a particular small sailing craft. That specification may have had more to with the builders' penchant for thriftiness in the choice of materials in a time of cheap labor than with iron being a better fastener. Today, the proven advantages of silicon bronze over mild steel make the nonferrous bolt the hands-down better choice.

And what about those plans that are conspicuous in their absence of construction details? Detective work is required to deal with them. Find a set of plans for a vessel of similar size and type. Chances are good that the scantlings will be close enough to be borrowed for your boat. Or pack your pad, pencil, and measuring tape, and check your local boatyard and maritime museum for kin to the boat you wish to build. Boatyards are great, as you can see modern techniques and materials at work. Museums are

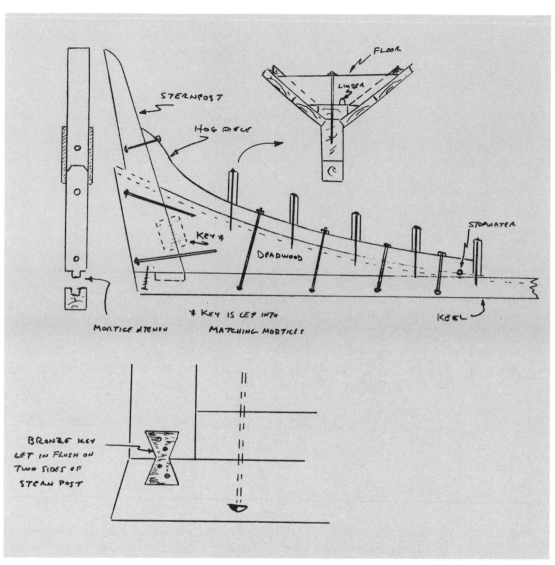

STERNPOST

FLOOR

LIMBER

HOG PIECE

STOPWATER

KEY *

DEADWOOD

KEEL

MORTICE & TENON

* KEY IS LET INTO MATCHING MORTICES

BRONZE KEY LET IN FLUSH ON TWO SIDES OF STERN POST

9-2: Keel for a Crosby catboat ca. 1885.

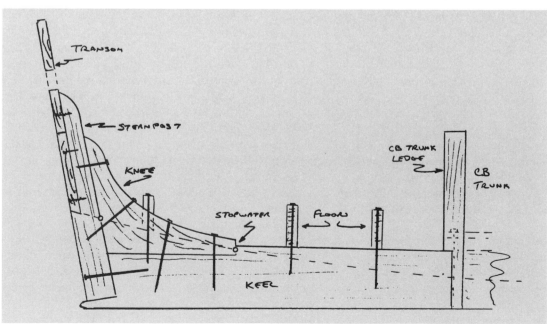

TRANSOM

STERNPOST

KNEE

STOPWATER

FLOOR

CB TRUNK LEDGE

CB TRUNK

KEEL

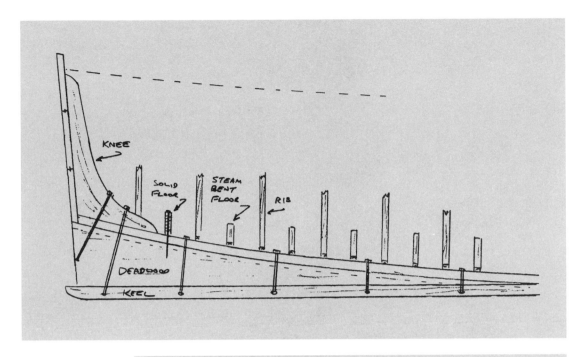

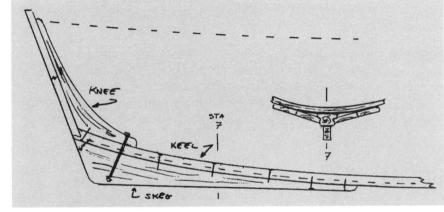

9-4: The steam-bent keel of the Catspaw dinghy.

9-5: Cross section of the keel of a row-boat with a keel batten and steam-bent floors.

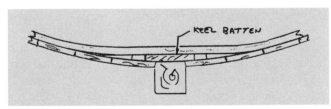

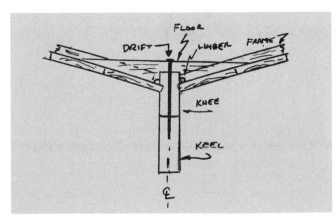

9-6: Cross section of the after end of the keel of a Crosby catboat, ca. 1885.

invaluable, too, not only for evidence of time-tested methods that work but also for those that do not.

STARTING OFF

Begin by making patterns for all the sawn parts of the keel assembly. Some plans come with paper patterns that can be traced directly onto your pattern stock, but most do not. In the latter case it's back to the old lofting board to lift patterns with the same nails-on-edge technique used to pick up the shape of the stem (see Chapter 8, The Stem).

After the patterns have been cut and fit, they can be used for choosing construction stock. Whenever possible, use your pattern to maximize the sweep of the grain of the stock. Trace the pattern onto the stock and cut.

Note: Before starting the cut, check one last time that your bandsaw is indeed cutting square. Keel stock tends to be fairly beefy stuff. A cut that is off by a few degrees can

9-7: A keel being made up directly on the lofting.

cause quite an error over a thickness of a couple of inches of stock, perhaps causing you to undercut the line on the opposite side.

When hand planing keel pieces, check regularly that the surface is being cut square, with no crown to prevent a joint from closing. As when building the stem, fashion your most difficult fits first, leaving extra stock on your negotiable edges, which can be trimmed to size later on.

Use caution when laying out and cutting the area of the keel that makes a joint with the stem. This joint is easy to get wrong, leaving you with a boat that is a bit shorter than you thought it might be.

LOCKING THINGS TOGETHER

On a boat with a complicated but light keel assembly, such as a Whitehall, builders will sometimes use a mortise-and-tenon joint to lock the sternpost to the keel. The same boat might be fitted with a hardwood key let into two opposing mortises to strengthen the joint between the sternpost and the deadwood.

Another way to link a sternpost and a keel is with two brass or bronze "butterfly" or dovetail plates let into both sides of the joint so they are flush (i.e., inlayed), and fastened. The plates act as dovetails do in cabinetry, keeping the pieces from pulling away from each other, while sandwiching them and restraining them from moving side-to-side.

ASSEMBLING THE PIECES

Whenever possible, use the lofting board as an assembly jig. (See Figure 9-7.) Cleats nailed down on the perime-

ter of the drawn backbone assembly will help keep everything aligned and will ensure the assembly will fit the setup molds.

DON'T FORGET THE STOPWATERS!

Remember that stopwaters are not just for the stem alone. Any underwater joint that passes through the rabbet needs to have a stopwater in the apex of same.

DRILLING AND BOLTING

After all the keel pieces have been well fitted, the next task is to fasten the entire assembly together. Generally, this is done with carriage bolts, drift pins, or, occasionally, screws. Take the time to lay out the fastenings so they do not conflict with the stopwaters, floor fastenings, centerboard trunk, etc. This is yet another area in which your lofting will serve you well.

It is good practice to set the fastenings so they will be at a slight angle, rather than parallel, to one another. The mating pieces will be prevented from backing off from each other by the offset pins, which will effectually jam the pieces. It is also good practice to stagger the fastenings on each side of the centerline.

Note: For success in drilling, the pieces must be firmly clamped together, and the joints must be dry, with no bedding. Bedding will act like grease, and holding the pieces will be like trying to clamp a squid, as one piece will try to shoot by the next.

Because many keels require extremely long holes for the fastenings, now is as good a time as any to discuss making long bores, a technique that will useful in other areas of construction.

DRILLING LONG BORES BY THE EYEBALL METHOD

Actually it's the "eyeball and homemade aligning jig" method. Just a few quick-and-simple steps will allow you to bore a long hole at virtually any angle, accurately, cheaply, and quickly.

To get the hang of the method, drill a practice hole in heavy stock before going to work on the real thing.

Plan your work

First, lay out the location of the bore on the flat side of the stock, taking care, as above, to avoid stopwaters, bolts, and other impediments to success. Next, square down from the points on both sides where the layout line hits the edge of your stock and mark it. (See Figure 9-8.) Then, mark the bore entrance and exit points on the squared-down lines. With a punch or even a large nail, mark the starting points for the bit.

The theory of drilling from both sides toward the middle

Admittedly, at first blush, drilling in from both sides toward the middle seems to be a rather horrible concept. After all, if you are boring all the way through a massive chunk of wood and you are off the mark by just a little, what's the big deal? True enough. But what if, instead of that monster chunk, you were attempting a long edge bore through narrow stock? That little bit off might just send your drill bit poking out through the side of your work.

The method of boring from both sides to the middle is not a new one. Tunnel engineers have used it for centuries. The theory is predicated on the notion that you will know where you are going when you start; if you do go off course from one side, the deviation will only be by half as much as it would be if you drilled the whole distance. The tools needed to accomplish this feat are few: a couple of sharp bits, a drill capable of low-speed operation, a simple guide clamped to the drawn line and extended out beyond the stock, a sharper'n hell eye, patience, and a little bit of practice.

A bit about bits (and augers)

The type of drilling implement to use is rather a philosophical choice. Generally, practitioners belong to either the twist-bit faith or the barefoot-auger persuasion. Each device has its advantages.

The barefoot auger is the old-time (albeit difficult to find) favorite. It is called barefoot, because it lacks both the lead screw and the cutting spurs of the conventional carpenter's wood bit. It is available with either a straight shank for a conventional drill or with a fluted square end for use with a hand brace. Why no lead screw? The upside of a lead screw is that after it has started, it tends to draw the bit right behind it, wherever it is pointed. The downside is the same, because if the bit goes off course for any reason, it is very difficult, if not impossible, to get it back to running straight again.

Starting a barefoot auger can be tricky—some builders make a shallow "pilot" hole with a gouge—but it is the unit to use for boring straight

9-8: Laying out the starting points for drilling a long hole from both ends.

large-caliber holes. Barefoot augers tend to be quite pricey, however, and the stock sizes are not particularly long. This latter situation can be remedied by cutting the shank and welding an extension rod to it, taking care in truing it up. Occasionally, pre-customized models can be found at flea markets and antique stores at a considerable saving in price.

The ship auger is a close cousin to the barefoot auger, the basic difference being that the ship auger does have a lead screw. It can be handy for general construction work. The lead screw can be used to advantage when you need to follow a pre-existing small-caliber bore. (More on this later.)

By the way, do use caution when boring with large bits mounted in a heavy-duty drill. A "fetched" up bit can send you into an unexpected spin.

The electrician's (a.k.a., bell hanger's) twist bit was originally designed for the electrical trade and is available in lengths of up to 30 inches. This bit is just the ticket for those long, heart-stopping edge bores, such as through the side of the trunk cabin. As it is not as exotic a beast as the barefoot auger, it can be readily found in good-quality hardware stores and at a reasonable price. Again, you can make up your own by welding a piece of rod to a regular-length twist bit, but the time necessary to get it just right makes this a questionable economy.

A note on brad-point wood bits: While these are great for precision jobs, such as doweling furniture, they are less desirable for long-bore situations. Like the standard auger, once a brad-point bit has decided what direction it wants to go, be it right or be it wrong, it stubbornly insists on going that way.

No matter what kind of bit you use, make sure it is sharp. A dull bit can make the job slow, smoky, and sometimes surprising, as an improperly honed cutter can send your bit on an unexpected detour through the side of your work.

What about a drill press?

So you've just bought a new drill press, because the catalog copy suggested it would do everything, including

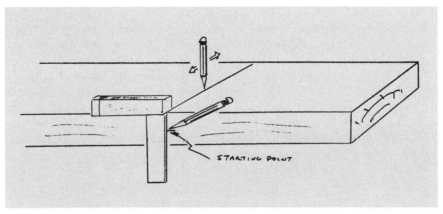

STARTING POINT

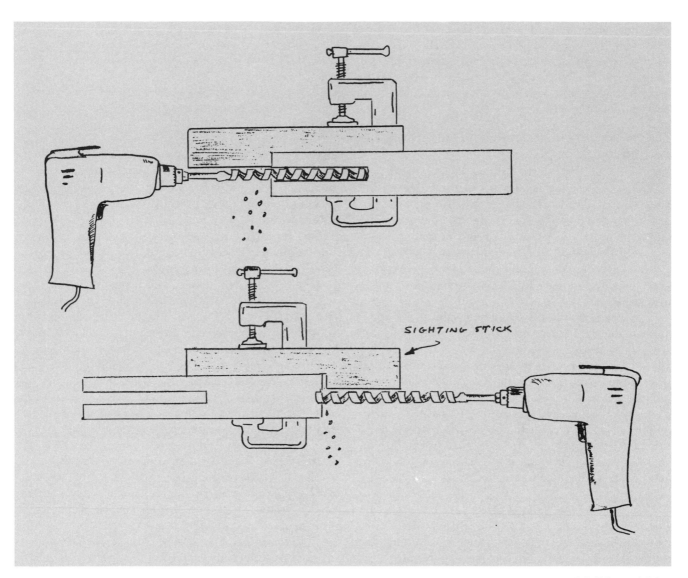

SIGHTING STICK

9-9: Using a sighting
stick as a guide for
drilling a long hole
from both ends.

replace your food processor. Wouldn't that be the tool to use instead of all this "eyeball" mumbo-jumbo?

Well, basically, no. A drill press is great for repetitive tasks, such as cutting bungs, or for anything that you already have, or can easily set up, a jig for. For most long-bore jobs, this is not the case. The majority of long bores tend to be specialty cases—holes drilled at weird angles in large unwieldy chunks of stock. By the time you have invented a jig and have convinced the drill press and stock to come to terms for just one hole, you could have bored a whole batch of holes accurately by eye. Just consider boring by eye a minor triumph of boatbuilder over machine.

Getting started

So, let's take that chunk of wood that we've drawn the lines on, clamp it to a stable surface that allows access to the drill, and clamp the guide to the drawn line. The guide can be as simple or as elaborate as the situation demands. Why not use the sliding rule from a combina-tion square? Let it extend, say, 4 or 5 inches outside the wood to be drilled.

Now it is time to select your weapons. If you were boring for a ¼-inch bolt, for example, a long electrician's or bell hanger's bit would be a good choice, and for propulsion, a good-quality, variable-speed ⅜-inch drill. Select a genuine electric drill—not one of those wimpy, anemic, battery-powered affairs. Take a moment to quickly bore a test hole in a piece of scrap to make sure the selected bit is as advertised—not too large, not too small. Then (although this is optional) replace it with a slightly smaller gauge bit. The logic behind this move is that if the hole you bore with the smaller bit is a wee off where the two holes meet, the error will likely be corrected when the hole is chased by the larger, final-size, bit.

Drilling the hole

Begin by placing the tip of the bit on the marked and punched center point and align the bit shaft by eye with the guide. This is the "eyeball" part of the enterprise and is actually a whole lot easier and more accurate than it sounds. The eye is remarkably good at seeing relationships, misalignments, and such. Just by shifting your angle of observation along the guide, you can check for miscues in the up-and-down and side-to-side dimensions. If you wish, a filler block can be clamped to the guide to reduce the gap between the bit and the guide as an additional visual aid in aiming.

We can now fire up the drill, all the while remembering to proceed with caution (habitual speed demons take note!). After checking the alignment one more time, commence drilling slowly. There is no need to really bear down on the drill, as the bit is sharp—it is, isn't it?—and will be doing most of the work. All you have to do is keep the bit on track.

As you go, pull out the bit often to clean out the accumulated chips, as a plugged-up bit can go off course, and continue to check your alignment with the guide. In no time at all you will arrive at the center (you will know this, because you have either been plumbing the depth with a rod from time to time or had cleverly marked the halfway distance on your bit with a piece of tape before you started). Continue just a little past the center point, remove the bit, and set up to attack the bore from the other side.

The opposite side setup and boring technique are exactly the same. Proceed cautiously as before. There is occasionally a bit of angst as the second bore approaches the center, probably because you still have wavering confidence in the technique. But persevere, and soon the bit will break into the previous bore dead on, or a least very nearly so. (Ah, ye of little faith....)

Blow the sawdust out of the hole and take a peek at your work. If the hole was bored with a slightly undersized bit, you can now chase it with the larger bit, which will clean the bore nicely. Or you can ream it clean with a custom reamer made by flattening the end of a piece of rod the same dimension as your drill bit and tuning the end with a file.

Where's the other hole?!

Oops! Occasionally, when drilling the second (return half) of the bore, you'll find that the breakthrough point seems alarmingly overdue. Not to worry. Just withdraw the bit and do a little investigation.

An overdue breakthrough can only be one of two things: the holes just haven't been drilled deep enough yet, which is good, or the holes are misaligned and will never meet, which is not so good but at least is fixable.

First, take a rod and plumb the depth of the two holes. You can just slide in the rod until it hits bottom and make a mark on it. Check the two distances against the stock you're drilling. If the plumb rod indicates the bores are indeed shallow, you are probably right on the money and drilling just a bit more will do the trick. If, however, the depth gauge suggests that the hole is plenty deep, you will have to run another test.

Insert a couple of extra-long rods of the appropriate caliber into each end of the bore, leaving a length extending out from the hole. Next, remove the guide and reclamp a long straightedge to the drawn reference line (the straightedge should extend out as well). The culprit should be revealed at this point, Dr. Watson, as one of the rods will be askew from the straightedge.

The most practical fix for this unpleasant situation is simply to drive in a glue-anointed dowel and, after the glue has set, rebore the hole. Be sure to cut a groove down the side of the dowel to let the glue at the bottom of the hole escape. This repair does little harm and the extra work it entails does tend to encourage greater attention toward accuracy the next time around.

Now, after a few more practice runs to make sure you have the hang of it, and to prove that the first one wasn't just a fluke, you'll be ready to go.

BACK TO THE KEEL

When all the holes have been drilled, the keel assembly can be taken apart

9-10: Shift your angle of observation slightly from side to side and up and down to "eyeball" the bit shaft true.

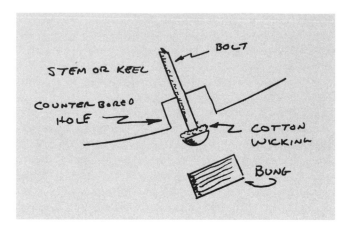

9-11: A properly installed keelbolt involves a counter-bored hole soaked with wood preservative, a few turns of cotton wicking under the head of the bolt, and a bung.

ving them home. (See Figure 9-11.)

After the backbone has been firmly fastened together and faired, give the entire assembly a good coating of red lead, or at least boiled linseed oil or Cuprinol, to keep it from checking.

CUTTING THE KEEL RABBET

In most cases, the technique for cutting the rabbet along the keel is the same as that for the stem. The rabbet, apex, and bearding lines can be lifted from the lofting with tick strips and plotted on the keel at each station. These points can then be connected with a batten and the lines drawn in with pencil. Then, as with the stem, cut spot notches with a chisel and a fid, and then connect the notches. If you are concerned about over-cutting the rabbet, just rough it out on the bench (or floor) and finish it off after the boat has been set up.

one last time, the bedding compound of choice can be spread on the mating surfaces, and the entire unit can be firmly fastened together. It is not a bad idea to dose the holes with preservative before this, however. To discourage leaks many builders will wrap a turn or two of twisted cotton or wicking under the bolt or drift washers before dri-

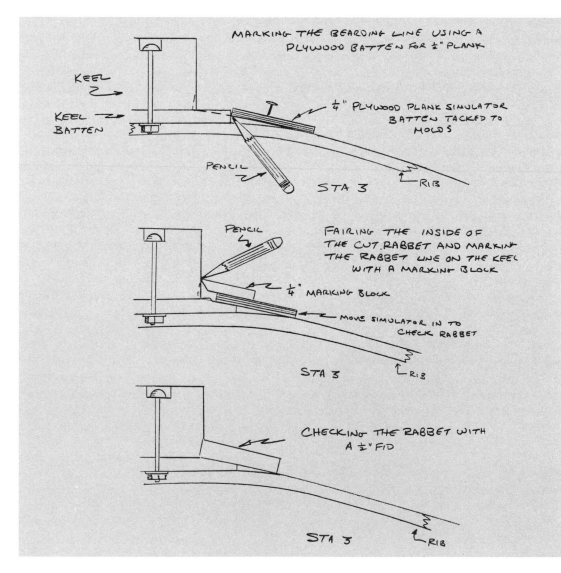

9-12: Using a plywood batten, marking block, and fid as aids in cutting the keel rabbet.

Divining the rabbet

Of course there will always be those cases that defy simple plot-and-cut techniques. The lofting might be a little questionable or murky, the keel assembly might have a keel batten that makes plotting the points difficult, the dimensions of the keel might have changed slightly after it was put together, or perhaps the boat you are building wasn't lofted at all but is being built from patterns, which reveal nothing about the rabbet.

These difficulties call for Plan B—The Empirical Rabbet Divination Technique. This method is easy, and with a minimum of care will ensure an accurate rabbet. It employs a "dummy" garboard plank that not only simulates the curve of the rabbet on the keel but also reveals the angle of the rabbet.

The first task is to set up the backbone assembly with the molds, all faired and ready for planking (see Chapter 11, The Setup), then round up some light plywood to use in making a dummy garboard. The plywood must be stiff enough not to sag between the molds, yet supple enough to make the twist into the stem rabbet. For most small craft ¼-inch luan will do.

Next, cut a strip, say 6 inches wide, from the sheet of plywood. This can be temporarily tacked to the molds and the transom as close to the keel as possible. Eyeball this strip for any sags. The curve should be as smooth as it would be on the finished garboard. Then, using a block of wood or a compass, scribe this "garboard" strip to fit the outer face of the keel. Remove the strip and trim it with a saw to the scribed line. Place it back on the setup with the edge of the strip touching the keel.

Cut another strip and repeat the procedure, fitting the piece to the forward end of the boat. After trimming, tack the forward strip in place and join it to the after strip with a gusset. You will now have a continuous "garboard" strip running from the stem to the transom; it will touch the keel along its length, and the forward end will fit into the stem rabbet (it will make the quick twist to land on the stem).

Again, sight down the length of the strip for fairness.

This is quite important, as the underside of this strip must simulate the underside of the real garboard; any glitches here will come back to haunt you later. On that merry note, let us proceed.

The line along which the underside of the strip contacts the keel is the bearding line, and it can be marked with a pencil. The angle the strip makes with the keel, or the keel batten if one is called for in your construction plan, is the angle at which the back side of the rabbet will be cut. This angle can be picked up at the stations or other predetermined intervals with a bevel gauge, recorded on a bevel board (see Chapter 15, Carvel Planking), and used when cutting the rabbet.

If your keel assembly has a keel batten, the majority of the back side of the rabbet can be planed into the keel batten with a rabbet plane. As you work, the dummy garboard strip can moved in toward the keel and landed on the keel batten to check your progress (and fairness). Use caution to avoid any hollows.

When you have the dummy batten next to the keel, the rabbet line can be marked. This is easily done by making a marking block with a bevel on the end. If the finished garboard is to be ½ inch thick, the marking block should be ¼ inch thick (¼ inch for the dummy strip and ¼ inch for the block adds up to the thickness of the plank). Just ride the block atop the batten as shown in the illustration, and mark the rabbet line in pencil.

The rabbet—the distance from the rabbet line to the apex—can be finished off with a chisel, or if there is a keel batten, it can be planed in with a rabbet plane (with the side of the plane riding on the already planed keel batten). Finally, the entire business can be checked one more time with the dummy batten and then with a ½-inch fid. Look okay? Then proceed with fitting the real garboard (see Chapter 15, Carvel Planking).

☞ A Few Odds and Ends

- A common configuration is the keel built of stock sawn to shape from patterns taken from the lofting. The curve of the top of the keel is the apex of the rabbet. A board keel batten is then bent to the keel with the apex of the rabbet following the joint, producing what amounts to a T-shaped keel. After the keel batten has been tightly fitted to the curve it can be clamped into place and drilled for bolts, so that the assembly is properly indexed. Temporary bolts can be placed, and the rabbet and bearding lines can be marked on the keel face from the lofting. The keel can then be disassembled and the apex depth line can be marked. Then, half

the rabbet can be planed as a bevel into the keelson to the depth of the apex, leaving the bevel a bit full for any possible correction after reassembly. The same can be done to the keel, this time planing from the rabbet to the depth of the apex. The keel can then be put back together, bedded, and bolted. The rabbet is now mostly cut, with only fine tuning necessary later after the molds are set up.

- Occasionally, the saw-cut curve of the after end of a keel deadwood will have a wider, saw-cut "hogging piece" fit to it (which acts like the keel batten to offer greater support to the planks). Fitting these two curves can be a real bear, involving plenty of planing, spoke-shaving, and unwelcome "shrinking" of stock. One easy way to get a perfect fit is to roughly trace out the dead-wood and the hogging pieces on their respective stock. Lay one piece over the top of the other, aligning them plumb, along their shared joint. Temporarily fasten one to another. Then, after checking that the top piece is fully supported, cut the curved joint with the bandsaw. (Be sure to first make a test run with your bandsaw to see if it is up to doing this.) You will now have a joint between the hogging piece and the deadwood that will fit perfectly. You can then align your patterns with the newly cut joint and retrace the deadwood and the hog onto their pieces of stock. All that remains is to cut the pieces to shape, and plane square and smooth.

- Long, narrow, stringbean keels found on pulling boats like the Whitehall can at times be problematic. The difficulty here is that they are floppy and difficult to keep straight. The builder must take extra precautions in blocking and bracing these noodle-like units at the setup stage to avoid bowing or hogging. Check the setup by eye and with a straightedge. Also, use care when installing the garboards, as the keel is a mighty attractive place to hang a clamp when you are trying to pull the garboard into place. Instead of the garboard moving to the keel, the keel is liable to move to the garboard!

- Many very light keels, for a good part of their length, will only have a bevel planed into them that acts as a rabbet. This means that they have only a rabbet line and an apex, with no extra backing such as that afforded by a full rabbet. Although this type of arrangement can be strong enough after the planking is on and the floors are in, it does demand the highest quality fits in the keel-to-plank seam. Many, if not most plans for boats of this kind are drawn to the inside of plank—to the apex line. Quite often, the offsets will give you a constant bevel that runs the entire length of the keel stick; i.e., a constant distance out for the apex, a constant height above base for the rabbet. This arrangement makes putting the bevel on the keel a breeze. It also makes getting a tight seam on the garboard much more difficult. The problem is that the garboard doesn't maintain a constant angle relative to the keel. The constant keel bevel requires a quirky reverse bevel on the garboard plank, which is difficult enough to fit in the first place. The quickest fix to this state of affairs is to redraw the plank's entry to the keel on the body plan—retaining the rabbet line but keeping the plank entrance to the keel square. This will cause the apex to move, in or out as the case may be, and will allow you to put the changing bevel on the keel.

- Sprung plank keels (the Catspaw is an example of this)

will often have the width at each station noted as either half-breadths in the table of offsets or directly stated on the construction plan. The keel's shape can be easily laid out by establishing a centerline on the keel stock, plotting the station points, squaring them out, and recording the offsets on the station lines. A thin batten can be sprung through the points and the line marked. That should be the correct keel shape as long as the correct station spacing has been used. But here's the rub: The keel is bent into an arc over the molds. If the builder uses the given station spacing (which is given in a straight line) to lay out and cut the keel, the keel will be too short when bent to shape.

What to do? If you have lofted the boat, simply tack a light batten to the curve of the keel as drawn. Mark the station intersections on the batten. Then release the batten and place it atop the centerline drawn on the keel stock. The station locations will now be "expanded" to the right spacing. When the keel is cut, it will now be the right length. No lofting? Springing a batten over the top of the molds on the setup jig will pretty much accomplish the same thing. Mark the station lines on the batten, release and mark the keel stock.

Also, to save time and labor, rabbeted plank keels of this type can have their rabbets rough cut on either the table saw or with a router. The rabbet can then be tuned up after the keel has been bent into place.

- Scarfing is a useful technique to use when it is difficult or impossible to get stock long enough for your keel. A scarf is a joint made by cutting or notching the ends of two pieces of wood correspondingly at an angle and bolting or gluing them together. Most keel scarfs are mechanical; i.e., fastened together with bolts. Rather than having the angled pieces run out to featheredges, the ends are nibbed or cut off square and the corresponding pieces are cut to accept the nibs. The generally accepted length from nib-to-nib of the angled cut of the scarf should be six times the depth of the timber (although Chapelle notes five to eight times the depth), and the depth of the nib should be about 25 percent of the depth of the timber.

A plain scarf is but two corresponding angled joints bolted together. For added security against slippage, this scarf can be turned into a keyed scarf by mortising matching notches across the face of the scarf and tightly fitting a rectangular key. If possible, the bolts should be staggered and laid out so as to not interfere with any other structures.

If, as an alternative, you go with a glued featheredge scarf joint, it should be cut to a minimum ratio of 12:1. If the keel is of oak, resorcinol glue would be a good choice of adhesive for this job, as most epoxies do not work well with oak.

☞ Boring the Shaft Log

The hole in the shaft log—that most challenging feat of accuracy—the mother of all bores. How on earth do they do it? Laser-guided teredos?

Indeed, drilling a long one-piece shaft log can be a sporty affair. Howard Chapelle's book *Boatbuilding* gives a good blow-by-blow account of the operation that just might engender in the builder a whole new appreciation of the outboard motor.

But perhaps the log does not have to be bored in one piece. Many times the shaft log can be laid out on the loft floor as two halves—one above and one below the centerline of the shaft. Sort of a square-sectioned wooden tube that could be sandwiched into the rest of the keel assembly. The long-distance bore can be roughed out as troughs cut into both halves of the tube. The halves can then be bolted together, and the passage chased out by running a long bit through the assembly. The accompanying hole in the sternpost would still need to be bored in the conventional manner.

How to rough out the "troughs"? There are a number of methods used to accomplish this task. Some builders favor the multi-saw-kerf technique. First mark the radius of the hole on the ends of the upper and lower sides of the log. Then set the table saw fence to start cutting near the inner edge of the marked radius. Run the halves over the table saw, with the blade extended just enough to come inside the marked half circle. Then set the fence over to cut nearer the center, and again raise the blade just enough to be inside the circle. And so on, until you have a series of furrows that run the length and depth of the trough on each side of the log. The furrows then can be cleaned out with a gouge or narrow hollowing plane.

Another method is the "follow the groove" approach. The theory behind this one is that if you have a pilot hole for the lead screw of a "ship" auger to follow, the screw will keep the auger on track. So how do you get the pilot hole? Pretty much in the same fashion as mentioned previously, only this time just score the upper and lower sides of the log dead on the centerline of the bore. Clamp the two sides tightly together and the two grooves produce the pilot hole. Make sure the auger is plenty sharp for this operation. It wouldn't hurt to practice this technique on some scrap stock just to get the hang of it.

Yet another tack sometimes seen is the square shaft hole. To do this, simply use your dado cutters on the table saw to cut half the channel out of each half log. The square trough can then be roughly half rounded with hand tools. After the two halves have been soundly bolted together, the hole can easily be trued up with the right-size bit.

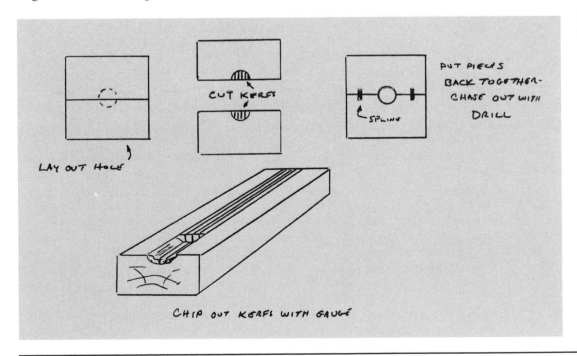

One method for boring a shaft log.

10 • THE MOLDS AND THE TRANSOM

Before starting to build the molds, a decision must first be made: Is this boat going to be built right-side up or, contrarily, upside down? At first, the answer seems a simple one—right-side up. After all, that's the way the boat is going to float, isn't it? Well, we hope so, yes, but there is more to the decision than that. There are pros and cons to either approach. Some of the considerations are plain old nuts-and-bolts issues, the others are matters of personal preference. Which option is best? Let's take a look at some of the arguments.

BUT FIRST, SOME TERMINOLOGY

The mold is the three-dimensional manifestation of the two-dimensional station curves drawn on your lofting. When set up on their respective station lines, a series of temporary molds will determine the shape of the hull for the boatbuilder in much the same way a dressmaker's dummy does for the tailor. The terms station and mold are not interchangeable. Only one side of the mold corresponds to the station. Remember, the station is only a paper-thin entity. The mold's job is to give strength and body to the station. Generally speaking, molds are made

to the inside of plank (dummies are made to the inside of dress). Occasionally molds are built to the inside of frame if the frames are to be bent directly over them. On some boats, sawed permanent frames take the place of the molds.

Ribbands are temporary batten-like wooden straps bent around the molds to which the steamed frames are bent. The ribbands not only dictate the shape of the frame but also give the setup of the hull strength and resistance to wracking.

The strongback is a sturdy foundation that supports the construction of the boat. It can be as simple as a series of posts under a keel, an I-beam, or even a ladder frame.

A cross spall is a straight piece of wood that reinforces the upper "U" shape of the mold. It is generally installed at a common waterline on all molds.

The construction baseline is an artificial line drawn parallel to the baseline on the lofting. It is most often drawn above the highest point on the sheer. It is most commonly employed on molds used in upside-down construction. Molds will all be made with their cross spalls fixed parallel to the construction base. When the molds are installed upside down on a straight, true, and level

COMMON WATERLINE

CROSS SPALL

SHEER

SHEER

GUSSETS

BASE

strongback, the cross spalls will self-level all the molds at their correct height relative to one another.

Now, on to the debate.

The considerations

Adherents to the right-side-up school of boatbuilding claim that for one-off (single boat) construction, this method is the only way to go. It is, in some ways, a simpler way of setting up to build the boat. The molds are simply erected on top of the backbone assembly. The ribbands are fastened to the outside of the molds and the transom, and into the rabbet. The frames are bent to the inside face of the ribbands (which correspond to the inside of plank). When planking the boat, the builder need only remove a ribband and replace it with the plank. After the last plank is on, pull out the molds, caulk the hull, paint it, and push it into the water. No problem!

"Not so fast!" cry our upside-down partisans.

"An oversimplification of the facts," grumble the disciples of the 180-degree faith.

True, at first blush, the Uprightistas do seem to have the easier approach. The upside-down technique requires more time in constructing a level strongback. The builder must expend a bit more effort to build all molds with an accurate cross spall located at the construction baseline. Then, because the upside-down method requires that the frames be bent over the ribbands, the molds must be modified to accommodate the ribbands. The most common method is to cut notches into the molds to let the ribbands in, so the outside face of the ribband corresponds to the inside face of the frame. And, of course, there is the business of lifting the boat off the jig and having to turn it over. Why bother?

The level strongback used in upside-down construc-

tion gives the builder a firm foundation to begin work. It also provides a surface on which to mark a strong centerline and perpendicular station lines. The molds, each built to the common construction base, will self-level when placed on the strongback. It is an easy task to slide the molds up the established station lines, match up the centerline, plumb, brace, and fasten. The marked strongback continues to assist you, as you can accurately bring the location of the stem over from the lofting board (you can even make a bracket for the stemhead to fit into). In addition, the location and angle of the transom can be picked up off the lofting, and a holding jig made to support the transom in just the correct position. The backbone assembly can then be set on top, and after aligning with the station and centerline, it can be set in place.

At this point, the right-side-up method's time advantage over its rival begins to dwindle. To build upright, the backbone first must be installed on a strongback or stocks, then plumbed and thoroughly braced in preparation for the installation of the molds. Setting each mold is a balancing act. The builder must align the centerline of the mold to that of the keel, while attempting to plumb the mold in two axes, ensure that it is perpendicular to the centerline in a third, and then brace it to something—the ceiling, the floor, or whatever is available. While, as each additional mold is added, the process gets a bit easier (as there is more to brace to), it still can't compare to the simplicity of the upside-down method.

Next, the matter of the ribbands: When building upside down, the ribbands do need to be set into the molds and care must be taken to make and install offset shims at the ends to ensure that the ribbands have the correct curve fore and aft. But this is no big deal; it takes only a few minutes. The dividend for this extra work

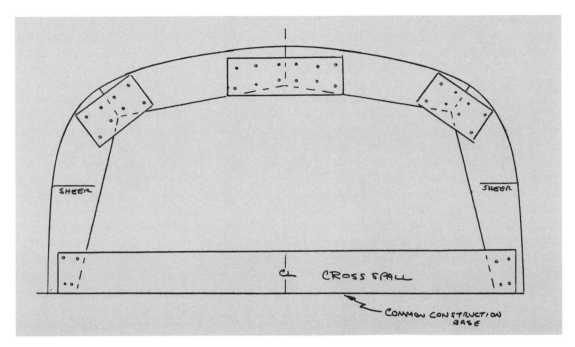

10-2: Mold for upside-down construction.

comes when you bend the frames.

As a rule, wood bends more easily around a form than when it is drawn into one. Frames in a boat have compound bends. Not only does the frame have to conform to the shape of the hull as drawn on the body plan, but also it must be twisted to fit the planks as they sweep up toward the ends. To add interest, if the frames are to be placed perpendicular to one another (as shown on many construction plans), a frame, as it is installed, will also have to be pulled back at the same time as the rest of the twisting in the other two dimensions is going on. What this means is that if you are building upright, you will be quite active. You will be doing plenty of twisting, clamping, and pounding with mallets on the frame heads as those hot, steaming frames are forced into place. Bending over an upside-down frame, although still an exercise in organized chaos, is much easier. You have the advantage of greater leverage, gravity is working in your favor, and clamping can be carried out in a more leisurely fashion.

Then, there is the matter of planking. Although, whether it is better to plank upside down or right-side up is mostly one of those points of personal preference, there are a few practical considerations. The garboard is generally accepted to be one of the more challenging planks to fit, as that long keel rabbet must be accommodated, and the hood end of the plank often must be steamed or boiled to allow the plank to roll into the stem. Fitting the garboard is a provocative task at best, but when the effect of gravity is added to the calculus, the effort can become downright exciting. The rest of the bottom planks, while not quite as persnickety as the garboard plank, are still more pleasant to fit when you are safely above them pushing down, rather than jacking

them up into place while lying under a gaggle of precariously affixed clamps. But again, this is only a personal preference.

A few final thoughts

Are you considering building more than one boat? If you are, the "permanent" upside-down jig might be the method for you, for as soon as you remove the first boat from the setup, the jig is ready for the next. If on the other hand, you intend to build only one or you simply don't have the storage space for a jig the size of a Volkswagen, perhaps right-side up is the way to go.

Finally, there is this practical question: If the boat is built upside down, do you have a way to turn it over? This may be a small matter if your pride and joy is a dinghy, yet another if it's a Friendship sloop. How many strong pals do you have who like boats? Do you really want to be a patron of Friendly Fred's Rent-a-Crane, and how much will the device cost?

After selecting your method, it's time to build those molds.

THE MOLDS

The shape of the molds will dictate the final form of the hull. A little extra time taken now to build them accurately will mean a lot less work and aggravation when setting up the construction jig. So use as much care in building the molds as you did when lofting them.

Construction specs

Your molds should be built of heavy enough material to contain the stresses of the ribbands and the planking to be wrapped around them. This can be upwards of hundreds

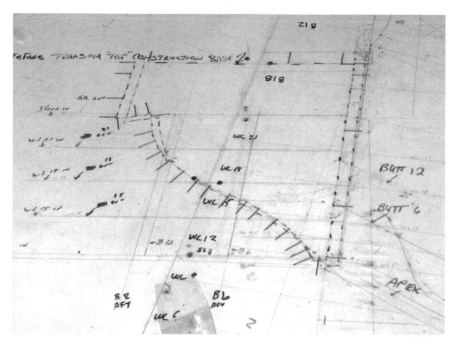

of pounds of pressure. Wimpy molds are no bargain, as they will require a lot of after-market reinforcement.

Use stock that is as wide as possible, since the molds, by nature, have a lot of shape cut into them. Also, if you are building upside down, there will be lots of notches cut into the molds after setup that could weaken the structure. Excessive parsimony when purchasing lumber can lead to a lot of expensive headaches later on.

White pine is a good choice for the molds, as it is easily worked, is soft and therefore less likely to dent the planks wrapped around it, and is relatively strong.

Although it's possible that a few molds (probably up forward) will be able to be constructed with a single wide board, the shape of most molds will demand that they be built up of two, or occasionally more, boards joined by rugged gussets. (Half-inch plywood makes a good gusset.)

The cross spalls need not be made of heavy stock, but they should be straight. In many cases, the spall acts as a base or reference line for the mold. Bows, swoops, and bends in this piece will make the job more interesting but hardly more efficient.

A matter of symmetry

Although occasionally the full station is shown on the body plan, the more common practice is to portray only half. Part of the reason for doing this is obvious—it saves space and cuts down on visual clutter. The other reason is symmetry and speed of production. Remember that Valentine's Day heart you made in grade school? You folded the paper in two, then cut out half of the shape. The paper was then unfolded and, there you were, perfect symmetry. It is thus with making the molds. When the molds are made in halves, you have a near guarantee that one side will be the same as the other. And because

10-3: To transfer the shape of a mold from the lofting to the mold stock, place nails on the lofting, their heads aligned with the curve of the station.

two pieces can be cut out for every one that is marked, working in halves saves time in assembly.

Placement of cross spalls

When building upside down, the cross spalls are usually placed at a common construction baseline. Some builders prefer using the sheerline or some other waterline height, but for all-around convenience in setting up, it's difficult to beat the baseline location. When building right-side up, select a common waterline near the sheer.

Inside or outside

Remember that the molds are built to the inside of the plank. If the designer drew the lines of the boat to the outside of the plank, the stations on the body plan will have to be reduced by the thickness of the plank. (See Chapter 7, Lofting Demystified.) Also, usually it will be necessary to notch out the molds to fit the keel and stem assemblies.

ONE TECHNIQUE FOR BUILDING THE MOLDS

Begin by roughly determining the size of the pieces that you will be using for the molds. Once again, the information on the lofting floor tells the tale.

First, cut a piece of 1- by 2-inch stock longer than your widest mold. Then tack it down to the body plan, parallel to the waterlines, at the topmost point of your right-side-up mold or the construction base of your upside-down mold. This is your construction stop, which, like the ledge on a drafting table, will aid in keeping everything square, aligned, and generally right where it ought to be.

Begin the job by roughly determining the size of the pieces that you will be using for the molds. Once again, the information on the lofting board tells the tale. Using two tapes, hold the end of one tape at the top (construction base) location and the end of the other tape at the centerline of the mold. Stretch the tapes out toward each other until they cross. Then, pivoting off the ends, swing the tapes in or out, until they just touch the station shape at one point. The point at which the two tapes overlap will give you the rough length of your stock. Cut two of each.

Next, roughly lay out your pieces on top of the drawn station line. The far ends of the stock will run out over the construction line on one end and the centerline on the other. The other ends of the stock will overlap each other, about halfway around the mold. Transfer the construction line and centerline onto the pieces. Roughly bisect the angle formed by the overlapped pieces and draw that line onto the top piece.

Okay? Then off to the bandsaw and cut each piece on the drawn line. Bring the pieces back to the body plan, aligning the cut ends with the centerline and construction line and the cut angled piece on top of the uncut piece. Trace that angle onto the uncut piece. Take the uncut piece to the saw, cut on the drawn line, then bring it back to the body plan. The two pieces should come together with a tight butt joint in the middle and meet the centerline and construction line at the ends. Temporarily, tack one piece in place with a couple of nails.

Getting the shape

The next job is to transfer the information from your body plan exactly onto the mold stock. The easiest way to do this is to lift up the other, unfastened piece and, using the tried and true "bed o' nails" technique, lay down a series of small nails with their heads following along the curve of the station. (See Figure 10-3.) Gently place the piece back on top of the station. Then squash the piece into the nail heads. Cautiously stepping on it with your logging boots is a good method (see Figure 10-4), as is kneeling on it in your knee pads. Avoid pounding on it with a hammer, as the vibration can cause the nails to scatter and provide false readings.

Lift the piece, knock off any embedded nails, and you will see that you have a series of dents in the wood. Use a batten to connect these dents or points into a fair curve. Lay this piece on the second one you cut for the same mold and tack the two together. Take the pair to the bandsaw, and cut the curve for both; also, cut the ends off the bottom pieces.

Return the pieces to the body plan and see how close the cut curve fits the drawn one. Touch them up with a plane and anchor them to the body plan with nails to keep them from shifting.

Repeat the exercise for the second pair of mold half pieces. After fitting, anchor them in place on the body plan as well.

Next, using your combination square, mark the waterlines and sheerline onto the edges of your mold halves. These marks will come in handy in the alignment process.

10-4: Lay mold stock over the nails on the lofting and carefully step on the stock. The heads of the nails will make their marks on the mold stock, thus transferring the shape of the station.

Assembly

You can now install plywood gussets that will join the two pieces of each mold half. First attach a gusset to the top side of the pieces while they are still tacked to the body plan. Drywall screws work well for this job. (Many builders like to add a dollop of carpenter's glue under the gusset as well.) After the pieces on one side of the mold have been joined, then another gusset can be fastened to the pieces on the other side of the mold.

After installing the gussets on the mold halves, you are almost ready to put them together to make the whole mold. But first, using a tick strip, pick up the half-breadth distances, measured out from the centerline, of each waterline and sheer. Transfer these to the other side of the body plan. Label each tick mark with the station number (later, you'll be glad you did). These marks will ensure that the both halves are equidistant from the centerline.

Separate the two mold halves. Then line up one of the half-molds with the drawn station and temporarily anchor it in place with nails. The other mirror-image side is mated up to it, butted on the centerline and against the construction line batten. The waterlines on the half mold should match the waterline tick marks on the body plan.

Give the whole business one more check for accuracy. Good? Then, join the two mold halves with a gusset fastened with screws and a shot of carpenter's glue. In the same manner, affix the cross spall at its appropriate location. (See Figures 10-5 and 10-6.) Don't forget to mark the centerline on the cross spall. Lift the mold off the lofting and repeat the process for the rest of the molds.

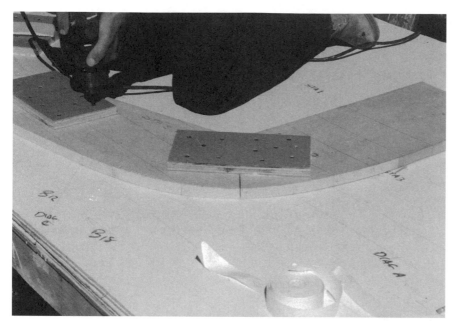

NOTES ON PLYWOOD MOLDS

Plywood can be used to build satisfactory molds, providing a few considerations are taken into account. To wit:

If El Cheapo 3-ply CDX softwood plywood is used, the chances are better than average that it will warp, becoming concave or convex (depending on your point of view). Braces screwed on edge to one side of the mold can help control this phenomenon.

Plywood, being a smooth, solid sheet, allows no bearing point to clamp your planks to. A series of holes (big enough to stick a clamp into) drilled a few inches in from the edge, or cleats screwed and glued to the side of the mold, will usually fix the problem.

The edges of plywood, especially the inexpensive stuff, do not hold nails well. This is an important consideration when fastening ribbands. The problem can be alleviated by adding softwood cleats to the edges of the plywood mold.

Plywood is hard, and the sharp edge of a mold can dent soft planking. This can be lessened by beveling the molds, but the cost in time is high.

WHAT ABOUT SAWN FRAMES?

The technique for building sawn frames is nearly identical to that used in building molds. Generally, the plans will give you the size of the stock (how thick and wide) to be used. Remember, that sawn frames must be beveled so the planking can lie against them. This means that sawn frames must be set up on the opposite side of the station from the molds, which will only touch the planking on one edge.

Also to keep in mind is that, if the sawn-frame boat you are building has built-in longitudinal pieces—chines, for example, or battens for batten-seam construction—these pieces will be let into the frames. Be sure your frame stock has enough "meat" to stand notching without weakening the frames.

THE TRANSOM

Back in the lofting department, we expanded the transom for the Catspaw Dinghy. This is the most common type of a transom for a small boat—flat, raked, with the planks running by and fastened to framing at the edge. The lines were drawn to the inside of plank, so we did not have to reduce the breadth of the transom by the thickness of the planking. We ended up with two half patterns—one for the outside or small face of the transom, another for the inside or larger face. (See Figure 10-7.)

In use, the two patterns are traced onto the panel made up for the transom—the smaller outer on one side, the larger inner on the other. The transom is then cut out to the larger side and spokeshaved to the smaller, which allows the compound bevel of the transom to develop automatically. The bevel should be quite accurate, too, as long as (1) the transom panel you used is the same thickness as that drawn on the lofting board, and (2) you take into account that the waterlines cross the transom at an angle and that the waterlines on your patterns must be offset from one another by that much as well. Also (as foolish as this may sound) you must be sure when you take that marked panel to the bandsaw that you are cutting out to the larger side.

But you say you prefer not to expand the inside face of the transom, and, anyway you are going to pick the bevels off the lofting, or that the patterns that came with the plans have the bevels included. Fair enough, but proceed with caution. Remember that you will be working to the small face of the transom, so leave yourself plenty of extra stock. The bevels picked up or given on the pattern may be accurate, but it only takes holding the bevel gauge at a slightly different angle on the stock from how the angle was picked up to change the bevel dramatically. It's therefore best to err on the side of caution, and, when shaving in the bevel, leave the transom a little full. The bevel can be fine tuned down to the lofted outside face line with battens and a spokeshave after the boat has been set up.

Don't forget to pick up the bevel at the very bottom of the transom where it meets the backbone. This can be captured from the lofting board. Depending on the rake of the transom, the bevel can add considerably to the vertical length of the inside face.

By the way, after the transom has been made, do not be in a hurry to sand off the centerline and those waterlines that are drawn on the faces. They can be invaluable

10-7: Patterns for the inner and outer faces of the transom of a skiff. Because the transom is further forward in the boat, the inner face of the transom is larger than the outer face.

later during the setup for checking the alignment and positioning of the transom.

Plywood transoms

Traditionally, transoms for plank-on-frame small craft are made from solid stock (see sidebar, Building Panels), but they can also be made from marine plywood. A plywood transom must be backed up with substantial frame and cheekpieces along the edges to provide something to drive fastenings into. Cheekpieces and reinforcing framing can also be used to advantage in larger transom construction, affording extra strength and fastening area, especially for boats propelled with outboard motors. If you use plywood, be sure to seal the edges well.

BUILDER, STAY THAT SAW

There is something about the construction of a transom that makes some builders want to trim off the top prematurely. They just can't help themselves. Maybe it's the understated elegance of the curve that mysteriously draws the saw, spokeshave, and plane to it. Perhaps the builder feels that if only the excess wood were removed, the boat would really start to take shape (even if the molds are barely up). Whatever the cause, you see the top of transoms finished before their time all over the place—occasionally with varnish added. Yet there are plenty of reasons to leave that transom top long for later barbering. For example:

• The chances are good that when the transom panel was built, the top edge of the panel was square to the centerline of the transom. When that transom is set up, the centerline will be plumb and the top will be level. It is an easy matter just to put a level across the top of the untrimmed transom to true it up. Not so easy if you have chopped off the top.

- Transoms can be tricky to hold in place, as they tend to be raked and are hanging out by themselves. When you have extra stock, you can screw or bolt directly to the transom, ensuring that the blasted thing isn't going to wander. When trimmed off, you are stuck with some sort of Rube Goldberg affair of clamps and pads to stabilize the unit—hoping all the time that it doesn't loosen up during construction.

- Garboard and broad strakes can prove tricky to fit to the transom, as there is little place to clamp. But that nice square transom top gives you a great place to hook a bar clamp and help pull that plank in. And as the top of the transom is actually waste, there is no need to worry about using clamp pads (which would likely slip anyway).

- After the boat has been planked and pulled off the mold, there is still lots of work to do. The sheer must be trimmed, floors fit, risers and thwarts installed, and so on. You'll be wanting to set the hull up plumb and square both fore and aft (to avoid building in twist). Up forward you can use a plumb bob. Back aft, there's that top of the transom to put the level on again! Plus there's all that extra stock to which you can safely attach brace "legs" without worry about injuring the transom.

- Then you'll be needing to turn the boat over to fair the hull, caulk the seams, and so on. You could build some padded sawhorses to place along the sheer to keep the boat from rocking and rolling, or you could rest the boat on the top of that untrimmed transom and the stemhead (which, of course, you wisely left long as well). What do you have? An automatic tripod.

- When the boat is nearly done, the transom can then be trimmed off, as neat as can be, with no worry about filling dings from slipped clamps or dropped tools.

Actually, there's quite a bit to be said for leaving the transom top long for a while. But don't let me influence you.

☞ Gluing a Panel

Gluing is a good option for a small-boat transom or the sides of a centerboard trunk. Keep in mind, however, that bolts and drift pins are a better choice for a panel that is repeatedly submerged, such as a centerboard.

As with most gluing projects, success lies in preparation. Begin by setting up your gluing table with a proper protective surface, such as polyethylene sheeting. Then assemble the necessary tools. Round up bar or pipe clamps, as well as several stout wooden cleats long enough to stretch across the face of the panel. While you're at it, break out about four C-clamps for holding the cleats in place. Add another piece of polyethylene the size of the panel, and you're in business.

To spline or not to spline

The jury is still out as to whether the use of a spline set into grooves strengthens or weakens a butt joint (as in a panel). The spline does, however, help to align the pieces when gluing, and that is a plus. If you choose the spline option, the groove can be quickly cut on a table saw. It generally is easier to cut the groove first and then make the spline fit to it than the other way around. Be sure the spline is not so wide as to keep the two sides of the joint from closing.

Gluing up

Prior to final assembly, take the time to familiarize yourself with the qualities of the adhesive you are using. For example, how much working time do you have? What is the required clamping pressure? Will the glue work on the wood species that you are using? Is the glue truly waterproof? And so on.

Then, put your gluing procedures through a dry run. One better method of clamping is to use the bar or pipe clamps in opposition—that is, on either side of the panel from one another. This can prevent building an unintentional bow into the panel. Some builders prefer the added security of wooden cleats clamped across the face of the panel to further prevent bowing. If you use the latter technique, don't forget to lay a plastic sheet between the panel and the cleats.

Tighten the clamps and check the dry assembly for bow and for tightness on both sides of the panel. If the setup looks good, then mix up the glue and get on with it.

☞ Building Panels—For Transoms, Centerboard Trunks, and Centerboards

Of the many standing power tools available to make your life easier and more productive, the jointer is perhaps the one that will see the least service. The reason is simply that, other than cross planking for a flat bottom, there are relatively few straight and square fits to be made on a small boat. For most situations, the builder can get by with good, clean cuts on a table saw and finish up with either a fore or jointer plane. This approach works well for a number of situations, including the building of the blanks or panels for transoms, centerboard trunk sides, and built-up centerboards.

There are good reasons for building panels from several pieces of narrower stock rather than a few really wide boards. Cost and availability lead the list. Wide boards generally cost more, are prone to more defects, and are more difficult to find these days. Another reason is the matter of stability. A wide board will have a greater shrink-and-swell cycle across its face and is more prone to warping, especially if plain-sawn wood is used—which is generally the case. A panel made up of narrow stock can reduce these shortcomings.

Select the stock

Obtain wood that is as clear as possible. Make sure that you allow yourself enough wood to build a panel large enough to accept your patterns with room to spare, and also to compensate for any miscues or sliding joints during assembly. (A lot of beautiful, but undersized panels have been assembled by overly thrifty builders.) Mill your stock to thickness with a planer, then cut it to width on your table saw, having first double checked that the blade is dead square to the table. Then saw the newly cut pieces to length.

Layout

Next, lay out your boards on the table next to one another in a rough approximation of the panel-to-be. This is the jigsaw-puzzle part. We have two concerns here:

The first is to compensate for the natural tendency of the wood to warp. The boards must be so arranged that the "heart of the tree" sides (determined by the curve of the growth rings on the end grain) alternate, which will help balance out any warp. So, when the boards are laid out flat, if the "heart" side of the first board is up, that of the next should be down, the third up, and so on.

The second concern is the alignment of the grain. The trick to making a great joint is to clamp two adjoining pieces together in a vise and plane them dead level and square as a pair. This technique is made a lot easier if the grain on the edges of those two pieces is aimed in the same direction.

Once you have your boards milled and layed out properly, place your pattern on top of the assembly and check that you still have enough stock. Then label the two sides of each joint facing you. The first might be A-A, the next B-B, and so forth. This will help you identify what should be next to where when it's time to glue or fasten.

Jointing

Now you must joint the edges. "Fold" the first two boards together, as if they were on hinges, and clamp them in a vise. Set them so that they are as square and level to one another as possible. Chances are good that you will need to add C-clamps at both ends of the boards to close them up tightly.

Your weapon of choice is either the fore plane or its longer cousin, the jointer. With the cutter set fine, the long bed will bridge the hollows and take off the high spots. (Save that sporty low-angle block plane or ubiquitous jack for your planking, with its rapidly changing curves and angles.)

Before starting to plane, check your tool one more time to see that the cutting iron is set so that it cuts square. Plane edge A-A with long continuous strokes, checking it often with a combination square. Also check that you are not planing in a hollow or a crown. Do this by placing a 4-inch aluminum level on the edge and sighting for light leaking under. Only a few passes with the long plane will be necessary, as the table saw cut should have done most of the job already. Not to worry, however, if after all precautions, you find the edge slightly (but uniformly) off from square, as when both boards are flipped and put together, the angles on the two pieces will be complementary and will still give you a straight panel.

After jointing A-A, proceed to B-B, and the rest. When all the edges are jointed, lay the boards down on a flat surface and lightly clamp with bar clamps to check the fits. When all is as tight as a drum, fasten all the pieces together.

11 • THE SETUP

After the molds have been completed, they are ready to set up. Whether you are building right-side up or upside down, the theory is the same: the molds must line up on the station lines drawn on the floor or the strong-back. But, which side of the station line—the forward side or the after side? Does it make a difference?

Common sense might lead the builder to install the molds in the same fashion as setting up studs when framing a wall in a house—all on the same side of each station, marching stem to stern, with a constant distance between each unit. Unfortunately, if that technique were used, one end of the boat will end up being too full.

MOLD SETUP RULE

Just as the battens did in lofting, the planks will be wrapping around those two-dimensional, paper-thin entities called stations. The station itself is only on one face of the built-up mold. The rest of the body of the mold is there only to support the station. What this means is that the plank will only be contacting one edge of the mold. So, here is a general rule:

Up forward, from the stem to the widest part of the boat, set up the molds on the after side of the station line; from the widest part of the boat to the transom, set the molds on the forward side of the station line. (See Figure 11-1.)

And here is an exception (which can be expected with every general rule):

When the mold is beveled to match the hull, and the station side of the mold is the widest, the setup rule is reversed. In this case, up forward, the molds will be set on the forward side of the line. Back aft, the mold will be set aft of the station line.

One example of the above is when building a sawn-frame boat, such as a dory. The frames are, in effect, also the molds, beveled to directly match the planking. Another example is when the molds are beveled to allow the frames to be bent directly over them rather than over ribbands. Many of the boats from the Herreshoff Manufacturing Company were built in this manner.

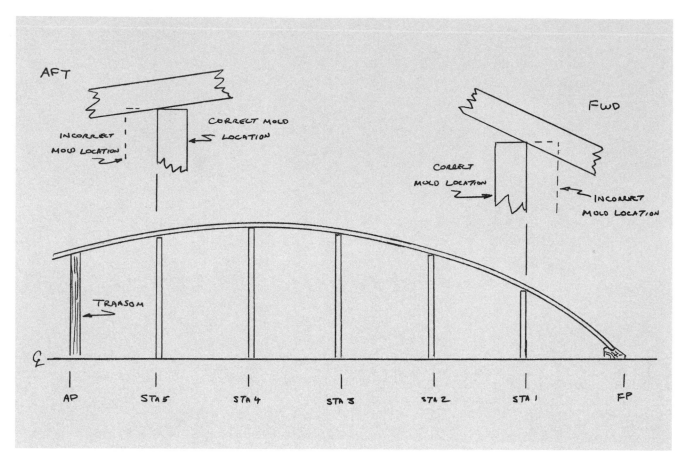

AFT

INCORRECT MOLD LOCATION

CORRECT MOLD LOCATION

FWD

CORRECT MOLD LOCATION

INCORRECT MOLD LOCATION

TRANSOM

CL

| AP | STA 5 | STA 4 | STA 3 | STA 2 | STA 1 | FP |

SETTING UP—BUILDING UPSIDE DOWN

On the floor

One method is simply to set up the construction jig on the floor of the shop. (The floor corresponds to the construction baseline drawn on the lofting and the bottom of the cross spall on the mold.) If you have access to a truly straight and level wooden floor that can be tied up for awhile, this can be the easiest way to go. The centerline and perpendicular station lines can be established directly on the floor or on wooden cross timbers. Cleats or brackets can then be screwed down to anchor the molds.

The molds are brought in and set up, aligned to the centerline, fixed to the cleats, plumbed, and braced. If the floor is concrete, an alternative method is to lay parallel wooden sleepers (4 by 6s, 4 by 8s) on the flat and fasten them to the concrete with anchor bolts. The sleepers can then be marked with the station lines and the molds erected on top of them.

The fly-in-the-ointment is that dead-level shop, barn, or garage floors that are available for long-term occupancy are in short supply. Add to this the fact that setting up on the floor locks you into whatever height the molds were built to, which may lead to no end of crawling, kneeling, and groveling to build the boat. Nonetheless, the simplicity of this method makes it very attractive for one-off sawn-frame construction.

On a strongback

Many builders opt to set up the molds on a ladder-frame strongback. The frame is a rectangular boxlike structure; 2 by 6s and 2 by 8s usually will suffice for a small boat. With two long outside rails and several cross pieces all the same length, it somewhat resembles a ladder (or a large, segmented fruit box with no bottom). The deluxe model often sports a centered, 1 by 6 board running fore and aft that is let in flush with the top side of the rails. (See Figure 11-2.) This board not only provides a site to mark the centerline but also tends to index the frame to prevent it from wracking.

The ladder frame offers several advantages over the floor setup:

a. It can be set up at a height convenient to the builder.
b. It permits the builder to set up on a concrete floor without having to drive fastenings into the masonry.
c. It allows construction in a shop with an uneven floor.
d. And last but not least, it allows the construction jig to be portable. Once the setup has been ribbanded out, the jig can be safety unfastened from the floor and the entire assembly can be moved. This not only permits reconfiguration of floor space during construction, but also allows the jig to be stored for reuse at a later date.

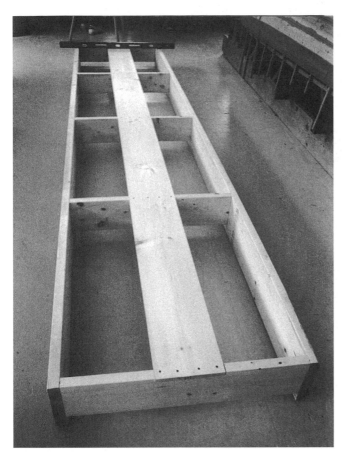

One method of building a ladder frame strongback

Begin by cutting the side rails and cross pieces to length. Clamp all cross pieces together and mark them for the centerline plank, then cut out the notches for the centerline plank to depth. Assemble the frame and square it up by measuring diagonally to opposite corners. Tweak it one way, then the other, until the diagonal measurements are the same. Then inlay and fasten the centerline plank.

Next, tune up the strongback. This takes only a short time and makes the setting up of the molds a breeze. Check for twist in the frame by testing with a level placed across the long rails at several locations. If necessary, drive wedges under the rails of the frame to bring it up to level. Once the frame is level, anchor it to the floor with screws.

Check the long rails for rise or dip, end to end. While there are many ways of doing this, including the use of lasers, the easiest (and cheapest) is the time-tested string-and-block technique. Begin by cut-

11-2: A ladder-frame strongback. The 1 by 6 board running fore and aft makes it a deluxe model.

ting three spacer blocks of the same thickness. At each end of the rail, drive a nail partly into the top surface. Tightly stretch a string (a chalk line will do) between the nails. Slide a block in under the string at each end. The key to this operation is the third block. Slid under the string at several locations, this "feeler gauge" tells the tale. If the block will not slide under the string, this registers a hump in the rail. A gap indicates a hollow. The string just touching the third block indicates the rail is straight.

Using anchor brackets and strategically placed shims, gently cajole the rails into place. Now you are ready to establish your grid.

Laying down the lines

Whether building on the floor or on a ladder frame, the next step is to lay down the construction grid. As with lofting, the place to begin is by striking a centerline. Next, plot the station, forward, and after perpendicular points on the centerline. Take the time to get this step right.

After properly plotting the station locations, you can then draw out the station lines square to the centerline. This is a straightforward operation, similar to setting up your lofting board. Using either a large square, or the 3,4,5 triangle method, draw your perpendicular station lines out from both sides of the centerline. Double check your work with trammel points. Okay? Then, without further ado, let's set up the molds.

11-3: Even the most precisely made molds will fail you if they are not set up properly. Take your time, check and re-check.

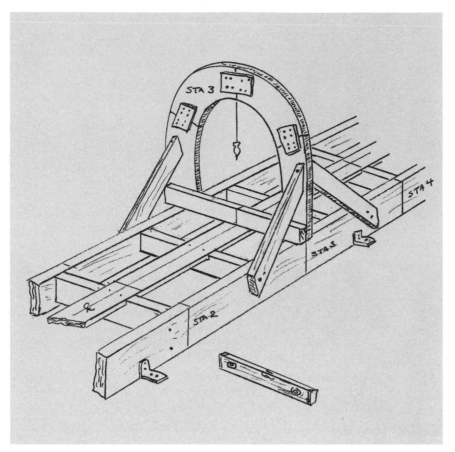

Setting up the molds

This is where all your front-loaded meticulous craftsmanship pays off. (You never doubted it would, did you?) Basically, all that remains to be done is to align the molds to their index marks, plumb, square, brace, and fasten.

The best practice is to start the setup with the 'midship mold and work toward the ends. (See Figure 11-4.) As the 'midship mold is generally the largest, it can be easily braced and will act as a keystone to which the rest of the molds can be buttressed. Start by aligning the station line of the mold to the station line drawn on the floor of frame. Then, line up the centerline drawn on the cross spall of the mold with the centerline on the floor. Temporarily anchor the mold with screws, so it doesn't get away. Drop a plumb bob from the centerline at the top of the mold to the centerline on the floor to check for miscues in the construction of the mold. If everything is copacetic, then, using the framing square and plumb bob, tweak the mold so it is square to the floor and brace it fore and aft.

Using the same technique, set up the adjacent molds, forward and aft of the 'midship mold. Check for plumb,

☞ Stations, Locations, and Accuracy

Setting up the molds is the big moment where the abstract 2-D world of lofting turns into 3-D. This is where, if a bit of care is taken, thoroughness in lofting begins to pay big dividends.

One common place for things to go awry is when laying out the station spacing. It's not difficult to get the spacing wrong, as the tape measure can slip and numbers can easily be misread (especially if the station spacing is inconsistent or the plans make continuous use of fractions). The best-made mold will appear to be wrong if it is set a couple of inches forward or aft of where it is supposed to be. So what to do?

One sure way to get the setup spacing right is not to measure at all. Instead, record the positions of all the stations, and the forward and after perpendicular, on a length of paper tape (or a long tick stick) just as they are drawn on the lofting. Then, just bring the tape to the construction site (floor, strongback, or keel), and transfer the points as drawn. If you are recording points on a keel,

be sure that you are using a waterline, or something parallel to it, to avoid error.

Another method that works for some small boats is simply to lay the completed backbone assembly right atop the lofting and square the station lines directly onto the wood.

Remember to use caution when marking station lines on bent, or sprung, keels. If the linear station spacing is first marked on the keel, then the keel is bent to shape, the station spacing will become shorter—an unwelcome surprise indeed.

One safe way to get the spacing right is to bend a wooden batten over the top of the keel as drawn on the lofting board and mark the station spacing onto it. When the batten is released and it straightens out, the station spacing will expand. The distances can then be recorded on the top side of the now straight but soon-to-be sprung keel. When the keel is bent, the station spacing will be correct.

and brace back to the 'midship mold. Then continue on until all the molds have been set up and braced.

Just a couple more things

Now is the time to make some final preparations prior to setting the backbone in place.

Install the transom jig that you drew on the lofting board. Although some builders prefer to wait until after the backbone assembly is in place to come up with a scheme to hold the transom, there is a lot to be said for setting up a proper holding device ahead of time. A well-designed jig will hold the transom plumb at the correct angle, at the proper height above base, and will aid in aligning the centerline. A little time invested here will save a lot of monkeying around later.

Install brackets at the top of each mold to fasten the keel to. L-shaped steel works well, but small wooden shelves will do the trick, too. Check the plans to be sure that the brackets will not be in the way of any frames. Install a bracket on the floor to hold the stem as well.

You can now drop the backbone assembly into place. The top of the stem should land right on the floor, the transom should fit into the bracket, and the station lines on the keel should line up with the stations. Line up the centerline of the keel with the centerline of the molds. Now fasten the brackets to the keel, the stemhead, and the transom.

11-5: An upside-down setup complete, with the backbone in place and before the ribbands are run.

Fair the setup

Check your work by wrapping a light batten around the setup from the stem rabbet (or bevel) to the transom. To ensure fairness, the batten must be tightly wrapped around the assembly. A floppy batten will provide false information, encouraging you to make unnecessary alterations to the setup. So, when checking for fairness, either clamp one end of the batten to the setup and pull against it, sighting for errors, or better yet, dragoon one of those frequently visiting shop kibitzers and put them to work.

As in lofting, what you'll be looking for is a nice, fair line that wraps around the hull, just touching each mold and landing nicely at one end in the rabbet and at the other onto the bevel of the transom. Untidy lumps that must be shaved down will quickly show up, as will gaps that must be shimmed.

SETTING UP—BUILDING RIGHT-SIDE UP

In building right-side up, the builder must use the same care as in the upside-down method. The whole business depends on establishing a proper centerline, correctly spacing the stations, and erecting the molds so they are plumb. The chief difference is that the keel is put into place first and the molds are placed atop the keel, which means that considerable effort must go into providing a decent foundation for the keel and setting it up properly to match the lofting. Also, the ends of the backbone must be thoroughly shored and braced either to the floor or the ceiling to keep them plumb, square, and in place. Having your waterlines and stations well marked all along the backbone will go a long way toward keeping your setup and sanity together.

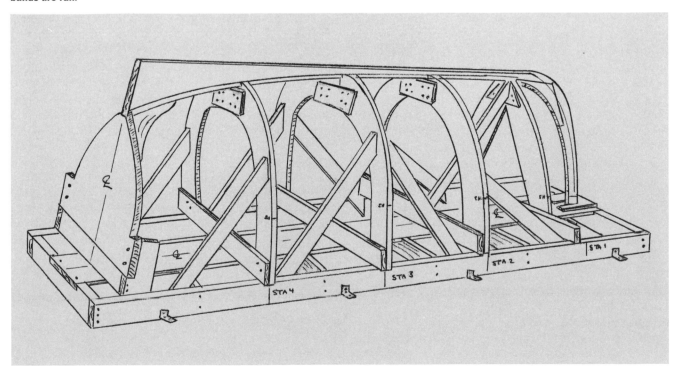

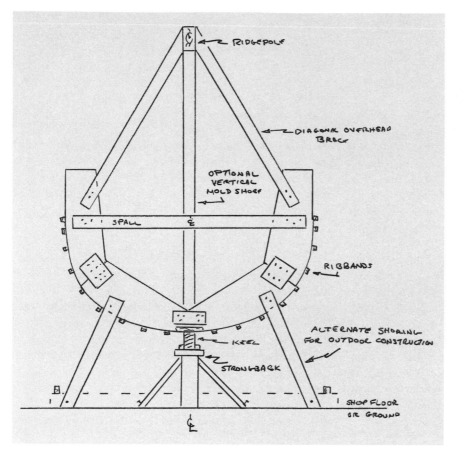

Labels in figure:
- RIDGEPOLE
- DIAGONAL OVERHEAD BRACE
- OPTIONAL VERTICAL MOLD SHORE
- SPALL
- RIBBANDS
- KEEL
- ALTERNATE SHORING FOR OUTDOOR CONSTRUCTION
- STRONGBACK
- SHOP FLOOR OR GROUND

11-6: Bracing a mold for right-side-up construction.

Setting up a light craft

When building a light craft right-side up, such as a pulling boat, often a strongback or a horse will serve as a good foundation. The horse is similar to a long sawhorse, with angled legs that can be fastened to the floor. On well-made strongbacks, the long horizontal beam is made in a T-bar or I-beam configuration to resist distortion. Some have additional vertical bracing at regular intervals along its length, as well as long vertical posts at the ends to brace to the ceiling.

If the keel is flat (as on a Whitehall), it can sit directly on the top of the straight beam. On the other hand, if the bottom of the keel is curved, a custom-curved beam top can be made (a bit like orthopedic shoes) for support, or more simply, spacer shims can be used. If you are using waterlines to check and align your molds, it is best to set the top of the beam level.

After the strongback is ready and a centerline has been established on it, the backbone assembly can be set in place. It is a good idea to anchor the keel to keep it in place. A very light keel may need blocking all along its length to keep it from rippling about like a serpent.

The stem and the sternpost must be plumbed and braced. Check with your plumb bob from the top of each to be sure you are dead over the centerline. Check the distance between the forward and after perpendiculars to be sure the distance is the same as it is on the lofting. And finally, make sure the transom is level, and at a right angle to the centerline. This can easily be ascertained by horning. (See sidebar, Horning, Isosceles, and It's All Greek to Me in Chapter 19, Interior Work.)

To help in alignment, your molds have been built with a cross spall that has a centerline marked on it and that has been set at the given waterline. To accommodate that centerline/waterline point we'll need to stretch a reference line from that same centerline/waterline height on the stem to that on the sternpost. A string stretched "humming" tight probably will be adequate for a small boat. For a better deal, consider installing a screw eye in the stem and sternpost, and running a thin wire, tightened by a baby "screen door" turnbuckle, between them. This rig almost eliminates sag, and cuts way down on frustrating string breakage.

Setting up the molds

Once again, start with the center mold. Compared to the upside-down setup, erecting the first right-side-up mold can be a sporty affair, a bit like balancing an egg on end. This is one operation where another set of hands would be really welcome.

Some builders will go so far as to construct a series of perpendiculars, one at each station. Installed just to one side of the centerline string and fixed at the keel and the ceiling or ridgepole, these members act as an aid to temporarily clamp the mold to while it's being aligned. The clamp can then be loosened enough to allow the mold to be plumbed, leveled, and horned into place. The tight string/wire will be your guide, not only to align the centerline of the cross spall, but also to check the height of the mold. The cross spall should just touch the string—neither pushing it up nor leaving a gap.

After the mold has been properly aligned, plumbed, leveled, and horned, it can be firmly braced, and the next mold can be tackled. Diagonal braces screwed across the top of the cross spalls during setup can help prevent wracking of the assembly. As soon as the molds are thoroughly fast, the setup can be checked for fairness in the same fashion as the upside-down setup

A few considerations for larger vessels

Commonly, a larger vessel will be set up with its keel supported on posts, stocks, or heavy blocking. When figuring

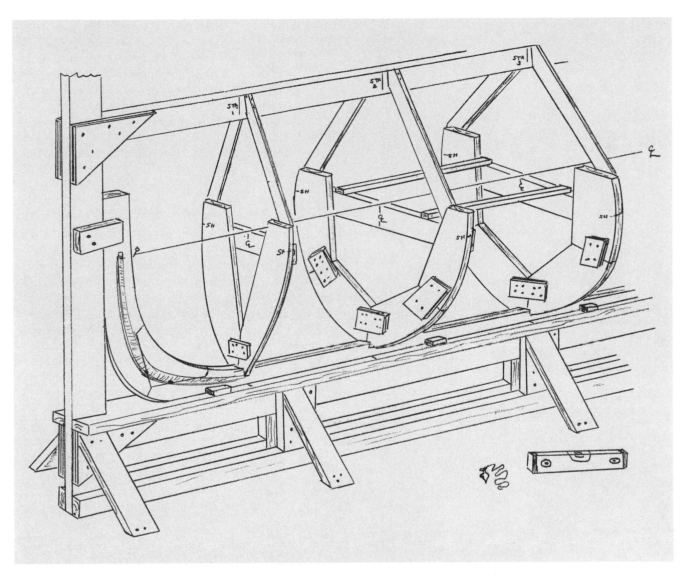

11-7: A right-side-up setup involving a strongback on which the backbone is mounted.

11-8: Ribbands being temporarily fastened to the right-side-up setup for a largish motor-boat.

Setting Up—Building Right-Side Up • 123

the height at which to build, consider whether there will be room to work comfortably when planking, caulking, and fairing the hull. Fitting a garboard is task enough without having to do it with a mirror and a shoehorn.

Begin by establishing a centerline on the floor and marking the stations on it. Many builders find it convenient to erect a post or block at each station line. If the bottom of the keel is curved, the use of a full-size profile pattern or template with stations and waterlines marked on it can be helpful in determining where to cut off the posts (or how high to build up the blocking). Firmly anchor the posts to the ground and brace them; any blocking should be well cleated to prevent shifting.

The keel can then be placed atop the posts and/or blocking, aligning it with the centerline on the floor and

11-9: This home-made tool is just the ticket for twisting ribbands so they will lie flat on the molds.

11-10: Alignment of ribbands for right-side-up construction.

the stations. Check that your reference waterline is level. Secure the keel in place with cleats on the posts (and blocking) and shores to the floor. Again, as in setting up the lighter boat, the stem and the stern of the vessel must be plumbed, squared, and properly braced. Then proceed with setting up the molds. Tune up the hull with your fairing battens, and then it is off to the ribbands. Or maybe not.

ON THE MATTER OF RIBBANDS

Generally speaking, most round-bottomed boats with steam-bent frames will require the use of ribbands in the setup, but not every boat requires them. Some notable examples are boats with sawn frames, semi-dories built over molds where frames are steam-bent in after planking, flat-bottomed skiffs and sharpies where sawn frames will be added after planking, construction jigs designed

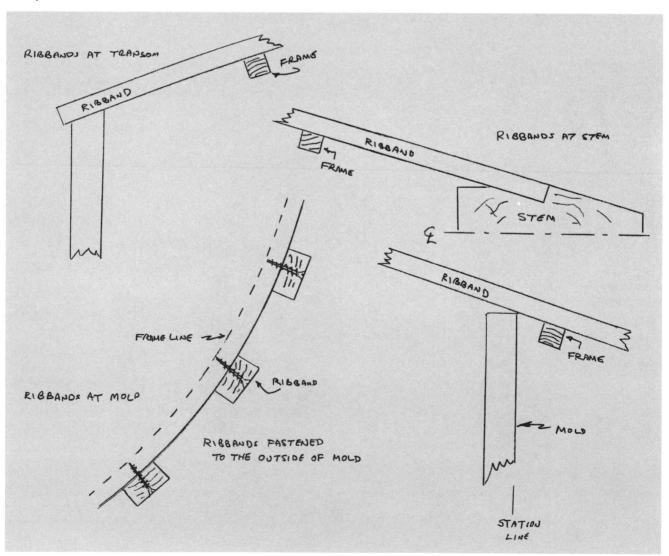

specifically for strip planking, and jigs designed for frames to be steam-bent directly over beveled molds.

Although ribbands can be added to the setup directly after the molds have been faired, many mechanics prefer to wait until after lining out the plank locations. (See Chapter 13, Lining Off the Hull.) One reason for this is simple clarity. It is lot easier to sight the lining-off batten when the view is unencumbered by a multitude of ribbands running at odd angles around the molds. Another reason is practicality when building upside down. If you are fastening with rivets, and your ribbands are spaced randomly over the hull, the odds are quite good that you will be driving at least some of those copper nails into ribbands. This can be quite disconcerting when attempting to lift the hull off the jig. Such a nuisance can be eliminated by aligning the ribbands between the lined plank marks. The last reason is aesthetic: The setup simply looks better when the ribbands are nicely placed, more or less following the planking marks.

The size of ribbands

Ribbands are rectangular in section and bent on the flat around the molds. Unfortunately, there are no hard-and-fast tables (that work) that will tell the builder the exact ribband scantling, or dimension, to use in a particular situation. This is because there are a number of factors to be considered, including: What is the spacing of the molds and therefore the greatest open space the ribbands will have to span? How much shape does the boat have? Will the ribbands be too stiff to render an accurate curve? How heavy are the frames that you will be bending? Will the ribbands be strong enough to stand the strain without distortion?

Another factor to consider is the strength of the wood being used. Spruce, for example, is stronger than pine, so the scantlings of a spruce ribband can be smaller than a pine one for the same effect.

The only way to be sure about ribband scantlings (unless you've built a similar boat lately) is to exper-

11-11: Alignment of ribbands for upside-down construction.

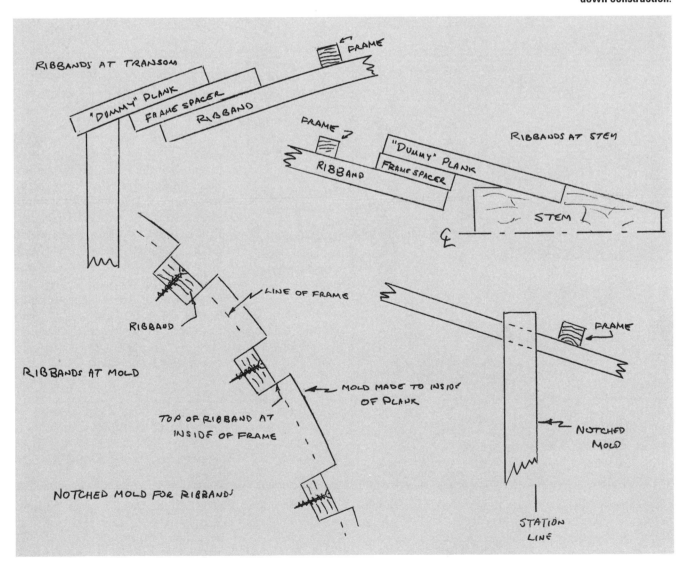

being bent over it?

Sometimes the builder needs to use a compromise solution to the ribband scantling problem, as in the situation where the mold spacing is relatively great, indicating a heavy ribband, yet the boat is quite shapely, indicating a light ribband that will easily follow tight curves. (Some Whitehalls and peapods fall into this category.) Perhaps the solution here is a laminated ribband. Resaw a 1¼-by ¾-inch ribband for two 1¼- by ⅜-inch ribbands. Each ⅜-inch stick will be floppy enough to be wrapped easily around the hull; when it is joined to its brother with either glue or fastenings, it will recover most of the strength of the original unripped ¾-inch piece.

A few general ribband rules

Select clear lumber for ribbands. Knots can weaken your stock and cause unfairness or "hard spots" in the ribband when bent. Whenever possible, use a stiff wood, such as spruce, fir, or yellow pine.

Ribbands should be put on in pairs—one on each side of the boat—to equalize the strain on the molds; they should be fastened with screws to permit easy removal. Drywall screws work well for this purpose. Pre-drilling and using washers will go a long way toward preventing breakage. Start from the center and work toward the ends. Bevel the edges of the ribbands to avoid injuring the frames when they are steam-bent over the ribbands. Ribbands should go on in one piece. If two short pieces must be joined to gain proper length, a scarf joint will provide a fairer curve than a butt splice.

Installing the ribbands

In right-side-up construction, ribbands can be fastened directly to the outside surface of the molds and the transom, and fit into the stem rabbet just as if they were planks. Later, when planking, the ribbands will be removed, one by one, as each plank is installed. (See Figure 11-10.)

Installation of the ribbands is a bit more complex when building upside down. (See Figure 11-11.) As the frames will be bent over the ribbands, and the molds are made (generally) to the inside of plank, notches must be

11-12: Offset filler blocks attached to the ends of the ribbands at the transom for upside-down construction. Note that some of the frames have already been steam-bent over the ribbands.

11-13: Offset filler blocks attached to the ends of the ribbands at the stem for upside-down construction.

iment. Saw out a sample ribband, say 1¼ inches by ¾ inch, bend it around the hull, and temporarily fasten it in place. Does it give you a fair line (compared to the fairing batten)? Did it "roll" into place, or did it fight you like an angry serpent? When it was screwed down and you leaned on it, did it deflect? Will it stand up to frames cut into the molds for the ribbands to be set into. The depth of cut is simply the total of the thickness of the frame plus that of the ribband. A simple marking gauge can be made for this purpose. To determine where to cut your notches, just bend a ribband around the setup molds and mark the outside edges. Then, using the gauge, mark the depth of the cut. Use a backsaw for cutting the sides of the notch; cut the bottom of the notch square. Check the depth with a sample ribband-and-frame "sandwich." With the ribband sample in place, the frame sample should be flush with the outside edge of the mold.

As with right-side-up construction, the ribbands are fastened to the molds with screws to simplify their removal.

To get the proper shape for the curve of the ribbands at the bow and the stern of the boat, an offset filler block must be attached to the ends of the ribband. (See Figures 11-12 and 11-13.) An easy way to do this is to cut the ribband just short of the stem and the transom. Make a couple of fillers that are the thickness of a frame and attach them on the outside of the newly cut ends of the ribband. Then just add a piece of ribband to the top of each of the filler blocks and extend the ribband into the stem rabbet and onto the transom, and fasten. This sandwiched "dogleg" arrangement will force the correct shape into the ribband.

Not to worry, this is a lot easier than it sounds.

☞ A Saw Cut Depth Device

When "letting" in notches for ribbands, chine logs, or battens in batten-seam construction, a plethora of saw cuts is required—all to the same depth. An easy way to speed this admittedly monotonous chore is to clamp a strip of wood to the side of your hand saw, parallel to the teeth, and use it as a stop for your desired depth of cut. All you need do is saw until your "fence" touches the work and you have arrived. (Do take a moment occasionally to tighten the clamps and check that the fence hasn't shifted.)

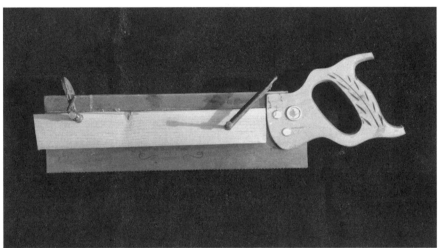

A fence clamped to the side of the blade of a backsaw.

The backsaw with fence in action.

12 • THE ART OF BENDING FRAMES

Builders have known for centuries that wood can be made to bend after it has been heated. There are a number of ways that heat can be applied, ranging from boiling the wood in caldrons, steaming it in boxes, torturing it with a heat gun, to holding it over an open fire. All these methods have their place, but for most boatbuilders, steaming is the way to go. The equipment is inexpensive and easy to make at home. The builder can easily and effectively heat long and lanky stock, such as that for stems, mast hoops, and planking, that would be impractical to heat with any other method. For bending frames, steam is unparalleled.

STEAM BOXES, OR, BABY, IT'S HOT INSIDE!

Every boatshop has its own version of the steam box. They range from exotic affairs that appear to have been salvaged from a Civil War locomotive to more humble units that may have previously produced moonshine. But whatever their outward appearance, they all contain the four basic components: a heat source, a boiler in which to make the steam, a pipe to direct the steam, and a "box" to contain the steam. All we're looking for here is a rig that will produce a lot of steam swiftly and safely. Let's start by taking a closer look at the components:

The heat

Most steamers use some sort of gas stove for boiling the water. These stoves are relatively inexpensive and require little maintenance. Some builders prefer the old-time plumber's stove, while the more progressive sorts opt for those 100,000 BTU outdoor Cajun catfish cookers available in large discount stores. Even a gas hotplate will fill the bill in a pinch. Whatever stove you choose, it must burn cleanly and put out a lot of heat.

Unfortunately, where there is heat there is the potential for fire. Before even considering setting up the stove, decide where it is to be located. The best place is outdoors, away from any flammables. The stove should be shielded from wind and set up on a fireproof mat. The base of the stove should be broad, with no possibility of tipping over. The tank should be set in a remote location and have an approved regulator and hose fitted to it. Without a regulator a gas stove is a potential Vesuvius!

Keep fire-fighting apparatus nearby. A garden hose ready to go is ideal.

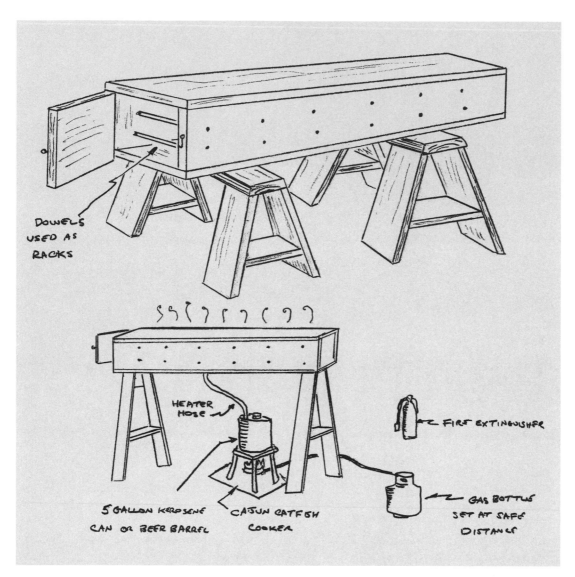

DOWELS
USED AS
RACKS

HEATER
HOSE

FIRE EXTINGUISHER

5 GALLON KEROSENE
CAN OR BEER BARREL

CAJUN CATFISH
COOKER

GAS BOTTLE
SET AT SAFE
DISTANCE

The boiler

Some builders will have a custom tank fabricated for them. A well-built tank can last for years and can have plumbing connections to introduce water, and even a gauge to check the water level. A more economical choice is an aluminum beer keg. These heavy-duty units are tough as boot leather and have a number of ports to attach plumbing fixtures. An emergency short-term alternative is a new, steel five-gallon gasoline can. (Steer clear of used cans; they may have unwanted vapors residing within.) While the bottom of a gas can will burn out in short order, it will generally last through the job and a replacement is readily available at the local auto supply store. Boatshop kibitzers will probably stand clear when you place one of these units on the gas stove—which is exactly what you want.

Whatever you use as a boiler, make sure that it sits safely on the stove and that the outlet is big enough to handle the steam that it produces. You don't want to build any pressure whatsoever in the boiler. Pressure is of no advantage in steaming and is very dangerous.

The pipe

For a permanent setup, a good way to convey the steam to the box is with a large-caliber pipe. For a temporary rig, automotive heater hose (the reinforced high-pressure type) works well. If you use hose, however, keep it from drooping down and creating a low spot that can collect water condensed from steam and cause a blockage. (See Figure 12-2.)

The steam box

The most popular steam box is a simple, long, rectangular shape built of boards, closed off at one end and with a door at the other, with a hole for the steam pipe or hose. A well-made box should allow good circulation of steam around the wood to be steamed. It should have cleats on the bottom and a couple of rows of dowels running from side to side down the length of the box; these are used as racks to hold the wood and keep the pieces separated from each other, with steam flowing around them unimpeded. Don't bother about caulking the box. You want

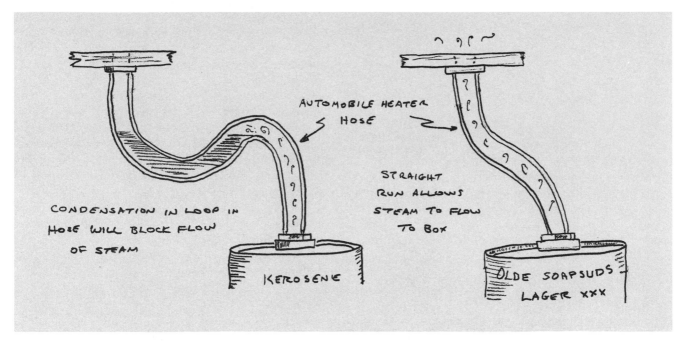

AUTOMOBILE HEATER HOSE

CONDENSATION IN LOOP IN HOSE WILL BLOCK FLOW OF STEAM

KEROSENE

STRAIGHT RUN ALLOWS STEAM TO FLOW TO BOX

OLDE SOAPSUDS LAGER XXX

12-2: The hose from the boiler to the steam box.

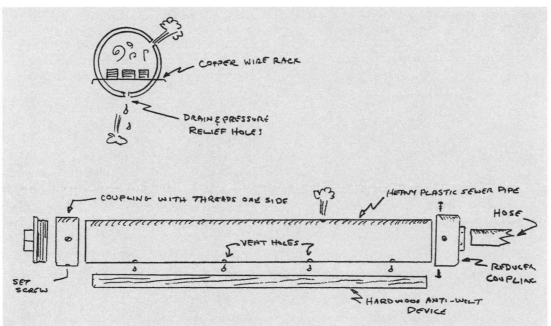

COPPER WIRE RACK

DRAIN & PRESSURE RELIEF HOLES

COUPLING WITH THREADS ONE SIDE

HEAVY PLASTIC SEWER PIPE

HOSE

VENT HOLES

SET SCREW

REDUCER COUPLING

HARDWOOD ANTI-WELT DEVICE

12-3: A steam box made from sewer pipe.

leaks. The only thing a tight steam box will do is slow or prevent hot steam from entering the box.

Another route to take is the plastic sewer pipe steam box. All the parts—pipes, flanges, caps—are off-the-shelf items. (See Figure 12-3.) The "box" can be assembled to any desired length. The pipe can be drilled for dowels or nonferrous wire for the shelves. Vent holes must be drilled at regular intervals to eliminate any pressure build-up. Brace the pipe underneath with wood to prevent it from sagging from heat over time.

WHAT STOCK WORKS

"Frames? Well, if you make up just enough you'll probably break 50 percent. But saw up twice as much as you need, and you'll likely have about half of 'em left over."
— anonymous cranky shipwright

Successful steam-bending is a bit like whipping up a gourmet dinner. Although having a great recipe and elegant (and pricey) cooking paraphernalia helps, the chef's secret weapon is well-prepared stock. This raw material is usually obtained from quirky purveyors, trimmed and sliced with care, then delicately cooked to perfection. It

BEST   WORST   REALITY

12-4: Cross sections showing frame grain alignment.

is thus with steam-bending.

So, what goes into selecting good frame-bending stock? There are a number of considerations, some of greater importance than others. Durability, rot resistance, availability, and whether the wood takes steam well are at the top of the list. Other elements, such as having quarter-sawn stock or a very specific moisture content, are of less consequence. Let's take a look at a few of the more important factors.

Choosing the stock

For most boat construction, it is difficult to beat white oak, your basic *Quercus alba*. This wood steams well, is rugged, holds fastenings adequately, and looks great when finished. The best for bending is straight-grained stock from butt logs.

Red oak is a close runner-up, but it has an open cell structure that draws water just like a bundle of pipette tubes and is less durable than its cousin.

White ash is a possible suspect. It is readily available, and strong for its weight, but it has an affinity for rot when it finds itself in stagnant fresh water.

All things considered, probably your best bet is to stick with the white oak if it is available. If it is not, break out the phone book and do some industrial research. Buttonhole your local boatyard manager, university extension service expert, and marine museum curator to find out what folks are using in your region (and why).

What to look for

Whatever species you decide to use, there are some common qualities to shop for. Frame stock tends to be fairly finicky stuff—intolerant of imperfection and funkiness. Time taken to select the right material will pay big dividends.

High moisture content is one of the keys to success. If possible, stay away from kiln-dried lumber, as the moisture has already been cooked out of the wood. Using it is like reheating leftovers. Instead, seek out recently cut wood, which is most likely found at a local mill. The technical books call for 12- to 20-percent moisture content, but unless you are a chronic gadgeteer who has an electronic appliance for every occasion, you won't have a moisture meter in your back pocket when you're prowling the wood stacks. Instead, simply ask when the wood was cut and if it has been kiln dried. If it has been cut within the year, you're probably in business.

After determining that your prospective stock has enough juice, eyeball it for failure-causing defects. Avoid decay, knots, rot, pitch pockets, and surface checks. The presence of any of these can cause premature and annoying failure.

Look for straight and uniform grain. A 1:15 ratio (meaning that over 15 inches the grain doesn't deviate more than one inch) is recommended. A smaller ratio is likely to cause difficulty. And beware of "interesting" grain—you know, the whorling stuff that so fascinates artistic cabinetmakers. Every one of those whorls is an invitation for a break.

Finally, stay away from sapwood, the light-colored wood closest to the bark. Sapwood is likely to have a moisture content different from the heartwood (causing bending problems); it is also non-durable, opening up the possibility of premature rot.

Preparing the stock

After selecting your stock, the next step is to mill it to size. If possible, cut your frame stock slightly oversize, then either plane or sand it to dimension. Aesthetics aside, the real reason for this tender loving care is to eliminate swirling saw-kerf marks on the frame that can foster cracking and breakage. Also slightly rounding or "breaking" the corners of the sawn stock seems to reduce split-producing stress while bending.

Which way should the grain of the wood lie? Most of the literature on the subject suggests that frames should be sawed with the annular rings lying parallel with the curve the wood will take in the boat. (See Figure 12-4.) Wood is said to bend easier this way and split less when fastenings are driven. In practice, the orientation of the rings seems to make little difference. Which is a good thing, because it is difficult enough finding straight, clear stock of proper moisture content without introducing unnecessary angst over whether the grain of the frame is running 17 degrees off parallel or not.

Where to buy frame stock

Chances are better than average that your local home-supply emporium or cabinetmaker's mart will not have what you are looking for. These places tend to specialize in kiln-dried standardized product, and filling oddball requests is not their forte. ("You want what? How about some yellow pine, it's the same stuff.") Your best bet is to search out a local sawmill, as lumber there is usually more reasonably priced, and the crew will generally be tolerant of unusual requests and more likely to have freshly cut lumber. And, if you play your cards right, and promise to restack the piles better than you found them, they will let you search through their inventory for the ideal bending stock.

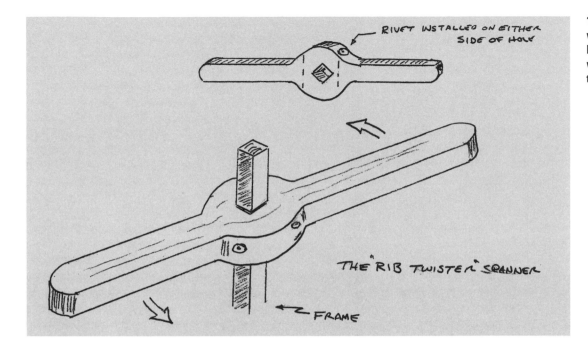

STEAMING TECHNIQUE

Success when steaming wood involves rapidly heating the wood for the right amount of time, then quickly bending it. Think lobsters here, not roast pork. Over-steaming will turn your wood into a limp piece of asparagus, lifeless and easily broken. The general rule is half an hour of steaming for half an inch of thickness (perhaps somewhat less for woods with plenty of moisture).

Wait until your steam box is up to temperature, with plenty of billowing steam leaking out, before introducing any stock to the box. Then, after donning your protective welding gauntlets, you are ready to go.

When doing production work, such as bending frames, avoid the temptation to load the box chock full. There are two reasons for this. The first is that large quantities of wood can act like a heat sink, lowering the temperature in the box and slowing down steam production. The second is that the steam-bending business is filled with surprises. Any hang-up in the bending process can cause spoilage of the remaining stock in the steam box. Indeed, it is not unusual for the impatient novice to spoil two-thirds of the stock in the box—one-third to under-cooking, the other third to overcooking.

To keep an eye on possible over- or under-cooking, it is a good practice to put a sacrificial piece of stock in the box that can be pulled occasionally to check on its condition. And to further pummel the cooking metaphor into the ground, remember the old bromide about the watched pot—nothing so slows down production as repeatedly opening the box to "see how things are doing."

ORGANIZATION

Planning ahead is the name of the game here. Although we're not talking the Normandy Landing, things do go a lot better if everyone knows their job and the tools are where you expect them to be.

Take the time to make a dry run through the exercise. Try bending a trial piece into place. Are there enough clamps to hold the bent stock? Are there enough gloves? How about pads for the clamps? Enough drills, hammers, and fastenings? How often will the water level be checked in the steamer, and by whom?

Develop a rhythm that will let you work quickly and efficiently while the wood is hot. Every second the piece cools outside the box is that much time you have lost from your window of bendability. Contemplative mellowness is out. What we're looking for is organized, deliberate, frenzy.

TOOLS FOR BENDING FRAMES

In any type of wood bending, you can't have too many clamps. This is especially true when bending in hot frames. Round up all you have and borrow some more. Make sure they are all well oiled. A rust-frozen clamp picked up at a critical moment is something you don't need. Also, as wood crushes easily when steamed, make lots of wooden pads or buttons (¼-inch plywood works well for this) to have on the ready for clamping.

Get out your wooden mallet. It will come in handy for persuading recalcitrant steamed stock to go where it should.

You will also need an electric drill, a drill bit to match galvanized nails (six-penny are good), and your favorite

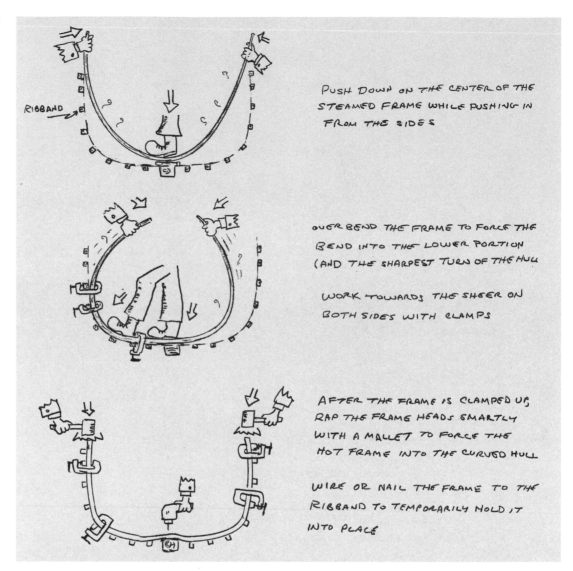

PUSH DOWN ON THE CENTER OF THE STEAMED FRAME WHILE PUSHING IN FROM THE SIDES

OVER BEND THE FRAME TO FORCE THE BEND INTO THE LOWER PORTION (AND THE SHARPEST TURN OF THE HULL

WORK TOWARDS THE SHEER ON BOTH SIDES WITH CLAMPS

AFTER THE FRAME IS CLAMPED UP RAP THE FRAME HEADS SMARTLY WITH A MALLET TO FORCE THE HOT FRAME INTO THE CURVED HULL

WIRE OR NAIL THE FRAME TO THE RIBBAND TO TEMPORARILY HOLD IT INTO PLACE

RIBBAND

hammer for fastening the frame temporarily to the ribbands. As an alternative for holding the frames in place, you can use aviation-type wire-twisting pliers and a spool of nonferrous wire. (Some builders in Maine, home of potato farms, use potato bag wire twists and twisters.)

By the way, beware of steaming oak in close proximity to iron or steel, as the acids in the wood will react with the metal and the oak will turn a luxurious bluish-black. Use wooden pads under clamp buttons and steer clear of iron steam boxes.

If you will be bending into an upright hull, make up a two-handled frame-twisting wrench. (See Figure 12-5.) This homemade tool will give you the leverage to twist the hot frame so it aligns with the fore-and-aft curve of the hull. Such a tool can be quickly made of scrap wood by sawing out a shape that is similar to two-handled tap-and-die tools. Customize the handles to fit your hands comfortably. Then, using a hand drill and a chisel, cut a rectangular hole the size of the frame in the center of the tool. For a deluxe version, add a long rivet on each side

of the hole to discourage the tool from cracking.

And don't forget leather welder's gloves, the type that extend up your forearms to protect them when pulling stock from the steam box.

SAFETY

Be cautious at all times, and accord the steam box the same respect you give the table saw. Steam scalds instantly. Never stand in line of the steam box when opening the door, and always wear your safety gloves!

SOME GENERAL NOTES ON BENDING FRAMES

If you are bending your frames either directly into an upright setup, or over a jig for upside-down construction, mark your frame locations ahead of time on the ribbands, using a light batten to draw the line.

Mark both sides of the frame on the ribbands. This

12-7: Pre-bending frames over a trap form.

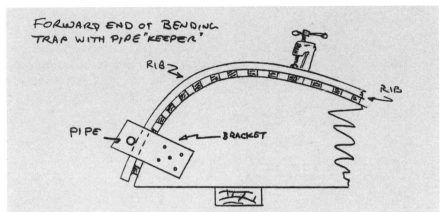

12-8: A pipe in a bracket fastened to the trap form holds the end of the frame.

FORWARD END OF BENDING TRAP WITH PIPE "KEEPER"

RIB

PIPE

BRACKET

RIB

12-9: Hold the shape of a pre-bent frame with a wood keeper strip temporarily fastened at the top and bottom.

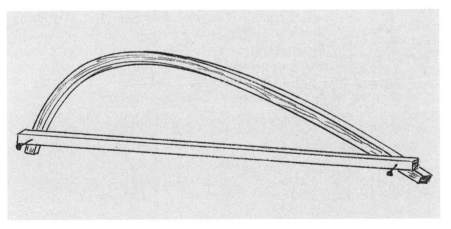

probably sounds excessive, but there will be so much action going on in the heat of the moment that you don't need to spend any extra time pondering the elemental question, "To be on the right side of the line, or the left?"

Begin framing amidships, where the bends are likely to be easier. To avoid distorting the ribbands by concentrating all your bending in one spot, alternate sides; bend one frame on the port side, then one on the starboard. Follow that by skipping a frame and bending one to the right of the first. Then skip a frame to the left of the first. Then fill in the missing frame to the right of the first frame, and then the left, and so on. The idea is to keep things in balance and to avoid any concentration of force.

BENDING FRAMES INTO A RIGHT-SIDE-UP JIG

The key to success when bending into a jig (as opposed to over one) is not to try to make the entire bend along the frame at once. A well-made frame will try to form a perfect arc when bent. A cross section of most hulls, however, is a fair curve but seldom a perfect arc. The chal-

lenge is compounded when bending a hot frame into a curve, as the frame will stubbornly try to straighten out every time you release pressure on it. So be prepared to wrestle your frame into submission, section by section, as if it were a hot python.

The job begins by checking one more time that everything, and everyone, is in place. You will be inside the jig with your heat-resistant gloves on. Your assistant, also with heat-resistant gloves, will pull the frame out of the steam box and deliver it to you with celerity. You will line it up with the marks, immobilize the keel end with a clamp, and begin bending it into position.

To force a frame into a tight turn of the bilge, you

12-10: Bending frames over an upside-down setup. Clamps are used to hold the hot frames to the ribbands.

That being said, there are still opportunities for things to go wrong, the most insidious being that the task looks so easy. An overenthusiastic builder can get ahead himself, happily bending one frame after another, only to discover later that the frames weren't properly pulled down to the jig, or that they were improperly located.

Before starting up the steam box, give the setup one last examination. Be sure that the ribbands are set into the molds at the proper depth, and that the frame locations are prominently marked on the ribbands.

It is a good idea to bend a few test frames to check for distortion of the ribbands. If it looks as though the ribbands will deflect, beef them up with a laminate on the bottom side.

When you start to bend the frames, set a pace that allows you to do a good job. Avoid the temptation to install all your clamps on the frame at once. Instead, work your way up the frame from the keel. In some instances you may need to work a little reverse bend into the upper part of a frame to force it into a hollow; then you can clamp it, and continue your bend to the sheer.

Check that the frames have been properly twisted against the ribbands at the sheer. This is easy to overlook, as the sheer is less obvious than it is in right-side-up construction.

The leverage that is such a boon to bending over a jig can cause problems if your frames are insufficiently steamed or if the ribbands are too light for the job. An undercooked frame can act as a pry bar, distorting the ribbands and imparting a washboard effect to the bottom of the boat that might not be noticed until it is time to plank.

may find yourself pushing the frame against the ribbands with your boot, while pulling the upper part of the frame in toward you to make a tighter curve. Now your cohort must clamp the lower part of the frame into the ribbands. Then you can push the upper part of the frame into the ribbands.

At this point, it may be necessary to begin pounding on the head of the frame with a wooden mallet to force more of a bend into the turn of bilge. Add more clamps. Check and see whether the frame is between the pencil marks and adjust as necessary.

Meanwhile, of course, the frame must be twisted to get it to lie flat against the ribbands. Slide on your homemade frame twister and tweak the frame in a corkscrew fashion, push it into place, and add more clamps. When all is satisfactory, anchor the frame to the ribbands with nails or wire, and move on to the next one.

BENDING OVER AN UPSIDE-DOWN JIG

Compared to bending into a right-side-up jig, bending over an upside-down one is a cakewalk. You have gravity and leverage working in your favor, and your feet will be firmly planted on the floor rather than dancing around the interior like a squirrel in a cage.

EMERGENCY RESAWING

There will be times and places that, no matter how many frames you try, they will keep breaking. There could be a number of reasons for this aggravating phenomenon. The wood could be too dry or have defects, or the steam could be not

12-11: When all else fails, partially resaw a frame and fasten it back together with rivets and/or glue after it has been bent in place and has cooled.

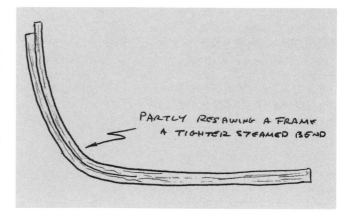

PARTLY RESAWING A FRAME
A TIGHTER STEAMED BEND

hot enough. Perhaps the wood has been overcooked, or undercooked, or perhaps the bend is just too great for a frame of that size.

Whatever the reason, partial resawing of the frame can sometimes save the day. What you need to do is resaw, or split, the frame with the bandsaw from the sheer to just past the point where the breakage has been occurring. (See Figure 12-11.) Do not resaw from that point to the keel. Now the frame can be steamed as usual; when bent, it will think it is two thin frames rather than one solid one and will easily make the turn. Clamp the frame and let it set. After cooling, the split frame can either be riveted and/or glued together.

Is a split frame weaker than a solid one? Probably, but not as weak as a broken frame.

YET ANOTHER ESCAPE

If a resawn frame has no appeal, try laminating one in place. Begin by stapling polyethylene film over the marked frame location. Mill up your laminations from a type of wood that glues well. Make the laminations quite thin, but twice as wide as the finished frame will be. (The extra width will compensate for the eventual shaping of the frame and will allow for the inevitable sliding of the pieces as they are clamped.)

Lay out all your laminations on a sheet of plastic on your workbench and thoroughly saturate them with epoxy glue. Then remove the oozing pile to the jig and securely clamp them in the proper place over the ribbands. Make sure the laminations are clamped tightly enough to close any gaps, but not so tightly as to cause glue starvation. After the glue has cured, the frame can be removed from the jig, sawed and hand-planed to shape, reinstalled, and fastened to the ribbands.

13 • LINING OFF THE HULL

Ah! There are few things that do as much to accentuate the beauty of a wooden hull as well-lined-off planks. Those sweeping lines that emphasize that rakish sheer. The glorious symmetry of the planks entering the stem rabbet. Proportion and harmony can lend even the most plebeian craft a dapper and jaunty tone.

Alas, the opposite can also be true. A poor lining job can make the best design seem out of balance, the finest construction appear slipshod and suspect. Worse, inattention to plank placement can cost time and waste material.

What to do? Little has been written on lining off and even less on how to do it. What literature there is evokes the image of wizened old codgers inscrutably dowsing for elusive plank locations with sacred square-sectioned battens. Mystical and arcane sorcery better left to wizards? Nay, the application of just a few practical and aesthetic considerations, and perhaps a bit of patience, should do the trick for you.

Not surprisingly, there are a few different schools of thought on how to approach lining off. There's the "eyeball 'em up as you go" fraternity, who prefer to lay out their plank placements as they proceed. This, they say, allows for mid-course correction and getting on with the job. Then there are the "predeterminators," those who would rather have the locations all buttoned up before the planking job begins so they don't have to deal with them later (or at least not very much).

No matter the approach you take, the considerations are the same. Above the waterline, optically and aesthetically, the planks should appear to be all the same size, even if they are not. The hood ends of the planks, at the bow where they enter the rabbet, should be roughly of equal width and should be sized to accept two fastenings. The same is true at the transom end. The middle of the planks must naturally be wider than at the ends but not so wide as to make them look like jumbo bananas. All the plank lines should sweep easily, with no "fishtails" or unsightly widening at the ends.

The effect of the rubrail on the perceived width of the sheer plank must not be forgotten. If, for example, the sheerstrake at its widest point is 2¾ inches and the rubrail is 1½ inches, to the eye that plank is now only 1¼ inches at its widest point.

Below the waterline is where all the work is done to fit in the rest of the planks economically and to make the topsides look good. It is here that you deal with the conundrum of fitting the same number of planks into a region of changing girths and complex hull shapes. Planks on a catboat, for example, may have to be quite broad amidships, only to suddenly narrow to accommodate a sharp turn of the bilge. (See Figure 13-1.) On a larger vessel, such as a Friendship sloop, plank widths might become so great as to necessitate splitting a plank into two narrower ones at a butt block.

STARTING OFF

Whether building right-side up or upside down, it is easier or at least less confusing to the eye to line all your planks before installing the ribbands. If you are building upside down and you have the ribbands let into the molds, you have a choice of either lining off all the planks at once or lining one plank at a time. On the other hand, if you are building right-side up and the ribbands are already installed, you will have to work around them, only removing those directly in the way of your plank.

At any rate, you will be needing some good-quality, straight-grained battens to do the job. When lining off all at once, it's good to have enough battens to allow you to leave one tacked in place for every plank. Then, when you have finished your lining, the entire planking job is revealed in all its glory, and you pretty much know what you are getting into right from the start. (See Figure 13-2.)

A NOTE ON LINING MARKS

While lining off the hull, you are likely to run into predetermined points that you will be bending the lining batten through. These might be indicated on the plans, or you might generate them yourself by mathematically dividing the girth—the distance from the top of the sheer to the keel—by the number of planks. Wherever these wonderful points came from, they will be dutifully recorded on the setup and a batten will be run through them. Then you could very well find that the line looks like the track of a Coney Island roller-coaster. Mon Dieu! What to do?

Remember that these points are only guideposts to the general location of the plank. Come as close as you can to these points while maintaining a nice, easy, fair

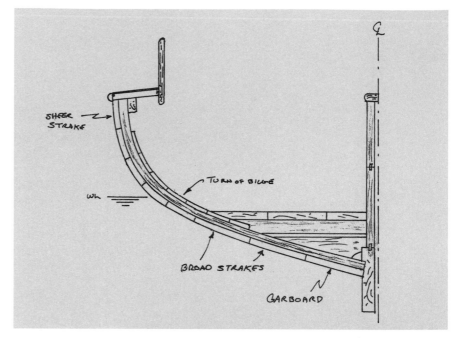

13-1: Plank widths on a Cape Cod catboat. Note that they become wider below the turn of the bilge.

13-2: Using battens to line off the planks.

line. What you see is what you get. Smooth curves not only look better, but also are easier to plank.

When dealing with lapstrake planking, the line that the batten is establishing is where the plank lands on the molds (or the inside line of the plank), not what you'll be seeing on the outside of the hull. To get a better idea of

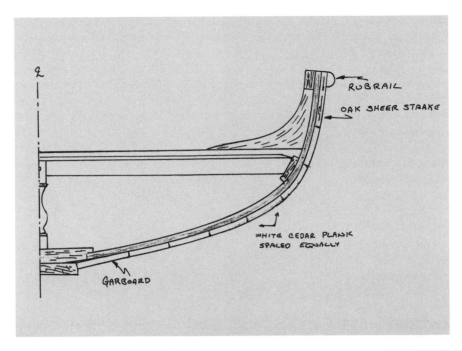

13-3: Compare the 'midship section plank widths on this Whitehall pulling boat with those of the Cape Cod cat-boat in Figure 13-1.

RUBRAIL

OAK SHEER STRAKE

WHITE CEDAR PLANK SPACED EQUALLY

GARBOARD

13-4: Lining off at the stem of a Whitehall pulling boat. The sheer-strake and garboard are determined first.

SHEER

BOTTOM OF RUB RAIL

BOTTOM OF SHEER PLANK

UPPER EDGE OF GARBOARD

STEM FACE

BOTTOM OF KEEL

the outside appearance of lapstrake planking, try using a batten that is the same caliber as your plank lap width.

LINING OFF A WHITEHALL PULLING BOAT

Let's start this business of lining off by doing the job on a 16-foot traditional Whitehall. Our example, a swift little beauty, was originally built in the 1890s, with the usual handsome touches—turned seat posts, sternsheets, a grate up forward, and a bright-finished sheerstrake. The plans indicate that there are eight planks per side, and that they all land on the transom. In addition, the sheerstrake is shown. Let's get to work on one side of the boat (we'll deal with the other side later).

The sheerstrake

Many boats, including our Whitehall, have prescribed measurements for an "accent" sheerstrake. These sometimes show up on the table of offsets, sometimes not. If the measurements are missing, and you really want to get that sporty oak sheerstrake just as it is portrayed on the plans, measuring the plans with a scale rule will provide decent enough information to do the job. These dimensions can then be plotted on the setup boat, a batten faired though them, and the line marked on the transom, the molds, and the stem.

The garboard

The garboard—the plank next to the keel—is perhaps the most daunting plank to line out, as its location seems to have been conjured out of thin air. Where does it start? Or end? And how wide should it be?

Let's begin at the beginning, which in this case is at the transom. Roughly divide the girth from the bottom of the sheerstrake to the rabbet by the remaining number of planks (seven). The last division next to the keel will be the width of your garboard (at least to start) at the transom. Next, go to the center mold and mathematically divide up the girth in the same manner used on the transom.

Now, for some artistic considerations. Compare the

widths at the center mold with those at the transom. Are they close, or are the center mold widths quite a bit greater than the transom's? If the center widths are a lot greater, how would a plank that wide look next to the svelte and sexy sheerstrake you just established? A trifle massive, you say?

Okay, why not increase the width of the garboard at the center mold a bit? The bottom is usually relatively flat in that area, so an increase in the width of the garboard would cause little problem. And a wider garboard means narrower planks above it—the plank next to the sheerstrake will no longer be distractively massive.

Deliberations on the shape of the garboard's hood end all have to do with how it will fit into the stem rabbet. The stem on the Whitehall is nearly plumb until the bottom, where it makes a quick arc and heads into the keel. The garboard must fit into this arc. If the plank enters the arc too high, all the succeeding planks will be too narrow, which is a problem, as you must be able to get two fastenings into each. If it enters the arc too low, the hood end of the garboard plank will be a narrow spear; twisting the plank into place and driving fastenings into it without breaking the hood end will be difficult.

To solve this dilemma, temporarily fasten your batten to the lining marks on the transom and the center mold, and bend it to a likely location on the stem. How does the line of the garboard look? Is the garboard too skinny? Is there enough room to get six more planks comfortably in above it? Tinker with the batten, up and down, until you strike a compromise that you can live with. Tack the batten in place, then sight along it for that fair line. Like it? Then mark the line on the stem.

The rest of the story

The rest of the plank locations can be determined in the same fashion as those for the garboard, using rough measurements to get started and "eyeballing" the batten to get the shape of the plank. This method is a little slow, but it gets the job done; on some hulls with complex contours,

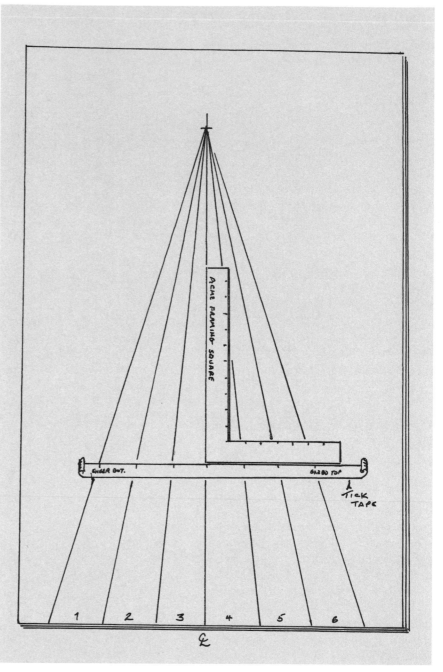

13-5: The incredible diminishing device being used with a tick tape and a framing square.

it's the only way to go. But on straightforward hulls such as our Whitehall, we can take a short cut with a special rig:

The incredible diminishing device

All right, maybe it's not incredible, but it is pretty handy nonetheless. This rig is a graphical proportional divider that works like those perspective techniques they use in art classes to make trees and railroad tracks disappear into infinity.

To make this elegant appliance, start with a drawing surface; a piece of plywood works well, as it's smooth and portable. Use one edge as a baseline, and from the center of it erect a perpendicular line. Next, record with a measuring tape the greatest distance on the center mold you want to divide up. Let's say that distance, from the top of the garboard to the bottom of the sheerstrake, is 38 inches. Divide that number by 6—your desired number of planks—and you get 6.33 inches, a most unhandy number to mess with. Rather than spend too much time on higher mathematics, simply boost that number to a more convenient one, such as 6½ inches or, better yet, 7 inches.

Next, mark off six 7-inch intervals on the baseline—three on each side of the perpendicular. Now make a mark high on the perpendicular. With a straightedge and a pencil, connect each of the six marks on the baseline with the central mark on the perpendicular. You'll now have a diagram that looks a little like a seven-poled tipi.

Using the device

To employ our diminisher, we first must measure and record the girths between the bottom of the sheerstrake to the top of the garboard at the molds, the transom, and the stem. Old-time boatbuilders used to do their measuring with a thin, flexible strip of wood that could be bent around the molds, et al., and onto which they could mark the girths. That's a good method, but a handier one is to use a paper strip, such as calculator tape or ticker tape (if you can find any). This is much easier to use, and it can be rolled up for use later on.

13-6: Transferring the plank lining points from the diminishing device to the molds.

Either way, bring the recorded distances for the first mold to the diminisher, along with a large framing square. Align one leg of the square on the centerline of the "tipi." Align the strip with the recorded distances on

the other leg of the square. Now slide the square up and/or down until the sheer and garboard points on the strip touch the outside legs of the "tipi." The intersection with the other legs will automatically divide the girth of that mold into six equal intervals. Mark those intervals on the strip, then take the strip back to the mold and transfer the intervals with a pencil. (See Figure 13-6.)

Repeat the operation on the rest of the molds, the transom, and the stem. After all that, it's simply a matter of springing battens through the points, tweaking the battens here and there for fairness, marking the planking lines, and there you have it. Ready to plank!

Well almost. There's just one more task.

Transferring the lines to the other side

Those hard-fought-for plank lines must be duplicated on the other side of the boat. To accomplish this, wrap the girth-measuring strips around the molds and transom of the first side of the boat once again to record the finalized plank locations, then bring them around and transfer the marks to the molds and transom on the other side of the boat. This method also will work for transferring the marks for the stem rabbet as well, or you can use the old two-pencil technique.

To use the two-pencil technique, position yourself so you are facing the face of the stem and can see each side of the stem equally. Hold a pencil in one hand on the first side of the boat so its point touches a lining mark at the stem, with the pencil itself aligned at a right angle to the stem. Hold another pencil in your other hand in the same fashion, riding it up and down on the stem until it is exactly opposite the first pencil. Make your mark. (See

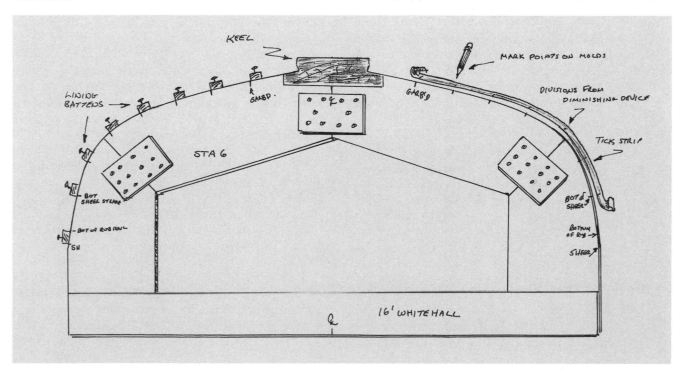

Figure 13-7.) Do this for each of the remaining lining marks.

Is that all there is to it? Yes. Accurate? You bet!

All that you need to do now is to run battens through the transferred points to check for any miscues and ink in your marks for permanence.

LINING A BALLAST KEEL SAILBOAT

Lining off the Whitehall was a straightforward job. The stem was nearly plumb, all the planks landed on the transom, and the hull was relatively narrow. With the exception of the sheerstrake and the garboard, the plank lines could be mechanically diminished. But what if we were lining a larger classical boat, such as a Herreshoff 12½-footer or similar type. Because of the shape of the 12½-footer—the long, graceful stem, the raked transom, and the fullness of the hull—simply diminishing would exaggerate the sweep of the planks, while probably giving us skinny planks at the bow with not much wood to hold the fastenings. To further muddy the waters, that elegant tuck at the transom requires us to take care to avoid very narrow planks that could break off or very wide planks that would require excessive sculpting to get them into place. Then there's the question of what to do with all that girth back aft; the planks must cover a great deal more "acreage" there than at the bow. Clearly this job will necessitate a more elaborate lining-off technique.

How many planks will it take?

Unfortunately, there is no hard-and-fast rule for determining how many strakes will be needed to plank a hull. Quite a few factors come in to play when planking, such as the changes in girth from the forward to the after section, the shape of the hull, and even what's available for planking lumber. Occasionally modern plans do indicate how many planks are necessary, but this is more likely an exception than the rule.

Probably the easiest way to deal with this dilemma is to do some research. Studying photographs of similar craft can go a long way toward unlocking the puzzle. Better yet, reconnoiter your local boatyards for boats of like kind. Be an industrial spy; take notes, make sketches. This information will be invaluable back in the shop.

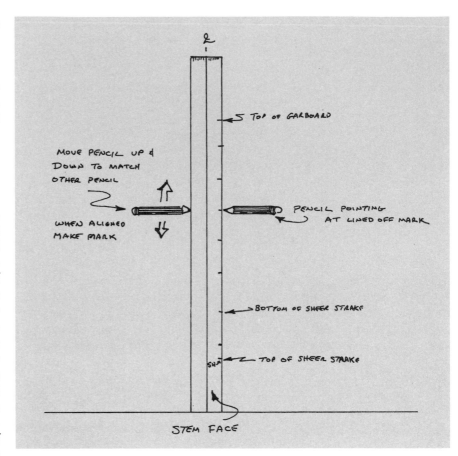

13-7: Using two pencils to eyeball the lining marks from one side of the stem to the other.

Taking care of the topsides

As with the Whitehall, the topside planks should appear to follow the sheer and be roughly the same widths. So, the first thing we want to do is make sure the sheerline is where we want it to be.

You say you marked the sheerline on the setup exactly where it was on the lofting, so it has to be okay? Well, maybe yes, maybe no. The sheerline that looked just dandy in two dimensions on the lofting board sometimes develops a mysterious hump in the forward quarter after the transition to 3-D. That's just another of those interesting surprises in the boatbuilding business.

At any rate, it's a good idea to wrap a flexible batten around your sheer marks and eyeball it from a few different angles to see if you like what you see.

After you have the sheer where you want it, remark the line with a pen so it doesn't escape. And, while you're in the neighborhood, mark the line of the bottom of the rubrail. This will come in handy soon, when you will be looking for the relative width of the sheerstrake.

Our next job is to determine a border line to work to. First, get out another batten that is wide enough to inhibit excessive edge-set, yet limber enough to follow the shape of the hull. Spruce is a good choice for this batten if you can get it. Now comes the artistic part. Using clamps, small nails, or a willing accomplice, temporarily hang this batten from roughly the load waterline at the bow to the load waterline at the stern.

The batten will hang below the waterline amidships—that's okay. At the stern it will be necessary to finesse the batten up and down until you find the place that will allow the bilge plank and the succeeding one to land on the transom and the sternpost rabbet without ending up as skinny "finger" planks that you can't fasten decently. After finding a location that looks as if it might work, tack the batten in place. Then go back to the bow and tack the batten there as well. Now you can move the batten up and down amidships until it pleases the eye and doesn't take on edge-set or otherwise become cranky. This involves a bit of creative tinkering, pulling nails and replacing them as you tweak the line of the batten.

After determining the location of the bilge batten, mark with a pencil the points where the batten hits the stem, the transom, and the molds. You'll most likely be able to hold firm to these marks back aft, but the chances are good that you will have to renegotiate them later in the bow.

Diminishing the topsides

Just as you did on the Whitehall, with a thin batten or a paper tape record the topside girths from the bottom of the rubrail to the top of the bilge batten at each of the molds, the transom, and the stem. Divide these girths by the number of planks, either mathematically or by using your trusty diminishing device, and record these divisions onto the setup. Spring your lining battens around the points and tack them into place.

13-8: Nibs at the hood ends of planks that enter the stem rabbet at a very low angle.

How do they look? This is a matter of baldfaced subjectivity: good lines are those that are optically pleasing to you. Are the planks defined by the battens visions of loveliness, flowing elegantly from the stem to the bow, or are they akin to a stack of bananas, chunky amidships with skinny, hard-to-fasten hood ends? If the former, you have it made and it's off to the bottom planks. If the latter, not to worry. Just try giving the hood ends a little more width by letting the battens drop a bit from the established marks at the stem rabbet while holding on to your marks at the stern and amidships. Stand back and appraise the situation from different angles. Usually a little bit of tinkering will do the trick. When you have the battens where you like them, mostly, mark the lines before they get away.

Below the waterline

Lining off the region below the waterline is done nearly all by eye. You will be dividing up a roughly triangular space, with the greatest girth aft of amidships, in which you must watch out for hood ends that are too narrow while keeping in mind efficient stock use and plank stability. But first, a few terms and considerations:

Nibbing planks

On many boats, the stem rabbet requires that the hood ends of the planks enter at a very low angle. Rather than having the upper side of the hood end extend into a long, wedge-shaped point that might be difficult to fasten or might split when a screw is driven through it, the plank is often notched or "nibbed" into the adjoining plank. (See Figure 13-8.)

Stealers

Stealers, despite their somewhat curiously larcenous appellation, are in reality transition planks. They are

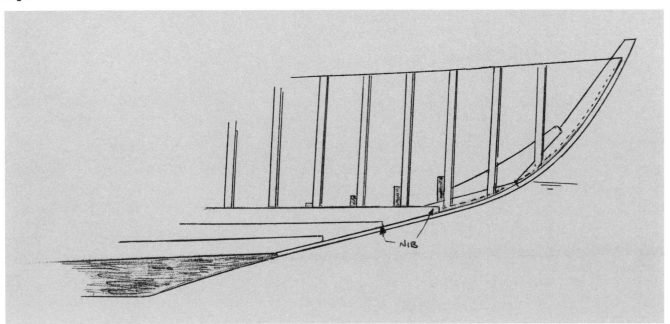

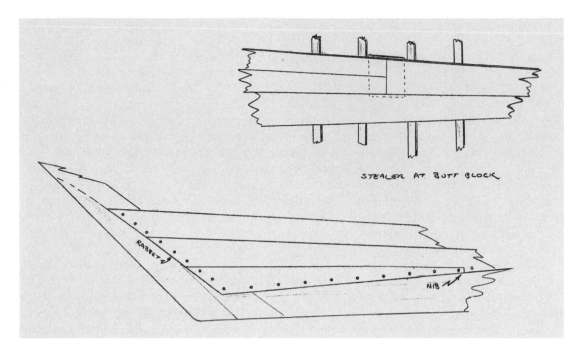

STEALER AT BUTT BLOCK

RABBET

NIB

generally short planks that are often used aft to split a troublesome too-wide plank into two more manageable, narrow planks. (See Figure 13-9.) An example of this might be when a very wide plank approaches a sharp turn in the bilge. It is to the builder's advantage to break that plank into two at a butt block to avoid excessive shaping.

A stealer can also be used to straighten out plank lines. Sometimes a triangular stealer is used with the pointed end nibbed into the adjoining plank. Occasionally, a stealer is used forward to consolidate two very narrow planks into one that would enter the rabbet with enough width to be properly fastened.

The garboard strake

To start lining out your garboard, look at the shape of the space you are trying to fill. You have determined how many planks you'll need to have and noted that there is considerably more girth to cover aft than forward. Also, very little shaping will be required to the lowest planks in the after section, as they will fit nearly flat into the rabbet at the sternpost. It should be possible to safely gain quite a bit of width aft, then to taper the plank forward until you nib the plank where it lands at the stem rabbet.

So, without further ado, wrap the batten around the setup at the proposed location, sight it for fairness, and clamp it in place. How does it look? Maybe it would look better if it were moved just a little? Fine, just loosen the clamps and skooch it over a bit. When the batten looks happy, tack it into place.

The broadstrakes

The broadstrakes are the planks closest to the garboard. After all the angst associated with the garboard, these should be a cinch to lay out. The concerns should be the same—wide planks back aft taper toward the stem as you continue to try to reduce the differences in girth. The chances are good that the hood ends will again want to be nibbed as they enter the rabbet. Again, when you are satisfied, affix your battens in place.

The proverbial light is at the end of the tunnel. Just a few more planks and you'll be done.

Finishing the job

You may be able to divide the remaining girths in a fashion similar to that of the topside planks. Then again, maybe not. Depending on your placement of the broadstrakes, you may want to tune your plank lines more to the specifics of the shape of the hull. For example, you might want a narrow plank or planks at the turn of the bilge; perhaps using a stealer back aft might be advantageous. At any rate, get those battens in place and give them the eye. Does it look like the boat you want to plank? Then mark the lines. You have work to do!

AN ALTERNATIVE

Are the plank lines still not as you'd like them to be? Consider carving a builder's half model onto which you can plot your plank lines. (See Chapter 24, The Builder's Half Model.) Paint the model flat white, draw in the molds, and sketch the proposed plank lines on the surface.

Topside planks look a little gross? Strakes too wide for that tuck at the transom? No problem. Just paint over the lines and start anew.

When you have the lines looking right, scale them off the model at the stem, transom, and molds, and record the points on the full-size setup. Fair the points with your battens, and you're off to the races.

14 • PLANKING STOCK

Before getting into the actual act of planking, let's further consider planking stock. While wood for planking in general has already been covered in Chapter 4, Wood for Boatbuilding, a couple of important matters remain: making short wood long, and repairing defects in planking stock that might otherwise be unsuitable for the purpose.

Getting wood of decent length for boatbuilding has been a challenge for ages. ("Blast!" Noah probably muttered, "This gopherwood is a half cubit too short!") Over time, as the great and noble trees of our forefathers have been cut, the situation has only become worse. To deal with this hardship, builders have come up with many creative solutions, one of the better being the mechanical scarf joint.

Scarfing, which dates back to the early Egyptian and Phoenician boatyards, joins timbers by means of matching bevels that are cut at the ends of the two pieces and fastened together. The fine ends are nibbed to avoid feather ends that can be weak in mechanical structures. The nibs also can act as a "parking brake" to prevent longitudinal slippage. For added security wedged keys or hooked scarfs often are employed. Well bedded and fastened mechanical scarf joints are quite strong and will provide yeoman service on heavy timbers, such as keels, clamps, etc.

SCARFED PLANKS VS. BUTT BLOCKS

Scarfs are all very well and good for massive keel timbers, you might say, but what about planks? This scarfing business seems like a lot of work and, besides, what's wrong with a butt block for making two short planks into a long one?

Although there's nothing wrong with using a butt block, there is certainly more to it than initially meets the eye. A well-made butt block can be a time-consuming bit of joinery, placement of the butt on the hull is always a consideration, and when you're all done with the block you still have to fit two individual planks. On the other hand, a plain or featheredge scarf, as opposed to a nibbed one, can be very easily manufactured in a near-production-line fashion. Gluing is a straightforward matter, and after the glued scarfs have been faired up, the plank can be spiled and cut from the joined wood as easily as if it were gotten out of naturally grown stock.

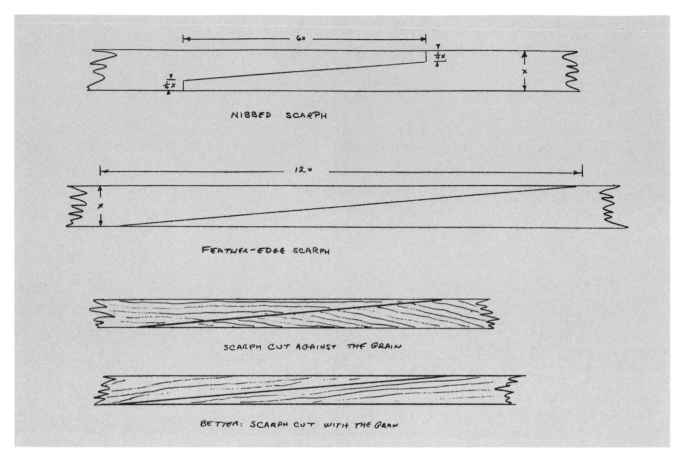

In addition, one of the bonuses of using scarfed wood for planking is that the builder can select the best parts of a couple of boards rather than resigning himself to dealing with the inconveniently placed knots, rot, or sapwood that invariably crop up in the otherwise "perfect" naturally curved stock.

THE ANATOMY OF A PLANK SCARF

The classic glued plank scarf should be made up of matching obliquely cut wedge-shaped slopes of roughly 12 to 1; in other words, the scarf should run 12 inches for every 1 inch of stock thickness. A properly glued scarf joined at this ratio should be as strong as the pieces of wood being joined. Although it is possible to get an adequate joint with a lesser ratio, say 8 to 1, there will be less glued surface. Therefore, the joint is unlikely to be as strong as a properly proportioned scarf and may even produce a "hard" spot when bent. The best joints should be cut with the grain rather than against it, and the joint surfaces should be smooth and true for better bonding (although thickened epoxy is much more forgiving of gaps than are older glues, such as resorcinol). Remember, when laying out the stock for your plank scarf, that the overall length will be decreased by the length of the scarf. In other words, two 10-foot boards 1-inch thick will only give you 19 feet of plank after they have been scarfed.

A CORDLESS HOMEMADE SCARFING DEVICE

Just how do boatbuilders get those uniform bevels, anyway? Even though the woodworking literature is chock full of dandy scarfing jigs that can either be purchased or made to accommodate a fancy power tool (likely as not, a plunge router) that you don't have, great results can be had with a homemade jig that uses hand tools, costs pennies, and takes about five minutes to manufacture.

The recipe

Find a piece of hardwood stock 18 inches long and 1 inch thick. Cut from the stock two 18-inch wedges that are 1 ½ inches thick on one end and taper to a point on the other. Find a softwood board 18 inches long by 12 inches wide. Line up the featheredges of the wedges to the edge of the board, align the wedges so they are roughly 10 inches apart and parallel to one another, and screw the wedges down to the board. That's the whole deal. (See Figure 14-2.)

The theory of this device is that the wedges, which are cut to a 12:1 ratio, act like inclined rails that control the final cuts of a long hand plane. The plane will be able to cut just so far and no farther. When the plane stops cutting it's time to stop.

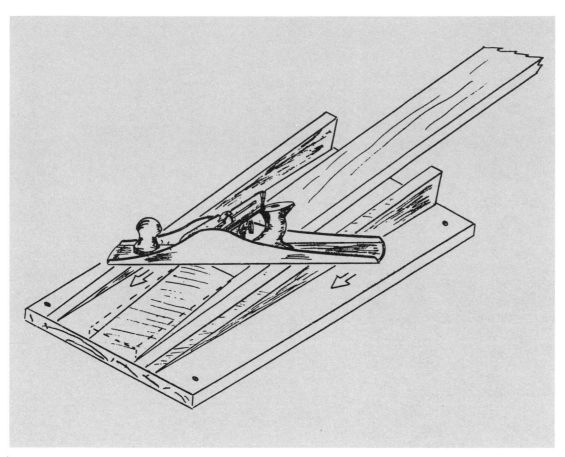

To use the rig

Simply line up the featheredge end of the jig to the edge of the workbench and screw it down. Then, insert the plank stock between the two wedges, line up the edge of the stock with the edge of the jig, and either clamp or screw the stock in place. Next, place a straightedge on the wedges and let it slide down until it contacts the plank stock. Draw a line across the stock and label it "end of scarf."

Next, staying clear of the pencil line, remove the bulk of the stock with a slick (a jumbo chisel), a round-bottom plane, or even a power planer. To finish the job, take a long hand plane (a Stanley #7 is a good choice), set the iron for a fine cut, and ride it down the rails diagonally. The bevel will be dead flat and end at the pencil line. Repeat the operation for the mating piece, and you're in business.

14-3: Stacking stock at a 12:1 ratio for scarfing with a portable power planer.

POWER SCARFING

For mass-production scarfing of straight dimensional stock for rails, battens, spars, and such, the hand-held power planer is a boon. Power may be involved, but the technique is decidedly low tech.

Starting from the edge of the bench, stack your pieces of square-ended stock, one atop the other, staggering each subsequent piece back from the leading edge of the one below at a 12 to 1 ratio, producing a series of steps. (See Figure 14-3.) For example, if the stock is 1-inch thick, the setback would be 12 inches. For ¾-inch stock, the setback would be 9 inches. For ½-inch stock, a 6-inch setback will do the trick.

Anchor the stepped stock to the bench to prevent movement, then use the portable power planer to knock the edges off the steps, gradually turning them into a continuous ramp. Finish off the job by using a long hand plane to true up the "ramp." Check for any crown or hollow with a straightedge (such as a 4-foot level). The

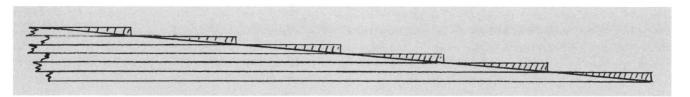

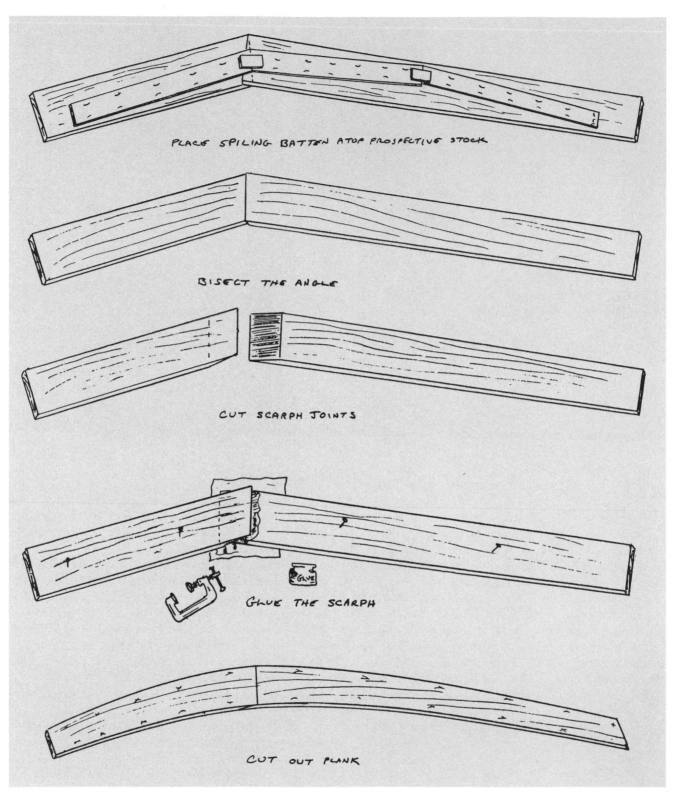

PLACE SPILING BATTEN ATOP PROSPECTIVE STOCK

BISECT THE ANGLE

CUT SCARPH JOINTS

GLUE THE SCARPH

CUT OUT PLANK

square cut ends will act as indicators as to whether your work is straight and true. When done, unclamp your stack and you'll have a series of pieces with all the same bevel, ready to be glued and clamped.

A DOGLEG SCARF

When scarfing planks that have a lot of shape, your assembled plank stock may have to be "doglegged" to accommodate the sweep. If so, that means the scarf must be cut and assembled at an angle.

To determine the angle for a dogleg scarf, take the completed spiling batten from the boat (we'll be covering how to create the spiling in the next chapter) and lay it on top of the two pieces of planking stock to be used, adjusting the pieces until the batten is covering all clear wood. The two planks will form an angle relative to one another. Roughly bisect this angle and cut it onto both pieces to be scarfed. When the stock is placed in the scarfing jig, it should be slightly askew, but the angle at the end of the stock will be square with the end of the "feather end" of the jig. Fasten down the stock and plane as before, and you'll have an angled scarf. Do the same for the second piece.

Achtung! Make sure to bevel the correct side of the stock (either the top or the bottom) to avoid having the "dogleg" embarrassingly pointed in the wrong direction. When done, assemble the scarf dry, and lay the spiling batten on top and check for fit. Still okay? Then off to the bench to set up for gluing.

GETTING READY TO GLUE

Assemble your stock on the bench and place a piece of polyethylene plastic under the joint to ensure that you'll be able to remove the plank after the glue has cured. Clamp the first piece to the bench and check one last time with the spiling batten for alignment. Make index marks as insurance against slippage. Be sure that you have all the clamps to do the job. After making a dry run and determining that everything looks right, break out the epoxy glue!

EPOXY GLUING TECHNIQUES

Nowadays, epoxy is probably the adhesive of choice for gluing plank scarfs. It's great stuff: waterproof, relatively inexpensive, forgiving of non-Chippendale joinery, and almost foolproof when properly applied. But if the builder attempts to cut a corner here, skip a step there, there will be great opportunity for things to go wrong—including something as disconcerting as having a scarf joint fail after the plank has been installed on the boat. To avoid an unwelcome surprise, let's take a moment to review some procedures that make the epoxy work.

Getting the mixture right

For reasons best known to adhesive pundits, not all epoxies have the same mixing ratios between the resin and the hardener. Indeed, ratios can, and do, vary within a single manufacturer's line of products. What to do? Check out the company literature and the label on the jug for the proper ratio and never vary it, as a weak and incomplete cure can result. After metering your potion out in the correct proportions, give it a good, thorough mixing. We are talking chemistry, after all; the idea is to get all those molecules working with one another to provide the best bond.

Getting the shop temperature right

The pot life and working time of mixed resin depend a great deal on the formulation of the hardener and the ambient temperature in the workshop, and the requirements vary from one glue manufacturer to another. One company might suggest that their product (with the proper hardener) may be easily utilized from the Arctic to the Congo. Another might specify that only normal room temperature will do and, in the event you may not be able to achieve that, will offer plans for a homemade autoclave powered by light bulbs. If in doubt about the specifications for your glue, it would be wise to consult with the manufacturer to avoid waiting weeks for the scarfed plank to cure in your igloo.

Watch for joint contamination!

Epoxy works best on joints that have not been contaminated by wax, oil, grease, or other slippery substances. How does a freshly cut surface become besmirched? Working habits are a prime suspect. Do you habitually wax the bottom of your plane? Is wax paper the parting agent of choice in your shop? Are you planning to glue up directly after changing the wheel bearings on the truck? 'Nuf said.

The dreaded glue starvation

Straight epoxy, mixed without added thickeners, is formulated to be thin to allow it to penetrate deeply into the wood fibers for a strong bond. This is a wonderful characteristic, except when gluing up a scarf joint. A scarf joint is by nature composed of large areas of end-grain in soft wood and can act like a sponge, drawing most of the thin glue right out of the joint, leaving little left to do the actual bonding. This can lead to failure of the joint. What to do?

A technique that seems to work well is the double-spread, or two-step attack. First, thoroughly saturate the two sides of the scarf with mixed, thin, straight epoxy. Next, spread the mating surfaces with a batch of premixed resin thickened with microfibers or colloidal silica (available from your friendly epoxy supplier). These additives, when blended into the pre-mixed epoxy, give the adhesive the body it needs to fill gaps and not run out of the joint before it cures. After the joint has been filled with this amalgamation, it is ready to be closed up and clamped.

The over-clamp syndrome

Many boatbuilders are graduates of the Resorcinol School of Herculean Clamping. If a little pressure is good, then lots has to be better, yes? In this case, no. Epoxy laminations require only contact pressure—just

14-5: Scarfing plywood with a portable power planer.

give way, or the wood? Likely as not, the glue joint is tougher than the wood. If that is the case, you're in business. Does the break occur in the joint? Give those manufacturers a call! They all have their service folks on hand whose business it is to solve customer problems, and they should have a solution for you in no time flat. The odds are good that when all is said and done you'll find this plank-scarfing business a mighty handy addition to your bag of tricks.

SCARFING PLYWOOD

Plywood can be beveled by hand for scarfing. The primary requirements are a flat bench, a sharp plane, and plenty of patience.

Align the panel to the edge of the bench and clamp it securely. Using a straightedge, draw an end-of-bevel line onto the surface of the panel. For tools, while all that is really necessary is a low-angle block plane and a longer bench plane (such as a foreplane), a hand-held power planer will definitely speed your work along. Plane from the end-of-bevel line to the lower edge of the panel, taking care not to develop crowns or hollows in the work. The line of the laminations will help you here as, when done, they should remain dead straight. Any undulations in the line will indicate that the bevel is out of whack. The glue lines in the plywood will quickly dull the edge of the plane iron, so keep that sharpening stone handy.

If a number of panels need to be scarfed, they can be stacked and hand power planed as described above.

An alternative to freehand planing is to use one of the aftermarket power tool attachments that allow you to cut accurate scarfs quickly and repeatedly. The Gougeon Brothers sell The Scarfer, which is a guide that can be affixed to the bottom of a hand-held circular saw. When run along a straightedge, the guide allows the saw to cut a scarf into the plywood. Another such device is a guide plate from John Henry, Inc., that can be attached to a hand power planer; the guide holds the planer true to the angle of the scarf.

Gluing a plywood scarf

Because of the extreme width of a plywood scarf, extra care is in order to ensure that the pieces are properly aligned and anchored. Fit the two pieces together and draw a line at the top shoulder of the bevel on the bottom sheet to index the fit. Check that there is no overlap or hollows (gaps) in the joint. Once again, a dry run of your procedure is in order.

If gluing a plywood scarf with epoxy, relatively little clamping pressure is necessary. Often a wooden strip placed atop the joint (with plastic underneath), with fasteners driven through to the underlying wood bench or floor, will do the trick. Another method of clamping less wide joints is to use a slightly bowed clamping block that

enough to hold everything in place. Over-clamping can pre-stress the structure and squeeze out most of the epoxy, again creating a glue-starved joint. It therefore makes sense to be circumspect with your clamping force. Also, using a hardwood or heavy plywood clamping pad that covers approximately the area of the joint will go a long way toward distributing clamping pressure over more area. (Don't forget to put an anti-stick polyethylene sheet between the block and the plank!)

Give the joint time to cure

Although the scarf may appear to have cured overnight, probably it won't have. Epoxy resin tends to continue curing over several days, gradually building to its full strength. Prudence calls for leaving the clamps in place for as long as possible, or at least placing the joint in an area of least twist to avoid prematurely stressing it.

Evaluate your technique

Try a little scientific experimentation. Glue up a few sacrificial scarf joints and allow them to cure. Then clamp them in a vise and do some destructive testing. Twist one joint into a corkscrew with a monster pipe wrench until it snaps. Hang another over the edge of the bench and pile on the weights until the plank breaks. Does the joint

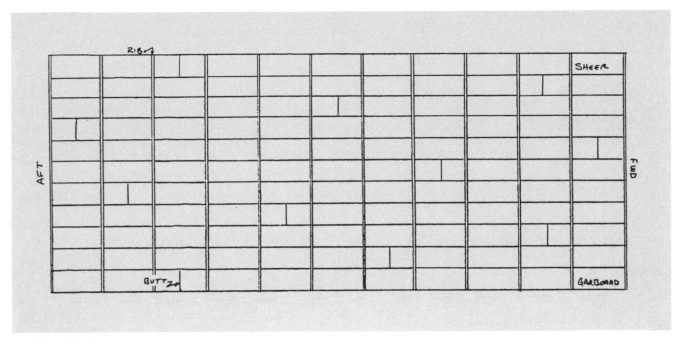

14-6: A possible layout of plank butts following the Rule of Threes.

is set over the joint, with the crown of the curve touching the center of the joint. C-clamps placed at each end of the joint will then draw down the raised edges of the block to the joint. (Experiment first, to make sure this rig works as advertised.) Don't forget to lay plastic between the panels and the bench!

BUTT BLOCKS AND THE RULE OF THREES

Although the scarf joint fastened with modern glue (especially epoxy) has obviated much of the need for the butt block, there are still situations where it is still the best remedy. Whether butt blocks are used because the shape of the hull demands it, or because a replica requiring a traditional look is being built, or because the builder is something of a neo-Luddite, distrustful of adhesives, they can be counted on to give years of yeoman service if fitted properly.

Occasionally one hears tales of frugal homebuilders who intend to build a 20-foot boat on the cheap. In order to save money, our thrifty heroes order an entire truckload of 12-footers that they butt right smack in the middle of the boat only to discover later that they have invented the zipper.

Alas, like just about everything these days, there are rules to be followed when using a butt block. The buttblock joint creates an inherently weak spot in a plank. When you consider that a butt block is basically just a wooden gusset holding two reluctant planks in place with a handful of fastenings, it is prudent not to have a whole nest of butt blocks all living in one region. Hence the general Rule of Threes—i.e., that butt blocks should be staggered by at least three frame bays, or three adjoining planks. The rule may not eliminate the weaknesses of butt blocks, but at least it diffuses the effects.

Besides following the Rule of Threes, you should try to locate the butts in areas of least twist in the plank, as there will be much less stress on the joint, not to mention your disposition.

Other considerations

Curiously, part of the appeal of the butt block to the prospective builder is its apparent simplicity in design. Indeed, the contrivance is usually perceived as almost an afterthought—merely a flat, rectangular plate of wood that can be knocked out in about 30 seconds and pretty much be stuck anywhere. Well, 't ain't so, McGee! There's a bit more to it than that.

The block should be made of a well-seasoned hardwood, such as oak, locust, or mahogany, and should be at least as thick as the bent frames. It must be cut to length to land between a pair of frames where the planks butt and shaped to snugly fit the curve of the hull and the planking—both fore-and-aft and top-to-bottom. It should be wide enough to overlap the adjoining planks a bit (at least ½ inch, top and bottom), as it picks up strength from its generous neighbors, which also help keep the butted plank fair.

The design of the block should take into consideration the inevitable rot-promoting fresh water that will want to collect on top of it. This uninvited liquid could come from leaks, or merely from condensation. Whatever its source, you don't need fresh water hanging around, being a general nuisance. There are a couple of ways to approach this. One is to chamfer the plank side of the block and fit it flush with the frames. (See Figure 14-7.) The triangular limbers so produced do a pretty good job

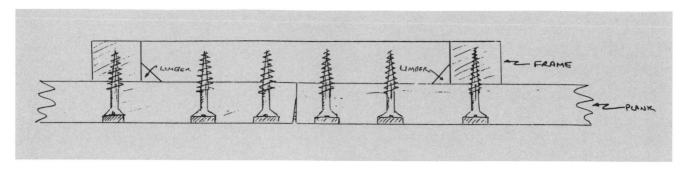

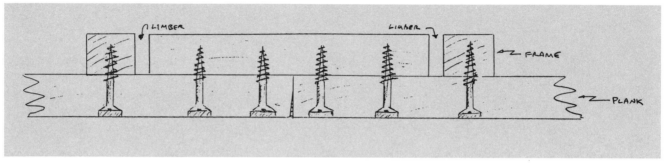

14-7 (top): Cross section of a chamfered-corner butt block.

14-8 (bottom): Cross section of a free-standing butt block.

of draining water as long as they don't get plugged up with trash or bedding compound. A more elegant method is to create gaps for the water to run down by, making the block shorter than the distance between the frames. (See Figure 14-8.) Some persnickety builders go so far as to cut a radius and bevel the top edge of the block to eliminate the possibility of standing water. (See Figure 14-9.)

Installing the block

After producing this masterpiece, it's a good idea to protect your investment by giving it a good shot of your favorite wood preservative. After a thorough anointment of this, the plank side should be coated with bedding compound. I prefer the good old-fashioned boatyard bedding compound for this chore. Although the newfangled synthetic flexible adhesives have many fine qualities, reparability is not one of them; once that stuff has cured, nothing short of blasting powder is going to break the butt block loose from the plank.

☞ Unacceptable Planking Stock Defects

Sapwood or spring wood

Sapwood is the live wood closest to the bark when the tree is felled. It is weak, absorbs moisture, and is prone to rot. It is generally easy to identify, especially after planing the boards, as it is often a different color from the good areas of the stock.

Large areas of rot

Rot can often be found migrating out from a black or rotten knot, or lying in the center of the log. Look for discoloration, and plumb it with a pen knife. Any stock that has rot that cannot be readily cut out and completely eradicated should be rejected.

Large knots

Avoid large knots, especially those that will lie in the narrowest part of a plank or any part of a plank that must take a good bend.

Cracks and shakes

These weaken the wood, are invitations to rot, and can cause leaks.

Spike knots

These are actually cross sections of knots or branches that extend across the surface of the stock. While usually not rotten, they weaken the structure of the wood, as they break the continuous grain and act as hard places when the plank is bent.

Warps, cups, and twists

Wood that is so distorted that the faces are no longer true planes can't be properly worked and will always cause problems.

Large pitch pockets

Pockets of pitch can be indicators of fiber separation and can weaken the wood.

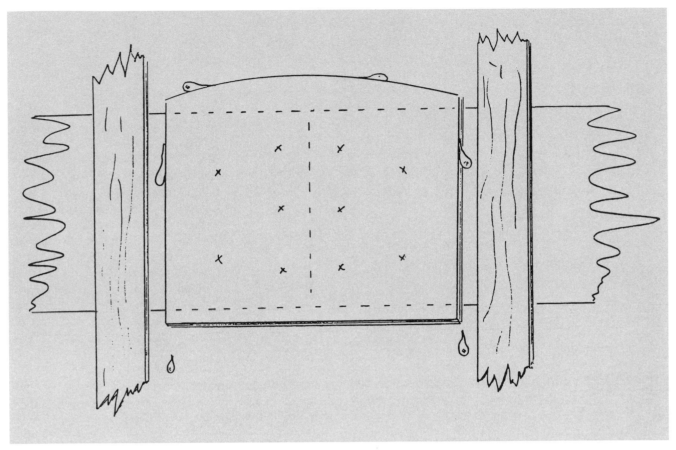

Generally, the same type and caliber of fastening used to attach the plank to the frames is also used to fasten the butt block to the plank ends. A common fastening schedule is 10 per butt—five fastenings on each side of the joint, with a row of three closest to the joint and a pair farther out.

And there you have it. Well, almost. Check to see that you have put a caulking seam on the butt ends of your planks. Okay? Then onward!

REPAIRING DEFICIENT PLANKING STOCK

The days—if there ever were such days—when a builder could cavalierly sniff and dismiss a piece of planking stock simply because it contained a small blemish or a knot are over. Good stock is scarce enough as it is, and expensive, too, without making perfection the sole selection criterion.

With today's high-strength waterproof glues and the proper techniques, rot can be exorcised, bad knots can be made better, and damage can be invisibly mended—within reason. We are talking about repair here, not resurrection. In repairing planks, as in most things, discretion should be exercised. There is some stock that cannot be used in boatbuilding and would be better used for sheathing a goat barn.

What are we talking about here are minor character flaws—mechanical damage to the edge of a piece, a small knot that is punky on top but solid underneath, a solid but loose knot (basically a dead branch that the tree grew around) that can be easily pushed out, and very light and localized surface rot that is not so pernicious or extensive as to weaken the board in any way. A small, solid knot, while troubling to purists, is acceptable—just try to keep the edge of a plank from running through it.

On the other hand, stock that has extensive damage or is of questionable merit is better treated by lopping off the afflicted area (if the impairment is localized) and scarfing in a new section, or rejecting the piece altogether and substituting better quality stock. These repairs, when made, can be done either on the bench or on the boat.

DUTCHMAN OR GRAVING PIECE

An area with a small, shallow (¼ inch or so) patch of rot can be repaired with a piece of inlaid planking stock, shaped like a diamond, longer than it is wide, called a dutchman or graving piece. As it is easier to make the receiving mortise to match the diamond than the other way around, cut the diamond first and then plane a slight taper into the edges—somewhat similar to a bathtub plug. Place the diamond over the afflicted area and trace

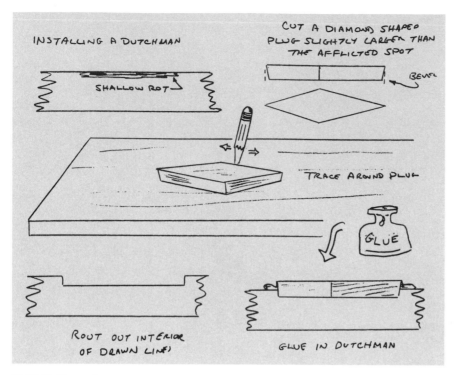

14-10: Making and installing a dutchman.

So you say that after you hung the plank on the boat you found a couple of loose knots that popped right out when you pushed on them? Well, good riddance. Better you found them now than later. To repair them, break out your brace and a conical plumber's reamer—the type that resembles a jumbo, narrow countersink. Poke the reamer into the knot hole and give it a few cranks, cleaning out any ambient bark. Then, with a penknife, whittle a tapered plug from scrap planking stock to fit the reamed hole. When the fit is snug, saturate the hole and the plug with unthickened epoxy, then apply a dollop of thickened epoxy and insert the plug firmly. (No need to hammer in the plug—you only risk splitting the plank.) After the glue has cured, trim off the plug inside and out.

A trifle barbaric, you say? Mais non, mon ami! Actually, the tapered hole provides greater gluing surface than one that is parallel sided, the whittled plug has no end-grain to soak up glue, the widest part of the plug is on the outside of the plank, the job is done after the plank has been hung so there is no bending stress, and the work doesn't involve an electrical cord.

Crescent patch

For a minor repair to the edge of a plank, you might consider a crescent-shaped patch. Start by cutting an elliptical patch and tracing the shape onto the offending plank edge. With a spokeshave shape the area to receive the patch. Apply glue as above and clamp the patch in place. After the glue has cured, trim the patch to size.

Laminated patch

The laminated patch, a variation on the crescent patch, is also good for making a minor repair in the edge of a plank. With a batten, spring a small elliptical curve around the area requiring repair and scribe in the shape with a pencil. As before, hollow out the area with a spokeshave. Then mill up a couple of thin pieces of planking stock for laminates, butter everything up with glue, and, with clamps, draw the laminates down into the hollowed-out area. After the glue sets up, trim the patch to shape. This method works well for making repairs in rounded areas as well, such as damaged toerails and spars.

around it with a pencil. Then using a flat-bottomed mortising (plunge-cutting) bit in a router, remove the stock from the middle of the area in question. (Rot must be totally eradicated down to good clean wood. Don't depend on your glue to penetrate and encapsulate any questionable areas.) Then, with a sharp chisel, clean up the edges of the mortise.

After cutting the mortise, check the fit with the dutchman. If the fit is good, file a small relief weep hole in the edge of the patch to allow a little glue to leak by and relieve the hydraulic pressure that will build up when clamping. To get around glue starvation, saturate the area with adhesive; if using epoxy, thicken the mix with microfibers. Clamp the dutchman in place. After the glue has cured, the excess patch can be trimmed off with a saw and planed smooth with a block plane.

When planking with a piece of stock that has been fitted with a dutchman, if possible place the dutchman-side of the plank on the inside of the hull; this will keep the dutchman in compression.

Plugging a knot

A quick repair to a basically sound knot with a porous or punky end can be made with a round plug cut with a plug cutter. The bad area can be drilled out with a Forstner bit; just bore deep enough to get into sound stock and glue in a plug of the proper size. Boring all the way through the stock and gluing in a circular plug is not a good idea, however, as the excessive amount of end-grain exposed on both the hole and the plug increases the possibility of glue starvation and potential failure.

15 • CARVEL PLANKING

Carvel, or smooth-seam, planking is probably the most universal system for covering a hull. From the simple flatiron skiff to the complex Friendship Sloop and the bulbous catboat, carvel planking can be counted on to do the job.

Sounds good? It is, though as with anything else, carvel has its intricacies, not the least of which involve the garboards—the two planks on each side of the hull adjacent to the keel. (To avoid confusion, I will discuss one garboard on one side of the hull; obviously, the garboard on the other side of the hull will be a mirror image of it.)

THE GARBOARD

For the home builder, the garboard strake is the hobgoblin of planking. Indeed, fitting it is generally approached with roughly the same enthusiasm as that for a root canal. Horrifying tales of ill-fitting, too-short, over-clamped, and broken planks abound. Just what exactly is the deal about this plank?

Well, admittedly, the garboard can be problematic, even a bit of a challenge at times, but its sinister reputation is somewhat overblown. The qualities that set the garboard apart from the other planks and makes it interesting are shape and twist, and the need for accuracy when dealing with them. Unlike almost all the other planks, there is little room for cheating on the fit of the garboard. The plank must snugly follow a shapely rabbet along the entire length of the keel and onto the stem. To compound the issue, the strake then must make a corkscrew twist as it approaches the stem, defying easy checking of the fit. On the bright side, as the garboard is usually the first plank to be hung, it rarely needs to be beveled.

The secret to success in getting out a garboard is the use of patterns and the accurate recording of data. This is not the job for the free spirit or abstract artist—what we need for this job is a good old-fashioned tax accountant and surveyor.

Establish the top edge

Begin by establishing the upper edge (closest to the sheer) of the garboard plank with your lining-off batten. This line should be as fair as possible, as it sets the pace for all the planks to come. Having established it, you are ready to make a pattern or spiling batten.

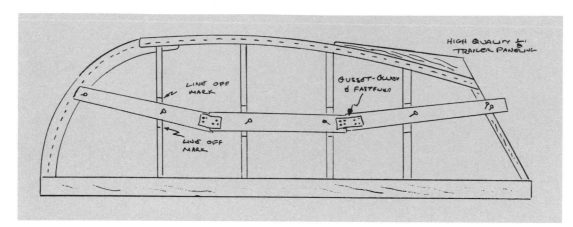

The theory of spiling

The theory of spiling is that the builder can generate a plank by first capturing the perimeter of the plank's shape on the boat. This can be done by recording a series of reference distance points onto a long template, or spiling batten. That template can then be removed from the boat and tacked to a piece of planking stock. By reversing the process, the distance coordinates can be reestablished as a series of dots on the planking stock. The builder need only connect the dots with a long, flexible batten, draw the line, and, Eureka!, he has the shape of the plank. All that is left to be done is to cut out the plank on the bandsaw, and plane in any necessary bevel and shape.

The spiling batten

The spiling batten is a flexible pattern affixed to the boat with either clamps or tacks, onto which the builder can record the length, width, and curvature of a plank. Think of it as an undulating reference table that is as long as the plank, on which the dimensions of the plank are recorded where they occur.

15-2: Using a compass to spile the garboard.

The batten is made up of thin strips of wood that are narrower than the actual width of the plank. While almost any thin wood stock works, a good choice is recycled ⅛-inch plywood paneling. It is uniform in thickness, it resists springing (or edge-set), and best of all, it is cheap.

Resistance to edge-set is a big plus. Many of the difficulties that builders have with their spiling can be traced back not to incorrect technique in recording information but to the recording of that information on a funky spiling batten—usually one that was sprung into place by a thrifty builder in a vain attempt to save money or time. When the falla-cious batten is removed from the boat, it will straighten out, and the new plank developed from this batten, even if it has all the right dimensions, will be shaped all wrong. To avoid this unwelcome (but interesting) surprise, piece up your batten right on the boat with two or more shorter sections, rather than one long, floppy piece. Then splice the pieces together with plywood gussets while the batten is still in place. (See Figure 15-1.) Adding a little glue under the gussets will also help deter the "hinged" batten phenomenon.

Spiling with a compass

Although there are a myriad of implements used to spile planks, one of the most popular is the pencil compass. The pencil compass method uses one of those dusty concepts you learned in high school geometry class: If you strike an arc with a compass, then by swinging two more arcs—using any two locations on the first arc as a starting point—the intersection of the two arcs will be at the fixed point from which you drew the first arc.

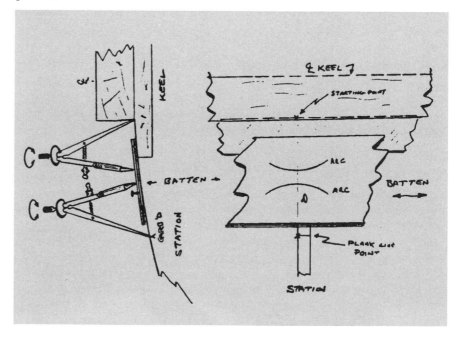

To apply this Euclidian marvel to spiling the lower edge of the garboard, simply set your compass to a convenient distance and, starting from the middle line of the rabbet in the keel, move along the length of the boat, swinging a series of arcs onto the spiling batten. (See Figure 15-2.) How many? It depends. The more complex the shape, the more points you need. Then, bring the compass down to the lined-off marks on the frames and/or stations and swing those arcs up onto the batten as well.

Remove the spiling batten from the boat and tack it to the planking stock. Then, from the series of arcs on the pattern, swing your intersecting arcs onto the planking stock. (See Figure 15-3.)

A caveat: Do not change the compass setting while spiling the plank, as it will produce perplexing inaccuracies that you don't need.

Yet another way

When spiling the keel rabbet, sometimes you'll find yourself working in quarters that are too tight to use the compass. One way out of this dilemma is to manufacture a notched wooden "spiling block" to help you capture the desired information. One end of the block rides along the middle line of the rabbet, while a pencil rides against the other side of the block—scribing a line on the batten. (See Figure 15-4.)

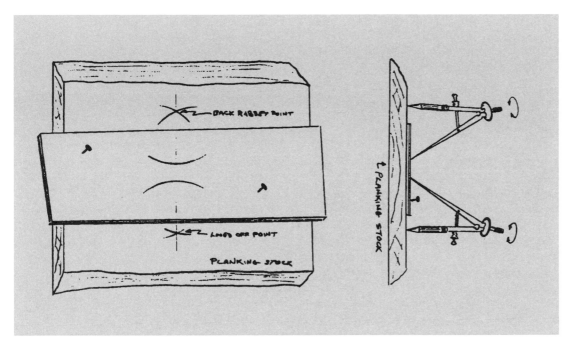

15-3: Spiling with a compass.

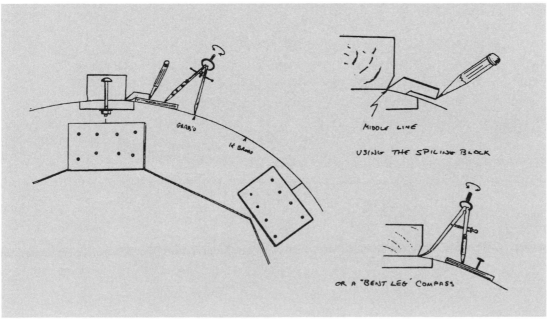

15-4: Spiling the keel rabbet.

☞ When It Absolutely, Positively Has to Be Right

Most spiling techniques are prone to small inaccuracies due to worn pencils, failure to keep the scribing compass perpendicular, or miscues in recording measurements. These erroneous readings are usually of small concern, easily corrected by fairing a batten past a misplaced point. If the line is off a bit, a little judicious planing here and there can fix the problem and the difference can be made up on the next plank. Occasionally, however, there are times when you will need a higher degree of accuracy, such as when making a shutter plank or if you are fitting a very expensive piece of wood and want to get it right the first time. At times like this, the divider/grid method shines.

Divider/grid spiling affords a high degree of accuracy, because instead of requiring a pencil compass to draw intersecting arcs, it employs fixed dividers that record the spiled distances on a grid line. The accurate pinpoints of the divider eliminate the sometimes ambiguous readings from intersecting arcs or any discrepancies caused by worn or broken pencils. Here's how it works:

As above, tack a spiling batten in place. With a straightedge (the rule from a combination square works well), draw a series of lines on the batten that are aligned with an edge of the frames and/or molds. These lines form your grid.

Next, lock your dividers to a constant opening. At the first grid line, place one point of the dividers at the intersection of the line and the plank apex, swing the other point down to the grid line on the spiling batten, and poke a small hole into the batten and circle it. From the circle draw an arrow pointing to the plank and label it with the number of the frame. (See Figure 15-A.)

Then, follow the grid line down to the point where

15-A: Make grid lines by tracing one edge of each frame onto the spiling batten. Use dividers to pick up and record the spiled distances on the grid lines.

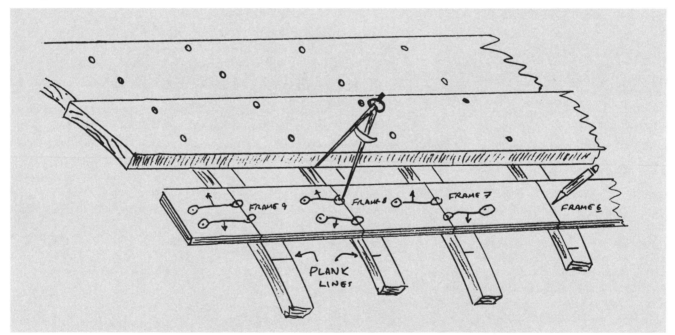

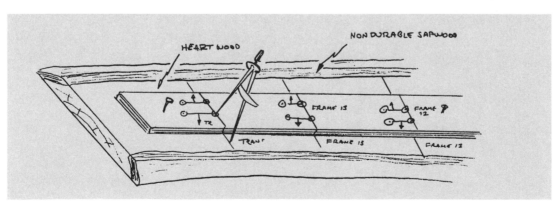

15-B: Lay the spiling batten on the planking stock, carry the grid lines onto the stock, and transfer the points with the dividers. Note that the spiling batten is on the "outside of tree" side of the planking stock.

it encounters the lined-off location. Place one leg of the dividers there and swing the other leg up to the grid line on the spiling batten. Again, poke a small hole into the batten and draw a circle around it. And as before, draw an arrow, this time pointing to the lined-off point. Repeat this operation at each grid line, then remove the batten from the boat.

To transfer the spiled marks to the planking stock, tack the spiling batten to the stock. Align a straightedge with the "grid lines" on the spiling batten and carry those lines onto the planking stock by marking both above and below the batten in pencil. Reverse the process with the dividers: place one leg on the point in the circled hole, swing the other leg in the direction of the arrow to the grid line on the planking stock, and poke a small hole and circle it. (See Figure 15-B.) Do this for each of the two marks on each grid line, then spring a fairing batten through the points and draw the line!

Tedious? Sort of. Accurate? You bet.

When transferring the line to the planking stock, reverse the process. Follow the scribed line with one side of the block and ride the pencil on the other side, transferring the line to the planking stock.

Scribing the hood-end pattern

Although it is possible to generate the hood end of the plank by spiling, there is so much shape in this area that the chances of getting the shape wrong are better than average. This problem gets worse on a double-ender, such as a peapod, where miscuing by just a little can make all the difference between whether a plank fits or does not. The solution is to make a pattern that tightly fits the hood-end rabbet by scribing the shape onto a piece of plywood with a pencil compass. (Remember, when scribing with a compass or dividers, always keep the points vertical in relation to one another.) After you have cut and fit the hood-end pattern, attach it to the spiling batten with a gusset. (See Figure 15-5.)

Transferring the data to the planking stock

No matter what spiling method you use, before removing the batten from the boat, check one last time to see if you have forgotten anything. Have you picked up all the reference points, including the stations, and labeled them? If the boat has a transom, have you noted it on the batten? How about those gussets connecting the strips and the hood-end pattern? Are they rugged enough to hold everything together?

Okay? Then off with the batten, and let's go shopping for a plank.

Choosing the stock

One of the under-appreciated qualities of a pattern (the spiling batten included) is that it allows the builder to make the most efficient use of the construction stock. Pull a few likely suspects from the planking pile and lay the batten on top of each. Look to see if the stock has enough sweep for your garboard. Can you avoid the sapwood? Are there any defects that could weaken the plank? Any rot?

When you find the plank that has your garboard hiding inside, tack or clamp your spiling batten down to it so it can't shift. Now you are ready to transfer your data to the planking stock.

Trace around the hood end, and record the rest of the spiling points onto the plank. Make sure all this information is well labeled on the planking stock. And don't forget to note any references, such as stations, frames, or the end of the transom. You'll be glad you did. When that's all squared away, you can remove the spiling batten. Its time to connect the dots.

Springing the marking batten

To join the marks on your stock, you'll be needing a long, clear strip of stiff (but flexible) softwood, also called a batten. Spring this marking batten through your intersecting arcs on the planking stock and onto the hood-end pattern. Hold it in place with small nails tacked alongside. Avoid driving the nails into the batten or through your marks.

View the batten with perspicacity. Any untidy lumps

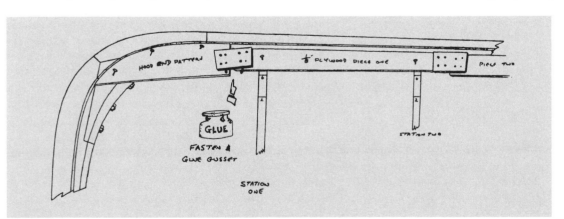

15-5: A pieced-up spiling batten with a hood-end pattern for the garboard in place.

or quirky bumps? Yes? Try pulling the nail at that location and see if the line fairs out. The chances are good that there will be a few cranky points out of the mainstream. That's the whole idea of using the batten—to winnow those maladjusted points for a long, fair sweep from stem to stern. When it looks right, draw the line.

A possible exception, or what's that dip doing there?

You say the batten makes a lovely fair line all the way along the rabbet from keel right on to the stem. It fairs through every point. Well, almost every point. There is this anomaly right about where the stem joins the keel—kind of a dip or hollow. Probably just a bad point or two. Best to fair by those malcontents and stick with the smooth line.

Hold on partner! Not so fast. The chances are good, in this case, that the dip really is there. Trust your spiling ("Trust but verify"—Ronald Reagan), even though the plank may not look exactly as you may have pictured it. Many garboards on traditional craft do have a dip where the plank starts to bend quickly into the stem rabbet.

Cutting out and shaping the plank

Stay to the outside of the line, because, as the old-timer says, it's a whole lot easier to plane down to the line than to add wood to a miscut plank. Finish the job using a jack or fore plane for the sweep and a block plane for the hood end, planing to the line and square with the sides of the plank. Then plane in any necessary hollow on the inside face of the plank to fit the curvature of the hull.

FITTING THE PLANK TO THE BOAT

After you have created your garboard, all that remains is to affix it to the boat. (See also Hanging Planks, below.) The garboard is a sportier plank than most to get on to the boat because of the twist necessary for it to land properly in the stem rabbet. The only sure way to get the requisite bend in the plank is to heat it, either with steam or a therapeutic hot water compress, to make it more pliable. After the plank has been bent and is cool, the wood will take enough of a set to allow final fitting and fastening.

Steaming is the most effective way to heat the wood. The drawback is that you must be highly organized, with all your clamps, pads, wedges, et al. —and maybe a helper—ready at hand when you wrestle the plank into submission immediately after the plank leaves the steam box. A more leisurely approach, especially for a builder working alone, is the topical application of heat right where you want by using boiling water and rags.

Here's how to use boiling water: Clamp the plank to the boat, roughly in the position where it is to be fastened. Wrap in rags the portion of the plank that is to be twisted in and slide a sheet of plastic behind it. Bring a caldron of water to a boil, don your insulated mitts, and pour a charge of water over the rags, thoroughly saturating them. Fold the plastic over the rags to keep the moisture in and hold the plastic in place with a spring clamp. Five minutes later, unwrap the plastic, reannoint the rags with boiling water, and rewrap the plastic. Repeat the drill every five minutes or so for about a half hour. Then pull the rags off, twist the hood end, now licorice soft, into the stem rabbet, and clamp it securely. Let 'er cool a bit, and the plank is ready for last-minute fitting.

After the fitting has been finished, all that remains is to fasten the garboard in place, starting at the hood end and working aft. Garboards should be fastened to both the floors and the frames when possible. And don't forget the bedding compound!

☞ Drain Plug

After a small boat has been in the water for awhile and is then hauled out, one often sees a harried owner clambering about the bilge attempting to scoop or pump out those final dregs of water. This healthful exercise would have been unnecessary if the builder had taken a few moments to properly install a garboard drain. Relatively inexpensive, this useful bit of plumbing will pay for itself quickly with the convenience it affords and earn the boatowner's lasting gratitude for your thoughtfulness.

THE REMAINING PLANKS

One of the beauties of carvel planking is that it can be easily varied in its width (or you can even add a stealer) to make up large differences in girth. Unlike a lapstrake

☞ Planing the Edge Square: The Ten-Second Rabbet Plane

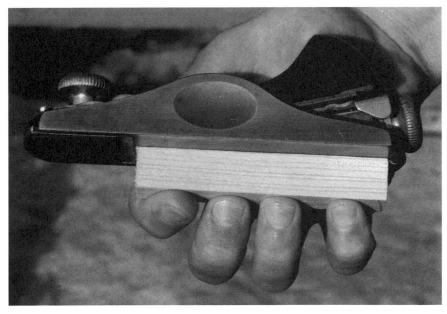

Curiously, one of the more challenging tasks while planking is keeping the square edge of a plank square when planing down to the line. Part of the problem is that light planking affords such a narrow base for the plane to ride on that it tends to roll, even if you are using a diminutive block plane. What to do?

You can assiduously check your work with a square every few moments. Or, you can dig out your old rabbet plane with the fence, set it up, and attack the job. Or you can simply grab a small square-cut block and, while you work, hold it tightly to the sole of your block plane, which is now a quick-and-dirty rabbet plane. Try it, you'll like it.

---

plank, which has difficulty with compound shapes due to the physical limitations of getting a flat plane to fit around a curve, a carvel plank is unfazed by demanding shape, as it is actually carved or sculpted to fit the hull. The question is, just how do you determine how much, and where, to shape the strake? After all, the carvel strake starts its life as a piece of flat, milled lumber.

Begin work on the next plank up from the garboard by assembling and attaching the spiling batten in the same fashion as for the garboard and by making your marks the same way. Use your compass to record the locations where the previous plank lands on the frames or molds for one edge of the new plank, and record the "lined off" marks for the other edge. Capture the shapes of the hood end and the transom end as you did for the garboard.

At this point accommodation must be made for the shape of the hull. The inside of the plank must be hollowed or "backed out" to fit the changing curvature of the frames. (See Figure 15-7.) The depth of the hollow must be determined, as this will dictate how thick your planking stock must be. For example, if the plans call for ½-inch planking, and

15-7: The planking stock must be thick enough to allow for hollowing the back of the plank to match the curve of the frames.

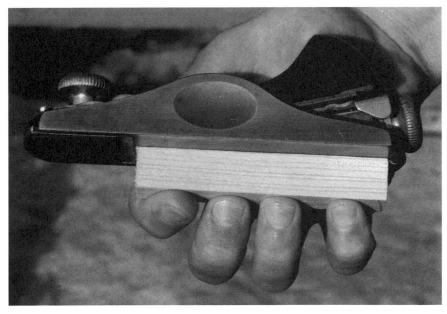

FINISHED PLANK THICKNESS

the amount of necessary hollow is ¼ inch, you will need to start with a board that is ¾ inch thick to make your plank. (While this may seem bothersome, it is lots better than starting out with ½-inch stock, hollowing out ¼ inch, only to discover your plank is now just ¼ inch thick.)

Next, the mating edge of the new plank must be dealt with. Unlike the garboard, where generally both edges are cut square, this plank and the rest of them must be beveled on at least one edge (two if you use a shutter plank). This needs to be done to avoid the inevitable gap on the outside that would be formed by two square-edged planks placed at an angle to one another. The angle of the bevel will change over the length of the plank. And, of course, an additional caulking bevel must be cut into the edge of the plank before it is hung.

This sounds like a lot more work than it really is. Actually, you've already done the tough part in spiling the plank. All you need to do is use a couple of homemade tools and follow a few simple techniques. So let's start with:

A MATTER OF BEVELS

After spiling the plank, the batten can be removed from the boat and the bevel for the new plank can be recorded. As this is a compound bevel (i.e., constantly changing), it must be picked up at several locations along the length of the plank. What is the interval? It depends on the shape of the boat and the location of the plank. If the plank is near the sheer where the sides are nearly flat, with very little curve, the bevel needs to be recorded at only a few,

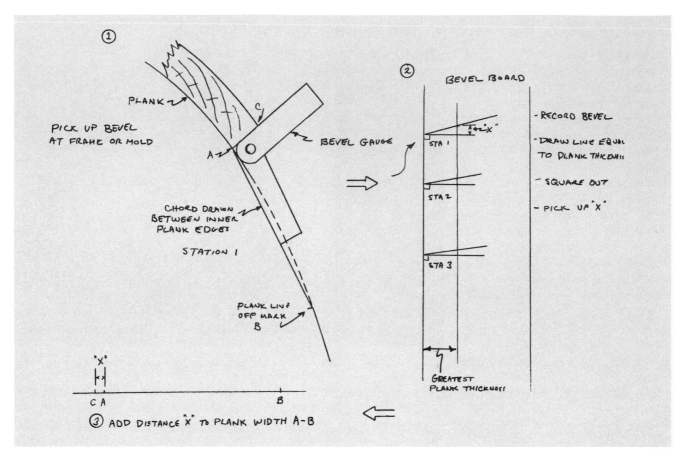

1 PLANK
PICK UP BEVEL
AT FRAME OR MOLD
BEVEL GAUGE
CHORD DRAWN
BETWEEN INNER
PLANK EDGES
STATION 1
PLANK LINE
OFF MARK
B
"X"
C A   B
3 ADD DISTANCE "X" TO PLANK WIDTH A-B

2 BEVEL BOARD
STA 1
STA 2
STA 3
GREATEST
PLANK THICKNESS
- RECORD BEVEL
- DRAW LINE EQUAL
  TO PLANK THICKNESS
- SQUARE OUT
- PICK UP "X"

15-8: Picking up the bevel from the edge of the plank already hung.

widely spaced points. On the other hand, if your boat is a curvaceous little pulling boat and the plank is at the turn of the bilge coming into a sporty wineglass transom, the bevel will be winding like a serpent; prudence calls for taking numerous readings.

So where exactly do you pick up this bevel? Simply laying a straight-legged bevel gauge on top of a frame and recording the relative angle of the adjacent plank will likely produce an inaccurate reading, because, generally, that is not how your new plank will be landing on the boat. The inside of the plank will be hollowed out, allowing the plank to fit snugly to the frame from the edge of the previous plank to the "lined-off" plank location on the opposite edge. So, the bevel that you are actually looking for is the angle that is formed by a line or chord that is drawn on the side of the frame (from the bottom edge of the spiled plank to the top, where it touches the adjoining plank), then up the square edge of the adjoining plank. You can either pick up the bevel along the side of the frame as described, or you can customize your bevel gauge by grinding in a hollow on one leg to compensate for the curve, and use it on top of the frame.

After picking up the bevel, record it on a straight-edged piece of wood, called a bevel board, that can fit in your back pocket. Just hold one leg of the gauge against the edge of the bevel board and trace the angle indicated

by the other leg onto the flat side of the board. (Don't forget to identify the bevel with the number of the frame or the station where you picked it up.)

Move to your next location, pick up the bevel and again record it on the bevel board. Repeat the operation along the length of the plank until you have captured and recorded all the bevels you need.

How thick the plank?

Next, you must determine the greatest thickness of your planking. To do this, go to the frame or station location that has the greatest curve and plank width. Measure the distance from the chord described above and the crown of the curve. If the height of the curve is $\frac{1}{16}$ inch and the plans call for $\frac{9}{16}$-inch planks, you must mill your planking stock to $\frac{5}{8}$ inch for that plank.

Lay down the shape of the plank

You can now select and plane down your stock. Actually, select stock for two planks, because if care is taken, you should be able to get matching planks for each side of the boat at the same time. (Just remember that the beveling and hollowing on one must be the mirror image of the other.)

In the same fashion as for the garboard, lay the spiling batten atop your stock. Watch for obvious defects, rot pockets, and sapwood. Check with your dividers that you won't be ending up with half a knot in the edge of your plank. When all looks well, tack the spiling batten to the stock, and, with a compass, transfer your points from the batten to the plank. Label your points and the station or frame locations, and note on the stock which side of the plank will be beveled.

Add a little, and cut out the plank

Now you must modify the spiled shape slightly, because when the plank was spiled the side to be beveled was measured to the "middle line" formed by the previous plank and the frame. If a batten is sprung through those points and the plank is cut out square-edged, the effect when this plank is beveled is that it will become smaller on the inside face (the one in contact with the frame). This will cause the plank to come off the lined-off points on the square side when clamped in place and may even make the plank difficult to fit.

So, to remedy the situation, add just enough extra to the spiled marks so that after the plank has been beveled,

the shape of the inside surface will be exactly what it ought to be. This modification will be calculated on our amazing bevel board.

First, set your marking gauge to the thickness of the planking—let's say ⅝ inch—and draw a line on your bevel board that is parallel to the straight edge of the bevel board. Note that each of your bevel lines intersect this line. Now, hold your combination square against the straight side of the bevel board and slide it to the beginning of one of your bevel lines. Draw a line square in until you hit the newly drawn parallel line. The distance from the point where the squared line hits the new parallel line to the point where the bevel line hits the new parallel line equals the distance to add to the point developed from spiling. Voila!

Using either dividers or a tick strip, pick up these distances and add them to the outside of the "to be beveled" side. In other words, add the Frame 1 distance to the Frame 1 spiled mark, and so on. Then transfer the points to the plank stock.

15-9: Beveling the edge of the plank.

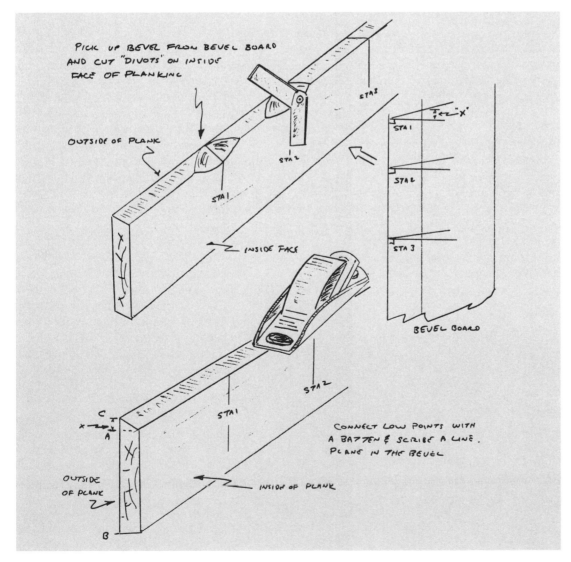

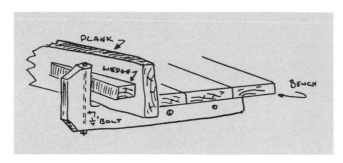

15-10: A handy wedge device for holding a plank at the bench for shaping.

You can now spring your fairing batten through the points and draw the line. The line for the lower (square) edge of the plank runs through the original spiled points. The line for the upper (beveled) edge of the plank runs through the new points.

The plank can now be cut out on the bandsaw, or with a hand-held circular saw if you are careful. As usual, leave the line when cutting. Place the plank (or planks, if you cut out two) in a vise and plane the top and bottom edges square. With that out of the way, you're ready to put on the bevel.

Recording the bevel

To establish the bevel, you must take the same distances that you picked up previously from the bevel board and record them on the inside face of the plank. There are two methods—mathematical, and "spotting."

The mathematical method

In the same fashion that you added extra territory to the outside face, you will subtract it from the inside face. Using dividers or a tick strip, make a mark for each location by measuring down from the newly planed edge. Then tack on a light batten so it just touches the points. Check the batten for fairness, then draw the line with a pencil.

Note: Be sure you are putting the bevel line on the correct side (and edge) of the plank. Odd as it may seem, the opposite has been known to happen. The easiest way to prevent this is to label the plank with a pencil.

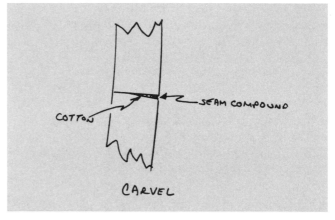

15-11: Cross section of a carvel seam.

Spotting

Put away the dividers and break out a spokeshave, chisel or penknife, and your bevel gauge for this approach. First, set the gauge to the angle for the first point on the bevel board on the gauge, then take the gauge to the corresponding point on the plank. Carve away a small divot on the edge of the plank until the angle of the divot matches that of the gauge. Pick up the next angle from the bevel board and repeat the operation on the plank. Continue until all the points have been marked with divots. Then, as in the mathematical method, tack a batten on the plank so it just touches the low end of each divot and draw the line. Remove the batten, and (finally) you are ready to plane in the bevel.

Planing in the planking bevel

Clamp the plank in a vise and mark the outside edge of the still-square plank with a pencil. Then, using a hand plane, remove the wood between the line of the edge and the line of the bevel. The compound bevel will develop automatically.

The caulking bevel

Carvel planking is designed to produce a seam that is tight on the inside and slightly open on the outside, creating a slight bevel or outgauge that allows the seam to be caulked with cotton. (See Figure 15-11.) Some builders cut the caulking bevel nearly all the way to the inside edge of the plank. Others cut the bevel only to a

15-12: A filler block to support the garboard next to the keel.

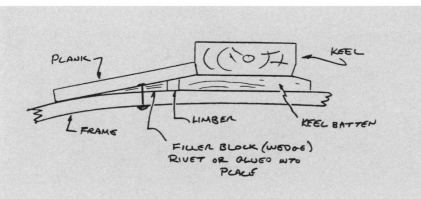

depth of two-thirds of the seam, preferring to leave the inner third of the plank edges in firm contact with each other. A general rule for the gap between the edges of the planks at the outside of a seam is 1/16 inch to 1/32 inch for each inch of plank thickness. Practically speaking, for most small craft, just an extra shaving planed off the beveled edge of each plank will provide a sufficient caulking seam.

Backing out the plank

To fit the curve of the frames, the inside surface of the plank must be hollowed or "backed out" along the entire length of the plank. This chore is generally done with a plane with a convex sole. Commonly, the "backing out" plane is a wooden smoothing plane that has been modified by rounding; that is, it is given a bit of camber. The iron is ground to suit. For production work, some builders use a portable electric power plane with knives specially ground for the job.

As with the bevel, the amount of backing out that is required will change along the length of the plank. One way to determine the amount of hollow is to use templates of thin wood (1/4-inch plywood works nicely). These are held against each frame, scribed, labeled, and then cut out on the bandsaw. These can then be used "dipstick" fashion to check the progress of the backing out at each frame location. Another way to go is to use a set of universal tem-

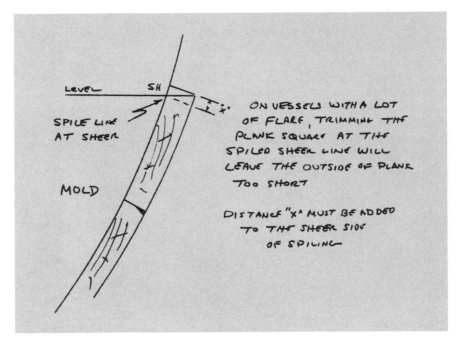

15-13: Leaving extra stock at the top of the sheer plank.

plates to check the hollow (see the curve capture device in Chapter 3, Homemade Tools).

Take the time to back out the plank fully from edge-to-edge. A partially hollowed plank—one that is either too shallow or has a flat area on each side of a hollowed center—will never fit well. The plank will not mate properly to the adjoining planks and will drive you crazy as it rocks up on one end, then the other, as you try to clamp it in place.

After backing out the plank and checking it one more time, it's time to hang that plank!

15-14: Using offset clamping pressure when hanging a plank when nothing else will work.

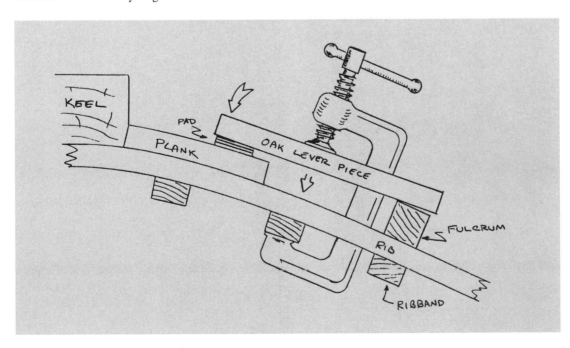

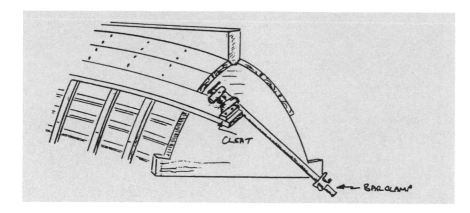

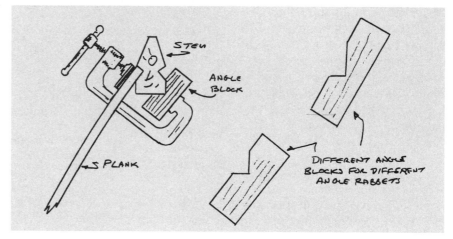

15-15: Using a temporary cleat and a bar clamp to pull a plank down to the edge of the transom.

15-16: Using angle blocks for grabbing the inside corner of the stem when clamping the hood end of a plank.

15-17: Using angle blocks and a bar clamp for pulling the hood end of a plank in to the stem rabbet.

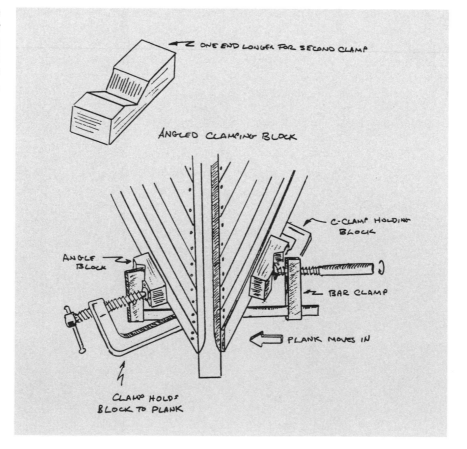

15-18: Edge-setting a plank with an edge clamp (left) and wedges (right).

If you are working alone, work out a way to support the far end of a plank while you work on the near end. Some builders set up a bar, parallel to the line of the plank, that the plank can slide along as it is swung into place. Others set up a hangman's-noose-like affair from the ceiling to suspend the plank; simply insert the far end of the plank into the sling, and the plank can be easily swung back and forth in "sky-hook" fashion.

Begin hanging the plank at the hood end and work aft, clamping as you go. Check the fit of the plank as you clamp, making sure that the edge-to-edge fit is okay and that the hollow of the back of the plank matches the curve of the frames. Keep in mind that screws, rivets, and clench nails are not clamps, so don't count on them to pull in the plank. These fastenings are designed only to hold what you have clamped in place; any pull you might get from them is pure serendipity.

Just one more thing— the sheer plank

Remember when making the sheer plank that the marks on the frames and molds represent the outside upper corner of the sheerstrake viewed in profile. If you just spile to the inside sheer mark and cut the top square, the outside upper edge of the sheer plank will probably be too low. The more flare a boat has forward, the more this is likely to be a problem.

In any event, it is good policy to leave a little extra along the entire length of the top of the sheerstrake as an insurance policy against any minor faux pas in the spiling process. (See Figure 15-13.) It is a simple matter to plane off any excess wood; it's much more difficult to add on wood if the plank turns out to be too narrow.

HANGING PLANKS

Hanging a plank is another of those jobs that work better if you plan ahead. First round up plenty of clamps. Standard C-clamps are a perennial favorite, but sliding-jaw bar clamps or the "Quick Grip" type can be set faster and are easier to use if you are working alone. To avoid crushing the plank, whip up a box of wooden "buttons" or pads to use under the clamps. Keep in mind that the depressions caused by clamp pads seem to swell out beyond the original thickness of stock.

Edge-setting the plank

The chances are good that the plank will need to be "edge-set" to pull it in tightly to the adjoining plank. There are a few dandy clamps, available commercially, that are designed expressly for this purpose, but wedges will do the job as well.

If you will be using wedges, be sure to have a good supply on hand in advance. Make them long and narrow, of softwood (scrap planking stock works well).

15-19: A special clamp for edge-setting planks.

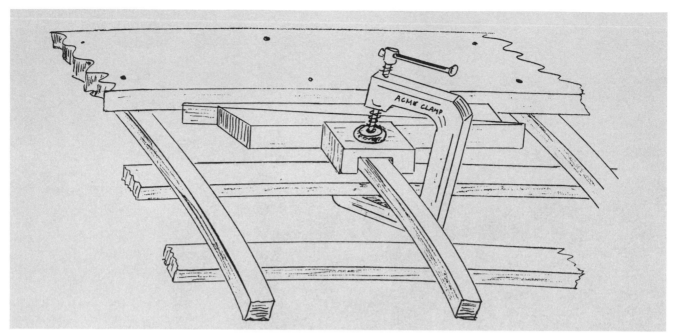

To use the wedges, clamp a hardwood block to a frame a short distance away from the new plank. For a deluxe version of this block, cut a U-shaped notch into it to fit around the frame and help keep the block from slipping. To make a super nonskid block, use spray disc adhesive to stick a small square of sandpaper, face out, to the block; the sandpaper will give the block just enough traction to keep it from sliding when pressure is applied.

Holding two wedges parallel to the plank, and in opposition to one another (point to point, so they will overlap), insert them into the gap between the block and the plank. Then, using two hammers simultaneously, tap on the butt ends of the wedges. As the wedges slide over each other, the plank will be forced edgewise. You may have to temporarily loosen your clamps in the region where you are wedging to allow the plank to slip edgewise. The long length of the wedges will afford plenty of area for friction to keep the wedges from backing down after they have been set and to prevent damage to the side of the plank.

Using wedges at 90 degrees to the planking is not recommended. If you simply must do this, at least pad the plank edge well with a long piece of wood to avoid crushing the edge with your wedges.

Cranky plank?

Having a difficult time fitting the plank into the rabbet? It could be that the plank is too thick. If you needed to increase the thickness for hollowing to accommodate the curvature of the hull amidships, the plank may now be too thick up forward, where hollowing may not have been required. Try reducing the plank thickness up forward to the specifications in the plans by planing the outside face of the plank.

Some types of wood will fight you more than others. Maine white cedar will bend in easily, while

15-21: Planking a hull right-side up. It's easy enough to poke your head inside and check the seams.

WILL ANSEL

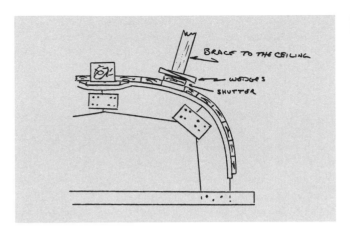

15-22: Forcing in the shutter plank with wedges against a brace to the shop ceiling.

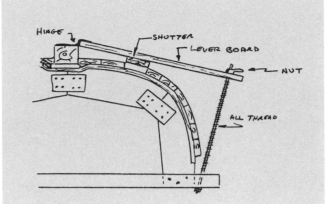

15-23: The hinged plank press at work.

mahogany will resist and Western red cedar might snap from the pressure. If you have problems, use the boiling-water technique described above for fitting the garboard.

How tightly should the planks fit?

While ideally adjacent planks should fit tightly at the inside of the seam, the reality is that the planks won't quite match up in a few places. Not to worry. As long as the gap is very occasional and is less than $1/32$ inch or so, and the seam opening is wider on the outside, you are probably in good shape. A hollow seam—one that is wider on the inside than on the outside—is another matter, however, as it is miserable if not impossible to caulk properly. Better to remove the plank and remedy the situation.

Of course, it's one thing to check the seams on the inside when you are building right-side up. You can just poke your head in and take a look. Any bum seams will stick out like a sore thumb. It's quite another situation to check for seam tightness when building upside down. It can be mighty inconvenient, not to mention claustrophobic, to have to constantly crawl into the jig to check on those seams, especially when they look so darn good on the outside. Unfortunately, over-optimism combined with the failure to check those seams can lead to some rather eye-popping surprises on pulling the boat off the jig and flipping it over.

The trick is to make checking for gaps easier. One way to do this is to use a trouble light. After tightly clamping the plank into place, hold the lamp on the inside, next to the seam. If the seam is tight, no light will be visible from the outside. If the seam is open, it will act like a pinhole camera and intensify the light, making spotting the problem from outside the boat easier. Security without spelunking!

THE SHUTTER PLANK

For the home builder working alone, the easiest route when planking is to start with the garboard plank and work toward the sheer. This method allows more flexibility when spiling (i.e., corrections are easily made) and requires a bevel on only one edge of the plank. There are times, however, when the builder will find it advantageous to plank up from the garboard and down from the sheer toward a predetermined plank that will require little twist and/or steaming in fitting. The term for this last strake to be worked into place is the shutter plank.

Using a shutter plank offers the builder lots of opportunities to employ high skill, as not only must the spiling be highly accurate to fill the gap exactly, but also the plank must be beveled on both the upper and the lower edges. Added to this is the usual backing out of the plank and the bending of the unit into place. And then there is the matter pulling the plank into position.

Many builders prefer a "driven fit"; i.e., fitting the plank, shaving by shaving, until it goes in halfway, then driving it the rest of the way by holding a heavy oak block against the plank and pounding it with a hammer. Walloping it in works well enough when you have a helper to support, swing, and twist the plank. But what if you are working alone?

Shutter plank clamping devices

The difficulty with shutter planks, of course, is the lack of any convenient purchase point for a conventional clamp to draw the plank in to the frames. Hence, most builders use an interesting array of props and shores emanating from the shop floor, ceiling, and walls (with the occasional house jack thrown in), all employed to cajole the reluctant victim into place. (See Figure 15-22.) These techniques work surprisingly well—as long as you have some place to brace against. But what if you're building upside down in, say, a large metal warehouse or out-of-doors? This is the time for a little outside pressure. I offer the following for your consideration:

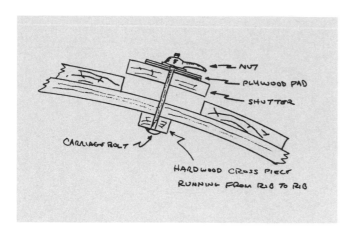

15-24: The bolted shutter press is not for the faint of heart.

The hinged plank press

The plank press is merely a hinged oak lever that pushes the plank down into place and holds it there until it has been fastened. (See Figure 15-23.) The neat part about this rig is its versatility. The pressure exerted on the plank is positive and adjustable, as it comes from a bolt-rod nut being tightened on a threaded rod. The whole device is interconnected, so you don't have to worry about it falling apart if you are working by yourself. If you want to check a fit, merely slide the plank in under the lever, affix the forward end, and tighten down the bolt-rod nut. Need an adjustment? Just back off the bolt-rod nut, make your adjustment, and tighten the rig back down into place. With any luck, the plank'll pull right home to the frames. Of course, maybe it won't—but it's an easy matter to repeat the process with the press and get it right the next time.

The bolted shutter press

The bolted shutter press is a device to be used in moments of great exigency and not by the squeamish. Devotees of highly finished interiors and those who blanch at slight imperfections need not continue. But those of stout heart, read on.

The shutter press is basically a homemade clamp that is able to put all of its pressure exactly where you want it.

(See Figure 15-24.) It does this with one purchase point on the inside of the frames, the other on the outside of the plank, exactly where you want it. A bolt-rod nut cranked down on a threaded rod between the two very effectively pulls the plank into place. Unfortunately it requires that a hole be drilled in the plank. But only as big as the diameter of the rod.

Actually, this rig works really well. The inner bearing surface is a piece of oak that spans a couple of frames and distributes stress. The outer surface is a large square of oak or plywood that protects the plank from being crushed. The bolt-rod nut permits you to "sneak up" on the job, allowing incremental tightening until you get just enough pressure for the plank to land properly. The entire rig is limber enough, though, that if plank adjustment is necessary, you can simply back off the bolt-rod nut and the plank will be free to move.

Drawbacks? Well, there is that hole. Just plug the blasted thing and tell people it was a knot.

Thoughts on fastening planks

As a general rule, plank fastenings should not be countersunk/counterbored to hold a bung more than the thickness of the plank.

Make sure that the fastenings are the right caliber and length for the job. If using screws, holes for them should be drilled to the proper size and depth. The Fuller-type countersink/counterbore is the best all-around tool for this job.

Temper your enthusiasm with the drill. If two holes per frame will do, four are definitely not better. Most planks on small craft require no more than two fastenings per frame—three only occasionally.

The garboard and the first broadstrake (the plank next to the garboard) should be fastened to both the floors and the frames when possible.

Never start fastening from the ends of the plank and work toward the center. You could end up with an embarrassing bulge, or "bubble," in the center.

When fastening your plank, starting from the stem and working toward the stern, all your fastenings will be

15-25: Plank fastenings at the transom must be driven parallel to the face of the transom, not at a right angle to the face of the plank.

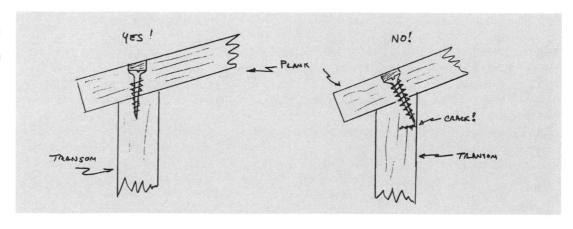

driven at 90 degrees, or nearly so, to the hull. Except at the transom. If a fastening is installed at 90 degrees to the edge the transom, the chances are good that it will either break out of the inside face of the transom or the head of it will be cut off when you trim the planking where it overlaps the transom. To avoid such grim possibilities, drill the hole parallel to the plane of the after face of the transom. (See Figure 15-25.) This is easy to do. Just hold a straightedge along the side of the transom as a sighting stick and eyeball your drill parallel.

Don't forget to lubricate screws! And if you are using a power screwdriver, be circumspect when setting the screw. The last thing you need is to wring off a screw or crack the plank in a final burst of speed.

☞ General Flathead Wood Screw Sizes for Planking

Plank Thickness	Screw Size
³⁄₈″	³⁄₄″ #7
¹⁄₂″	1″ #8
⁵⁄₈″	1¹⁄₄″ #9
³⁄₄″	1¹⁄₂″ #10
⁷⁄₈″	1³⁄₄″ #12
1″	2″ #14

SOURCE: *BOATBUILDING MANUAL*, BY ROBERT M. STEWARD

FILLING THE SCREW HOLES

After all your fastenings are in, and you are sure that they are set deep enough that you won't run your plane into them when fairing the hull, you can fill the holes. You have two choices here: bungs (plugs) or putty.

If you will be finishing the hull bright, the only way to go is the bung route. Bungs can be purchased ready-made or cut from scrap planking stock with a bung cutter. There's much to be said for buying your bungs ready-made, unless you have a trained baby ape with a long attention span to do the cutting, as you are probably looking at making a thousand or more. On the other hand, if you are not planning to stain the hull before varnishing, cutting the plugs from scrap will give a much better chance of matching the bungs to the planking.

Set the bungs with a good quality glue, being careful to line up the grain with that of the planking. Use care when cutting off the bungs. The safest method is to cut them proud with a backsaw or one of those sharper-'n-hell Japanese saws, then pare them down with a chisel, taking care not to chip them out of the hole.

If the boat is to be painted, putty may be the answer. The question is what kind. The old favorite is the one-part "surfacing compound" that comes in a tin. Relatively cheap and easy to apply, it does have the drawback of tending to shrink as it dries, requiring several applications to fill the hole properly. Then after the boat is in the water, the putty often swells, leaving bumps in the surface of the planking.

Then there is polyester putty (a.k.a., Bondo). This product is a two-part mix—one part, the putty; the other part, the catalyst. This putty cures very quickly. Unfortunately, when cured it is also very hard—harder than most planking. When sanding and fairing planking filled with cured polyester putty, the puttied holes are like knots, always wanting to stand proud like baby mesas.

The best putty-type product seems to be two-part epoxy fairing compound. While more expensive than other types, it doesn't shrink when dry or swell when wet, it sticks well in the hole yet can be pried out if necessary, it is soft enough that it sands much like the wood substrate, and it has a longer working time than its polyester cousin. Who could ask for more?

As good as epoxy fairing compound is for filling countersunk fastening holes, working with it can be, at

☞ Trimming Frame Heads

When planing the sheer to its final sweep, it seems like a natural time to also trim off the top of the frame heads to match the sheer. There are situations where it is an advantage to leave the frames running long (maybe an inch or two) for just awhile longer. One such situation is if you will be installing through-riveted inwales and outwales. In this construction, a through hole will be drilled and a rivet will be run through the outwale, the sheer plank, the frame, and the inwale, where a rove will be driven over the nail, the excess nail nipped off, and the end peened.

Difficulty arises when the nail is driven through the hole. If the bored hole is slightly undersized and if the frame has been trimmed off at the sheer (quite close to the rivet hole), there is a good chance that the frame head will split. If, however, the top of the frame was left long, when the nail is driven it will not split the frame. The frame can be safely trimmed afterward. If leaving the frame heads long is impractical, make sure the hole is bored large enough to allow the rivet to slide through without stressing the frame.

By the way, for good looks, when you finally trim off the tops of the frame, "break" or slightly scallop the forward and after top edges of the frame symmetrically with a rattail file.

best, a tedious and thoroughly messy business. The stuff always seems to spread out and cling to all surrounding surfaces, ensuring energetic sanding to remove the offending residue. That is, unless one used the method invented by John Brooks, a professional boatbuilder from Mount Desert, Maine.

All one needs for using John's method is a roll of standard masking tape. Using a drill press and a Forstner bit, drill a series of holes the size of a standard countersink into the face of the tape. Now you have a roll of perforated tape. Use it by tearing off a piece, the hole in which can be placed over the counterbored hole. Fill the hole, peel off the tape, and you are left with a tasteful epoxy bung that can be easily sanded flush.

REMOVE THE PLANKED HULL FROM THE JIG

Before removing the planked boat from the construction jig, take a moment to ask yourself a few questions:

- Have all the screws that held the backbone to the jig been removed?
- If you are planning to make the final cut of the top of sheer plank when the boat is upright, have you transferred the sheer marks from the molds to the inside of the sheer plank?

- Have you lightly traced the station lines from the molds to the hull? Station lines can come in mighty handy when laying out the interior.
- Have you made cross spalls (spreaders) to help hold the hull's shape after it has been lifted from the jig? Many times a hull will either spring out or draw in when removed from the constraints of the jig. A cross spall is just a piece of stock going from sheer-to-sheer with cleats fastened to it that conform to the inside and outside faces of the sheer plank. Mark the location of the cross spalls on the sheer. Then you can pop the boat from the jig. If the hull changes shape at all, it can easily be brought back to where it should be by dropping in the cross spalls.
- After the hull has been removed from the jig and before you begin to install interior furniture—risers, thwarts, knees, bulkheads etc.—brace the hull carefully. Check with a level and a plumb bob to be sure that the boat is fully stabilized and braced plumb and square to avoid any pernicious twist. Diagonal bracing to the stem and the transom, and blocks along the keel, will hold the boat in traction, right where you want it until the internal structures take over the job.

16 • LAPSTRAKE PLANKING

Lapstrake planking—known as clinker in Britain—has a lot going for it. It is perhaps the most elegant of the many planking systems. The sweeping lines of a well-lined out hull are a joy to behold. The process of lapping the planks and fastening them together stiffens the individual planks and allows them to be thinner. This nature of interconnected structure allows the boat to be built lighter than its carvel counterpart, particularly in the framing, while still maintaining its strength.

Lapstrake is also popular for its ability to stay tight without caulking, even after long periods of time out of the water. This quality made it a preferred construction method for the old wooden lifeboats.

For the home builder, the system has much appeal, because all the planking is of uniform thickness throughout the boat. There is no need to determine planking thickness or to back out the planking. Wood can be milled off-site and used as delivered.

As the planks overlap each other in lapstrake construction, spiling is nowhere nearly as persnickety as it is for carvel. If the width of a plank is less than it should be by 1/16 inch, it is no big deal. There still will be plenty of overlap for the seams to be tight and strong.

Lapstrake allows versatility in setup and construction technique as well. Since the planks are fastened to one another as construction proceeds, the boat can be built over simple molds. Frames can then be bent into the planking after the job is done. On the other hand, if one wishes, the boat can also be planked over a conventional ribbanded mold with pre-bent frames.

THE NO-FREE-LUNCH DEPARTMENT

Of course, no system is without its own problems. In lapstrake, looks and practicality dictate that the planking locations must be properly determined before you start to plank. A poorly lined carvel hull can be camouflaged with a smart paint job. Bad lines on a lapstrake hull will be there forever to remind you of your blunder.

More importantly, the location and width of the lining marks will determine whether you can fit the plank on the boat at all. In carvel planking, if you have a wider plank than you wish for a particularly sharp turn of the hull, all you need to do is use thicker stock and hollow out the inside of the strake until it fits. Lapstrake planks are like planes (or facets) coming around a curve. If a plank is

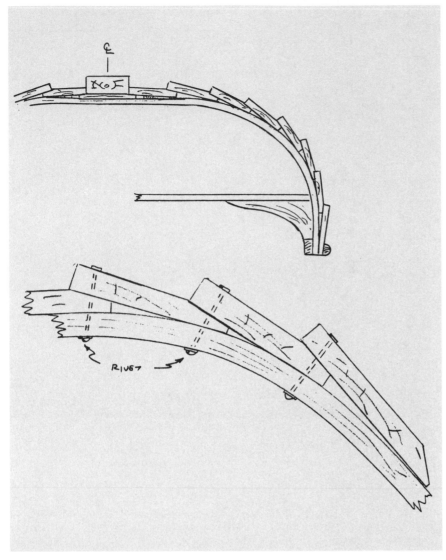

16-1: Lapstrake planking.

sheer. There can be no shutter plank.

And just because lapstrake planks are all milled to the same thickness and cut out square doesn't mean you don't have to deal with bevels. Bevels are just on another part of the plank as compared with carvel, and, as with carvel, these are compound bevels.

As if that isn't enough, there is that little matter of getting the planks to come in flush with one another at the bow and the stern....

GETTING STARTED

As with carvel construction, the place to start is with the lining off of the planks. This process is similar to lining off carvel planking, except that the width of the laps must be taken into account. While the planking lines on some hulls can be diminished mechanically (see Chapter 13, Lining Off the Hull), for most boats, the better part of the job must be done by eye. Pay particular attention to craft that have a long, flat run underwater, then a tight turn to the bilge. You may have to use wider planks in the flat section to allow you to use narrow planks when coming around that tight turn.

While lining off, you might find that you must plane flats on the transom to allow the planks to land tightly there, or you might at least have to back out the planks slightly for the last foot or so.

To picture what is actually going on as you line off your planking, it is helpful to mill your lining-off battens to the same width as the laps and the same thickness as the planking. For example if the planking is ½ inch and the width of the lap is ¾ inch, then make the batten ½ inch by ¾ inch. When tacking down the batten, align it so it lies with one edge touching the lined-off marks on the mold, with the body of the batten on the "keel" side of the marks. Setting the batten this way allows one side to show you the edge of the first plank, and the other side to show you how far the second plank will lap over the first.

too wide for a tight curve, the plank may not be able to land on the adjoining plank properly, or worse, it will be left sticking off the curve like a tangent. Long, narrow hulls lend themselves more easily to lapped planking; some hulls are simply too complex for lapstrake.

A notable disadvantage of lapstrake planking is that the raised edge of the planks, especially if they are of a softwood, such as cedar, can be easily abraded and chewed up by sand and rocks when the boat is hauled up a beach.

Since the strakes are interconnected in lapstrake planking, there are more fastenings to install than in carvel—roughly three times as many. As the planking is by nature thin, lap fastenings are generally set flush with the outside face of the plank. The plank must be finished off on the outside before installing. And, in nearly all cases, plank splices must be scarfed, as butt blocks are impractical.

Due to the nature of the planking process, lapstrake planks can only be hung consecutively, from the keel to the

☞ A Device for Checking the Laps

Wondering if the plank that you lined off at the turn of the bilge will be too wide to lap properly on the adjoining plank? Check it out with a homemade reach-around gauge. This simple device will give you a quick ballpark reading on the width of the plank and help you determine whether it needs to be changed.

As discussed elsewhere, one easy method to picture what is actually going on as you line off your planking is to mill your lining-off battens to the same width as the lap width and the same thickness as the planking. By placing one edge of the batten on the lined points, you illustrate the outside edge of the plank. The other side of the batten illustrates the lap line on the plank — the line that you will be spiling to.

To make your gauge, take a straight piece of wood a little longer than the expected width of the next plank. Cut a shallow rectangular notch into the side of the gauge (see illustration). Hold the gauge so the notch fits over the lining batten and hold it so one edge of the notch is touching the "lap" line of the batten.

Align the other side of the gauge so it touches the lined-off mark for the next plank. The gauge is now simulating how the new plank will lie at that location. If the gauge only touches at the "lap" line and the "new plank" line, the plank width is probably fine for that location. But if the bottom of the gauge contacts the curve of the mold or frame and prevents the gauge from touching the lap line, the plank is too wide and should be relined.

The lap gauge simulates how the plank will lie at that location.

Using a lap gauge.

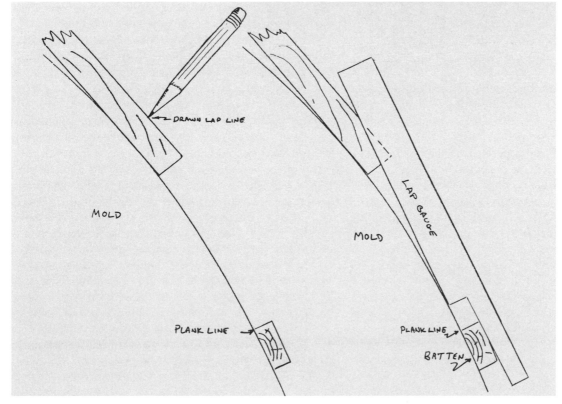

SPILING

Spiling a lapstrake plank is quite similar to spiling a carvel plank (see Chapter 15, Carvel Planking). The notable difference is that with carvel you record from the lower edge of the previous plank, while with lapstrake you record from the lap line that is drawn on the face of the previous plank. (See Figure 16-2.) With the exception of the garboard strake, the spiling batten should lap over onto the previous plank.

Spile the garboard plank exactly as in carvel construction, then lay it out on the stock, cut it to shape, and square up the edges. Then mark the lap line at the given width with a pencil. If no lap width is specified on the plans, a constant distance of ¾ inch, more or less, will do the trick.

BEVELING THE LAPS

Beveling the laps is where lapstrake construction gets interesting (but not difficult). Mating the first and second planks actually involves two operations: (1) putting the compound bevel on the lap on the first plank, and (2) dealing with the ends of the planks so they come out flush when they fit into the rabbet or against the transom. Let's deal with the bevel first.

In most situations, all of the bevel will be cut on the top outward edge (the sheer side) of the preceding plank. The lapped area of the plank must be beveled off to allow full contact from the edge of the plank to the marked lap line, with no hollows or gaps on either side of the lap when the two planks are put together.

It is quite an easy matter to get the bevel at the molds. All the tools that are necessary are a spokeshave and a short rule or straightedge. Using the rule to simulate the next plank, put one edge of the rule on the next plank line at a mold and lay the length of the rule against the corner of the plank to be beveled. With the spokeshave take a little off the lap and check it with the straightedge. Shave a little more, and check again, and so on, until the rule lands at the pencil lap line and lies flush along the spoke-shaved bevel. Do this at each mold. All you need to do then is connect the spotted bevels, and you are in business.

To connect the spotted bevels, some builders remove the plank from the boat (it would have been temporarily clamped in place at this point), clamp it to the work bench, and plane in the bevel with a jack plane. Other

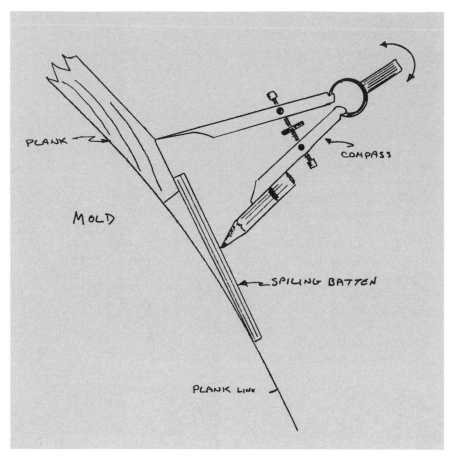

16-2: Spiling a lapstrake plank. The key here is to spile from the lap line on the previous plank.

dead-eyed mechanics plane freehand right on the boat. This can be tricky, as miscues can leave lumps and hollows along the length of the bevel.

A third approach to connecting the spotted bevels is the batten-and-gauge method. Begin by tacking a stiff batten to the molds at the upper edge of the points lined off for the next plank. Next, make a stepped lap gauge. Start with a straight, rectangular-sectioned piece of wood, longer than the plank is wide. On the gauge, draw a line that parallels the edge of the gauge that is the same width as the batten. Cut along that line for about two-thirds of the length of the gauge. Then cut into the previous cut from the outside edge, which will give you a stepped gauge.

Take the gauge to one of the spot bevels that have been cut in the plank. Place the gauge on top of the mold, with the notched part of the gauge riding on the batten. You will produce the same result as when you used the straight rule to get the bevel. Use a sharp block plane, set fine, to cut the bevel, and ride the stepped gauge along the length of the batten to check your work; the correct bevel can be quickly and easily planed into the plank.

Don't forget to take a moment to check the length of your bevel for roundness or "crown" with a straightedge. That bevel should be dead flat. Any crown will drive you nuts when you are trying to pull the planks together with the clamps.

Still in doubt? Leave a little extra thickness on the bevel, check the fit by clamping the new plank in place, and take off whatever is necessary to make a perfect lap.

DEALING WITH THE ENDS

At the bow, and at the transom of some boats, the planking comes in flush. There are three popular methods to achieve this: the dory lap, the ship lap (i.e., a half lap), and the rabbeted-to-a-featheredge lap.

The dory-lap solution

This approach uses matching bevels on the adjoining planks to bring the ends in flush with one another. One method that works well is to clamp the plank in place and capture the bevels along its length as described above. Then take the plank to the bench and plane the entire bevel in with your jack plane.

Next, starting from about a foot from the end, gradually plane or roll the bevel so that the end of the bevel at the ends of the plank comes to a featheredge. Check the bevels for crown and fasten the plank without further ado.

If you wish to test the fit, the adjoining (new) plank can then be clamped into place and the lap bevel checked along the run of the plank. While it is clamped up, trace the lap line on the inside face of the new plank. Also mark the location of where the "dory lap" part of the bevel begins. Otherwise, you can just trace the lap line onto the inside face of the new plank with a marking gauge and note the point at which the bevel starts.

Take the new plank to the bench. At the bow end of the plank, plane a bevel into the marked lap that starts at nothing at the one-foot-aft mark and goes to a feath-eredge at the hood end. That takes care of the forward end of the plank. The after end is another matter.

If the sides of the transom are straight, as on many runabouts, the lap bevel at the transom end of the new plank can be planed in to a featheredge in the same way as the forward end of the plank. If the transom is rounded, as on most pulling boats, the planks will be lying atop one another at an angle as they come around the curve. To check what is needed for a bevel, place your bevel gauge on the transom next to the latest plank and swing the blade out to capture the angle of the feath-eredge "dory lap." That angle you have just captured is what you want on the bottom side of your new plank lap. (Note: It also may be necessary to plane a "flat" on the transom to allow the plank to land properly.)

Take the gauge to the transom end of the new plank, and with a chisel or spokeshave cut a notch that records the bevel. Then from the one-foot-mark, plane in your rolling bevel to that notch and no farther. That should do it. Clamp the plank in place, and check the fit. It should be mighty close.

Ship lap, or half lap

Another way to achieve the same result is to use match-ing half laps at the plank ends. This can be easily done by using a rabbet plane fitted with a fence that can be set to the lap width, or by tacking a piece of batten along the lap line and using it as a fence. While the plank is still on the bench, starting from 12 inches or so from the ends, plane a square-sided rabbet into the lap surface of the plank. This will be a straight, inclined plane starting from the 12-inch point and cutting down to one-half the plank thickness at the ends (on transoms with a lot of shape, leave a little more thickness at the ends).

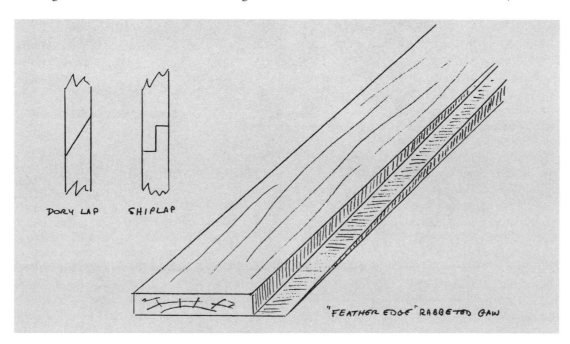

16-3: Three ways to bring in the ends of lapstrake planks flush at the stem rabbet and the transom.

DORY LAP   SHIPLAP

"FEATHER EDGE" RABBETED GAW

16-4: Wooden bar clamps with lever cams being used to put pressure on the laps while the fastenings are driven.

Hang the plank as usual, and then bevel the lap edge of the plank as described above. A small amount of bevel must be worked into the rabbet as well. Be conservative with this, though. More bevel can be worked in as you fit the adjoining plank.

The next plank can then be spiled and gotten out as before. The new plank can be temporarily clamped in place on the lap line, and the edge of the plank beneath can be traced onto the bottom of the new plank. Also mark the point where the rabbet begins. Remove the new plank and plane in the matching rabbet on the bottom side. Replace, and check your fit. If, after clamping up, the lap looks good, fasten the plank.

Rabbeted to a featheredge

This method, popular in England, involves cutting with a rabbet plane a ramp-like rabbet (or chase) that tapers to a featheredge on the lapped edge of the first plank. Although this featheredge business sounds mighty fragile, it's not as bad as it sounds, as the edge is backed up by the rabbet in the stem and the transom back aft. The advantage is that nothing has to be done to the underside of the second plank.

To cut the rabbet start by placing your newly cut and square plank on the bench, face up. Mark the lap line in pencil. Next, tack down a batten along the lap line as a guide for the rabbet plane. Repeat the operation at the transom end, but check before planing to a featheredge, because if your transom has a lot of shape, you may need more thickness at the end of the "ramp" to accommodate the plank bevel.

Install your plank on the boat and bevel it as described above. When you reach the rabbets, make a shorter version of the stepped gauge and just continue the bevel right into the rabbet. The stage is now set for hanging the next plank. No extra shaping will needed on the mating side of the new plank.

16-5: Using a bar clamp against a temporary cleat to bring a lapstrake plank in to the edge of the transom. As in usual plank-hanging procedure, clamping began at the bow and has proceeded aft.

FASTENINGS

For fastening the laps in most small craft, two, maybe three, fasteners between the frames are plenty. For light planking, clench nails are a good way to go. They are quicker to install than rivets, and you can work single-handedly. (Use caution at the ends, where the featheredges are.)

For more heavy-duty work, rivets are a good choice. A rivet is more time consuming to install than a clench nail, but the large ring (the head and the rove) offers a bit more security. A rivet can be reset and tightened if necessary, and is easier to repair. It is easy to get your fill of riveting, however. Even a small boat can contain a few thousand rivets. If you are planning to build a number of boats, a short aircraft-style air hammer with a riveting set would be a good investment. (Along with a good set of ear plugs.)

Occasionally, for industrial-strength planking, such as that used in 1950s vintage outboard runabouts, machine bolts, nuts, and washers can be used. These bolts tend to be very strong and are easy to repair; for most situations, however, they are overkill.

For fastening the planks to the frames, usually screws or rivets will do. Check your plans carefully for sizes and specifications. Some lightweight craft have slim frames that will accommodate rivets but will split if screws are used.

Remember, your fastenings are only intended to hold what the clamps have already pulled tightly together. This is especially true at the laps, as it is their snug wood-to-wood connection that provides strength and watertight fit. Before fastening, round up as many deep-throated clamps as possible. If using deep-throated C-clamps, be sure to protect the lap with wooden pads.

An alternative to the garden-variety steel clamp is the sliding wooden-jawed bar clamp. Light, and easy to use singlehandedly, it offers a good depth of throat, usually 8 inches, to reach in to close the lap joint. Rather than using a turnscrew to achieve final pressure, the wooden bar clamp uses a quick-acting cam. (See Figure 16-4.) Yet another route is to make your own clamps (see Chapter 3, Homemade Tools.)

As with all clamping, start at the bow and work aft.

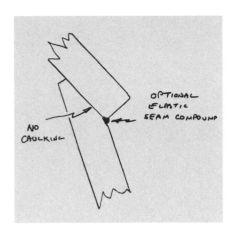

16-6: Lapstrake planking is not caulked, but some builders groove the apex of the lap between two planks and run in a bead of synthetic compound.

CAULKING THE LAPS

Over time, the working of the hull and a multitude of shrink-and-swell cycles will cause even the best-fit laps to open up and the boat to resemble a colander. To make things worse, these open seams can trap paint and other detritus during spring fit-out. This foreign matter can jam the planks open, preventing the tightening of the seams after the boat has been launched. In the past, boat owners have attempted to appease King Neptune by smearing ceremonial compounds, waxes, or tallows on the outside of the laps. If this "fix" worked at all, it usually didn't last long.

A better repair is to take a hooked tool, such as a reefing iron (see Chapter 3, Homemade Tools), and cut a small groove in the "apex" of the lap between the two planks. A bead of synthetic caulk, such as one of the polyurethanes, can then be run in the groove and tooled to a concave shape. (See Figure 16-6.) The caulk will cure to a rubber-band-like consistency, and will stretch and compress as needed. Many boatbuilders are using this technique on their new craft as well, as it guarantees the customer a tight boat right from the get-go.

What about coating the entire lap with this tenacious goop when planking the boat? Wouldn't that take care of any future leaks? Probably. Also, it's likely to take care of any future repairs, as the planks will be inextricably vulcanized to one another.

17 • Centerboard, Centerboard Trunk, and Rudder

In many ways centerboards and centerboard trunks have earned a justifiably bum reputation as bugaboos. Indignant charges of "They are sure to leak!" and "The board always jams!" too often ring true.

The problem lies in some builders' halfhearted attempts in dealing with what is, after all, a large hole in the bottom of the boat. A centerboard trunk is subjected to a considerable amount of working over its lifetime, and it should be properly affixed to the keel with fastenings that can be tightened and braced by floors and, if possible, linked to other structures with knees.

The Installment Plan—Now or Later?

The trunk can be installed either before planking or afterwards. If the trunk is to be installed prior to planking, the center molds must be modified to accept the trunk. To get the information, it's back to the old lofting board. Draw the trunk assembly onto the profile and transfer the necessary heights of the logs and sides to the body plan. There, you can draw the cross section of the trunk onto the affected stations. The molds will probably need a bit of beefing up to compensate for the large slot that will be cut in them. If the trunk is made to patterns that came from the lofting, all should go well.

Which is better, now or later? Either works well. The trunk is probably easier to fit when the planking isn't on, but there is a bit more work in setting up the jig. On the other hand, scribing and fitting the logs after the planking is on might be tight work, but the setup is simpler. Either way you go, however, the location of the centerboard trunk should at least be marked on the keel right from the start and even the trunk slot cut (a softwood wedge or plug can be set into the slot if the builder is concerned about movement or subtle closing of the slot).

Cutting the Slot

One easy way to cut the slot in the keel is to drill a hole the same diameter as the slot width at either end of the slot. Pick up the angle of the ends of the slot from the lofting. The holes can be connected with a circular saw and a sabersaw. The ends of the slot can be left round, as the ends of the through-the-keel tenons on the ledges can be shaped to fit the round ends. This saves time in

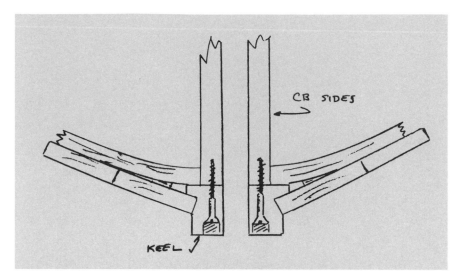

CB SIDES

KEEL

**17-2: A centerboard
trunk in a catboat.**

CENTERBOARD

TRUNK SIDES

FLOOR

BED LOG

PLANK

KEEL

**17-3: A centerboard
trunk in a semi-dory.**

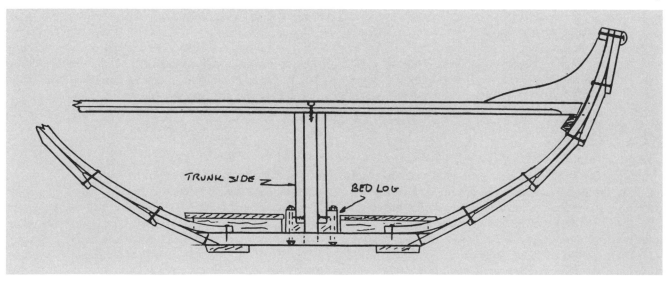

TRUNK SIDE

BED LOG

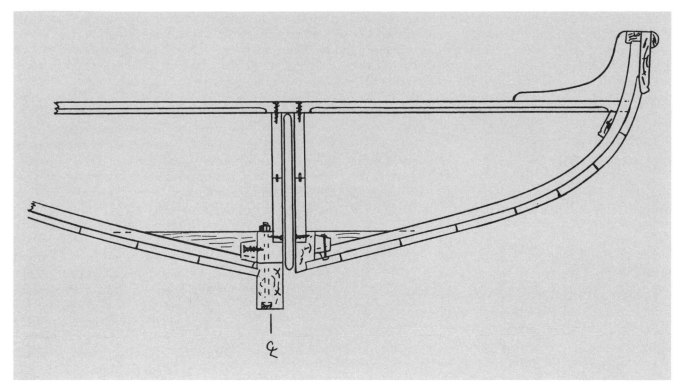

17-4: Offset center-
board trunk in a
Whitehall pulling
boat.

squaring up the ends; also, the round shape probably relieves some stress in the keel.

BUILDING A TRUNK

One common type of trunk is built with simple, usually splined, softwood panel or plywood sides that are fastened to hardwood ledges (centerboard trunk posts) fore and aft. Often the ledges are notched like a tenon to allow the inside-of-trunk portion to extend all the way through the slot. The outside shoulders of the posts will be allowed to land on the top of the keel assembly where they can be bedded. (See Figure 17-5.)

As with the garboard plank, the panel-to-keel joinery of the trunk must be of the highest quality. Any gaps now can lead to leaks later. After the panels have been fitted to the bottom tightly, the post-to-panel joint can be clamped up and drilled for screws. The assembly can then be taken apart, bedded well with either boatyard bedding compound or a flexible adhesive, which will allow movement while adding strength, and put back together again, with cotton wicking in the joints. (Gluing the panels to the rest of the trunk assembly isn't recommended.)

The trunk can then be put into place, and the fit to the keel checked—especially important to check is that the shoulders on the ledge indeed allow the trunk sides to land tightly on the keel. With the trunk firmly clamped in place, the holes for screws or drifts can be bored. Then the trunk can be removed just one more time, bedding and a strand of cotton wicking applied, and the trunk

replaced and fastened home.

While such a technique is adequate, and successful enough, for some boats, there are drawbacks to it. The only line of defense against leaks is that relatively narrow panel-to-keel joint. If, over time, leaks do begin to occur along that joint, it will be difficult to tighten the trunk if screws were used (as they have little "bite" in the soft wood) and almost impossible with drifts.

A better approach, if the width of the keel will allow it, is to build the trunk using through-bolted rabbeted bedlogs.

BUILDING A RABBETED BEDLOG TRUNK

A bedlog is a fore-and-aft-running base for a centerboard trunk. It is usually a heavy piece of hardwood timber, such as oak, fit to the inside curve of the keel. Into the inner face, a rabbet the thickness of the centerboard side panel will have been cut. The outside of the bedlog has a series of holes bored vertically into it. Eventually, when the bedlog is in place and tightly fitted to the keel, these holes will be continued into and through the keel for through bolts.

Care needs to be taken to get a good joint between the bedlog and the inner surface of the keel. Putting carpenter's chalk on the keel and rubbing the bedlog against it will show up "high spots" on the bedlog. (Be sure to remove any chalk before bedding and installing the trunk.)

The construction of the bedlog centerboard trunk is quite similar to the basic trunk described above. The ledges are made in an identical fashion and are attached to the panel or plywood sides in the same method. The main difference is, instead of the trunk side panel being fit and vertically fastened to the keel, the panel is fit to the rabbet in the bedlog (which faces the inside of the trunk) and side fastened to it with either screws or rivets—similar to fastening a plank to a rabbeted stem. Although some builders spline this joint, a thorough bedding with a flexible adhesive should give it plenty of watertightness. The trunk can then be assembled, again checking that the fit to the keel is perfect, that the entire assembly is plumb in the boat, and that the "shoulders" on the tenons do not prevent the joint from closing up. If all is well, the holes in the log can then be continued down through the keel with a long bit.

The next step is to devise a proper gasket for bedding the trunk to the keel. Although in the past builders might have used rubber or canvas impregnated with white lead, today, a good coating of Sikaflex or 3M 5200 will probably suit the bill.

The grand finale here is the installation of the bolts. First, it will probably be necessary to countersink the holes just drilled on the bottom side of the keel for the bolt heads. (It is sometimes helpful to temporarily plug the holes with a short dowel to keep the counterbore from skidding). Anoint the holes with a shot of preservative.

Before installing the bolts, check (1) that they are long enough and (2) that they have enough threads cut into them to allow them to pull the whole assembly up tight. Then install the bolts (don't forget to wrap a twist of cotton wicking around the head). Tighten the bolts gradually, as though you were bolting a wheel onto your car or torquing an engine head. When the bolts are all tight you should have a good squeeze on the gasket and a trunk that should be leakproof for years.

CENTERBOARDS

A traditional centerboard is essentially a panel held together with drifts and bolts. It should be built up of individual boards of a heavy wood,

17-5: The ledge and its relationship to the other parts of a centerboard trunk.

17-6: The construction of a typical traditional wooden centerboard.

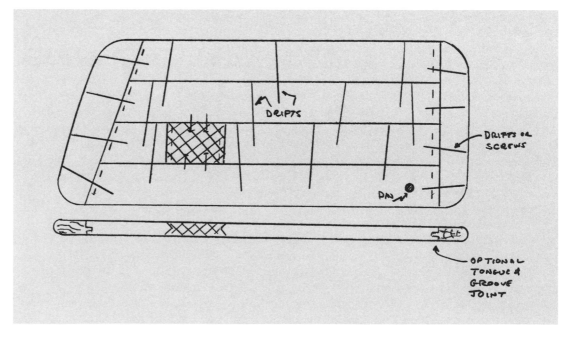

such as oak, with the grain alternately reversed to inhibit warping. The boards will generally be fastened together with drift pins. There may be some through-bolts, and often, to stiffen the board and discourage warping, tongue and grooved wooden cleats at the ends running 90 degrees and fastened to the rest of the boards. (See Figure 17-6.)

For ballast, the lower end of the board will have a square or rectangular aperture left open for lead. To hold the lead, nails can be driven into the edges of the inside of the hole and left standing proud, or the edges can be chamfered (beveled) to a "V" shape, which will allow the lead to flow around the V and lock itself in place.

17-7: An installed centerboard trunk in a small open boat. The centerboard is raised and lowered with a lanyard running through a hole in the centerboard trunk cap and tied off to a bronze cleat.

DRILLING FOR CENTERBOARD DRIFTPINS

To drill for the driftpins that will hold the individual pieces of the centerboard together, make up a pattern for the centerboard—it takes just a moment and will pay big dividends later on. Mill out the stock that you will be employing. It's not a bad idea to leave the stock just slightly over-length to allow for any possible miscues in construction; you can always trim the assembly later.

Find a flat spot to lay out your milled stock for the centerboard, side by side. How do they look? Do they all fit nice and square, snugly next to one another, or are there a couple of questionable members in the congregation with warped personalities? Give the nonconformists the bum's rush; this job has enough interesting qualities without introducing more. Pull the entire assembly together and immobilize it, using either bar clamps or blocks-and-wedges. Everything still lying flat and tight? If so, we're off to the races!

Transfer the shape of your trusty pattern onto your laid-up stock. Then take a few moments to number the boards and to lay out the locations of the drift pins, the through-bolts, the pocket for the poured lead, etc. It's also not a bad time to make up all those pins and bolts—then you'll have them for when they are needed and you'll be sure of the caliber of the rod and its length. Few phenomena are as disappointing as the belated realization that you've either drilled holes the wrong diameter for your rod (probably too large) or that the holes are drilled too shallow.

Okay? Good.

Release the assembly from its clamps. Now, let's start with the second board in from the edge. Using the tried-and-true method described in Chapter 9, The Keel, drill all the holes from the edges toward center. Next, clamp board one to board two. Make sure those two rascals are snug and dead flat relative to one another, as whatever you have now is what you'll end up with later. You can now use the holes drilled in board two as a doweling jig. Simply run the bits through the bore and into the adjoining board. It has to line up, and it has to run true—at least as long as the holes in board two are true.

For the drift pins, simply drill in to your predetermined depth; a long, undersize bit or a brazing rod make a convenient depth gauge. Don't forget to clean the bit. As for the through hole, you have a choice: either bravely blast all the way through, trusting the "doweling jig" to carry the day, or sneak up on it by drilling halfway with the "jig" and meet it from the other side as done previously.

Now the two boards' positions can be stabilized by either placing short dowels in a couple of the drift pin holes between plank one and two, or you can simply drive in the drifts and be done with it. Before choosing the latter course, however, check that you have a drill long enough to bore the full length of your bolts. Such a precaution can avoid considerable consternation later on.

On to board three. Drill the holes for the drifts in the same fashion as with plank one, then align and clamp the board tightly to boards one and two. Again run the bit through the bore and drill into board two. Then you can chase back through the bolt holes in boards one and two into board three. (Again, either going all the way through or using the time-tested two-ends-to-the-center method;

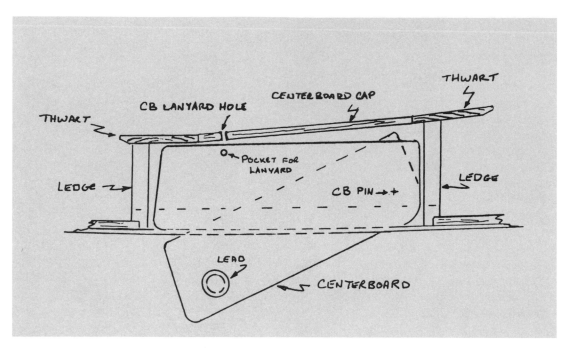

see Chapter 9.) Index once again with dowels or pins, and then it's on to boards four, five, and so on until all the holes have been drilled. You can now drive in all the drift pins, if you haven't done so already.

All that is really left after that is to countersink for the nuts and heads of those long bolts. Remember that the centerboard still needs to be trimmed off, so make those holes deep enough to take that into account!

Now we are just about ready to install the long bolts. Before doing so, however, I always like to chase the long bit one more time down the bore, just to eliminate the possibility of a chunk of crud being hung up in there someplace. Then install the bolts, trim off the centerboard, and there you are!

By the way, yes, plywood does make a nice centerboard.

GOING UP?

For lifting and lowering the board there are a number of options. One of the simplest is the lanyard or pennant option. The lanyard is attached to the board by feeding it into a small hole drilled into the top edge of the board, which leads into a larger "pocket" hole drilled partway in from the side of the board. A stop knot can be tied into the end of the lanyard, and the knotted end can be nested in the pocket hole. A copper patch can then be tacked over the pocket hole. The lanyard is threaded up through a hole in the centerboard trunk cap and made fast to a tie-off cleat. (See Figure 17-7.)

Another excellent system employs a lifting handle shaped a bit like an old-time fireplace poker. It is attached to a metal strap let in flush with the side of the centerboard. This arrangement, although a bit more complicated than the above, is quite effective, as it allows you to

push down on the board if the need arises.

To hold the centerboard in place in the fully raised position, consider installing above the waterline a bronze keeper pin (sort of a parking brake) that passes through both sides of trunk and the centerboard. Drill the pin for a lanyard that can be attached to the trunk.

On the matter of the centerboard cap: if a lanyard is used to lift the centerboard, consider lining the hole in the cap with a copper-tubing fairlead and installing a piece of brass half-round on top of the cap for the line to run over on its way to the jam cleat. Both of these will go a long way toward extending the life of the cap.

THE PIVOT PIN

The centerboard pivots on a pin. The hole in the board to take that pin must have some sort of bushing, as a pin constantly working against wood will eventually wear and oversize the hole. A small piece of pipe whose inside diameter is slightly larger than the specified pin and set in epoxy fits the bill nicely. A second option is a pipe nipple threaded into the wood. Yet another is to let in two bronze plates with matching holes on either side of the centerboard and rivet them in place.

Placement of the pin is important. If it is above the waterline, there is little worry of leaks. The same can be said if it is installed in the exterior part of the keel (outside and below the planking). If the pin is to be below the waterline, but inside the boat, the arrangement becomes a bit more complicated. When installing the bolt that will act as your pin, put a rubber washer underneath the washer on either side to ensure watertightness.

When tightening the pivot pin bolt there is sometimes a tendency for the sides of the trunk to be pulled

17-9: Tools for melting lead—a cast-iron pot, a ladle, and a propane-fired burner.

the canister) should be worn, as should a leather apron, a face shield, gloves, and rugged shoes. Check the weather, as even the smallest amount of water can cause the melted lead to spatter. Set up your operation so that any breeze is at your back, blowing the fumes away from you.

Set up the centerboard so it is dead level. Fasten a plate of either steel or hardwood to the bottom of the cutout aperture in the board. (See Figure 17-10.) If possible, clamp for extra security. Be sure the cavity is completely dry.

While the lead is melting stir it occasionally with a wooden paddle and remove any dross or slag that floats to the surface. Be sure that you have melted enough lead to fill all the space in one pour. (New molten lead will not stick to already cooled lead.) Work the lead to remove any air bubbles, and slightly overfill the opening to produce a lumpy, convex meniscus, as the lead will tend to slump as it cools. The lead will flow around the carved "V" in the opening, or the proud nails, locking it in place.

together, binding the centerboard. One way to prevent this is to use 5-minute epoxy to hold bronze washers on each side of the board at the pin hole. The epoxy will keep the washers in place while you get them into the trunk and will act as shims to keep the board from binding. Eventually the glue will fail, but no matter—by that time the washers will be in place, doing their job.

Another lead-pouring technique is to use two plates, one to cover the bottom of the aperture, the other the top. Drill a fill hole and a vent hole in the top plate. Pour the molten lead into the fill hole until it is visible in the vent hole.

After the lead has cooled, it can be smoothed with conventional woodworking tools.

POURING LEAD CENTERBOARD BALLAST

Melting and pouring lead is not something to be left to last-minute decisions. Although it is a very low-tech operation, several nasty repercussions are possible if you approach this operation in a cavalier fashion. One of the least of these could involve the local fire brigade.

I might mention that if the thought of molten lead gives you the heebie-jeebies, you might try another approach that some builders are using, which is to mix lead shot into a slurry of epoxy and trowel it into the aperture.

Molten lead is not only extremely hot, but also the fumes it gives off are toxic. The melting stove should be set up level, outside in an area protected from wind, on a gravel or other protective surface. As always when working with flammables, a fire extinguisher should be handy. The implements for working with lead are a cast-iron pot and a ladle, available from old-style hardware stores. (See Figure 17-9.) Personal protective garb is a must. A proper canister mask (check the ratings on

A PLYWOOD CENTERBOARD

At the risk of hearing cries of heresy from the more adhesophobic among us, let us consider the positive aspects of an epoxy- and fiberglass-sheathed plywood centerboard. A board made of a high-quality mahogany marine plywood, such as Bruynzeel, at the same dimensions as the conventional centerboard will

17-10: Lead ballast poured into an aperture in a centerboard, cross-sectional view.

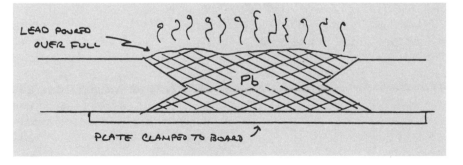

LEAD POURED OVER FULL

Pb

PLATE CLAMPED TO BOARD

☞ Weight of a Square Foot of Lead

Thickness Inch	Lead in Pounds
$^{1}/_{16}''$	3.691
$^{1}/_{8}''$	7.382
$^{3}/_{16}''$	11.074
$^{1}/_{4}''$	14.765
$^{5}/_{16}''$	18.456
$^{3}/_{8}''$	22.148
$^{7}/_{16}''$	25.839
$^{1}/_{2}''$	29.53
$^{9}/_{16}''$	33.222
$^{5}/_{8}''$	36.923
$^{11}/_{16}''$	40.604
$^{3}/_{4}''$	44.296
$^{13}/_{16}''$	47.987
$^{7}/_{8}''$	51.678
$^{15}/_{16}''$	55.37
$1''$	59.061

One cubic inch of lead = 0.410 pound

17-11: The rudder on a North Haven dinghy. Layout of the grain of the wood is critical in a shape such as this.

be extremely stable. Installing the aperture for the lead is easy, requiring only a hole saw to make a round hole that can have its edges chamfered to the "V" with a rasp. The bushing for the pin can be let in conventionally and anchored with epoxy. If there has been a pocket drilled for a lanyard, it too can be saturated with glue. Then the entire board can be sheathed with fabric and epoxy. Add a little graphite powder to the final coat of epoxy to increase scuff resistance and the overall durability of the coating, and you have a centerboard to be reckoned with.

Not sold on the idea of a plywood centerboard? Well then at least install a "push down" hole in the trunk cap on the off chance you may need to poke a rod down to encourage a recalcitrant swollen plank board out of the trunk.

NOTES ON FIXED-BLADE RUDDERS

Rudders for small craft come in numerous shapes and styles. Most are a variation of the fixed-blade type. The rudder has much in common with the centerboard, including unequal exposure to moisture and to stress.

The shape of the rudder can be easily lifted from the plans by laying out a scale grid on the plans and transferring the shape in full scale on a plywood pattern.

The traditional technique for constructing a rudder is to build it from two or more boards. This is preferable to using a single piece of stock, even if a wide enough piece were available, as more than one piece is a deterrent to warping.

Care needs to be taken when laying out and aligning the stock for the rudder to avoid weak "short" grain in the narrow portion of the rudder where it runs along the transom. If the grain in that narrow neck should run parallel to the transom, you might consider adding fore-and-aft through bolts to help the rudder resist breakage from twisting. The narrow portion of the rudderhead can also be reinforced with rudder cheeks that are through riveted in place.

Wood for rudder construction should be well seasoned; oak or mahogany are good choices. When the rudder is assembled, reverse the end-grain from one piece to the next, so the tendency of one piece to warp in one direction will be cancelled out by the next piece's tendency to warp in the other direction. If the pieces are fastened together with drift pins, the pins should be driven at slight angles relative to one another to lock the assembly and keep the pieces from pulling apart. A cleat installed across the bottom edge of the rudder, if the shape of the rudder allows it, can help deter warping.

Generally speaking, the rudder should be tapered or faired as it runs aft to the trailing edge of the blade. This tapering can be done with either a hand or power plane, and finished off with a disc sander. The leading edge should be either rounded or tapered as per the plans.

As with the centerboard, when all factors are considered, a plywood rudder, especially one laminated from a couple of sheets of plywood is a mighty attractive

alternative to the plank variety—it could even become one of tomorrow's classics.

17-12: Traditional built-up outboard wooden rudder on a small motorboat.

18 • STIFFENING THE HULL

Once the hull has been planked, it can be removed from the building jig and the fitting out can begin. Although much of this work is straightforward, albeit time-consuming, a major point must first be considered: How can the shape of the boat be kept from changing while the work is done?

STABILIZING THE HULL

The easiest way to stabilize the structure is by using cross bracing or spalls. The best time to make the cross spalls is when the boat is still on the construction jig, just before the boat is lifted off. A spall can be just a length of wood that is long enough to run across the boat from sheer to sheer, with wooden cleats fastened to it that are fitted to the inside and outside of the top of sheer. That way, if the boat wants to spring in or out after it is removed from the jig, you will be able to cajole it back into place with the already-made cross spalls. (Just remember to mark on the spalls which is the fore side and which is the after, and to note on the sheer of the hull exactly where these wonderful devices are supposed to fit.)

Oops, you say you forgot to make your cross spalls before removing the hull from the jig? Then go back to your molds and measure the widths at the sheer. With the assistance of a pipe clamp and a tape measure, check these widths at the appropriate places on the sheer of the hull; if they are off, push or pull the hull back into position.

After you are sure the hull shape is where you want it to be, you must affix other temporary bracing to hold that shape, as the cross spalls must be removed to allow access to the sheer. Cross pieces can either be attached to the untrimmed frames still standing proud of the sheer, or they can be positioned slightly below the point where the inwales will be fitted. That done, the cross spalls can be removed, and you are ready to proceed.

FLOORS

Floors are the vertebrae of the hull's backbone. They strengthen and hold the bottom in shape, so it is important that they are well fitted. There are a number of ways to obtain the shape of the floors, including lofting the forward and after faces of each one and fitting them before the hull is planked. However, the easiest method for the home builder is simply to scribe the fitted shapes of the floors directly from the planked hull.

Fit to the hull after planking

Begin by scribing and cutting the hull contour onto pattern stock. Although the shape can be traced directly onto the planed floor stock, lightweight pattern stock works faster, is a lot cheaper if you spoil a piece, and allows you to be more efficient when selecting your actual stock for construction.

Before removing your fitted floor pattern from the boat, record the bevel(s) of the hull planking onto the pattern with your bevel gauge. Then trace the shape onto the hardwood floor stock. Be sure to allow extra stock on the top side of the floor to allow for "shrinkage" of the floor timber as it is trimmed to fit the hull. Use a block plane and a spokeshave to work the bevel into each floor until it fits tightly to the hull.

Trimming the top

If the sole will ride above the top of the floors, or if nothing else depends on the top of the floors being at a specific height, you can simply mark the height above the top of the keel onto the floor and use a small level to provide a level line across the floor. This can then be trimmed on the bandsaw and planed square.

If, on the other hand, the floorboards are to be mounted directly on top of the floors, a bit more care must be used. In areas where there is sweep, spring a batten down into the curve and work the tops of the floors down until the batten lies flat against the generated angle.

A technique that works well in an area that runs dead flat over a number of floors is to first trim the forward and aftermost floors in the series so they are dead level. Then, make up a straightedge with a notch cut into it that is a little wider than the thickness of the floors. Remove all the middle floors except one. Dropping the notch over that middle floor, which will be taller, bridge the forward and after floors with the straightedge. The straightedge creates a plane that can then be marked onto the "tall" floor by sliding it along athwartships and marking it with pencil. Trim the "tall" floor and install it. Drop another floor into place and repeat the process.

After the floors have been fitted, they should be well dosed with preservative, or painted with red lead.

Fastening the floors

The fitted floors can now be fastened in place. The easiest way—although perhaps the less sporting one—to determine where the fastenings through the planking are to go is to place each floor in the hull at its final location and trace around it onto the planking with a pencil. Remove the floor, and with a fine drill bit bore pilot holes through the planking from the inside to the outside.

Replace the floor and drill back into it from the outside. The floor can be fastened to the keel either with screws for a small boat or with drifts for a large one.

☞ Don't Forget the Limbers!

A limber is a passage cut along the outside face of a timber, most often thought of in floors but also in bottom of the maststep, edges of the chines, sides of butt blocks, and any other piece that might impound water. The limbers in floors should be cut before they are installed. Make them of ample size to allow easy passage of water and line them up.

A practice not often seen any more, but popular in the past, was to run a light-caliber brass chain, called a limber chain, through the entire series of limbers in the floors. The ends of the chain, fore and aft, were accessible to the crew. The crew could grab an end and haul the chain back and forth, clearing any accumulated debris. Call the device a sort of nautical sewer snake.

KNEES

Knees are among the most important structures in a boat. They can be thought of as brackets or gussets that reinforce and brace. Their uses are myriad throughout the hull. They can be found stiffening the transom at the sheer, reinforcing the transom-to-keel joint, interconnecting the hull with the deck beams or thwarts at the sheer, and even underpinning the centerboard trunk.

The traditional knee uses the naturally grown curved grain found in the branches and roots of apple, oak, and hackmatack trees. When one considers the way the near-right-angle hackmatack root buttresses the entire tree, or the way the apple tree branch bears the weight of the fruit, one understands the strength of these naturally grown structures. For years, knees from grown crooks were the standard in the boatbuilding industry, but unfortunately the timber for them has become scarce and is available commercially only from a few specialty outfits.

Small boat builders, professional and amateur, can of course stalk and capture their own grown knee stock if they plan ahead. Occasionally, as an alternative, a builder can get by with a knee cut from relatively straight stock, but this is the least desirable option, as at least part of the knee will have short grain, which will be weak and may possibly fail.

Fortunately, for small craft, the strength of the naturally grown crook can be simulated with a steam-bent knee or even improved upon with a laminated knee.

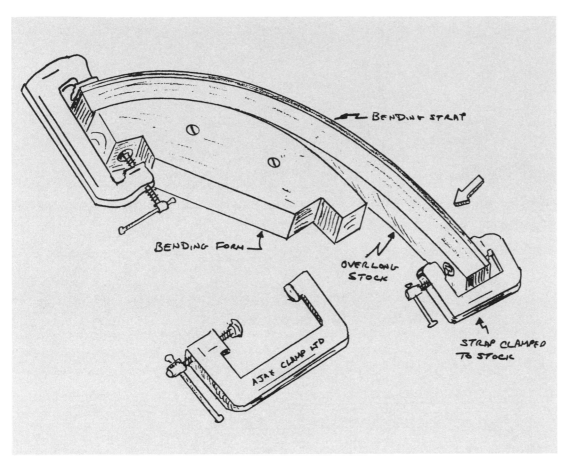

STEAM-BENT KNEES

The first step in the preparation of a steam-bent knee is to cut a bending jig from a stout piece of wood that will conform with the desired inside concave face of the knee. As with any steam-bending, the jig must have a little overbend built into it to accommodate a certain amount of springback in the stock.

The second step is to select and mill your stock with care, using only green stock and discarding any in which the grain runs out to the side or has any defects, such as rot, knots, or checks. (See Chapter 12, The Art of Bending Frames.) The stock should be milled with extra length to provide leverage when coming around the turn. To prevent side buckling, the width of the piece should be greater than its depth. Indeed, if the stock is wide enough, two knees can be cut from one bent piece.

The third and perhaps most important key to success is to use a bending strap. A metal tension strap clamped to both ends of the piece being bent will compress the inner face of the curve while preventing the outside fibers from stretching and causing failure. It will also hold the wood against the jig and restrain it from straightening out while it cools and hardens up. (See Figure 18-1.)

Note: Beware of using black iron for your strap if you will be bending oak, as iron in contact with steamed oak will impart a deep ebony color to the knee.

After the stock has taken its set, it can be fit either as a free-standing curved unit with an open back, or with a filler piece glued or mechanically fastened to the outside of the curve, which will provide a close approximation in appearance to a naturally grown knee.

LAMINATED KNEES

The laminated knee offers the best of all worlds. It is rugged, defect free, and good looking—at least if one can suppress the urge to use garishly contrasting woods. The fabrication technique is very nearly the same as making a laminated stem. (See Chapter 8, The Stem.) Perhaps the greatest difference is that the curve of the bend of the bending jig for the knee is greater than that for the stem, necessitating thinner laminates. All else—the quality of the stock, gluing procedures, organization and preparation—are the same.

Begin by cutting a gluing/bending jig of the correct size. Cutting angled flats on the side of the jig opposite the curve will allow easier clamping. Cut an experimental batch of laminations and run a trial clamp-up. Check to see that the strips close tightly without leaving gaps. Will you need custom, curved clamping blocks? As with the steam-bent knee, if the laminations are wide enough, two matching knees can be made from the same piece. If the trial run looks right, the knee can be glued up and left to cure.

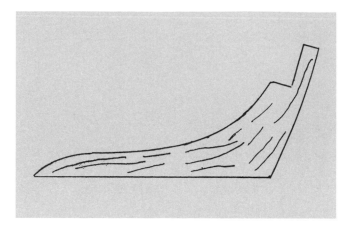

When the glue has set, the knee can be cut and fit in exactly the same fashion as the grown crook.

MAKING A PATTERN

A pattern for the knees can either be developed by eye or taken directly from the plans.

Method #1—By eye

First fit the pattern stock to the two critical sides that will be joined to the structure. This can be done by scribing. The elegant, visible inside curve can be drawn freehand or by using a ship's curve.

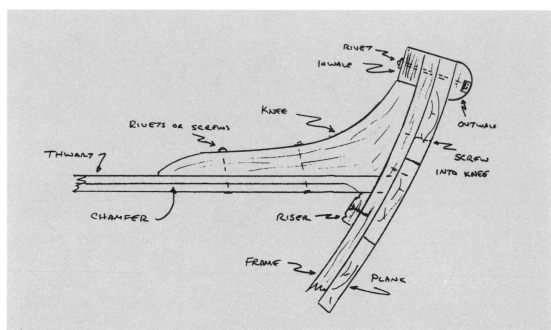

18-3: A fitted thwart knee.

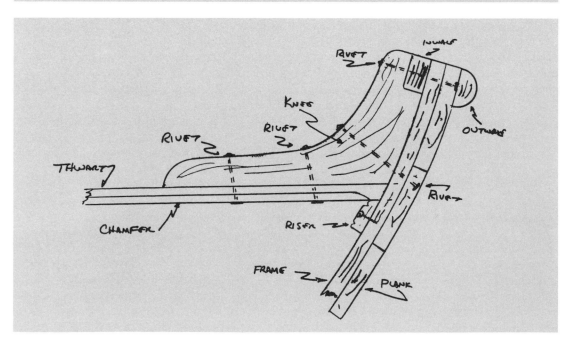

18-4: This fitted thwart knee isn't as elegant as that in Figure 18-3, but it's stronger.

Method #2—From the plans

Draw, in scale, a grid over the knee on the plans. (A one-inch grid works well for small craft, two- to three-inch for larger boats.) After fitting the two sides of the hull with the pattern stock, draw the grid full size onto the pattern. Mark the intersections of the curve of the knee on the scale grid and transfer them to the full-size grid. Connecting the intersections with a flexible batten and drawing the line will give you the curve of the knee visible inside the boat.

FITTING THE KNEE

With the pattern at the ready, you can proceed to fit the knee. Keep in mind that even with a pattern for the piece you should always cut the stock oversize, as knees have a habit of shrinking as they are being fit.

Fit the easy part first—i.e., the side with the least amount of shape. For the transom knee, for example, the easy part would be the flat beveled side that joins the transom. For the thwart knee it would be the flat side that lands on top of the thwart. Next, fit the curved, compound angle where the knee touches the hull. Then fit any notches or tabs, such as where a knee joins an inwale. And, finally, after all else is done, cut the long, curved outside.

A NOTE OF CAUTION WHEN USING KNEE PATTERNS

Keep in mind that the pattern is only a two-dimensional representation of the shape of the knee. What this rather obvious statement means is that the pattern does not give you the full picture of what's really going on. For example: You have spent a goodly amount of time fitting a knee to a raked transom. This has been a tricky business,

with a lot of bevels to contend with. You are ready to cut the final (visible) curve on the knee. You place the pattern on top of the knee, you trace the shape onto it, you take the knee to the bandsaw, you cut square, right to the line. You take the knee back to the transom and find it's all wrong! Egad, what happened?

The rake of the transom is the culprit here. Although the pattern is accurate for the top of the knee, if you cut the shape out square, the knee will be too shallow on the bottom side. The reality here is that the angle of the cut must be roughly the same angle as the rake of the transom. One of the easiest ways to get this angle is to trace your pattern on both the top and the bottom of the knee. Then, cut square to the bottom side and spokeshave to the top, and the angle will develop virtually automatically.

Note: The outside, decorative curve of a knee pattern should be considered negotiable. Difficulties in fitting the knee to the boat may require changes to the pattern if the knee runs out of stock.

DRILLING AND FASTENING

Getting the fastenings to be right where you want them can be a tricky business. Many times holes for transom knees are drilled at the wrong angle, causing the fastenings to emerge from the side of the knee. Or worse, the bored holes miss the knee altogether, requiring artful repair to a structure that is often to be varnished.

One solution to this conundrum is to first drill a pilot hole from the inside out, then chase back from the outside in. Begin by clamping the fitted knee in place and tracing its locale on the hull with a pencil. Then, using a bevel gauge, capture the angle at which it lies

18-5: Quarter-knee camber at the transom.

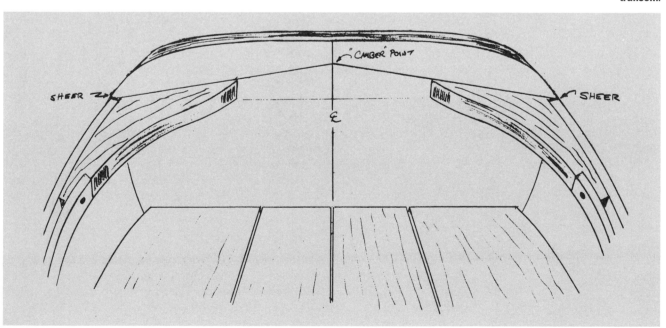

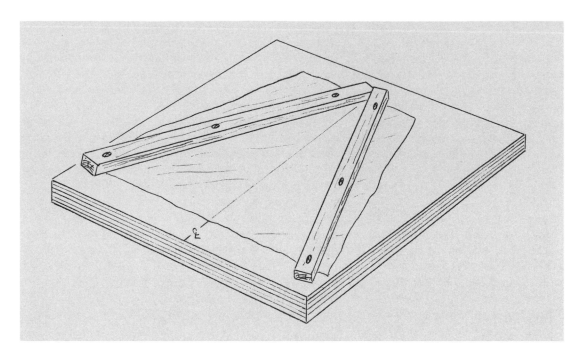

18-7: Marking the stock for a two-piece breasthook.

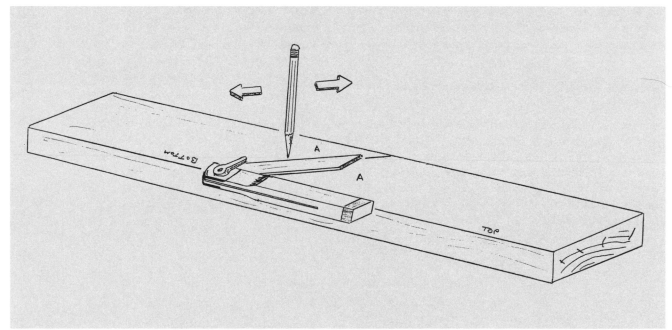

against the transom; this is the angle at which the fastening holes must be drilled.

Unclamp the knee and remove it. Draw a line midway between the edges of the knee already traced on the transom in pencil. Lay out your fastening locations on that line. Note: If the knee is highly visible, such as one on a varnished transom, a bit more elegant appearance will be achieved if the fastenings are laid out symmetrically.

For drilling the pilot hole, fit a long, undersized bit into your drill. Then, using a bevel gauge as your guide to the proper angle, drill from the inside mark to the outside.

The knee can then be clamped back into place. With a countersink/counterbore of the proper size and using the pre-drilled pilot hole as a guide, bore back from the outside, into the knee. The bored hole has to come out exactly right.

Unclamp the knee, apply a thin coat of bedding compound to the edges, clamp it back into place, and fasten.

THE BREASTHOOK

Ah, the breasthook! 'Tis the keystone in the arch, the gusset in the truss, the nautical nexus. Or, more prosaically, it is the triangular wooden plate fitted inside the planking just abaft of the stem that helps unite and tie the entire bow structure together. Any way you slice it, it is vital to the

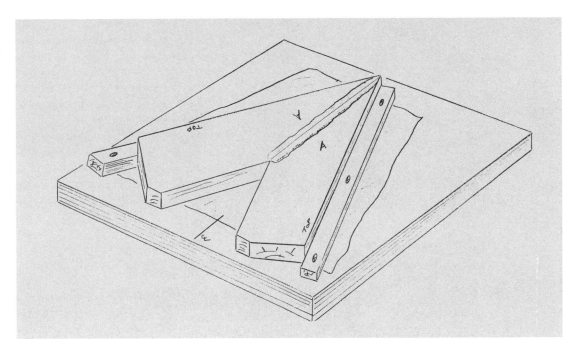

structural integrity of the boat. For the working or decked-over boat, the breasthook only has to be well joined and rugged. In the open boat, it also has to look right.

TYPES OF CONSTRUCTION

A breasthook can be made from a natural crook with suitable grain, such as apple, hackmatack or oak, of laminated stock, or even of joined, solid pieces. Any of these will do a good job. The decision as to which to use is a combination of the practical (is the stock available, and how long will it take to fashion the piece?) and the aesthetic (does it look good?).

If the proper stock is selected, a naturally grown breasthook can be a handsome thing, indeed, but it is not for the impulse shopper. Running out to the backyard with the chainsaw at the last minute and lopping a chunk off your spouse's favorite McIntosh simply will not do (for a number of reasons). To avoid unneeded shrinking, warping, and cracking, be sure your stock is well seasoned. (True devotees of the natural crook have been known to collect their wares years in advance.) When shopping for a natural crook, inspect the article carefully. What at first glance appears to be the perfect piece may just be the product of two trees grown together and therefore structurally weak. Also be on the lookout for insidious rot, common in apple wood, and insect life residing within.

Laminated breasthooks, just as the laminated knees described above, can be exceptionally strong when glued properly. The plusses and minuses are the same as for laminated knees.

Glued-up breasthooks, joined in two halves, can be quite durable, are a cinch to make, and can have a hand-some, bookmatched mien. Built from dry, off-the-shelf, straight-grained stock, such as oak or mahogany, these basic units are stable and economical, and require no special expeditions to the wood lot. For the home builder with limited specialty tools, this type of 'hook might offer the most straightforward route.

A GLUED-UP BREASTHOOK

Making the jig

Job one is to whip up an assembly jig. No fancy materials are needed here. Just rustle up a square of ½-inch plywood roughly 18 inches square to serve as a base, two pieces of 1- by 2-inch pine for the sides, a handful of drywall screws to hold the whole business together, and a piece of clear, 4- or 6-mil polyethylene large enough to cover the plywood for a non-stick surface.

Next, determine the approximate angle of the shape of the breasthook as it fits into the bow of the boat. This can done either by picking up the angle with a pocket bevel gauge from the plans or by simply tracing the actual angle onto a piece of pattern stock laid atop the planking where it enters the stem, then picking up the angle with a bevel gauge.

Record the triangular shape that the breasthook will fill on the plywood base with a pencil. Then bisect the angle. (If you can't remember how to do that, break out your old high school geometry book.) This will be your center or "joint" line. Capture this bisected angle on a piece of wood—you'll be needing it later. You can now staple the plastic over the plywood.

Align the 1 by 2s along the outer edges of the triangle on the face of the base, fasten them with drywall screws, and you're in business.

18-9: Bar clamps are used to force the two pieces of the breasthook tightly into the assembly jig.

18-10: Test-fit the glued-up breasthook in place. The dotted lines represent the final after edge.

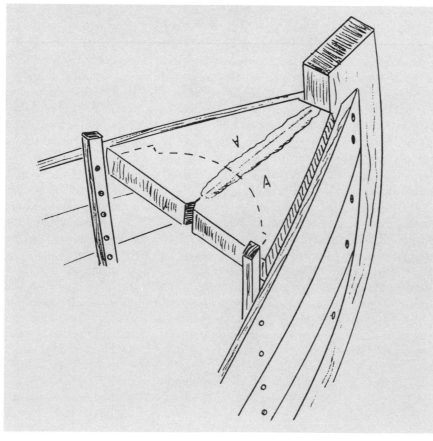

Getting out the stock

What to look for? Sound, clear, and dry stock is what is needed for this job. Check out the plans for dimensions. Keep in mind that these are finished measurements. You may want to allow for extra thickness to permit a bit of camber, or curvature, to be carved into the top of the breasthook. Also, check that your stock will allow you to cut the pieces a little over size, as, like knees, a roughed-out breasthook has a habit of getting too small, too fast. That little extra wood may just save the day.

After finding the perfect piece of wood, you are ready to cut. Set your bevel gauge to the bisected angle and, while holding one leg on the edge of the stock, mark the angle all the way across the stock. (See Figure 18-7.) Take the wood to the bandsaw and cut along the line. Then, flip over one piece and put it together with the other piece, sawed-edge to sawed-edge. You now have the makings of your book-matched breasthook blank.

Lock the two pieces together, side-by-side, kerf-side-up, in a vise and plane them smooth and square. When the pieces are almost there, check the fit by sliding the pair into the jig. The fit will be perfect when the pieces are snug against the 1 by 2s and the joint at the centerline will be tight. (See Figures 18-8 and 18-9.) When you have achieved that, you are ready to glue.

Gluing and clamping

Before gluing, make a dry run to iron out your technique. You'll be needing a few C-clamps for holding the stock down, and two pipe or bar clamps to pull the stock into the jig. The principle here is that the more you pull the stock into the V-shaped jig, the tighter the joint will be. The C-clamps are there to keep the pieces from rolling up when they are drawn in. When all looks right, whip up your glue, butter up your pieces, and clamp 'er up!

Note: While epoxy is usually the glue of choice for this job, not all epoxies are formulated to work well with acidic woods, such as oak. Peruse the manufacturer's recommendations—you may wish to switch to another adhesive, such as a resorcinol.

Cutting and fitting

Now the breasthook is ready for fitting. While it is helpful to develop a pattern for the breasthook from the plan as an aid toward symmetry, it should be used only as a guide. A breasthook is a melody of tapers, compound angles, curves, and cuts. If you simply trace the pattern onto the blank, capture a bevel or two, and fearlessly zip the piece through the bandsaw, the odds that the piece will come out right are fairly low. You need to sneak up on this bit of joinery. So, before firing up the saw, let's take a look at a couple of matters that are common to whatever type of breasthook stock you use.

Do you wish to have a bit of camber on top of the 'hook? Then the blank must be installed slightly above the sheer. This will affect how far up you will bevel the sides of the blank that will lie against the planks. Notching the 'hook around the stem is recommended. A well-done job looks great, and a poorly fitted one does not; furthermore, a notch adds no strength and provides a rot-promoting water trap. There's much to be said for eliminating the notch—just beveling the forward side of the 'hook to fit the after face of the stem and leaving the sides of the stem open as limbers. This technique is fast and has an understated elegance.

Begin the job by squaring off enough of the forward point of the blank to allow it to lie on top of the sheer and up against the stem. Then, using your bevel gauge, pick up the angle of the after face of the stem relative to the breasthook. Take the blank to the handsaw and bevel the squared-off end to fit the stem.

Next, put the blank back onto the sheer. Line the blank's middle joint up with the centerline of the boat. Then, holding the piece so that it doesn't shift, trace the inside face of the planking onto the bottom side of the piece with a pencil. Again using your handy mini-bevel gauge, capture the angle of the planking relative to the blank. (Note: this may be a compound bevel.)

At this point, label the top and the bottom of the 'hook. This will help you to keep track of what you are doing. Okay? Then off to the bandsaw.

Following the curved line drawn onto the bottom of the piece, make a square cut. This will bring your scribed line to the top edge of the blank. Now mark the desired camber height line along the newly cut edge. Set the bandsaw to the lowest (least) angle that you picked up with the bevel gauge and, with the "top" side up, cut the angle into the side of the breasthook blank, following along the drawn camber line (the edge of the 'hook will

18-11: A roughed-out breasthook temporarily fastened in place. Note that the top surface is higher than the top edge of the sheer plank. That's to provide enough wood for the camber.

remain square above that line).

Then pop the 'hook into the vise and clean up the cut surface with a low-angle block plane. Check it with the bevel gauge and make any necessary adjustments to the angle of the sides. Of course, the trimming and fitting of the angle will make the 'hook "smaller," allowing it to drop into place. When it drops in, you may need to trim the forward angle of the 'hook relative to the stem to accommodate the breasthook's final location.

After final trimming, the breasthook should fit snugly forward, port and starboard. (See Figure 18-10.) Use clamps to hold it in place, then drill and temporarily fasten it in place with screws. (See Figure 18-11.)

Tabs, curves, and cambers

The next job is to mark off the "tabs" on the breasthook that the inwales will be fastened to. The tabs are the same width as a frame, so simply use a piece of frame as a spacing gauge and mark both the top and bottom on each side of the 'hook. Mark where your right-angled end cuts are. They should be equidistant from the bow end. Take the breasthook back to the vise and make your cuts. A supersharp Japanese saw (a.k.a., Piranha-on-a-Stick) is just the ticket for this job. Reinstall the unit in the boat and check your fits with a short piece of inwale stock. The inwale should easily land flush on the new tab. Mark where the inboard side of the inwale contacts the breasthook. It is from this point on one side to its counterpoint on the other that the after face of the breasthook will be drawn.

This is where the breasthook pattern (remember that pattern?) comes in. This curve of the after face has little

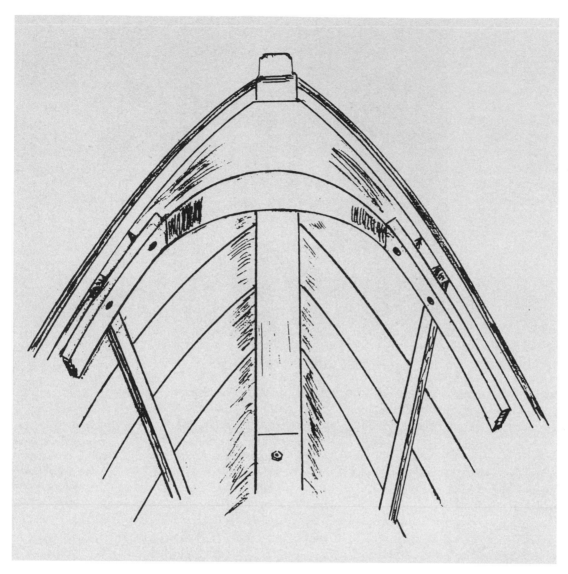

to do with strength but lots to do with good looks. The eye expects a nice, continuous curve that connects the inboard end of the port inwale to the same point on the starboard one. This can be gained from the pattern; alternately, it can come from a light batten sprung between the two inwales. That curve, when it is cut, should be beveled to mime the rake of the stem; there should be no bevel if the stem is plumb. The easiest way to make this bevel is with a bandsaw, cutting the curve plumb, then finishing with a spokeshave.

All that remains is to plane in the camber. With a block plane and a spokeshave, work from the centerline to the sheerline. The height of the camber will be greatest aft and least right behind the stem. After the curve has been shaved in with artful symmetry, give it a final rubdown with sandpaper and you're almost there!

The newly cut camber will make the after face of the 'hook look thicker in the center than it is where it meets the inwales. (See Figures 18-12 and 18-13.) A quick remedy is to set your marking gauge to the depth of the

inwale and draw a line parallel to the camber onto the after face of the 'hook. Spokeshaving a bevel to that line on the underside of the hook will provide the subtle illusion of equal thickness.

And there you have it—cut, fit, and all ready to go. And don't forget the bedding compound!

A couple of extras

For extra security, a through-bolt can be added after the 'hook has been fitted. A bronze rod threaded with nuts and washers at either end in countersunk holes fits the bill nicely. Also, if your boat is one that is often lifted by the breasthook, try customizing the hook with a handhold depression sculpted underneath.

INWALES AND OUTWALES

The inwales and outwales, when installed, build into the sheer a type of sprung truss or girder that really beefs up the strength of the boat. Although these members are straightforward in their positioning, as always, there are a few points and stratagems to consider.

Inwale aesthetics

Just as one expects "virtual camber" in the breasthook and transom knees, so is the case with the inwales and outwales. Having the inwales set in slightly higher than the sheer, as though you were planning to run a deck over them, looks great. Conversely, inwales that are set so you can run a straightedge from top-of-sheer-plank to top-of-sheer-plank will leave you, well, flat.

So how do you obtain this jaunty inner uplift? One way is simply to do it by eye. Lightly clamp the inwale to the frames and slide it up or down. When you get it where you want it, mark the location.

Another method often used is simply to use a square to line up the inwale with the sheer. This works well enough as long as there is enough flare in the sheer. This method works less well if the sides are plumb, and really less well if there is tumblehome.

A third, near surefire technique, is to use the beam camber pattern. (To make it, see Chapter 21, The Deck.) Situate the pattern atop the sheer, running across the boat from side to side, then simply slide the inwale up to the bottom of the pattern, clamp, and mark the location.

Outwale aesthetics

Many construction plans call for the forward end of the outwales, or rubrails, to be reduced in dimension—in thickness, and sometimes in width as viewed in profile—to account for a trick of perspective as they approach the stem. If a rail is left at its full dimension throughout its length, it actually seems to the observer to grow in size, giving it a chunky sort of mien. The solution is to make the outwales a little thinner forward. To the eye they look as thick as the rest of the rail back aft. Go figure.

Configuration

A typical arrangement is the "open wale," in which a sandwich is created, consisting of the outwale, or rubrail, attached to the sheerstrake, fastened through a steam-bent frame, and finished off on the inside with a sprung-in inwale. For overall practicality, this approach is my favorite, as it allows plenty of ventilation and also permits you to easily dump water from the hull by rolling it up onto the sheer. It is, therefore, the one I will describe here.

Installing the inwale

The place to begin is with the inwale, the fitting of which has a bit more to it than would first seem possible. Plenty of poorly joined and not-quite-long-enough inwales have made their appearance over the years. The problem arises because fitting the inwale seems so easy—just chop it off and stick it in. The catch is that it is a sprung fit into the "tabs" on the breasthook and the transom knee. If the proper fitting to the inner girth of the hull isn't taken into account, the inwale will come up short every time.

To begin, make your inwale over long. Using a bevel gauge, pick up the bevels of the fit of the inwale to the breasthook, mark the end of the inwale, and cut. Fit the end of the inwale into the "tab" of the breasthook, spring the inwale in place along the sheer of the boat, and clamp it at your positioning marks. It will be too long at the transom knee, so just let it run out over the knee.

18-13: A finely fitted breasthook, flowing into and out of the stem, the forward-most frame pair, and the inwales.

Chances are good that the fit at the breasthook will be close, but not perfect. So break out your favorite backsaw or Japanese trim saw and run it through the ill-fitting joint between the breasthook and the end of the inwale. The saw will take a little off from each side of the joint. With a wooden mallet, tap the after end of the inwale forward. Check the fit. Still need a little more trimming? Saw and tap again until the fit is perfect.

Next, pick up the bevels necessary at the transom-knee end. With the inwale still clamped in place, mark where you think the cutoff point should be for the after end to fit the transom knee. Then give yourself an extra ¼ inch. Mark the bevels, remove the rail, and make your cut.

Replace the inwale in the boat as before, clamping and checking the position, only this time place the after end in the tab of the transom knee. The bow end will be just a little too long to fit into its tab. Not to worry. Saw through the joint at the after end, and slide the inwale aft. With a few more saw cuts in the joint back aft, the forward end should snap into place.

Remove the inwale, bed the joint, and put the inwale back. If the outwale is to be fastened with screws, the inwale can now be fastened with rivets. Check first that it is still clamped to the marks, and then drill for the first rivet from the center of the inwale through the frame and sheer plank. Then drive a copper nail from the sheer plank side and peen it over a burr, or rove, on the inwale side.

If the inwale is to be through fastened to the outwale, just clamp it in place until the outwale has been fit.

Installing the outwale

Compared to the inwale, the outwale, or rubrail, is a cinch to fit, as all it has to do is accommodate the sheer and be beveled to fit the stem. The backside (sheer plank side) of the outwale should be hollowed slightly to match the curve of the hull and to allow for bedding. Make it long enough to run out past the transom; the excess can be trimmed off after fastening.

After the outwale has been properly clamped into place, the fastenings can go in. If the outwale is to be screw fastened, walk off the screw locations with a pair of dividers; using a countersink/counterbore, drill for the screws, then drive them.

If you are fastening with through-rivets, begin by fastening the forward end of the outwale into the stem with screws. At each frame bore from the center of the outwale to the center of the inwale using a sighting stick; counterbore for plugs on the outwale side. Drive and peen the rivets, and finish up at the transom knee with screws. Trim off the end of the outwale at the transom, and shape the end as necessary.

FINISHING UP

The tops of the frames can now be trimmed off. A super-sharp Japanese saw works well for this. To protect the outwale and inwale from sawtooth marks while you do this, use a protective pad—simply a piece of cardboard with a hole the size of the cross section of a frame cut out of the middle. Finish off the job by using a long fairing board to tune together all the pieces—the outwale, the inwale, the frame tops, and the sheer plank.

19 • INTERIOR WORK

No end of work is required to finish off the interior of a boat, everything from risers to oarlock pads. Let's look at the tasks, one at a time.

RISERS

Risers are the fore-and-aft interior stringers or members that support the thwarts; they are fastened to the inside face of the frames on each side of an open boat. Generally, they are fastened to the frames either with rivets or screws. Installing the risers is a straightforward operation.

The first task is to determine just where each of the two risers lie in the boat. The location of the top of the riser is generally given on the construction plan, either numerically as offsets or illustrated well enough that it can be scaled down from the sheer with a scale rule. Keep in mind, however, that any distances given or scaled on the profile plan are measured vertically, and not along the curve of the hull. You are likely to be more accurate if you square down the prescribed distance from a straightedge spanning the boat from sheer to sheer. It is not at all uncommon for the top of the sheer on one side to be

slightly higher or lower than the other side. Double check those installation marks with a level (you did level the boat up, didn't you?) to ensure that the thwarts will lie on the same plane. Then spring a batten through the marks for a fair line, mark the inside face of the frames, and you're ready to start installing the risers.

Spiling

Although some boats are of a shape that allow the risers to be sprung or edge-set into place, others, notably those craft with a lot of sheer or with a wide, heavy riser, will require that the risers be spiled. The technique is similar to spiling the hull planking (with the exception that the operation is an inside job).

Tack the spiling batten to the inside of the hull, and record the marks from the inside of the frames onto the spiling batten. To get the bottom edge, draw a line equidistant to the first line by the width of the riser.

Making the riser

The shape of the riser can be transferred from the batten to the riser stock, and the riser cut out. Or, if you are working with expensive wood, a pattern of common stock can

19-1: This may be a small boat, but the interior is still complex and fitting it properly is time consuming.

THWARTS

Curiously, a builder who would never consider trying to get out a plank without spiling will, nonetheless, reject the notion of using a pattern to fit a thwart, or a bulkhead. You see it all the time. "A waste of time," grumps our friend, "Let's just get on with it!"

But all three operations—getting out planks, thwarts, and bulkheads—have much in common. Usually, costly and difficult-to-come-by stock is used, and the work itself involves complex fits with compound bevels that must be right on. The material is hardly the stuff to be throwing away in a trial-and-error process, as if it were a common 2 by 4.

The miracle of patterns

A thwart can be a particularly sporty unit to fit to the hull. This is probably because it looks so darn simple. The novice installer, throwing care to the winds, will plunge into the fray with his ever-so-pricey mahogany plank, confident in the knowledge that in only a few moments of masterful scribing, cutting, and shaving the job will be over, and he will soon be off to more challenging stuff. Bad move.

What our tenderfoot has neglected to account for is that the hull tapers, not only fore-to-aft but also downward toward the keel. If that is not enough to add interest to the project, the bevel at the ends of the thwart is likely to be compound as it lies against the hull. Blissfully unaware, our plucky builder commences to scribe, cut, and shave—dashing from boat to bench and back again countless times until he makes his final cut, only to discover that the seat is now too short! Uh-oh!

"Well, maybe there's enough stock left to use for the next seat," says the speed demon, "And this time it'll work!" Maybe.

That's a tough way to run a railroad, though, when there is an easier way. With a pattern.

be made that will allow you to check the fit before cutting the real thing.

Installing the riser

If the riser has been properly spiled, it should lie in place easily, without having to be forced and without a tendency to roll up. The job will require clamps with the deepest throats you have to hold the riser in place for fastening; further offset clamping pressure might be necessary. (This is a job where an extra set of hands can be helpful.) As the fastenings will be visible, lay out their locations beforehand and then install.

19-2: A pattern for fitting a thwart.

THWART PATTERN

When making a pattern for a thwart, first determine the location of the thwart on the risers from the con-

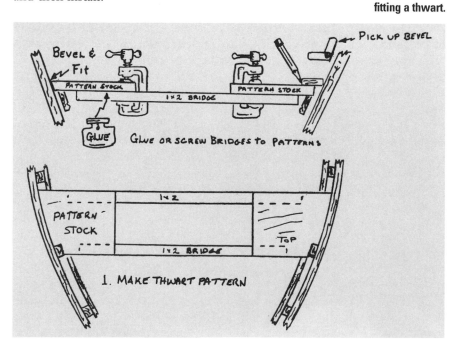

struction plans. Occasionally this site is given numerically, but chances are better than average that you will need to measure for it with your scale rule. Then check the squareness of your marks on the boat by measuring back to a point on the centerline, either at the stem or the transom. Those location marks you've established should be equidistant from the centerline point.

Next, dig out two pieces of short stock that are the same thickness and width as the finished thwart will be. (Ratty cedar works well for this.) Then find a couple of pieces of 1- by 2-inch stock that are just a little shorter than the length of the thwart. These will be for "bridging," or connecting, the end pieces.

This type of pattern is based on the premise that the most difficult part of whipping up a thwart is capturing the proper shape of the thwart at the ends where they contact the hull. After you have the ends, you can connect them with the "bridge stock," which will give you the necessary thwart length.

To begin, temporarily clamp a piece of the short pattern stock (a.k.a., the end template) at the location of the thwart on the riser. Use a block of wood and a pencil to scribe the curve of the hull and the cutouts (if any) for the frames onto the pattern stock. Then pick up the bevel with a bevel gauge.

Next, set the bandsaw to the angle picked up with the bevel gauge, and cut out the scribed curve on the pattern stock. Bring the end template back to the boat and clamp it in place. It should fit just right (or be

19-3: Checking the fit of the pattern in the boat.

very close). Repeat the procedure for the other side. Then glue or fasten the bridging rails to the bottom side of the end templates, lining them up parallel to the athwartship edges of the patterns. And there you have all the necessary information in one place to manufacture the thwart with no further trundling back and forth to the bench. (See Figure 19-3.)

Making the thwart

Now, put the completed pattern, bottom side up, on top of your thwart stock and trace the shape. (See Figure 19-4.) Label it bottom. Cut out the shape square on the bandsaw, which will bring your lines to the other (top) side. You can now cut or plane in the bevels. (Check one more time before you do to make sure that the bevels will be cut on the correct side of the thwart; an error here and you will make an inverted piece that probably won't fit.)

That's all there is to it. It has to come out right—the first time.

Still not convinced it's worth the effort? Do you want to try it without the pattern? Well then, at least start with the longest thwart first....

UNDER-THWART BRACES

If the thwarts require transverse bracing to prevent flexing or "oilcanning," the proper length and fit of the brace can be obtained in much the same fashion as the shape of the thwarts. First mark the landing points of the

19-4: Using the pattern to make the finished thwart. Trace the pattern onto the stock, cut the thwart square, then cut in the proper bevels.

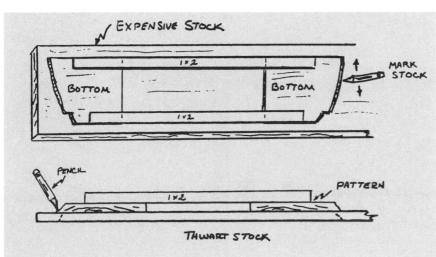

19-5: A finished thwart in place, locked there with a thwart knee and fastenings into the seat riser.

counterbore. Disassemble one last time, bed, reassemble, and screw. That's it!

MAST PARTNER AT THE THWART

If the plans call for a mast stepped through a thwart, the size and location of the hole, and the angle of the sides of the hole to follow the rake of the mast, can be predetermined on scrap stock and fastened to the center of the thwart pattern. This can be traced onto the thwart stock at the same time as the rest of the information. Keep in mind that, just as when cutting the ends of the thwarts, there are angles that have to be dealt with to avoid cutting a mirror image of the hole, rather than the proper shape.

One way to ensure the correct location of the partner is to index the edges of the center (mast partner) part of the pattern onto the thwart stock and square those edges around to the other side. Then make light plywood patterns, with exactly the same dimensions as those you just traced, for the top and bottom faces of the center of the thwart pattern—holes and all. Label them appropriately.

brace on the riser. Then fit the two ends of the brace to the riser, using pattern stock of the same dimension as the brace, and connect them with a third piece of pattern stock. This shape can then be transferred to the brace stock, cut out, and fit.

A thwart brace can be made much better looking without substantial loss of strength with the addition of decorative scalloping on the bottom edge. To ensure symmetry, make a half pattern of the desired scalloping—actually, a pattern that is a bit longer than half, with a centerline—that can be flipped over onto the port and starboard sides of the brace. Then it's a simple matter of tracing and cutting.

To ensure a good fit of the brace to the risers and the thwart, put the thwart in place on the riser, making sure all the fits are tight. Clamp the brace to the thwart with deep-throated clamps, and trace both sides of the brace onto the bottom side of the thwart. Remove the thwart and the brace from the riser. Unclamp the brace from the thwart. Draw a line on the thwart to locate the fastenings between the two brace lines, and drill index holes from the bottom up.

Now, reinstall the thwart and the brace in the boat, and clamp them in place. From the top side of the thwart, drill down through your index holes into the brace with a countersink/

Trace the top pattern on top of the thwart, the bottom on the bottom. Check with a pair of dividers that the top and the bottom are indeed where they are supposed to be. Then cut your hole undersized

19-6: A fitted forward thwart with knees. Note that the edge of the thwart has been chamfered.

☞ Horning, Isosceles, and It's All Greek to Me

Horning is a technique that utilizes the isosceles triangle to establish a line that is square to the keel. Fast and easy to accomplish, it has many applications in the construction of a boat, including determining and checking the transverse locations of molds, transoms, bulkheads, thwarts, and oarlocks.

The theory

The isosceles triangle has two equal sides. Picture it as two matching right triangles put together back to back, the equal sides acting like the hypotenuses. When horning, we have a centerline, comparable to the matched-up sides of those triangles, that intersects the base of our isosceles triangle. The distance out from that centerline intersection to those outside hypotenuse-like legs is equal. So much for the geometry review.

A practical application

The plans say that the thwart for your spiffy pulling boat should be installed at frame 13. All well and good, but back when you steam-bent those frames in, you considered yourself lucky that the blasted things bent in at all, never mind in the exact position indicated on the plans. The chances are better than average that they weren't all installed 100 percent symmetrically.

Not to worry. Cut yourself a piece of straight, light stock (1 inch by 2 inch), long enough to reach across the boat, riser to riser, at frame 13, and lay it there. Using two tape measures, take the ends of the two tape measures to the centerline on the inside of the stem. Bring the other ends to the points where the straight stick touches the riser on either side of the boat. Swing the stick until the tapes read the same. Those equal readings indicate that the stick is now running square to the centerline of the boat. A thwart installed in place of the stick will also be square to the centerline.

On the matter of oarlocks

The same technique will work for the positioning of the oarlocks. Roughly establish the locations of the oarlocks as given by the plans. Again, use a straightedge that will span the boat, from sheer to sheer. Select a center point, either on the breasthook or on the stem head; as before, using either

your measuring tapes or trammel points on a beam, tinker the straightedge back and forth until the two "legs" of the triangle are equal. C'est tout! You are ready to row.

Fair enough, you say, but what if the designer, in a weak moment, forgot to establish the oarlock locations on the plans? Actually, this is a common omission on boat plans. Part of this is due to deference to personal preference—rowers have their own ideas about the placement of oarlocks, just as car drivers have the same about the adjustment of their seats. Sometimes the decision on placement is made on more mundane criteria, such as: Where will the darn things fit?

At any rate, to my knowledge there is no hard-and-fast formula for determining the exact position of the oarlocks for a particular boat, other than clamping the oarlock pads in place and jumping into the boat with a pair of oars and trying them out. But there is a general rule of thumb that seems to work in a majority of cases: center the 'locks 12 inches aft of the after edge of the thwart. So just square up from that "mid-thigh" edge of the thwart to the sheer and move aft a foot, and you should be pretty close.

Putting the isosceles triangle to work in boatbuilding.

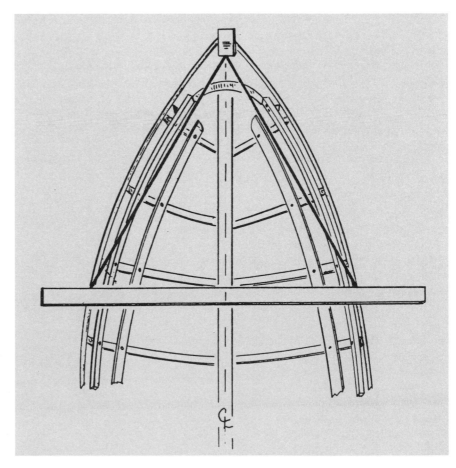

19-7: A rather long thwart stiffened with an under-thwart brace and supported with a turned post.

For example, to fit a one-piece plywood partition that is bordered by a cockpit sole, a centerboard trunk, a deck beam, and a curved hull:

First, get out the largest part of the template by using either a solid piece of cheap plywood or making up a wooden frame. Fit it to the centerboard trunk and sole. This is easy to do as the two structures form a square corner, and the rest of the pattern can be a loose fit to the beam and the hull.

On a piece of scrap lumber, scribe the camber of the deck beam. Cut out the curve, and affix the scrap, with its new radius, to the pattern.

Then make up pointers from pieces of scrap wood the same thickness as the future bulkheads and affix them to the pattern at several locations to capture the hull's shape. With a bevel gauge, take and record the bevel between the pattern and the hull at each pointer.

If you use scrap pieces to pad out the pattern to the hull, the work will take longer, but you won't have to record the bevels separately. (This technique is the same as for determining the end shape for the thwart pattern.)

Remove the pattern, lay it on the bulkhead stock, and trace off the shape. If you used pointers to determine the shape against the hull, spring a batten through the points to mark the curve. (See Figure 19-9.) Cut in the bevels, and there you are!

and work out to the drawn lines.

With the hole for the mast cut, the reinforcing mast partner can be fitted to prevent the thwart from splitting. This is simply a piece of stock with a hole cut in it that is of the appropriate diameter and rake to match the hole in the thwart, fastened to the bottom side of the thwart. It can be either a piece of hardwood with its grain running 90 degrees to the grain of the thwart or a piece of good-quality marine plywood. Drill, bed, and fasten. If desired, the hole can be lined with leather to protect the mast from wear.

MASTSTEP

The location of the maststep, the member that restrains the heel of the mast, is determined from the plans or lofting. The step should be made of oak or similar rugged, rot-resistant wood. In some small boats it is mounted directly on the backbone; in others it may span a number of floors. The maststep must be well fitted and fastened to resist any movement. Add limbers to prevent any water build-up and subsequent rot.

By the way, there is much to be said for installing the maststep early in the game when there is more access to the inside bottom of the boat.

BULKHEADS

There are a number of ways to capture information for fitting a solid bulkhead. One accurate method requires making up a "dummy" bulkhead—actually a pattern—that will give all the dimensions necessary for the finished article.

19-8: A pieced-up bulkhead pattern.

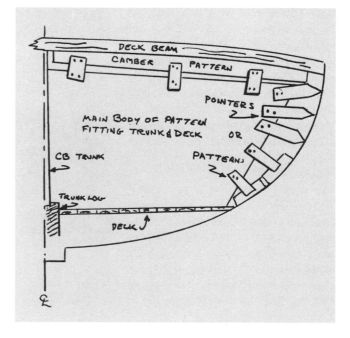

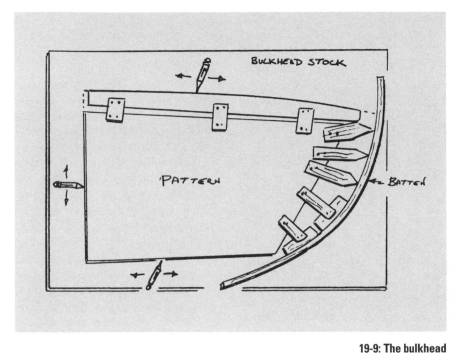

19-9: The bulkhead pattern laid on the stock.

STERNSHEET BENCH

The sternsheet bench in a pulling boat, if the plans call for one, can be a challenge for the home builder to get right. At first blush, the job appears to be straightforward enough—just another one of those scribe-and-fit deals. But consider everything that is going on here:

The bench is actually made of two side benches and a center "keystone" at the transom. (See Figure 19-10.) The sides must follow the curve of the hull and, for a good fit, the outboard side must have a compound bevel to lie against the frames. It must fit the rake of the transom and be well joined to the adjoining thwart. The chances are good that, due to the curve of the riser, the bench will have to be sprung into place. And, of course, the side of the bench on one side of the boat must be shaped the same as its mate on the other side and also be level with it. It's enough to make you want to throw an aluminum lawn chair back there and be done with the problem.

If that is not an option, then it's back to patternmaking.

The framing

Let's start with the foundation (or at least the framing). If your bench is of the Whitehall horseshoe or U-shaped type, which runs from the after edge of a thwart to the transom and back up to the thwart on the other side of the boat, you will need to install a number of supporting cleats and braces. A support cleat is required on the bottom of both sides of the after edge of the mating thwart. Made of oak, with its grain running fore and aft, or heavy mahogany plywood, half of the length of this cleat will extend beyond the after edge of the thwart for the bench to land on.

Next, a cleat must be installed on the transom; the top of this cleat must be beveled to allow the bench to land on it. The position of the cleat might be noted on the construction plan; if not, it can be generated fairly accurately by springing a batten along the top of the riser and letting it extend until it touches the transom.

By the way, if you have left the waterlines drawn on the inside of the transom, you can use them as references to ensure the cleat is level.

Finally, an athwartships riser-to-riser brace that supports and connects the two halves of the bench must be installed. The top of the brace must match the top of the risers. Check to be sure that it is level.

Eventually, there will be an inboard brace running fore and aft from the thwart to the riser-to-riser brace, but that will be scribed to fit later.

19-10: Here's what we're shooting for: an elegant Whitehall sternsheet bench, two side pieces, and "keystone" joining piece.

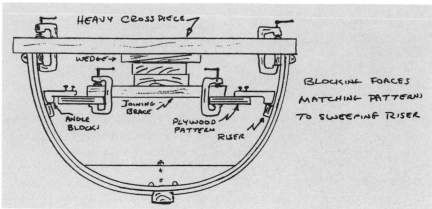

Labels in figure: HEAVY CROSS PIECE · WEDGES → · ANGLE BLOCKS · JOINING BRACE · PLYWOOD PATTERN · RISER · BLOCKING FORCES MATCHING PATTERNS TO SWEEPING RISER

19-11: Patterns for the sternsheet bench.

19-12: Use angle blocks to record the shape and the bevels of the outside edge of the bench.

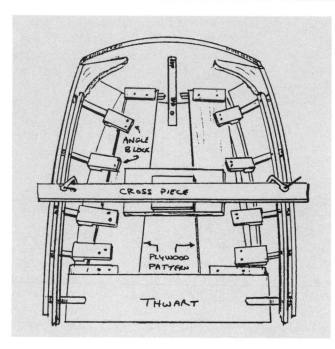

Labels in figure: ANGLE BLOCK · CROSS PIECE · PLYWOOD PATTERN · THWART

The pattern

The next job is to roughly scribe two pieces of plywood for the bench patterns; ³⁄₈ inch plywood works well and will be used in this example. These don't have to be fancy, but they must be of a size and shape to contact the fore-and-aft cleats, the riser (at least in a few spots), and the athwartships brace. After cutting out the pair, put them in the boat as close to the bench's location as possible. Connect them by clamping a couple of pieces of straight stock across from one piece to the other. This not only will keep them from rattling around in the hull, but also will keep them level relative to one another. At this point, the pattern, which is straight on its surface, will probably only be touching the fore-and-aft cleats.

Now, clamp a rugged timber brace from sheer-to-sheer about halfway along the length of the bench. The purpose of this prodigious brace is to give you something to block against as you press the pattern (and later the bench itself) down into the curve of the risers. Using scrap blocks and wedges, force the plywood down until it

touches the tops of the risers and the cross brace equally. The bottom of the plywood is equivalent to the bottom of the bench.

For our next act, we'll take pointers or pieces of scrap wood the same thickness as the future benches and fit, bevel, and affix them at several locations to capture the shape of the bench. (See Figure 19-12.) Our bench will be butted against the inside surface of the frames. Although it is certainly possible to make our pattern fit to the inside edge of the hull, with all the requisite notches for the frames, there is little to be gained either in strength or in looks. We would only be gilding the lily, as it were.

Make the pointers of the same stock thickness as the finished bench. They don't have to be very wide—an inch or so should do it. Draw a line the same thickness as your plywood pattern stock on the side of the pointers (³⁄₈ inch in this example), and with the bandsaw, cut in about halfway on this line and then cut out that piece of stock. The cutout portion of the pointer can now sit on top of the plywood; the bottom of the pointer will be even with the bottom of the plywood, and the top will represent the top of the bench.

You can now fit the pointers against each frame along the length of the bench. Each pointer will have a different bevel on the end of it, reflecting the changing shape of the hull. The pointers can then be glued to the plywood at each frame location. Now, take two pieces of stock (which is the bench thickness, minus the ³⁄₈ inch in this example) and pick up the end that touches the thwart and the transom (don't forget the bevel).

Now we have pretty much all the information we need to make the side benches—except for the inboard curve. The construction plan will show this curve, and the information can be scaled from it and marked on your pattern. This will allow you to figure out how much stock you will need; chances are good that it is going to be more than you thought. You'll be needing a little bit more, too, because the inboard edge of the bench should be over size to allow for the "shrinkage" of the bench while it is being fitted.

Making the bench

Remove the patterns from the boat, and lay them upside down on your stock. Trace the forward and after ends onto the stock. This is the bottom of your stock and should be labeled as such. Make marks at the end of each of the pointers, spring a batten through the points, and draw the line. Then take the stock to the bandsaw and cut it out square (remember to leave extra stock on the inboard side). Transfer the bevels to the bench stock from the pattern with your bevel gauge. Before breaking out your spokeshave, check one last time that you are putting the bevel on the correct side.

After planing in that rolling bevel and cleaning up the ends, the two bench sides can be brought back to the boat and tried in place. They will probably seem a bit long, but that's only because they must be sprung into place. As you did with the pattern, use blocking and wedges against the hefty cross brace to force the bench sides home.

With the bench sides bent into place, the points for the curve for the inboard side can be reestablished, a batten sprung through them, and the cut line traced.

At this juncture the size and shape of the middle "keystone" piece (or pieces) can be laid out on top of the bench sides. Remove, cut the inboard curve on the bench sides and the line for the keystone to specs. Spring the bench sides back into place one last time and install with screws to the cleats and the riser.

Make a pattern for the keystone and use it for making the piece, but leave the actual stock long on the inboard side for fitting. After you are satisfied with the fit of the keystone, including the uniform spacing between the pieces, draw the inboard curve and saw it out. The keystone can now be installed.

The last thing to do is to scribe the under bench curve onto the pattern stock for the inboard brace. Cut out and fit the brace, and then install it.

A lot of work, you say? Perhaps, but then, what a grand bench it is!

OARLOCK PADS

Little is written about oarlock pads, and they are rarely shown on construction plans—which means that these little pedestals for the mounting of oarlock sockets are usually left to the eloquent and discerning good taste of the builder. Having said that, I must admit that there are some awfully clunky looking ones out there.

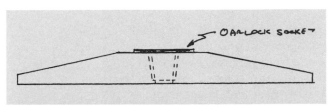

19-13: Profile of a typical oarlock pad.

19-14: An oarlock pad may seem simple, but one that is poorly designed can have a bad visual effect on a good boat. This one—long, low, and with crisp lines—has a fine appearance.

Some of the elements that help to make these utilitarian appendages look more elegant are:
- Symmetry in construction and installation. (See sidebar, Horning, Isosceles, and It's All Greek to Me.)
- Proper length (10 to 12 inches works well)
- Sides shaped generally to follow the sheer.
- A short, flat area on top, tapered on each side down toward the sheer. This looks good, and it is also one less place for lines to get hung up on.
- Mortising the top of the pad to allow the top of the socket to lie flush is time consuming and probably provides yet another place for water to lie.
- If slotted screws are used (oval heads are nice), the slots should line up with each other if at all possible, but don't lose any sleep over it if you try your damnedest and they won't.
- And don't forget to bed the pads.

FLOORBOARDS

The design of the floorboards is many times left to the last minute, and the width and length of the slats determined by whatever scrap lumber is left over. Although floorboards can be thought of as disposable or at least renewable items, they shouldn't look that way. A handsome little pulling boat with floorboards that look like a pile of scrap kindling someone just threw in can be a disappointing thing indeed. A few points to consider:

Will the floorboards be removable? Or at least will a section be removable to allow access for cleaning, bailing, and reaching a garboard drain? Removable sections can be held in place with small turnbuttons made with ½-inch brass half-oval molding, drilled, countersunk, and screwed in place atop a small washer.

How wide should the individual boards be, and how far fore and aft should they run to be practical? Symmetrically laid boards look best—that is, boards of equal width, working out in either direction from a board running down the centerline.

What spacing between the boards is to be used? The easiest method to maintain a consistent spacing when drilling the floorboards and fastening them down is to use spacer blocks of equal thickness—plywood works well for this.

Finally, consider spiling your outermost board to shape. It really does save a lot of time over the trial-and-error method.

20 • EXTERIOR WORK

Fairing the Hull

Few builders would claim that fairing the hull is their favorite task, at least not with a straight face. The job is, no question about it, a lot of work. Yet, there is a satisfaction in it, as the shape of the hull is transformed from faceted and rough as a corn cob to smooth, with the flowing lines that were imagined in the designer's eye. Fairing is a partnership of the visual and the tactile: It is not enough to use the eye alone; the touch of the hand is required to pick out nuances in unfairness. And what other operation offers the opportunity for as much healthful and mettle-testing calisthenics?

Plane facts

To begin, plug or fill the holes created by the countersunk fastenings, taking a moment to reset any screw or rivet that appears to be countersunk too little. Next, use a smoothing or jack plane to knock off the high ridges of the plank edges at the seams. Work fore and aft, joining those edges level to one another. To avoid pulling too much grain, keep the iron sharp and not set too deeply.

Next, begin planing the hull on a bias, or diagonally, at roughly 45 degrees to the run of the planking—first in one direction, then at 90 degrees to the first. Work vigorously, but don't try to take it all down to shape on the first pass. You'll have better quality control if you remove the stock in stages. In areas with hollow, perhaps below the waterline up forward, or back aft as you come up into a wineglass transom, you may have to employ a backing-out plane or spokeshave to work in the proper shape. Use your hand to detect any unfairness.

By now, you (or more likely your prized Stanley #5) have probably discovered a few more fastenings that need resetting. Do that, and then continue fairing until the hull looks and feels right. There will be some plane marks, but all in all, the shape should be just about right. Rake away the shavings. The next stop is the disc sander.

Disc sanding

The disc sander with a foam pad is a boon to any mechanic having to fair irregular surfaces. This is not the fast-turning disc grinder with the stiff disc of yore, where any faux pas or miscue meant disaster. The modern disc sander turns at a much slower speed than its ancestor, and the foam disc it is fitted with is much more forgiving, while still allowing for plenty of control. The introduc-

tion of hook-and-loop sandpaper encourages you to change the paper at the proper time rather than wait until there is no grit left on the paper at all.

20-1: Using a pistol-grip caulking roller. That's a traditional caulking iron in the foreground.

There is still a bit of skill required in the operation of a disc sander, however. The operator must keep the disc flat to the hull and keep the machine moving in the same diagonal pattern as when using the hand plane. And remember: This job requires eye protection and a top-quality face mask.

The sanding board

For the final fine-tuning of a hull, nothing works quite as well as the good old-fashioned sanding board. This humble device is usually a homemade affair, consisting of a long section of board or plywood of the desired flexibility and length, with handles affixed at each end. The sandpaper is attached to the bottom of the board with either adhesive goop or mechanical fastenings. A ready-made, plastic version is also available from hardware stores; it is lighter and easier to use than the homemade type, and features a hook-and-loop sandpaper system that encourages the operator to change the paper at the proper time. Used with finesse in the same diagonal fashion as the plane and disc sander, the sanding board can fine-tune and join a hull to a bottle-like smoothness.

When does it all end?

How far to take the fairing process depends on how persnickety you choose to be. Theoretically, the fairing process could be said to continue right up to the application of the final coat of paint. The hull should be touched up with the sanding board after caulking, and then as glazing compounds and trowel cement are used and the undercoat and subsequent top coats are applied. It is probably safe to say that a boat meant to be used will require less tedious fairing than the one meant for display.

CAULKING CARVEL PLANKING

Few subjects, at least in the boatbuilding realm, inspire more spirited, dogmatic, and otherwise opinionated debate than the matter of caulking. The literature is replete with cautionary tales of one sort or another. And true, boats can be over caulked with dismaying results; for example, enthusiastic practitioners have been known to break out the inside of planks with a caulking iron. Nonetheless, while perhaps the technique is a bit more art than science, there is no reason why, with a bit of care, the builder shouldn't have success caulking a small carvel hull—particularly one built with softwood planking, which is more forgiving than hardwood.

A little theory

Unlike a lapstrake hull, where all the planking is interconnected, a carvel-planked hull is like an Easter basket pinned only at the frames. Caulking with cotton not only seals the seams but also joins and stiffens the hull, almost as if the seams were splined. (Often, caulking cotton will make an impression or dent in the edge of planks that can be seen when the planks are removed for repairs.)

Cotton can be set with either a roller alone, or a caulking iron and mallet. For most of the seams in a small boat—if it is well planked—the caulking roller is the weapon of choice. However, the garboard seam, the stem rabbet, and any irregular seams are probably best done with an iron and mallet.

Before caulking, vacuum the seams to remove any detritus from the fairing process that might gum up the works. Butt joints should be caulked before the adjoining seams, leaving "tails" of cotton sticking out, top and bottom, that can be melded later into the plank seams. Many builders prefer to caulk the tightest seams first, the theory being that driving the cotton might just edge-set the planks enough to close up any looser seams. Beware of over caulking, however, as it can strain the planks and fastenings, and put the frames in tension. Caulking the garboard last with an iron and mallet will button up the entire hull. It's a good idea, if you are working alone, to shift sides occasionally to keep the hull in balance.

Cotton wicking and the caulking roller

Probably the best method for getting the cotton between the planks of a small boat is to roll it into the seams with a caulking roller or wheel. The cotton is set by downward pressure applied to the roller wheel. (See Figure 20-1.) The roller can also be used to open and unify the appearance of the seams before rolling the cotton.

The caulking roller is used in much the same way as the tool used to install insect screening in aluminum patio doors. The business end of the tool is a tapered wheel, which is set into either a straight or pistol-grip handle. Of the two, the pistol grip is more comfortable to use, affords better control, and is, ergonomically speaking, a better tool. (See how to make your own in Chapter 3, Homemade Tools.)

While it would seem that the caulking mallet and iron would do a better job of setting the cotton (those tools make more noise, don't they?), actually the weight of your body concentrated on the fine edge of the roller wheel probably equates to quite high pressure in pounds per square inch. In fact, you can roll cotton right into the face of a piece of cedar with very little effort. (Try it, you'll see.) This phenomenon is something to keep in mind when using a caulking roller, as it is easy to get off

20-2: Caulking cotton is first tucked into the seams in loops and then driven with an iron and mallet.

20-3: Here all the seams have been caulked and the ends of the cotton are hanging at the hood ends.

track and unintentionally implant cotton where there were no seams previously.

A good type of cotton to use with a roller is the twisted type, called wicking, which is somewhat like kite string and sold by the ball. Leaving a few inches of tail free at the end of the seam—this will later be set with a iron when the garboard is caulked—hold the wicking parallel to the seam and then firmly roll it into place. If your wicking runs short, be sure to overlap the previous piece with the next one by a couple of inches.

Caulking with an iron

Caulking irons come in a variety of sizes, but for many small craft a narrow iron with a driving edge of $\frac{1}{32}$ or $\frac{1}{16}$ inch will do the trick. Occasionally a bent iron—that is, one with a bend on the flat—is useful for caulking alongside the keel. As for the tool for driving the iron, while the old-time caulking mallets with the slotted, cylindrical mesquite head complete with iron rings are still available, a fine job can be achieved on a small boat with a generic wooden carpenter's mallet.

Caulking cotton comes in one-pound skeins, much like yarn. The strands can be divided to vary the thickness of the cotton needed for the job. The coil can be unwound and fed into a receptacle—perhaps a cardboard box or a

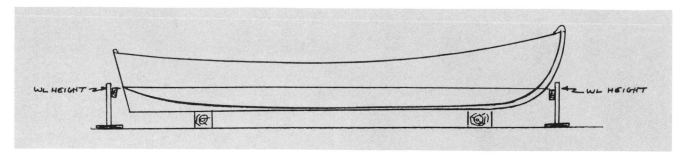

20-4: To begin scribing the waterline, set up the hull so it is level athwartships and the waterline heights at the bow and the stern are level relative to one another. Set up horizontal straightedges at the bow and stern, with the top edges aligned with forward and after waterline marks.

paper bag with its edges rolled over—like rope down a hawsepipe. This will permit the cotton to feed out again, allowing easy, untangled retrieval when doing the job.

Initially, soft caulking is lightly tucked into the seam in loops or "bights." (See Figure 20-2.) The size of the loops can be varied to compensate for differences in the width of the seam. Then the cotton is driven into the seam with the iron and mallet. When working down a seam, keep the iron square with the seam while moving it in a slight "rocking" motion, driving the cotton in. "Tracking" the back corner of the iron in the already tamped-in seam will help greatly in keeping the iron from going off course. The iron should have a solid feeling to it when the caulking is properly set.

Beware of over-vigorous use of the mallet, as it is easy to drive too far and break the cotton out of the back of the seam. Also, use a light hand when caulking around the transom to avoid forcing the planking away from it.

An alternative to caulking around the transom is to lay down a strand of wicking on the edge of the transom before fastening the planking to it. Of course, this must be done during the planking stage, not now.

Painting the seams

After the seams have been caulked, brush paint into the seams to stabilize the cotton, keep it from "puffing" back out, and isolate it from moisture. A cheap, throwaway china-bristle brush that has been given a "Mohawk" hairdo with a wide chisel makes a good applicator for working the paint into the seams. While any oil-based paint works, genuine red lead is likely to offer more preservative value than any other.

Paying the seams

Tune up the surface of the hull one last time with a plane and a long board, and then fill the seams with compound. Seam compound provides an initial barrier against leaks, helps keep the water from worrying the cotton, and provides the seams with a nice uniform appearance after painting. The compound also keeps the seams clear of paint that can harden and impede the swelling of the plank.

For seam compound, old-time

20-5: Stretch a string from the forward straightedge to the after one.

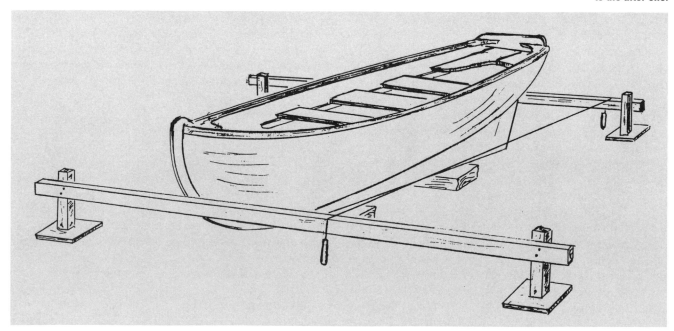

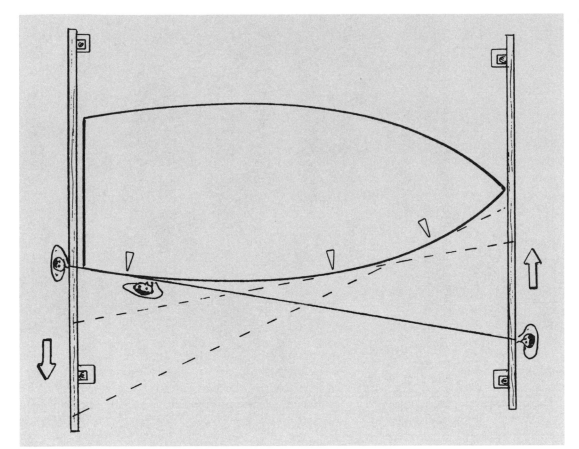

mechanics used such potions as pine tar and whiting, white lead putty, or even asphalt roofing tar. Today's commercial seam compounds work well enough, although they are really only good for one "squeeze."

You might want to consider one of the modern flexible compounds, such as Life Caulk, which will come and go with the planking. Keep in mind, however, that the flexible seam compounds are strong adhesives and will cling to the plank tenaciously; this can make future repairs a bit difficult. Mask the seams before working-in adhesive compound to avoid a difficult to clean-up mess. Tool the seams with the back of a teaspoon before the compound sets up for a better-looking job.

Once the seams have been payed, many builders like to seal the hull, inside and out, with primer to stabilize the planking and to prevent shrinkage.

Scribing the Waterline

There is nothing like a sharp waterline to sparkle up the appearance of a boat. The contrasting color of the most workaday antifouling paint can perk up an otherwise humdrum topside paint scheme and lend a feeling of tasteful elegance to the hull. And a crisp line rising to the bow will give your boat a look of saucy swiftness even when she is lying at anchor.

On the other hand, a funky waterline that looks as if it had been applied with a mop on a moonless night will have the opposite effect. Even the most handsome hull will have difficulty overcoming the deleterious effects of a wavy, irregular waterline.

The question is, just what is the best way to establish the waterline, outside of hiring a crane and slowly lowering your boat into a vat of bottom paint? As with most boatbuilding situations, there are a number techniques that will work. Which is best depends less on philosophy and more on the tools you have, and the size of the boat and where it is located. But whatever method you use, the place to start is at the beginning, and the end, of the line.

The starting points

The first thing to do is to establish where the waterline falls at the bow and the stern. If you are building new from a contemporary set of plans, the chances are good that the location of the painted waterline location will be shown somewhere on the prints. While this indicated line is no guarantee that the vessel will actually float as illustrated, it's likely that it is pretty accurate. The points where this line hits the bow and the stern can be scaled from the plans, and then marked on the stem and the centerline of the transom.

Another place to get your starting points is from the load water line (LWL), the theoretical line of flotation, established on your lines plan and lofting. You might even

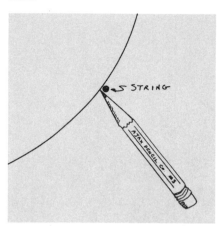

20-7: Bring in the taut string until it almost touches the hull, then make your mark.

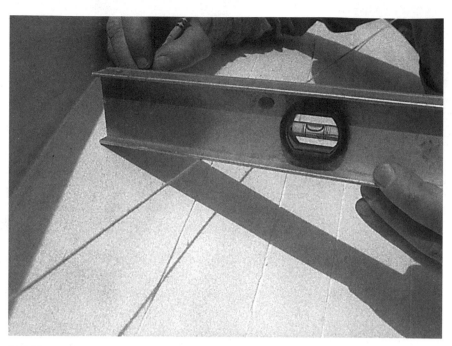

20-8: Here, where the string cannot be brought all the way in to the hull, a level is being used to carry the plane the rest of the way in. (In this case, the waterline is being marked on an upside-down boat.)

have drawn this line on the backbone, and it might still be visible. If not, again, its location can be scaled. Of course, this is just the line or plane of flotation. You must add thickness to the line, so that when the waterline is painted it will be visible.

If you are re-establishing a waterline on an older hull, the job becomes a bit more complicated. Over time, the original line established by the builder can disappear. This can be from repeated painting and other refinishing over the years. Or the scribed line could have been obliterated if the hull has been replanked and repaired. Do not despair, as some minimal detective work may turn up some vestiges of the old waterline.

Using a pocket knife to scrape away old paint, look for signs of a scribed line on the side of the stem or on the transom. Not there? There may be other clues. In the past, some progressive builders installed benchmarks to aid in the reestablishment of a waterline. Sometimes as an indicator they used a screw set flush with the surface with its slot in the horizontal position. A marker like this was usually installed in the forward face of the stem and the centerline of the transom. Try removing the stemband; underneath there might be an unplugged, exposed screw. Back aft, check low on the transom or on the sternpost for an anomalous screw. Still nothing? Then it is time for the dip-and-mark method.

Strange as it may sound, actually launching the boat into a calm body of water, such as a pond, can be the most effective method for determining the level of flotation fore and aft. It is not, however, the best way to mark the entire length of the waterline, as ripples in the water will throw you off. So just wade in and mark the line at the bow and the stern. You can finish the job back on dry land.

With any of the above approaches, it doesn't hurt to set the end of the waterline a little higher at the bow than the stern. If all goes well and the boat floats right where you expected it would, the line will have a slight, but debonair, lift forward. If, on the other hand, the boat floats lower forward than you had expected, the line will look just right, and you can tell everyone that you planned it that way.

Waterline theory

When setting up to determine the waterline, keep in mind that what you are really doing is creating an artificial plane around the boat that simulates the one provided by the water. A number of instruments can be used for the job. A transit, a contractor's water level, or even a laser (if you should happen to have such an item) can be helpful. For the small boat, however, the job can be done easily, and on the cheap, by using a string, a carpenter's level, and a couple of straightedges.

Whatever device you use, it is essential that the boat be set up level athwartships. And, in most cases (other than with the string-and-straightedge method), the waterline height at the bow and the stern should also be set level relative to one another. (See Figure 20-4.) Many builders prefer to run the waterline while the boat is still set up in the jig, as the boat is already immobile and level athwartships.

The strings-and-plane technique

After leveling the boat you are ready to run your line. The tools required are few and simple: two straightedges (as long as possible), a spool of carpenter's string, a long level (4 feet is good), a short "pop" level, a few clamps, four short 2 by 4s, four sawhorses, a pencil, and two helpers or two sash weights.

Job one is to set up your fore-and-aft horizontal planes—the long straightedges—even with the waterline heights that you have established on the stem and transom. This is where the sawhorses and 2 by 4s come in. Clamping the studs vertically to the horses will make four stands to which you can clamp your straightedges. At the bow, align the straightedge so it just touches your marked line and is dead level. Firmly clamp the straightedge to two of the stands. Repeat for the transom. You now have your two horizontal planes.

Next, stretch the string from the top of the forward straightedge to the top of the after. (See Figure 20-5.) The idea here is that a tightly stretched string running from one straightedge to the other can be used to bring the plane in to the side of the hull where you can mark it. Success hinges on keeping the string taut; a limp string will provide an interesting but unacceptable line. The best, and quickest, approach is to round up two assistants to guide the line in to the hull and keep it taut. If help is unavailable, a sash weight suspended from either end of the string works well to keep the line taut yet easily adjustable.

Marking the line

Beginning at the bow, slide the string along the forward straightedge plane as close to the stem as possible. Back aft, slide the string across the straightedge away from the transom so the string makes a diagonal between the two planes. Then, move the string in toward the hull until it almost touches. The reason for not touching the boat is that the tension on the string will cause it to "roll" up the hull and provide an inaccurate reading. Mark the spot on the hull with a pencil. (See Figure 20-7.)

Next, move the string out a little on the forward straightedge and in a little on the after one until the string nearly touches another spot on the hull. Again, mark the spot with a pencil. Continue the process, moving one string in and one out until you have a series of marks along the length of the hull. The number of marks that are necessary to give an accurate line depends on the shape of the hull. The more complex the shape, the more marks that will be needed.

In some places where there is hollow in the hull, usually up forward near the stem, you will not be able to pull the string all the way in to the hull. No problem. Simply get the string as close as you can, and then use a short "pop" level held to the bottom of the string to carry the plane the rest of the way to the hull. Mark the spot with a pencil. (See Figure 20-8.)

Scribing the line

By tacking a long, thin batten to the hull, the line can now be marked. For the best result, tip the batten a bit so only one edge touches the hull. As with lofting and spiling, run the batten through the majority of points, bypassing any obvious anomalies.

Once the batten is tacked in place, eyeball it carefully. Is it a nice, smooth line with no cranky spots? If so you are ready to mark the line for all posterity. While a pencil line is fine for a one-shot paint job, a scribed line is best if you want to be able to locate the line year after year. One of the better ways to scribe the line is with the last tooth on a hacksaw blade. Simply ride it along the edge of the batten, and the tooth will turn up a nice furrow like a chisel plow. When you are done, remove the batten and proceed to the other side of the hull.

Waterline weirdness on lapstrake hulls

The waterline on a lapstrake hull is rather a contradictory individual, in that, to appear straight in profile, it must be crooked, or more aptly, a jagged bolt of lightning. This is because the line must pass over the "steps" of the laps at an angle. A proper line crossing laps at an angle will travel along the face of a plank until it reaches the edge, where it then must backtrack somewhat along the step. When the line reaches the next plank below, it will then continue along that plank. Keep this in mind when you are laying out your points. Eyeball the line in profile to check for fairness; use short battens to scribe it.

20-9: Painting to the waterline is easy if you have a proper line scribed for all to see.

21 • THE DECK

There are many ways to frame out the deck of a small boat. Which system is best is dictated less by specific deck dogma and more by the preferences of the designer, the proclivities of the builder, and sheer practicality. The options range from simple sawn deckbeams bolted to the side of the frames, to elaborate laminated beams with dovetailed ends mortised into a sturdy clamp and shelf. What might work on one boat might be totally inappropriate on another. Given that homily, there is a universal thread running through all the framing systems: they must be well thought out and executed, as the deck framing ties the boat together.

Of all the many systems, perhaps the choice for small craft is the one in which the deckbeam is notched to fit, land on top of, and be bolted vertically through the clamp. This construction style is straightforward, so you can easily get the job done. Although it lacks the locking qualities (and persnickety joinery) of the mortised dovetail, or half-dovetail joint, it is still quite strong.

CHECK THE SHAPE OF THE HULL

Before starting the deck framing, check to make sure the boat's shape hasn't changed. Measure at several locations, and compare the readings to the molds. Then, just as when installing the inwales in the open boat, brace the hull to prevent movement, in or out, with stretchers (transverse ties) temporarily fastened to the frames.

By the way, there will never be a better time than now to paint the interior of the boat, even if you have to wait for the paint to dry before getting on with the deck framing. You'll be glad you did.

Oh, yes, if your station locations at the sheer are still visible, don't paint them out yet. They will help in laying out the beam locations.

THE CAMBER PATTERN

The camber, or the crown, of the deck is usually given on the plans. The designer may use a minimalistic approach to express this convexity, such as including a statement such as "Camber of deck = 2 inches over 4 feet or greatest beam." Then again, if the plans are a bit more "uptown" you may be provided with a graphic represen-

☞ Generating Camber

Scientifically

The theory behind this method is that properly dividing the arc of a circle and measuring the distance from those divisions to a baseline will give you offsets that can be plotted on stations drawn on a baseline. A batten can be sprung through those points, developing a parabolic curve that will become your pattern. (This is much easier than it sounds.)

Assume that the designer has specified a camber of 2 inches over 4 feet of beam. Begin by drawing a baseline 4 feet long. At the 2-foot mark, erect a perpendicular centerline. Next, divide the baseline into four equal parts on either side of the centerline (in this case, at every 6 inches.) Erect a perpendicular station line at each division. Working from the centerline, label the stations A, B, C, and D—D being at the ends of the line.

Set your compass to a radius of 2 inches. Setting the point of the compass on the centerline intersection of the base, draw an arc from the base to the perpendicular, which will produce a quarter circle. Next divide the 2-inch

radius on the baseline into four parts, each being ½ inch. Okay? Then, in the same fashion as above, label each division A through D, D being where the arc meets the base.

Now just divide that arc into four parts. Start by opening out your compass a little bit more, perhaps to 3 inches. Place the point of the compass at the intersection of the arc and the baseline, and swing an arc up toward the centerline perpendicular. Next, place the point on the intersection of the original arc and the centerline perpendicular, and swing a second arc down toward the base until it intersects (or crosses) the first arc. With a straightedge, connect that intersection to the baseline/centerline point. Where the straightedge crosses the original arc is the halfway or 45-degree point. Mark that point and label it "B." Now place the compass point on the 45-point "B" and swing it up until it intersects the upper arc and down until it strikes the lower arc. With your straightedge, connect the new upper arc intersection and the baseline/centerline point. Where it crosses the original arc is the 22½-degree point. Mark and label it "A."

tation similar to those used for sparmaking. These usually illustrate a compressed arc, complete with stations and a centerline labeled with heights, drawn out from a base. The idea here is that to get your real-life camber curve all you have to do is lay out the stations as shown at their proper spacing, mark the indicated heights on the stations (and the centerline), spring a batten through those points, mark the arc with a pencil, and use it for a

pattern with which your beams can be made.

If the designer does not provide a graphic camber curve, you can break out a pencil compass and your high school geometry book, and generate the crown yourself right on the lofting board, or you can do it mechanically.

21-1: Typical framing for the deck of a small craft.

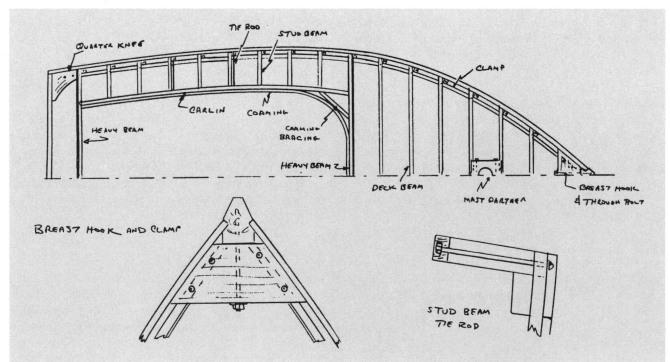

Repeat the drill for the lower arc intersection. This will give you the 67½-degree point. Mark and label it "C." Then with a pencil and straightedge connect A to A, B to B, and C to C. These connected points are your "offset" distances that will be plotted on the station lines.

Using either a divider or a tick strip, pick up distance AA and plot that on stations A on either side of the centerline station. Do the same for BB, and CC. The height at D, of course, will be zero. Spring a light batten through the plotted points and the centerline height. Make up a pattern. This curve can then be transferred directly to the deckbeam stock.

Mechanically

If the scientific method doesn't appeal or if the curve developed in that fashion leaves the boat with a "flat" look forward, you can make a mechanical device to obtain the curve. To do this, measure the boat's greatest beam at the sheer (in this example, let's assume it is 4 feet.) Lay out that distance on a baseline drawn on the lofting floor. Drive in a small nail at the end points. Lay out the camber height (assume it to be 2 inches) on a perpendicular drawn at the centerline. Drive a small nail at that point as well.

Then get yourself two pieces of straight stock that are longer than the width of the boat—perhaps 4 feet 3 inches—and position them against the nails so they touch in a teepee or wide V fashion in the center. Join the stock with gussets, fastenings, and glue. With a rattail file, make a half-pencil-deep groove in the bottom of the V and put a pencil in it.

Take the device to the boat and set it up as shown in the illustration. Hold or clamp your deckbeam stock to the frame at the proper location. The device will ride on the top of the sheer from right to left (or vice versa), with the pencil in the groove creating a curve on the deckbeam stock. That curve represents the camber of the deck.

Two ways of developing the camber curve: scientifically (top) and mechanically (bottom).

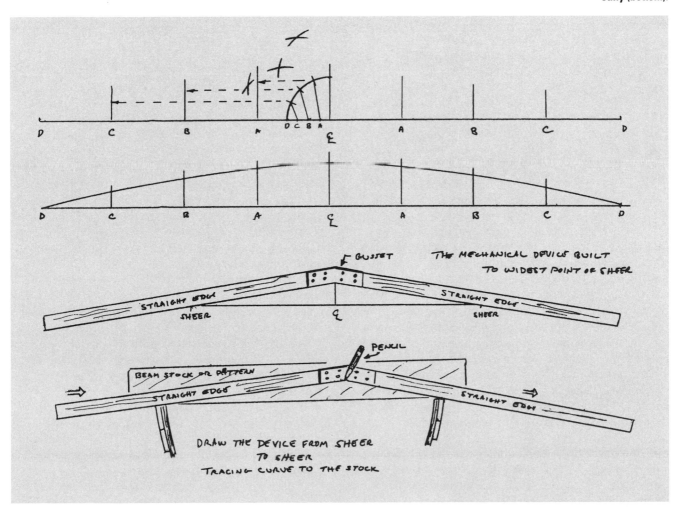

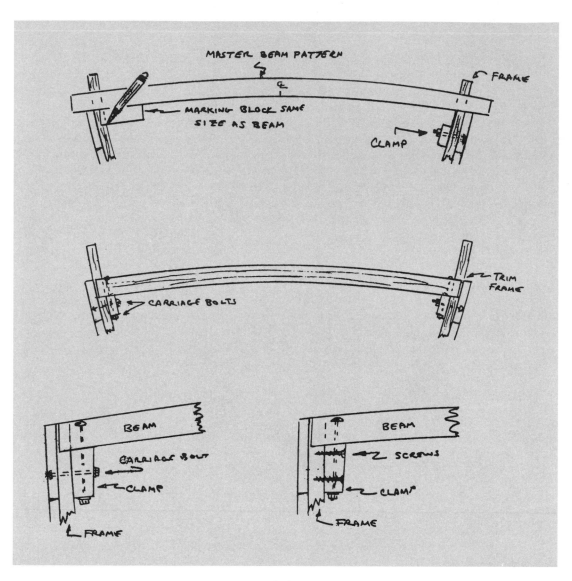

SHEER CLAMP

One way to determine the location of the sheer clamp is simply to square in from the sheer plank and measure down. Or, if the boat has a lot of changing shape, you can use the deck-beam pattern. Lay the pattern across the boat from sheer to sheer; slide a block the same dimension as the deckbeam (or slightly under, if you are notching the beam deeper) along the underside of the beam pattern until it contacts the frame, and make a mark.

At this point, it is handy to have a piece of dummy clamp stock to check your fit with the beam block. If the boat has plenty of flare, the deckbeam will fit nicely on the square-edged clamp, with possibly a little notching required on the inside-of-boat face. If, on the other hand, the sides of the boat are plumb, or have tumblehome, the joint between the beam and the clamp will be open or gapped on the inside. To get a full landing, bevel the clamp—pick up the bevels along the run between the beam block and the frame. Or, alternately, the square-topped clamp can be moved upward by the amount of the gap shown between the bottom of the beam block and the dummy clamp, and a notch made on the outboard side to accommodate the camber.

It may be advantageous to whip up a full-size pattern of the clamp to check your fits and length to avoid unpleasant surprises later on. The forward end should fit against the stem.

On some light craft you may be able to get the clamp out of one piece of stock, otherwise it will have to be scarfed. In the good looks department, chamfering the lower inside edge of the clamp is a nice touch.

While many times the clamp can successfully be sprung into the hull, it is sometimes more easily fit if it has been spiled. Although it may be possible to wrestle the clamp into place cold, softening it up in the steam box can make things go a whole lot easier.

Once the two sheer clamps—one on each side of the boat—have been bent to the lines on the inside of the boat and well clamped, they can be fastened to the frames with screws, or with rivets or carriage bolts.

To finish up the job in the bow, the two sheer clamps should be carriage bolted to the bottom of the breasthook. The breasthook in a decked-over boat need not be anywhere as fancy as the one in an open boat; all it has to be is functional. Such a breasthook can be a well-fitted piece of hardwood, with the grain running athwartships. It can be installed a little above the sheer so a bit of camber can be worked into it. Some builders install a through-bolt running fore-and-aft to the forward face of the stem, while others use screws from the 'hook to the stem. The breasthook should be well embalmed in red lead, bedded, and fastened to the sheerstrakes.

Back aft, the sheer clamps can be bolted to the bottom side of the transom quarter knees or blocking. Again, all should be red-leaded and bedded.

DECKBEAMS

Traditional deckbeams are sawn of such woods as oak, fir, yellow pine, or hackmatack, working wherever possible with the natural grain of the stock. Beams can also be sawn from glued-together planks, or laminated of planks vertically glued together, or laminated from many thin pieces of wood, such as spruce, fir, or mahogany, bent over a bending jig, and glued with epoxy or resorcinol.

Although a deckbeam can be of equal thickness from top to bottom, it is not unusual to cut a different camber on the bottom of the beam (making the beam deeper in the middle) than on the top. On some small, light craft the bottom of the beam can be cut straight from end to end; this will make it stiffer, albeit heavier. Which type to choose is dictated by construction scantlings, builder preference, or more mundane considerations, such as the availability of stock.

And whichever it is, for that touch of understated elegance, after shaping, you may wish to chamfer the lower edges of the beam.

Allow for springback

Anything sawn from a large piece of rough stock is bound to change shape in the sawing, so it is a good idea to give yourself a bit of insurance by cutting a sawn deckbeam in two steps: First rough-saw it oversize so any movement that can happen will happen, then lay down the pattern again and re-cut. Even a laminated beam can spring back when released from the laminating form, so plan ahead for it when building the jig.

Finding the beam locations

Siting the beams properly and making them square to the centerline not only gives you a better-looking job but also makes life easier when installing such components as the mast partner and hatches, if they are called for by the designer. To determine the beam locations, check the plans.

To place a beam, begin by laying a straightedge across the boat, sheer to sheer, at the rough location. If the stations are still marked on the sheer, you will have a good reference to work from. Otherwise, you can scale from the drawing or measure directly from the lofting, the distance square back from the stem. Then using two measuring tapes, "horn" the straightedge square by measuring from the points where the straightedge hits both sheers to a common point on the centerline at the stem. When the two tapes read the same, the straightedge will be square across the boat. Then double-check the distance measured back on the centerline from the stem. Mark the beam locations—both the forward and after sides!—onto the sheer and move on to the next beam.

Fitting the full-length beams

After rechecking that the camber is correct, fit the longest beam first. Work carefully, as this one will set the tone for the rest of the beams.

The beam and usually the clamp will have to be notched to fit. This is an interesting bit of joinery; to get the hang of it, try a dry run on an expendable piece of cheap stock cut to the same dimensions as the real thing. After fitting, the beam should be bolted to the clamp.

Note that some builders like to place blocking (hardwood fillers) between the frames to aid in fastening toerails or hardware; this will affect the end fits of the

21-3: Deckbeams notched at the ends over the clamp.

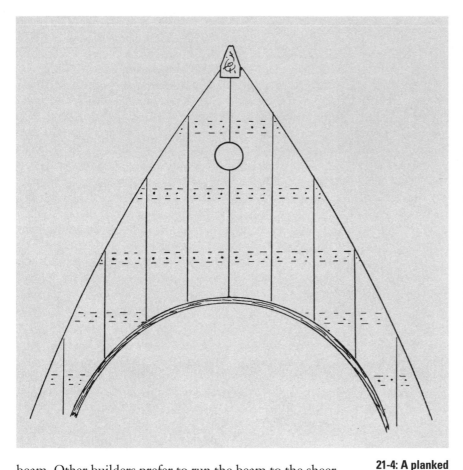

21-4: A planked deck with curved coaming in place for a catboat.

beam. Other builders prefer to run the beam to the sheer plank. It is good practice to leave a gap between the ends of the beam and the blocking or the sheer plank to promote air circulation and prevent rot.

Proceed forward to the next beam and fit it. Some builders prefer to lay out each forward beam separately, rather than use the common beam pattern, to avoid a "sagging look" in the deck forward as viewed in profile. The crown of the beams can be checked with a centerline string stretched from the breasthook to the center of the first long beam that has been fitted.

Once the deckbeams have been fitted and installed, check for unevenness across the tops with a straightedge, and true up any inconsistencies with a plane. Any small unevenness that might be left will most likely be faired out by the deck planking.

Cockpit opening

There are a number of ways to fit the stud beams and carlins for the cockpit opening. One way is make the carlins first, and that is the way we will do it here.

To get the shape of the carlins, begin by mortising the carlin receiving notches in the fore-and-aft deckbeams. The notches should correspond with the angle at which the coaming is to lie; this angle will be found on the plans. Then clamp a stiff batten to the tops of the full-length beams and across the cockpit opening, run-

ning it against the inboard edges of the mortise notches on the beams. Measure to check that you have maintained the proper width of the side deck from the sheer. (If the batten appears floppy, it may be necessary to brace it at the sheer.)

Cut and put in place a piece of pattern stock—cedar or light plywood will do—that lies alongside the batten and fits into the deckbeam notches exactly. Scribe the under-the-batten shape onto the pattern stock. Also, pick up the bevels where the carlin intersects the deckbeam. Remove the pattern and draw a line parallel to the one just traced that represents the bottom side of the beam. Now cut out the pattern and use it to mill out the real thing.

Spring the carlin into place between the fore-and-aft full-length beams, and check the shape and height of it with the camber pattern. Okay? Then, repeat the exercise on the other side. After fitting, remove the carlins.

Next, cut out the stud beams—make them a little over length—using the camber indicated by the deckbeam pattern. Notch, fit, and bolt them to the clamp in the same fashion as the full-length deckbeams.

Spring the stiff batten over the cockpit area as before, only this time run it on the outboard edge of the fore-and-aft beam notches; i.e., the batten will be closer to the sheer by the width of one carlin. The stud beams can be clamped to the batten, allowing you to check that they are all parallel to each other. When they look good, trace the outboard-edge-of-carlin line onto the tops of the stud beams. Then, with a bevel gauge set to the angle of the coaming, trace down from the batten line onto the fore-and-aft faces of the stud beams. Saw to these lines, trimming the stud beams to length.

Replace the carlin, and draw it to the stud beams with bar clamps. Check everything one more time with the deckbeam pattern and if it looks good, fasten with screws from the carlin into the ends of the stud beams.

To make the entire assembly more rugged and to tie everything together, tierods (long bolts) can be added; run them from the carlins to either the sheer clamp or the frames. Also, for support from below, a few hanging knees can be fitted from the deckbeams to the hull; alternately, wood or bronze struts can be run as needed from the carlins to frames.

Curved coaming

If a curved coaming is to be installed, it must be supported by blocking added to the deckbeam assembly. The curve, and its attendant blocking, will (or at least should) be given on the construction plans. This curve can be lifted from the plans by tracing a scale grid on the drawing and then transferring it to a full-size grid on a piece of plywood and cut out. This curve pattern can then be fastened to the top of the beam assembly. Springing in a piece of flexible plywood to this estimable curve, to act as a stand-in for the coaming, and clamping it into place will tell you what you will need in the way of blocking.

Mast partner and more blocking

The mast partner at the deck for a small mast can be made from either a single or two pieces of hardwood with through fastenings running either side of the mast hole or, perhaps even better, of several thicknesses of high-quality mahogany marine plywood laminated together. The partner should be let in on the centerline of the deck at the location prescribed on the plans and fastened to the deckbeams. After the camber has been worked in, the top of the partner should lay flush with the under side of the deck.

Blocking that acts as a base for deck hardware—cleats, deck blocks, etc.—can be installed in a similar fashion between the deckbeams. The blocks spread out stress and offer a stout foundation for the fastenings. Bed everything well.

Finishing the job

Check the entire deck framing assembly one last time for trueness, use straightedges and wide plywood battens laid on the flat. Tune any high spots with a plane and a fair-ing board. Then paint at least the tops of the beams, the blocking, et al., with red lead or other suitable primer/preservative. On to the deck.

TYPES OF DECKS

When it comes to small craft, you have a number of choices when it comes to the deck. Deciding which to choose depends on the builder's taste, penchant for tradition, and practicality, and the availability of materials. While a conventional laid deck may look great, at least when new, almost any style, unless it is installed over a plywood subdeck, is likely to leak at some time in its career. On the other hand, a canvas-covered deck as found on Crosby and Beetle catboats is orthodox as all get out, is easy to repair, stays tight for a mighty long time, and is quite as handsome as its more effete, bright-finished brethren. (See Figure 21-4.)

For the ultimate in low maintenance, it is difficult to beat a plywood deck covered with epoxy and Dacron. The plywood imparts structural strength, and the Dacron sheathing adds abrasion resistance and the non-skid qualities one associates with canvas. Indeed, a plywood-Dacron deck looks a great deal like a canvas deck. Whatever type is chosen, longevity should be a prime consideration.

STRIP-PLANKED DECK

Just as in a strip-planked hull, a strip-planked deck—narrow wood strips, fastened together—is quite strong. (Conversely, it can be difficult to repair.) This technique is commonly used when the deck thickness is ½ inch or greater. To minimize movement of the wood, the strips

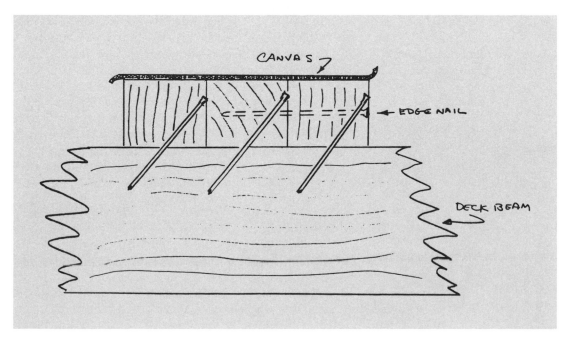

21-5: Cross section of a strip-planked deck. The strips are blind-nailed into the deckbeams and edge-nailed to each other between the beams.

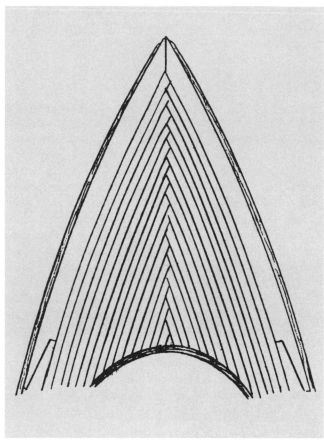

21-6: A herringbone strip deck.

less; spray-on disc adhesive can be used to fix sandpaper to it.) Some fastidious builders will even go so far as to wet down the deck with water to raise the grain; then, when the deck has dried thoroughly, they will sand the deck bottle smooth.

One easy way to check for fairness is to apply marking line chalk to one side of a batten roughly 4- to 6-feet long. When the batten is drawn over the surface of the deck, high or irregular spots will pick up the chalk.

PLYWOOD DECK

For many boatbuilders, plywood is perhaps the most practical material for a deck. It is rugged, adds strength to the assembly, is resistant to leaks, and can be laid relatively quickly. Its initial cost varies directly with the price of the type of plywood chosen. A plywood deck can be painted, left au naturel, stained and varnished (as on many lapstrake runabouts), or covered with canvas or epoxy and fabric. Plywood also can make a suitable subdeck for a laid plank deck if the job is properly done and maintained. If a deck is expected to see a lot of rough service, two layers of plywood, laminated with epoxy and the joints well staggered, can be used.

High-quality mahogany plywoods take varnish well and can be quite elegant in appearance; they also can be very slippery underfoot. For practicality, it is difficult to beat fabric-covered plywood. But whatever route you choose, be sure to go with good quality marine stock; checks and delamination are problems you don't need.

Before laying down the plywood, check the deckbeams for fairness with a straightedge. To ensure fairness along fore-and-aft joints between sheets, backing battens can be let into the deckbeams.

Sections of plywood decking are usually cut out in pairs. When fitting, pay particular attention to the mating of the pieces at the fore-and-aft joints and at butt joints. Trying to make any gaps by edge-setting the stock will probably reward you with an array of curious bulges and depressions, rather than the preferred smooth camber.

A good strategy to avoid having to "make the plywood fit" is to rough-cut the curve that will follow the edge of the deck and concentrate on the straight joints. Once the straight joints are perfect, temporarily anchor them and scribe the final curve of the deck edge on the plywood. The plywood can then be trimmed close to the line, with just a bit left to be planed off after all is finally fastened down.

By-the-by, after the plywood is fitted and before it is fastened down, some forward-thinking builders take the time to paint or otherwise finish the underside of the plywood. This is an especially smart idea for those who are prone to claustrophobia, as they won't have to paint in small spaces when the boat is finished.

After smearing bedding compound on top of the

should be cut and installed so the grain is vertical. One installation method is begun by springing the first strip plank to the curve of the sheer and fastening it to the sheer plank. Then, as the planking proceeds toward the center, the strips are nailed sideways to one another; often, they are glued as well. In addition, the strips can be either toenailed into the deckbeams (similar to installing flooring in a house) or face-nailed into the beams with ring nails, countersunk, and puttied. (See Figure 21-5.) At the center of the deck, the strips can either be fit to a central fore-and-aft "king" plank or joined at the centerline in a herringbone fashion with one another. (See Figure 21-6.)

Fairing, caulking, and sanding

A wooden deck, laid or strip-planked, once it has been fastened down, must be faired. Begin by working diagonally with a hand plane in one direction, then the other. After most of the high spots have been removed, use (with circumspection) a power disc sander with a flexible foam pad to join the surface.

A laid deck can be caulked by opening up the seams with a seam roller, rolling in a strand of cotton, and sealing. Then, give the deck a final tune-up using a fairing board. (A fairing board can be quickly made by adding handles to a piece of plywood, 4 inches by 2 feet, more or

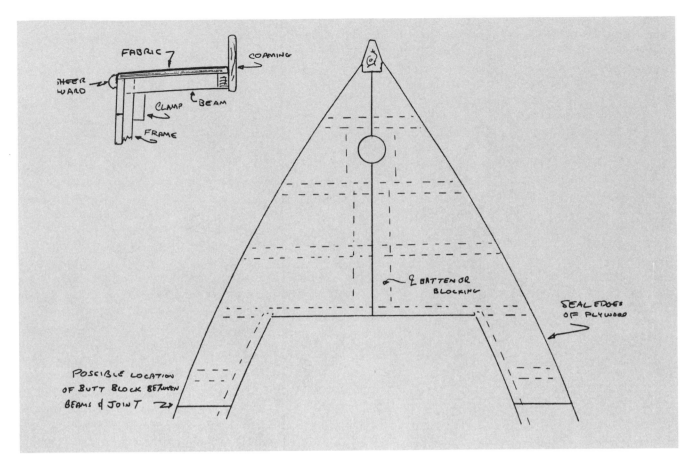

21-7: A plywood deck covered with fabric set in epoxy.

deckbeams, you can begin fastening with either screws or ring nails. Work from the centerline out to the sheer. Like any type of planking, it is important that the plywood makes good contact with the framing you are fastening to. Use props and shims from the shop ceiling to push the plywood down to the deck framing. After fastening, trim the edge of the deck at the sheer and, if you will be covering the plywood with fabric, radius the edge. Bung over the countersunk fastenings or fill with a stable putty, such as epoxy fairing compound, and you are ready to paint the surface of the deck or cover it with fabric.

EPOXY AND FABRIC

Plywood covered with epoxy and fabric makes for a most durable and good-looking deck. Fiberglass is the old standard in fabrics, as it offers durability, affordability, and high strength. Also worth considering is Dynel, a stretchy acrylic fabric that conforms easily to shapes, is nonirritating to the skin, highly chemical resistant, and has good abrasion resistance. On the flip side, it resists lying down on flat surfaces and is not as strong as some other fabrics. Some builders cover their decks with fiberglass cloth and epoxy, others prefer Dynel and epoxy, yet others may opt for a fiberglass underlayment for strength

and a top layer of Dynel for its nonskid quality and abrasion resistance.

The application of whatever cloth you choose is straightforward, as the plywood surface is relatively flat. Before laying down the cloth, be sure the surface is free of any contaminants, such as wax, grease, or oil. For good adhesion the wood surface should be as dry as possible and should be sanded to provide "tooth" for the epoxy to lock onto. As with any gluing project make a dry run to ensure you have your procedure down, your tools, gloves, trays, and rollers at hand, and enough helpers to do the job. Consult the manufacturer, or the manufacturer's spec sheets or manual, for working times, recommended procedures, and lay-up schedules for its product.

Applying the cloth over a dry surface, then wetting it out with epoxy, is the preferred method, as it allows the builder to position the cloth and remove any wrinkles before the sticky resin makes that difficult. Leave enough fabric to allow for trimming.

When wetting out the cloth, saturate it completely and work from the center to the edges. The second layer of cloth (if used) can be laid right atop the wetted-out first. Watch for air bubbles, wrinkles, and dry spots in the fabric while the epoxy is still fresh. The cloth can, and should, be trimmed with a utility knife after it has reached its initial cure or green stage. Additional coats of epoxy can be applied as per the manufacturer's instructions.

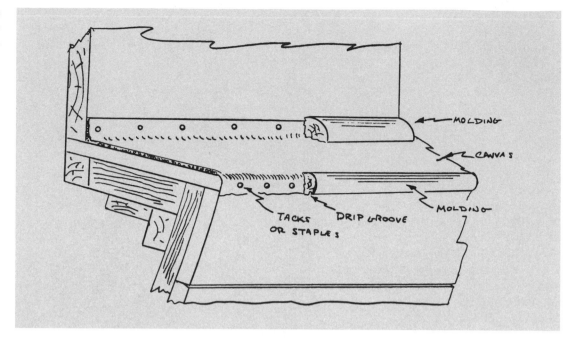

MOLDING

CANVAS

MOLDING

TACKS OR STAPLES   DRIP GROOVE

21-9: A planked deck ready to be covered with canvas. Coamings and moldings will be added after the canvas has been laid.

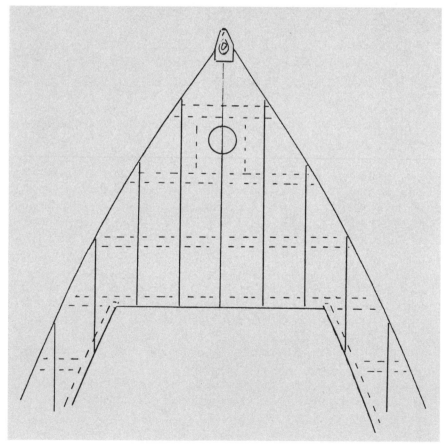

When the epoxy has cured, the deck can then be painted. It is very important to check the manufacturer's pre-painting instructions to avoid the dilemma of perpetually uncured paint.

CANVAS DECK

Amidst all the hoopla about space age sealants and whiz-bang epoxy- and Dynel-covered plywood, one would think that the notion of covering decks with canvas had gone out with the buggy whip and gargoyle carving. Alas, another victim of better living through chemistry. Or is it?

It's difficult to compare canvas to modern glued deck coverings, as they are such different beasts. While the new materials do a great job, there is much to be said for canvas decks on small craft. Like canvas on a traditional cedar canoe, the canvas covering a deck allows the planking below to move during shrinking and swelling cycles without worry about cracks or leaks, and the nap on the surface provides a non-slip surface. Furthermore, canvas is easy for the amateur to apply and repair without an advanced degree in chemistry.

Compared to the concerns about tightness and appearance of a caulked planked deck, the canvas-covered deck requires less than cosmetically perfect wood; i.e., slight defects are permissible. There are no caulk compatibility questions to be answered, no caustic bleaches to be handled, and no messy deck oils to contend with. Indeed, canvas only requires an occasional coat of paint to keep it in good condition. Although canvas is nowhere nearly as

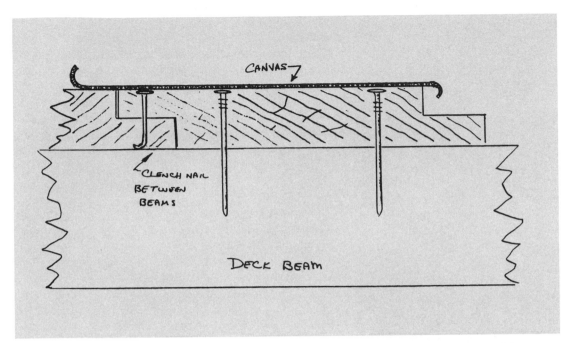

21-10: Cross section
of a canvas-covered
ship-lap planked
deck.

CANVAS

CLENCH NAIL
BETWEEN
BEAMS

DECK BEAM

21-11: Two types of
seams when joining
deck canvas.

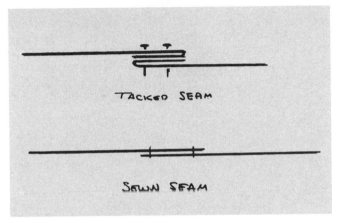

TACKED SEAM

SEWN SEAM

bulletproof as the synthetics, a properly applied and maintained canvas deck will be durable and leakproof for years. And best of all, it looks great.

Decking options

The deck underlying canvas can be of either plywood, strip planking, or conventional planking, as all you are looking for here is a fair and durable "subfloor." The canvas and the paint will take care of the business of beauty and the matter of watertightness.

If you opt for the plywood route, the technique of installation is the same as it would be for the epoxy- and fabric-covered deck discussed above. The same is true for strip planking, though that is a labor-intensive method.

If you go for an old-fashioned planked deck, for wood you can use cedar, pine, or cyprus with success. The installation of the planking is relatively straightforward. One option is to run square-edge planking fore and aft. (See Figure 21-9.) If the planking will not be seen from underneath, fairly wide stock can be used. If it will be seen, tongue-and-groove with beveled joints or ship-lap stock could be used. (See Figure 21-10.) (A caveat on tongue-and-groove decking: Over time, the edges could warp and show up as ridges in the canvas.) To help prevent any unsightly warping or twisting, the planking should be well fastened with nails, with the heads set just below the surface; bronze ring nails will work well here. Any end-to-end (butt) joints in the deck planking should be backed up by butt blocks, and they should be well staggered. Fill any nail holes with quality putty. Radius the edges of the deck slightly to allow the canvas to roll over them without becoming snagged or cut.

Fair the deck as described above. Then vacuum and tack the deck free of any dust and debris—any stray bit of grit or sand will stand out like a boulder under the finished canvas—and paint it with thin, oil-based paint.

Canvas

Before purchasing your canvas consider its anticipated use. No. 12 cotton duck is suggested for light decks, while No. 10 or No. 8 is recommended for heavier traffic. For extra durability and longevity in high-traffic areas, you might consider one of the synthetic canvases now available. If possible, buy the duck wide enough to cover the deck in one piece (widths are available up to 144 inches in the U.S.). If a full-width piece is not enough, the fabric should be double sewn in a straight seam that will run down the centerline, or it can be joined at the centerline by a double fold that is tacked in place. (See Figure 21-11.)

Stretching the canvas

Stretching your canvas into place is one of those jobs best done with help. Before starting, go over the deck with a

tack cloth one more time. Also check to be sure the canvas is perfectly dry.

21-12: Spreading elastic compound into which the canvas will be set.

The canvas must be set in an elastic compound to help preserve the fabric. (See Figure 21-12.) In the past, white lead was used for this purpose. These days, some builders use thick paint, while others prefer a 50/50 concoction of oil-based seam compound and marine paint blended to a creamy, brushable consistency. Canvas cement is sometimes employed, but be aware that down the road when it's time to replace the canvas, removing the cement will demand some tough scraping. In addition, movement of the deck planking as it swells and shrinks can strain cemented-down canvas to the point of splitting.

Coat the deck with elastic compound. Begin the job by stretching the canvas fore and aft along the centerline and drive fastenings to anchor it. Then, pull the canvas smoothly and tightly across the top and over the edge of the deck, taking care to keep any centerline seam straight, and avoiding any creases and/or wrinkles. Some builders wrap the canvas around a broomstick to get a good purchase on the goods. Others use canvas-stretching pliers. "Iron" out any bubbles with a fiberglass air roller or wooden block prior to fastening. Drive your fastenings— ½-inch to ¾-inch copper tacks or bronze or monel staples roughly every 1½ inches—as you stretch, making sure they are located where they will be covered by trim or rails.

Cutting an opening for a cockpit

After the canvas has been fastened around the perimeter of the deck, and after ensuring that the boat is well braced up, you can add weights to the cockpit area to remove any slack in the canvas, or simply get in and walk on the canvas for the same purpose. Then tack or staple the canvas to the edge of the cockpit. When cutting the canvas, leave a margin of extra fabric, about 4 inches, inside the cockpit and other openings to allow purchase for any remedial stretching.

Painting the deck

Dampen the canvas with a wet sponge to tighten it, then follow with a coat of oil-based paint thinned to allow it to penetrate the fabric properly.

Note: Even after it has been moistened with water, the fabric will soak up a considerable amount of paint. Make sure you have enough. Brush on a couple more coats to ensure a uniform, non-mottled appearance, but don't try to fill the weave of the fabric completely, as the canvas will become brittle and the surface will become slippery.

Finishing up

All that remains is to cover the cut edges of the canvas to ensure weathertightness and a smart appearance. Coamings for the cockpit and hatches will do this anyway; in other areas, the fabric can be trimmed out with perhaps a half-round molding (along the side of a cabin) or by installing a guard or rubrail (on the sheer plank). To ensure a watertight fit, some builders will "back-out" or slightly hollow their rubrails and slightly undercut the right angle on the inside of their moldings. They do this for a weathertight fit on the outside edges of the trim and to allow room for the flexible bedding compound underneath. Fasten the trim pieces with screws, taking care not to drive them into a deck seam, where they will have little holding power. Trim any excess canvas with a utility knife.

COCKPIT COAMING

A steam-bent coaming adds an elegant touch to an open boat. It is, however, yet another feature that requires a full-size pattern to be fitted correctly. The coaming is either bent to the interior framing of the cockpit or mounted on the deck along the side of the cockpit opening. The latter positioning is probably the more challenging of the two, as there will be no cockpit frame to clamp to, and the bottom edge of the coaming must fit the fore-and-aft curve and the side-to-side camber of the deck. The interior-mounted coaming, however, has its own quirks, as it may have to be notched and trimmed at the proper angle to allow it to land on the deck forward.

Making a pattern

To make a pattern use either light wood stock or thin plywood. The wood stock is perhaps easier to trim to size, while plywood is a bit more stable and resistant to change of shape. The fitting of the pattern will require considerable scribing and trimming. Clamping blocks, cut to the angle of the coaming and fixed to the deck, can be helpful—especially if the coaming is mounted on the deck. Fit the bottom edge of the pattern first, scribing, recording, and cutting the necessary shape, notches, and bevels. Then clamp the pattern in place, scribe in the top edge as shown on the plans, and trim to shape.

Cutting the stock

When selecting your stock look for the clearest material with the straightest grain possible, especially in the region with the greatest bend. When cutting the stock, allow a little extra length and width to accommodate any beveling and miscues in the scribing process. The stock on the upper edge can easily be trimmed off after the bottom edge has been fit.

Steaming the stock

There are two ways to go when bending the coaming: Either bend it over a jig or directly into the boat.

Of the two choices, bending over a jig is definitely easier. You can position your clamps exactly where you want them and have greater control over the bending process. On the other hand, to bend over a jig requires building a jig; it also involves an accurate guesstimate of the amount of overbend to build into the jig to compensate for spring back. (Some woods will fight you more than others; oak is relatively compliant, while mahogany dislikes bending and will spring back quite a bit.)

Bending the coaming directly into the boat will eliminate the need to build a full jig, but it wouldn't be a bad

21-13: At the cockpit the canvas is folded over the edge and tacked or stapled in place.

idea to fix in place clamping blocks to hold the coaming in the correct location and the proper angle. It generally is more difficult to pull a curve into a piece of wood than to bend it over or around a shape. The coaming will want to straighten out and come away from the edge of the cockpit, so you must have plenty of clamps and pads ready to prevent that from happening.

Which is the better method depends on circumstances and preference. If only one end of the coaming must be bent, perhaps the jig is the way to go. On the other hand, if the coaming is a continuous arc bent into the forward end of the cockpit, as it is in some catboats, you may prefer to bend it right into the boat. Whatever method you choose, leave extra stock at the ends to be trimmed later, as you will have enough to think about when bending the coaming without having to wonder whether the piece will be long enough or not.

Trimming and fastening

After the coaming has cooled and taken its set, fit and trim it to size. Any connecting or bracing blocks should be made and fit at this time as well. Drill for the fastenings, bed, and install.

22 • SOLID-WOOD SPARS

For traditional small craft, it is difficult to beat solid-wood spars. Decidedly low-tech in construction, such spars require little or no gluing, no exacting assembly table, and no specialized tools. They are easily shaped with hand tools.

SELECTING SPAR STOCK

Stock should be reasonably clear of knots, and free of shakes and sapwood, and should be ordered a bit over length so you will be able to trim off any end checks or cracks. The type of wood to use depends greatly on local preference and availability. If you can get it, Sitka spruce is a very good choice, indeed. Known for its tight, straight grain, with limited defects, it is light in weight, yet strong and stiff. Expect to pay a premium price for the privilege of using this exceptional wood.

Good alternatives are the Eastern spruces, which, if selected carefully, have very similar qualities to Sitka spruce. There was a time, not that long ago, when, if you lived in the Northeast, it wasn't much of a chore to go down to the local lumberyard and find some pretty decent-sized dimensional lumber just right for sparmak-ing. Alas, in recent years the lumber industry has mined this resource heavily, and high-quality spruce timbers (4 by 4s, 4 by 6s, etc.) have become difficult to come by.

A good alternative to solid timber is to laminate your spar blank from spruce boards, which are still readily available. (See Figures 22-1 and 22-2.) Lamination allows you the golden opportunity to "inspect" the interior of the spar before it is glued up. On the other hand, your spar will only be as good as your glue joints, so be sure to properly prepare your stock and follow the glue manufacturer's recommendation to the letter. And lay out the stock so the end-grain of the boards alternates—the rings facing one way on the first board, the opposite the next, and so on. This will help deter warping, which is sometimes a problem in solid-timber spars.

LAYING OUT AND CUTTING

The level of detail offered the builder regarding the taper of the spar will depend on the plans. Some plans offer highly technical data, with regular stations and offsets given to sixteenths of an inch. Others may provide information in the form of an arc of a circle onto which has

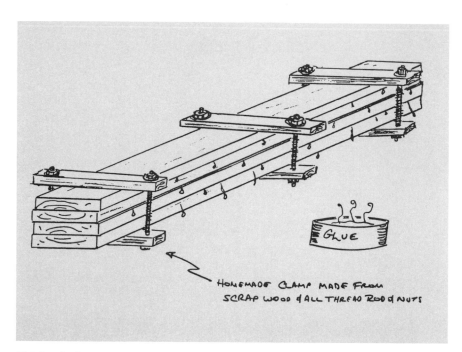

22-1: Laminating a spar from spruce boards.

on its face. Then, as before, record your offsets for the half-breadths onto the station lines, fair with a batten, and scribe the lines in pencil.

Now it's back to the bandsaw to slab off the two new sides. Plane smooth, and you have a spar with a four-sided taper.

Note: If the plans call for letting in a sheave or lifting mechanism, it is easier to do this now while the spar is still at its squared-off stage rather than later when it is rounded. (See Figure 22-4.)

FOUR WILL GET YOU EIGHT

The next step is to take the spar from four-sided to eight-sided. Although the layout for this can be figured mathematically, the easiest way to go is to use a sparmaker's gauge. This elegant device automatically, and proportionally, divides each face of the four-sided spar into three parts and provides guidelines for planing the four sides to eight.

Making the gauge

While sparmaker's gauges can be configured differently, they are all basically set up the same. Usually, the body of the gauge is made of straight stock. On it four holes are laid out in line. The two outer holes are for pins that pass through and extend beyond the body. The inner two are for pencils.

been drawn radii that represent half-diameter measurements at specific stations. Still others may show no numerical data whatsoever, requiring the builder to establish station lines and to scale the dimensions off the plans.

Whatever the plan's presentation is, the technique for initial shaping of the spar is the same. Begin by surveying the stock. You will have to work around knots and any sweep or set in the stock.

Measure and cut the stock to length, then strike a centerline on one face of it. If you are using a solid, rather than laminated, piece of stock, align the centerline with the center or heart of the tree. This should reduce the spar's tendency to warp. From the plans, establish the station locations on the centerline and square them out in either direction. On each station, plot the half-breadth of the spar measured out from each side of the centerline. Then spring a batten through the points to fair the line, and mark it with a pencil.

Take the spar blank to the bandsaw and, after checking that the blade is set dead square, slab off the two sides of the spar, making sure that you are cutting to the outside of the lines. Smooth the cuts down to the lines with a long plane.

The next job is to square down the station lines onto one of the newly cut and planed sides—this side will be square across but curved along its length—and establish a centerline

22-2: When laminating a spar, use lots of clamps and space them closely.

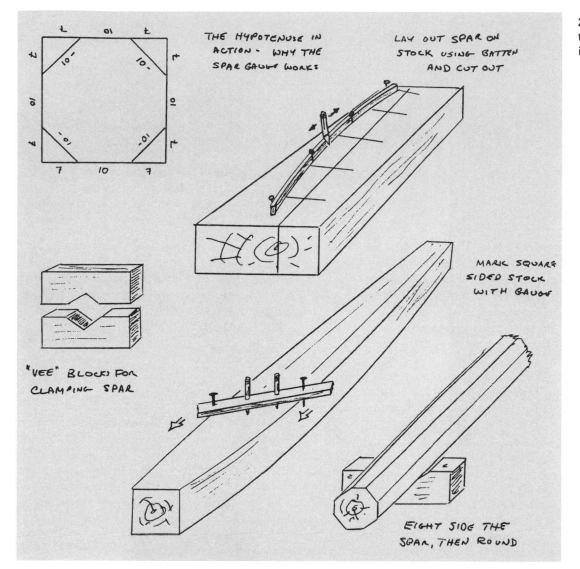

THE HYPOTENUSE IN ACTION - WHY THE SPAR GAUGE WORKS

LAY OUT SPAR ON STOCK USING BATTEN AND CUT OUT

MARK SQUARE SIDED STOCK WITH GAUGE

"VEE" BLOCKS FOR CLAMPING SPAR

EIGHT SIDE THE SPAR, THEN ROUND

22-3: Laying out, tapering, and rounding a spar.

22-4: Cut in for a sheave or other lifting mechanism before rounding the spar.

Four Will Get You Eight • 239

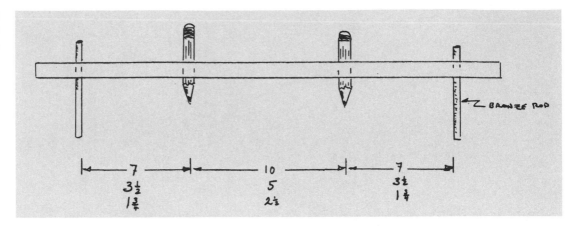

The body is laid out in 24 units—these can be inches, millimeters, cubits, or whatever. (See Figure 22-5.) It matters little what unit you use as long as you are consistent. The distance between the outer pins—not center-to-center, but innermost-edge to innermost-edge)—is 24.

Drill holes for the pins, then measure in 7 units toward the middle of the body from the inside edges of the pin holes and drill holes to take the pencils. Insert the pins and the pencils. The ratio of the gauge will be 7:10:7; in other words, 7 units from the inside edge of the first pin to the point of the first pencil, 10 units from pencil point to pencil point, and 7 more units from pencil point to inside edge of the second pin.

Using the gauge

The idea behind the sparmaker's gauge is that when held properly it will scribe two pencil lines on each side of a tapered, four-sided, square-sectioned spar—thus dividing each side, or face, into three parts.

To use the gauge, ride the pins along the outside edges of the tapering spar. (See Figure 22-6.) As the gauge rides along, the pins always touching the outside edges, the twin pencils will mark the spar. As the spar tapers, the pencil lines will get closer, but the ratio measured across the spar at any one point will always remain the same (or very nearly so)—7:10:7.

So what's the deal with a 7:10:7 ratio? It is the key to turning a four-sided tapered spar into an eight-sided tapered spar. It's all tied in to Mr. Pythagoras's theorem, which is that the square of the hypotenuse of a right triangle is equal to the sum of the squares of the two adjacent sides. So, if we plane a flat or facet from a 7-unit line on one side of a four-sided spar to a 7-unit line on an adjacent side, we have created a hypotenuse. Seven

squared equals 49. 49 + 49 = 98, the square root of which is just about 10, which is the 10 in the 7:10:7 ratio. Eureka!

So just plane off the corners of the four-sided spar from line to line, and you will automatically have an eight-sided spar. For faster results, set a hand-held circular saw to 45 degrees, and, staying to the outside of the lines, remove the greater part of the stock. Finish up the job with your hand plane.

ROUNDING THE SPAR

Although there are formulas for 16-siding and 32-siding, for a small spar it probably is just as easy to begin rounding off after the stick has been eight-sided. Knock off the edges of the octagonal stick with a plane, working along the length of the piece, more or less 16 siding the spar by eye.

After the spar has reached this stage in its shaping, it can become somewhat ungainly to clamp to or hold in a vise. A quick and easy way wrestle the spar into submis-

22-6: The sparmarker's gauge in use.

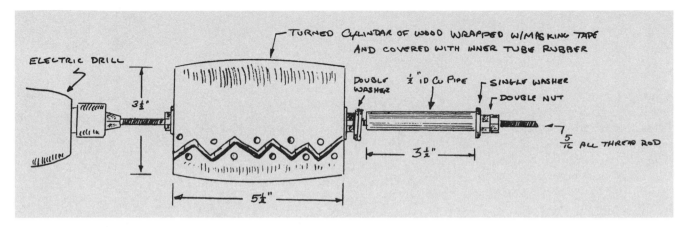

22-7: The McIntosh spar-rounding device.

sion is to make up a couple of pairs of clamping blocks. These are simply matched V-blocks, the depth of which is roughly half the diameter of the spar; they can be quickly cut from scrap on the bandsaw. Do you want deluxe versions? Line them with leather.

To use the blocks, put a pair around the spar and clamp the sandwich to a sawhorse. Relieving the pressure on the clamp will allow the spar to be rotated or moved fore and aft.

At this point the rounding can start in earnest. What tool to use? One route to go is to make a spar plane by converting an old-time wooden-bodied plane. Mill the base to a hollow along its length, insert the cutting iron in the plane, and scribe the shape of the hollow onto the cutting edge of the iron with a pencil. Grind the edge of the iron to shape, and sharpen it.

Making your own spar plane is worthwhile if you will be making a number of spars, but if you are working on only one or two, it may be gilding the lily. Another method is simply to use your flat-bottomed planes in a rotating or rolling fashion, moving in a slight diagonal manner around the spar, paring off the high spots as you go around. Just keep your iron sharp and set fine to avoid tearing out the grain. Reset the spar in the blocks several times to ensure you are getting the spar consistently round. Use your eye and a stiff batten to check for any developing hollow.

Once the spar is close to round, it's time to break out the sanding device for final tuning.

SANDING

A useful sanding device can be made in a jiffy. Slice open a new sanding belt, the type made for a belt-sander, so it will lie flat. Make two wooden handles and bolt them to each end of the belt. Use the belt "shoeshine" fashion around the spar to smooth any high spots left by the plane. This device is quick and easy to make, and it's cordless!

Another effective spar-sanding tool is one used by boatbuilder Bud McIntosh and found in many boatshops

since he wrote about it years ago: a drill-powered belt-sanding drum device. (See Figure 22-7.) The unit consists of a wooden cylinder or drum roughly 3½ inches in diameter. The cylinder can either be turned on a lathe so it is barrel-shaped—that is, thicker in the middle than at the ends—or a straight-sided cylinder can be swelled out in the center by wrapping it with tape. Rubber is tacked around the outside of the drum to act as a tire, and the center of the drum is drilled for an axle. Threaded rod (⁵⁄₁₆″ works well) is used for the axle, long enough so that a couple of inches extends beyond one end and about 6 inches beyond the other end.

Snug the rod to the drum with nuts and washers. For a handle, use a piece of ½-inch copper pipe, roughly 3⅓ inches long. Slide a couple of loose washers over the long end of the rod, then slide on the pipe, then another washer. To finish off the device, double nut the end of the rod, locking it but allowing the copper handle to spin.

You now have a device reminiscent of an industrial-strength prayer wheel. To use it chuck the small end of the rod into a variable-speed drill. Hold the drill in one hand, the copper tube handle in the other. Next, turn a belt-sander belt inside-out and slide it over the spar and the drum. Hold the drum so there is a slight pressure on the belt, and start the drill ever-so-slowly. (This is a dust-mask and eye-protection operation.) It takes a bit of practice to get the belt to track properly, but once you get it, you can go right to town. (See Figure 22-8.) Just remember to keep down the speed, and keep the belt moving along the spar!

As the spar reaches its final shape, switch to a finer-grit belt. To finish up the job, use a hollow hand-sanding block and fine paper, working in the direction of the grain to remove scratches.

Small-boat spars are generally oiled or varnished. The clear finish is important to allow regular inspection.

Notes on gaff jaws

When laying out gaff jaws, the curve of the jaws should follow the grain of the wood. Use stock that is tightly grained and defect free, and watch for short grain at the turn of the jaw, which can create a weak spot. If no suitable wood is available, you might consider laminated jaws.

If you are steaming wood over a bending jig for bent gaff jaws, you will have a greater chance of success by making the bending stock considerably longer than the finished jaws. The bending will go easier, and you will obtain a fairer curve. After the curve is bent, the shape of the jaws can be cut on the bandsaw.

To get a good fit of the jaws to the spar, first temporarily clamp the jaws to the spar. (This can be a bit of tricky clamping.) Be sure they are in the same plane with one another. Scribe the location of the jaws with a pencil, remove the jaws, and flatten the landing spot on the spar with a block plane. Slightly hollow the base of the jaws to ensure good contact. Then clamp the jaws back in place and drill for your fastenings. (Bronze rod peened over washers works well for this purpose.) Remove the jaws one last time, apply bedding compound, put the jaws back in place, clamp, and fasten. Tack protective leather inside the mouth of the jaws, and you are done.

22-8: The McIntosh spar-rounding device in use.

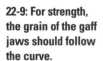

22-9: For strength, the grain of the gaff jaws should follow the curve.

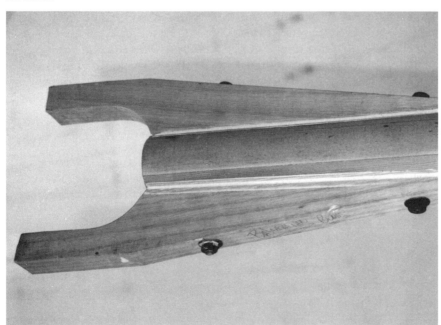

MAST HOOPS

It just isn't as easy as it used to be to find the perfect masthoop down at the hardware store. For some reason merchants are reluctant to keep 'em in stock. Hence, it's up to the builder to whip up these often-forgotten-until-the-last-minute units in the shop. Like most items, however, there's more to the making of a masthoop than would first appear. First-time manufacturers who attempt to freehand the operation may be plagued with scorched fingers and shattered stock, and produce an assortment of irregular, warped, ellipsoid-shaped hoops.

The difficulty in making mast hoops is that wood, even when well steamed, hates to make the tight turn required and will rebel by splitting out on the outside of the curve and becoming distorted. The solution is to use a bending jig that not only has a compression strap to keep your stock from failing but also is shaped properly to give you the elegant circular shape of a mast hoop every time. Where do you obtain such a wonder? You make it, of course!

Ingredients

The materials needed to assemble this handy rig are all standard off-the-shelf stuff. The basic bending form is a short length (say, 5 to 6 inches long) of plastic sewer pipe. Plastic pipe is great stuff; it is rivaled only by drywall screws in its versatility. It comes in a variety of diameters, is easy to cut with a hacksaw, will not stain steamed oak like black iron will do, and, best of all, is cheap.

For the compression strap, a piece of perforated, galvanized "pipe hanger's" strap, roughly 2-feet long, is a good choice. Employed by plumbers to hang pipes from floor joists, this soft, ductile, metal strapping comes in rolls readily cut with tin snips. The galvanization protects against unsightly staining of the bending stock, and the perforations allow easy drilling for rivets. Add a 4-inch piece of ¾-inch dowel for a strap handle, a few assorted screws, nuts, and bolts, and some scrap lumber for a base, and you're all set to go.

Assembling the jig

Begin by anchoring the plastic pipe "mold" to a portable base. One good way of doing this is to first trace the interior circumference of the pipe onto either a stout piece of hardwood or a piece of 1-inch-thick plywood. Cut out this circular slug with your trusty bandsaw, and fasten it to a rectangular board with screws and glue. Then just slide the pipe section over

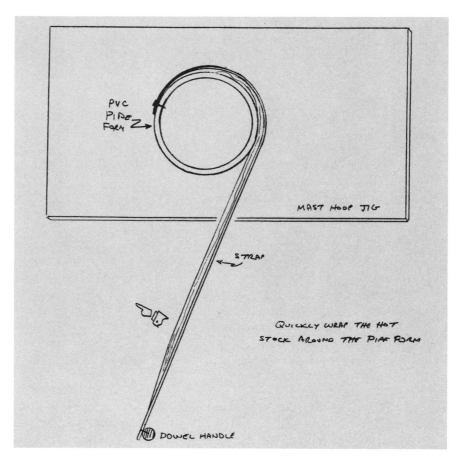

22-10: Bending a mast hoop in a jig, step 1.

the slug, and drill and anchor the pipe in place with screws. Then attach your bending strap to the piece of pipe with a screw and washer set no farther down on the pipe than you can reach with a deep-throated clamp. Next, fasten the dowel handle to the other end of the strap in the same manner. That's all there is to it. All that remains is to clamp your jig to a secure base that can be circumnavigated while you bend the hoop. A sawhorse screwed to the floor will do.

Mast hoop stock

This is the place to be fastidious in your selection of wood. Accept only straight and tightly grained stock that is defect-free and as "green" as possible. White oak is a good choice, as it bends well and is durable. Ash works as well. The wood should be milled smooth, with no saw marks, and the edges should be relieved or broken with sandpaper to aid in heartbreak-free bending. The ends of the stock must have complementary bevels, so when the stock is bent around the form into a hoop, the bevels will overlap, producing a scarf joint that can be riveted together.

How do you determine the length of the wood to be bent? Although it is possible to figure the proper dis-

tance mathematically, the easiest method is to wrap a piece of paper tape around the circular form, adding a bit for the overlap of the ends, to provide a ballpark length to work with.

As with any kind of steaming project, it's always a good idea to make up extra stock. At first, run all your stock a little bit long and then experiment with different lengths to see which one best fits the bill. (Remember to keep track of the measurements.) When you've found that perfect measurement, simply trim all the stock to that length, bevel the lap ends, and you're ready to start up the hoop factory.

Steaming

Proper steaming is the key to success. Not enough time in the box, and the stock will be too stiff and will probably break. Too much, and the stock will turn into so much overcooked asparagus and will probably break. What we're looking for is wood of the al dente sort.

Wait until steam is billowing out of the steam box. Only put in a few pieces of stock at first; then, after things get rolling, when you take one piece out, add a new one. How long to cook your victims? The generally accepted rule is an hour for an inch of thickness, half an hour for half an inch, and so on. The time will vary, however, as each piece of wood is a bit different. What really counts is speed. The stock is so thin that once it is out of the box

PULL AND CLAMP

LET COOL AND RIVET HOOP

COMPLETED HOOP

it will cool very quickly and stiffen up again whether you're ready or not.

Bending the hoop

When your stock is ready to serve, hold the bending strap out at a tangent from the pipe and align the piece to be bent so that one end contacts the pipe and the length of it is lying against the strap. Then, marching around the sawhorse, quickly and tightly wind the strap and stock around the pipe—a bit like winding the starter cord on a British Seagull outboard motor.

Immediately after bending, with a deep-throated C-clamp, hold the hoop in place against the pipe until it has thoroughly cooled. Then, while the hoop is still on the jig, drill through the holes in the bending strap into the lapped portion of the hoop stock. Remove the hoop from the jig, and insert a copper wire nail for a rivet (from the inside), back the head of the nail with a holding iron, drive a rove over the shank of the nail, nip off the excess shank, peen, and you have a complete mast hoop. Sand and varnish to taste.

In the event you will be making

22-12: A mast-hoop-bending jig, with strap. To the right is a deluxe "keeper" for temporarily parking the hoops.

a whole nest of hoops in production fashion and won't have time to stop and rivet each one, make up a set of "keepers" to temporarily park your hoops in until you have time to rivet them. These are just circular molds cut to the outside diameter of the hoop. For the deluxe version, cut a slot in one side of the keeper so you can drill and insert a nail while the hoop is still ensconced. Then when you're ready, just pop the hoops out, finish off the rivets, and hoist the sail!

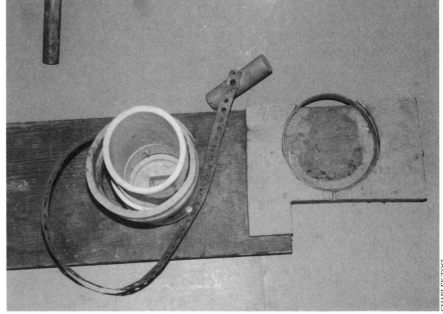

23 • WHAT LOOKS GOOD

A little while ago I found myself down at the county seat, on the waterfront. The town pier there is an egalitarian meeting place for boats—sort of a local pub for watercraft—and moored alongside were all manner of small craft. Chunky working skiffs jostled elegant pulling boats; up-to-date speedboats sporting metalflake finishes hobnobbed with traditional catboats. A few of these craft could make your heart sing. Others were homelier than a stump fence.

Just what is it that makes the difference? The cost of the boats doesn't seem to matter—many of the economy clam skiffs display a salty elegance and propriety that can't be beat. Meanwhile, some of the pricier yacht tenders and mass-produced luxury go-fast boats have all the grace of a varnished milk carton and the finesse of a butter tub.

Nope, rather it seems more to do with the little things: a subtle attention to detail, symmetry, and proportion, qualities that don't necessarily make a boat float better but surely make it look better. To that end, I offer a few admittedly highly-opinionated observations on what seems to make boats look good.

SHEER BEAUTY

Probably the first and foremost consideration is the sheerline, the subtle, graceful curve that defines the uppermost edge of the hull. Aesthetically, the line of the sheer is probably the most important feature on a boat and is also likely to be the most challenging for the home builder to get right.

Part of the difficulty in deciding what looks proper to the eye is that a great deal of experimentation in sheerlines by designers over the years has tended to muddy the waters. Flat or nearly straight, wave-shaped, "powderhorn," and even occasionally reverse sheers can be seen on the waterways. Some of these shapes work well enough; others don't. But for a traditional hull, it is difficult to beat a long, fair parabola that reaches its highest point at the bow.

Even if the builder opts for the traditional sheer and lofts the designer's work exactly as drawn on the blueprint, there is still a good opportunity for things to go wrong. This is because many times the two-dimensional representation of the sheer that the draftsman rendered with such care on the drawing board will leave much to be desired when built in three dimensions. The suppos-

23-1: The elements that make the difference between boats that look good and those that don't are subtle, and include detail, symmetry, proportion, and other elusive values.

poor spacing in the floorboards, or a coaming higher on one side than the other, there's no way you are going to miss it. You might get used to it, but miss it? No way. It'll be waiting for you every time you go near the boat. Using patterns, rechecking measurements, and working from a centerline when laying out components go a long way toward developing a handsome boat.

THE PLACEMENT OF FASTENINGS

Oddly enough, regularity in the placement of fastenings in a small craft can say much about quality. In this discussion the matter has less to do with whether the boat will hold together and more with what the eye expects—much like having all your buttons lined up on your shirt.

The easiest way to lay out the desired spacing is to draw a pencil line at the requisite distance in from the edge of the piece being fastened—a plank, a thwart, etc.—and "walk" off the intervals with dividers. The advantage of this technique is that in the long run it probably will save time, as you won't have to stop and decide just where to put in that fastening—the location will have already been marked.

edly long sweeping sheer may suddenly have developed a curious flat spot in the forward quarter, or may even display an apparent downsweep, or powderhorn. What goes on here?

The difficulty can be traced back to the drawing board. Oftentimes, the sheerline as portrayed on vellum, although technically correct (at least in 2-D), fails to take into account real-life perspective. This phenomenon will be most evident on vessels that are bluff or full forward, and have a subtle curve to the sheer, and must be corrected by the builder on the lofting board or by adding a little extra swoop to the planking as the boat is built. Often, as little as ¾ inch to 1 inch added to the sheer at the stem of a small boat will do the trick. Unsure whether your plans have this problem? Build a half model before you build the boat, and check it out. (See Chapter 24, The Builder's Half Model.)

SYMMETRY

Sym•me•try, n, 1. Satisfying arrangement marked by even distribution of elements, as in a design: a. balance b. proportion c. harmony.

Small craft are, in a way, a bit more of a challenge to get right than a larger vessel. The reason is that you can see all of a small boat at the same time. If there are mismatched knees,

23-2: The line of the sheer is one of the key elements in the handsomeness of a boat. As in this Whitehall, perhaps the sheer most pleasing to the eye is a long, fair parabola that reaches its highest point at the bow.

23-3: Even the most utilitarian of small craft is a delight to behold if the builder pays attention to the rules of symmetry.

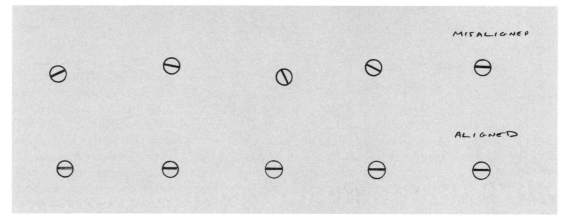

23-4: Screws—line 'em up and get all those slots going in the same direction.

MISALIGNED

ALIGNED

Keep in mind that if you are installing those good old-fashioned flat-headed slotted screws, and if their heads will be visible, it pays to take the time to line up the slots so they are all parallel with each other. (See Figure 23-4.) This really does make a difference. Lined-up slots impart understated elegance; randomly aligned slots sometimes look slipshod. I must mention, however, that try as you might there are times when the slots just will not line up. Don't lose any sleep over it. Boatbuilding is supposed to be fun, not an exercise in contortionism.

THE ALIGNMENT OF BUNGS

Bungs—wooden plugs that cover countersunk fastenings—may be small, but they have a large effect on aesthetics. Often, in the rush to finish up the job, a builder will simply drive the bungs without regard to the alignment of the grain. While this will be little noticed on a painted hull, its effect on a bright varnish finish will be profound, spoiling an otherwise beautiful bit of joinery.

Taking the time to align the grain of the bung to that of the surrounding wood will pay you back many times in enhanced beauty.

THICK MADE TO LOOK THIN

In the construction of small craft aesthetics is constantly dueling with its old nemesis, practicality. The thwart is a case in point. Structurally, it must be rugged enough to support the beefiest passenger; aesthetically, it must be light enough in appearance that the boat doesn't look like a coal scow.

What to do? Chamfer the lower edge of the thwart for a little creative marine trompe l'oeil. (See Figures 23-5 and 23-6.) The mind's eye loves to be fooled, and it really doesn't care if a thwart is a chunky 1¼ inches thick as long as it appears to be ¾ inch.

To lay out the chamfer, simply draw a line along the edge of the thwart, ¾ inch down from and parallel to the top. Then chamfer back 2 inches or so from this line on

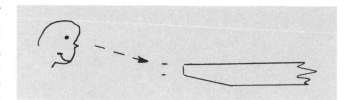

VIRTUAL CAMBER

Certain characteristics or traits are expected on a traditional small craft. Deck camber is an example, even when there is no real deck to be cambered. Certain parts of the boat should be shaped as if they were following the camber of an imaginary deck. The top of the breasthook, for example, should be arced, the inwales fastened square with the flare of the sheerstrakes, the quarter knees at the transom fitted with a bit of upward rake on the inboard side. Compare this to a boat where everything has been installed level, from sheer to sheer. The first looks crisp, jaunty, and ready to go to sea; the latter is rather bland, lacking nautical joie de vivre, more like something built for a catfish pond.

the bottom of the thwart. But before you break out the spokeshave, break out your French curve and end the line inboard of the riser by scribing an arc down to the bottom corner of the thwart edge, about half an inch from the riser. This is necessary because, while the eye appreciates the thin appearance along the length of the thwart it would be taken aback by thinness over the risers. If the chamfer were carried all the way to the ends of the thwart, the thwart would appear to be levitating over the riser—appealing, perhaps, to some mystics, but unsettling on a traditional wooden boat. The drawn curve brings the chamfered thwart back to full thickness before it reaches the riser. (This same technique should be used on the thwart edge at the centerboard trunk if the trunk is locked into the thwart.) All that remains is to shave in the chamfer, and your bit of optical legerdemain is complete.

One easy way to work camber into the breasthook is to install it oversize and sculpt it in place. For example, if your inwales are to be 1-inch wide, try making the breasthook 1⅜ inches thick and installing it with the extra ⅜ inch exposed above the sheer. Mark a centerline on top of the breasthook and, working from the centerline to the sheerline on either side, carve in the camber. Then, to maintain the look of the 1 inch inwale on the curved after face of the breasthook, scribe a line 1 inch down from the top that parallels the camber. Chamfer the bottom of the piece to the line in the same manner as the thwart, described above.

MORE VISUAL DODGES

Turning the post that supports the thwart on a lathe can transform it from blocky and utilitarian to understated and elegant without any loss of strength. A similar effect can be obtained by tastefully scalloping the under edge of a thwart brace.

Determining the angle for installing the quarter knees is quite straightforward. First draw a vertical centerline on the inside face of the transom. Onto the centerline, mark the desired height of the camber. Then, with a straightedge, draw a line from the centerline point to the sheer at each side of the transom centerline. And there you have it, the lines with which the top of the

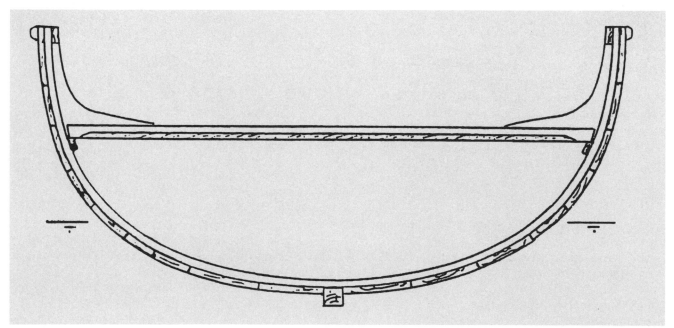

23-7: A gently scalloped under-thwart brace and a turned post subtly transform the ordinary into the extraordinary.

TAPERED RUBRAILS

If the rubrails, or outwales, are milled and installed at a constant thickness, say ¾ inch, they will appear to grow in width as they approach the stem. This apparent chunkiness seems especially noticeable on fine and sleek craft, and is yet another curious effect caused by perspective. No matter. Simply tapering the rails up forward seems to set things right. Before installing the rails, clamp them to the bench and, from a point about 3 feet back from the stem, hand plane in a taper from ¾ inch in width to ½ inch. That should do the trick.

BEADING

Beading is a useful artful dodge in wooden boat construction. Not only is beading handsome but also it is a useful visual distraction. A bead cut into the edges of a heavy thwart riser optically reduces the width of the piece; the riser retains its strength yet looks delicate.

Beading cut into the edges of shiplapped staving on a bulkhead looks to the casual observer like a tasteful detail—which it is—but more importantly, it creates shadow lines. (See Figure 23-9.) Some joints in the staving inevitably open more than others due to the normal shrinking and swelling of the wood; these

23-8: A symmetrical layout and uniform gaps between planks and floorboards always look good.

quarter knees are to be aligned.

Oh, and don't forget to check the knees with a pattern to see that they are symmetrical before installing them.

GETTING THE GAPS RIGHT

Gaps between parts are a necessary feature in a wooden boat to accommodate drainage, ventilation, and the normal shrinking and swelling of wood. They are visible everywhere: between floorboards, seat planks, interior ceiling or lining, and so on. If these gaps are uniform, they add to the good looks of the boat. If they are not, the workmanship—no matter how expensive the wood, how shiny the finish—will look shoddy.

Laying out those persnickety gaps individually with a tape rule is difficult, and then when you screw the pieces together the layout more likely than not goes askew anyway. True enough. What to do?

A better, faster approach is to park your measuring tape and slice up a batch of spacer blocks. A good size is ¼-inch thick, cut from a piece of ¼-inch plywood. Next, lay out the pieces to be assembled and fasten down the first piece. Position and fasten the next piece with spacer blocks between, and then the next piece, right on down the line. The spacer blocks will give you perfect ¼-inch gaps every time.

Virtual Camber • 249

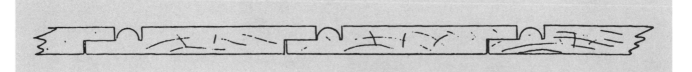

23-9: Beaded staving.

shadow lines divert the eye from this potential unsightliness—yet another boatbuilding sleight of hand.

FAIRED STEM

The stem is another item that is sometimes shortchanged in the rush to complete the boat. Often, you'll see a hull with graceful lines sweeping forward, but the effect of the lines will have been spoiled by the builder, who snubbed off the nose of the boat by beveling the side faces of the stem inward from the rabbet toward the centerline. The result is something like sticking a clown's nose on a gazelle: interesting, but perhaps not exactly appropriate for a traditional wooden boat. The stem will have a more classic appearance if the sides of it are faired to continue the curve of the hull.

MOTEL FURNITURE

Part of the beauty of a wooden boat that sets it apart from its fiberglass cousins in the harbor is its sharp, crisp lines. Well-defined shadow lines accentuate the elegant curves that are a signature of wooden craft. Yet so many builders will go out of their way to overly round off those fine features, giving the boat a Swedish-modern look similar to the overly rounded end tables and lamps that graced cheap motels in the 1960s. Being a little more circumspect in the use of a spokeshave and a router will not only produce a more handsome boat but will also will save time.

SURFACE FINISHES

Finally, there is the perennial question: Which finish is best? Admittedly, the degree and type of finish on a boat is a matter of personal taste. Beauty is in the eye of the beholder, and all those other good old bromides. Yet I would like to introduce this rather iconoclastic notion: There is such a thing as too much varnish.

This is not to say I dislike varnish. It is great—on other people's boats. Yes, varnish does allow you to see the beauty of the wood, and, yes, indeed it does—especially for bottle-finished mahogany speedboats—provide steady employment for a myriad of boatyards. But we are talking boats here, not grand pianos. A bright finish is time-consuming to keep up, it limits what you can do

23-10: A finely crafted wooden boat is handsome when its parts are crisply defined. Relieve edges, but don't round them excessively.

with a boat, and in many ways it can distract from the total beauty of the craft.

That said, I must add that prudent application of the "clear stuff" can enhance rather than overwhelm the lines of a hull. Rails, sheerstrakes, transoms, spars, and coamings are excellent candidates for varnish, especially when contrasted against a traditional enamel finish. A good enamel finish will be virtually maintenance free throughout the season, stand up to wear and tear, and, when well applied, look like a million bucks.

Actually, when looking for a yardstick to judge whether a finish job is practical or not, I give it the "Man's Best Friend" test. If you can take your favorite canine pal boating and if the boat still looks great when you get back, that's a good finish.

PAINTING

Volumes can and have been written on the subject of painting. Two statements can probably be safely made on the subject: (1) The amount of time and energy necessary to obtain a good finish is generally underestimated, and (2) There is great variance among practitioners as to the proper and (perhaps) only correct method to apply these liquids. Nonetheless, with a bit of care the builder, and occasional painter, can obtain a serviceable, good-looking, and durable coating on the boat with a minimum of angst. (See more about paints and painting in Chapter 6, Glues, Paints, and Potions.)

Painting weather

The ideal condition for painting is shirtsleeves weather—settled, little wind, no chance of rain. Fog should be avoided, as it will penetrate the surface of fresh paint. Don't paint too late in the day, as dew can settle on the new paint. Also, shun painting under the direct sun on a hot day; the brush will drag, the paint will set up too quickly, and the chance of blistering is great. On the other hand, cold and humid weather will delay the drying of the paint and encourage it to run.

All that being said, you may have occasion to paint on a non-perfect day, and if you do, be prepared to modify your paint accordingly (see below).

Which paint to use?

Marine enamels are truly specialty paints, formulated to take the worst the maritime environment can dish out. They are typically made up of a mixture of components, including resins, oils, pigments, solvents, driers, and adhesives. In addition, ultraviolet inhibitors are added to the mix of some paints. There are many choices for the builder, ranging from high-tech two-part polyurethanes to the traditional alkyd enamel. For most, the latter is the most practical and economical choice.

It is good practice to stay within the same family of paints on a job to avoid conflicts between the formulations. Always check the manufacturer's label on the can for recommended procedures.

Test panels

Test panels are a great way to experiment with new techniques and products. The best panels are those built of the same material you are refinishing and that are set in the same attitude and climate as the job. You will have learned a lot about the characteristics of a particular varnish after you have coated a vertical test panel with it. You will also know how much you like a new color before you have committed it to the boat. That glorious "Sea Foam" green on the paint chip may reveal itself to be a bilious "Bilge" green on the test panel.

Some of the new alternatives to varnish have their own curious hues of orange and yellow, so it is best to try them out on a test panel beforehand. Some builders go so far as to build up several coats on their panels and leave them exposed to the weather and sun to test the long-term durability of the product.

A sports car finish?

Keep in mind that the glossier the finish, the greater the chance that imperfections in the underlying surface will show. This is especially true with white. Consider using semigloss, or even flat. Many manufacturers offer flattening additives that can knock back a stock high-gloss paint a notch or two.

Amendments

Few if any paints are formulated to be used directly out of the can. Generally, they must be modified or adjusted to the conditions under which they are applied. The three most popular amendments are thinner, brushing liquid, and Japan driers.

Thinner is a fast-evaporating solvent that improves drying in cold climates (below room temperature). There is no hard-and-fast rule about how much to add, but generally thinner is introduced in small amounts, not to exceed 10 percent by volume, until the paint begins to brush out properly.

23-11: A boat with painted surfaces accented by varnished elements is sometimes more handsome than one with all paint, or all varnish.

Brushing liquid, or retarder, is thinner's alter ego. It is basically a slow-drying solvent used to ease brushing on warm or windy days and to allow for proper flow of the paint and leveling off of brush marks. As with thinner, there is no specific rule about how much to add to paint. Add brushing liquid cautiously until the paint feels right in the brushing.

Japan driers can be used when the paint absolutely, positively must be dry quickly. Add with circumspection, a few drops at a time, and check with the manufacturer for compatibility with the paint.

Keep in mind that the days when all paints were formulated pretty much the same are over. Cavalierly splashing in a dollop of a generic fluid called thinner can spell disaster for your paint job. If you are using an off-brand thinner, be sure it is compatible with the paint involved. If you are unsure, stick with the manufacturer's recommendation, even if its thinner is a lot more expensive. Following the rules is cheaper than having to do the whole job over.

Mixing

Proper mixing of paint is indispensable. Improper mixing can lead to inconsistency in color, covering, and brushability, as the bulk of the solids will be on the bottom of the can. The easiest route is to take your paint to a store with an electric shaker/mixer. A second method is to pour off roughly one-third of the paint into a clean can, then stir the contents of each can with a wide stirring stick, taking care to bring up the heavy pigments from the bottom. When the contents of both cans are thoroughly blended, pour the two cans back together and continue stirring. Hand-drill-powered mixers work well for this. When applying the paint, stir the contents of the can on a regular basis.

Note: As a general rule, do not stir or shake varnish, as bubbles can be introduced into the mixture. The only exception to this rule is satin finish varnish, which contains a flattening agent that must be evenly distributed through the mixture.

To avoid contaminating your original pot of paint with dust and other detritus, use small quantities at one time, poured into a second clean container. Paint strainers—paper funnels with mesh in the bottom—are handy and easy to use.

Brushes

Use only good-quality brushes. Some swear by short-bristle badger brushes, while others believe synthetic is fine enough for most jobs. What you don't need, though, is one of those extra cheap brushes that loses bristles faster than a hound dog sheds fur on a hot summer day.

Many builders have had great success using the thin yellow foam rollers that are used to apply epoxy. The painter will cut in the edges with a brush, and cover the rest of the territory with the roller. Bubbles in the finish can be removed by striking them with a wetted-out homemade "brush" that is made by slicing a roller into sections and cutting the pieces into "half moons." These crescents can be used as they are or mounted on a stick.

Whatever brush you choose, practice a bit with it to get a feeling for the tool. Be sure the brush is thoroughly wetted out before starting. Dip only the bottom third of the brush in the paint; as you brush, work back toward the ending spot of the last stroke. Paint an entire area at a time, as stopping midway in a large surface will leave a visible line. Stop if you must at a natural edge, such as a plank lap, a chine, or the edge of the transom.

Avoid the temptation to lay on paint heavily. Two light coats are much better than one heavy one. Work so you will always have light reflected from a newly painted surface. Trouble lamps strategically placed can help you spot unpainted areas that might go unnoticed in the shade. Unless the paint begins to sag, don't "touch up" slight imperfections. You can catch them on the next round.

Dust

Dust is the nemesis of the painter, and boatshops have plenty of it. Unless you are looking for a nonskid surface on your topsides, you must take steps to rid the shop of as much dust as possible. Some boatbuilders go so far as to wet down the floor with water to curtail any dust that might be kicked up while painting and varnishing.

Masking tape

Sad to say, there are inequities even in the world of masking tape, involving a wide range of qualities, quirks, and costs in the product. Hence, the painter needs to know the pedigree and track record of the tape being used to avoid difficulties. Generally, the better grades will be carried by marine suppliers or catalogs; as you might suspect, the best masking tape is likely to be more expensive than the homeowner variety available at your local chain hardware store.

The cheap grades of masking tape are mostly intended for noncritical finish work. They are notorious for allowing aggressive marine paints to creep under the edge of the tape, leaving you with an artistically irregular, some might say organic, line. They are also well known for their tendency to weld themselves to the side of the boat after a very short exposure to the sun.

There is a wide selection of masking tapes for different applications. There are flexible tapes, for curves and contours; fine-line tapes, for that extra-sharp color line separation; safe-release tapes, for use over delicate surfaces that other tape might lift, and long-mask tapes that can be removed easily, without resorting to a chisel, up to a month after application. Consider the job and select your tape accordingly.

Smoothing and filling

Fair the surface to be painted as much as possible with 100- to 120-grit sandpaper. On large surfaces, such as the hull, use a long board. Imperfections can be filled with a suitable filler, a fast-drying, tough, plastic material that is applied with a putty knife or a plastic spreader. In the past, standard one-part surfacing compound was the composition of choice. Although it has relatively good adhesion qualities and sands well, this material tends to shrink considerably while drying, thus requiring several applications. Many builders now opt for the two-part epoxy surfacing compounds. Easy to mix, albeit somewhat malodorous, this two-part concoction sticks to nearly any surface, does not shrink, and is soft enough to allow for easy sanding. Polyester putty (a.k.a. "Bondo") should be avoided, as its adhesion is suspect, and because it tends to be harder than many of the softwoods to which it is applied (similar to the hardness of a knot), making it difficult to finish flush with the surrounding surface.

After filling and fairing be sure to remove all traces of dust before starting to paint. Vacuum, wipe with clean rags, and follow up with a tack rag.

Undercoat

Apply an appropriate undercoat to fill and smooth the surface. Some high-filling undercoats, called sanding-surfacers, contain a large amount of talc that allows easy sanding and smoothing.

Undercoat is hydroscopic; it will absorb water and can cause blistering to subsequent layers of paint if left at the applied thickness. Manufacturers call for sanding off the bulk of the paint to a translucent film, leaving the filler only in the grain and the scratches.

Allow the undercoat to dry overnight, then sand with 120- to 150-grit paper, tack, and recoat with undercoat. Some painters will add a small amount of topcoat enamel (roughly one-part topcoat to five-parts undercoat) to the second coat of undercoat. Allow to dry overnight and then sand and tack.

Note: Undercoat is not durable and should be covered with enamel as soon as possible after it has dried.

Trowel cement

After the first undercoat has been applied and the hull is of a uniform color, previously undetected blemishes may suddenly appear. This is where trowel cement comes in. This product, formulated to be used over painted wood, is almost like a thickened paint; it is employed in a similar fashion to drywall compound to fill small scratches, dents, and wide, low areas of $\frac{1}{16}$ inch or less. After the cement has dried, the surface can be sanded smooth and tacked. Apply trowel cement in thin coats to avoid lumps.

Topcoat

Sand once again, tack, and apply the first topcoat. Allow the paint to dry a full 24 hours. Lightly sand with 220-grit sandpaper, and tack. Apply a second coat, and that should just about do it.

24 • THE BUILDER'S HALF MODEL

There is nothing quite like a half model, a scale representation of a hull split down the middle longitudinally. It catches the eye and the imagination in a way that no photograph or set of lines plans could.

The lure of the half model probably has something to do with the synthesis of the visual and the tactile. The model can be pivoted, rolled over, and rotated on its axis for viewing—qualities that no other medium outside computer-generated images can rival. But the model offers more than the electronic projections can: it can be examined by touch in the same way one tests the full-size hull for fairness.

Whether you are building a painted utility model as an aid in checking a questionable sheer or to lay out planking lines, or a varnished model simply for the pleasure of having it, it is a endeavor well worth doing. The tools required are few, the cost of materials is low, and the investment in time is small. All you need is a set of patterns, and you're in business. The question is, where do you procure those patterns?

HALF-MODEL PATTERNS

There are a limited number of commercially available pattern kits available, mostly the usual suspects: *Sovereign of the Sea*, *Cutty Sark*, perhaps a token Friendship sloop. Other than these, to get the patterns you want, you will have to make them yourself. But this isn't all that difficult. All you need is some cardboard (cut up breakfast cereal boxes will do), a utility knife, some spray mounting glue, a used-up ballpoint pen or a stylus, a few sheets of carbon paper, and the lines plan for the boat you wish to model.

Note that these instructions assume the lines plan for your boat is drawn to the outside of plank. If it is drawn to the inside of plank, just add the planking thickness to each station on the body plan and redraw the waterlines before making the patterns. The profile pattern does not need to be modified.

A half model is basically a "wedding cake" of wood built of laminated layers called lifts. The shapes of the lifts are shown on the lines plan as the waterline curves in the half-breadth view. To capture these shapes, take a large piece of cardboard, cover it with carbon paper, and slide it under the lines plan. Then, using your inkless ballpoint pen, trace around one of the waterline curves.

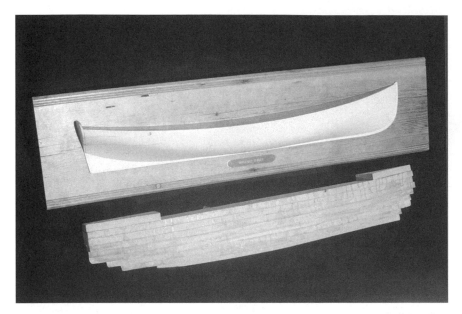

24-1: A half model of a Whitehall pulling boat and a glued-up block of lifts used to make it.

Also trace the centerline and the perpendicular station lines, and number them, as they will be used for reference later. Cut out the shape with scissors or a utility knife. Repeat the operation for a pattern for each waterline/lift and the sheerline. The profile view will show you how many lifts you will need.

Note that some plans don't show all the waterlines near the sheer, as the lines would overlap. If that is the case, simply use the sheer pattern for the upper lifts.

Next, slide your cardboard and carbon paper combo under the profile view of the hull and trace the profile. Also trace the horizontal waterlines and the vertical station lines; these will be used to index the pattern to the laminated block of wood that will be used to make the model.

If your boat has a deep but relatively narrow keel—a Maine lobsterboat comes to mind—a carved keel might be a bit fragile. A good alternative is to build and carve your model to the rabbet line, and add a keel and stem afterwards. If you decide to go this route, trace an additional profile pattern drawn to the rabbet line, rather than to the forward edge of the stem and the bottom of keel. Then whip up some patterns for the stem (from the rabbet to the stem face), and the keel (from the rabbet to the bottom of the keel). And while you are at it, you can also trace any other patterns derived from the profile plan, such as for a rudder or swung-down centerboard.

Our final patterns are for the stations. Derived from the Body Plan, they are the Rosetta stone of the operation. The station patterns control the shape of the hull of the model from the outside in exactly the same fashion as the construction molds control the shape of the full-size vessel from the inside. A station pattern could be called a negative template, as you will be cutting out the shape of the station from the cardboard and using the piece that remains as a template to be fit over the model as it is carved to check the shape.

The station patterns can be made in two ways. The first is to cut a square of cardboard the size of the body plan and slide it and a piece of carbon paper under the plan. Trace around a station, from the sheer to the keel and up the centerline. Draw in the horizontal waterlines on both the hull and the centerline side. Label the station and the waterlines. Remove the cardboard and, using a utility knife, cut out the cross section of the station, leaving a shape that looks like a little arch. Do this for each station.

The second method is to make several photocopies of the body plan and, using spray adhesive, mount them on cardboard squares. Then, as in the first method, cut out the station patterns.

Now you are fully armed with a set of patterns.

TOOLS

You will need a good chisel, a standard spokeshave, a combination square, a hand plane, and a half-round rasp. A ½-inch gouge is handy but not necessary.

Edge tools are only as effective as they are sharp, so include a good sharpening stone in your kit and use it often. Have on hand a selection of coarse, medium, and fine sandpaper. And beg, borrow, rent, or buy lots of C-clamps. You'll be needing them.

You should have access to an electric planer if you are milling your own stock, and a bandsaw to cut out the sheerline. If you don't have a bandsaw, a sabersaw (blades come in lengths up to 7 inches) will work for the sheerline and the profile shapes; a hand plane can be used on the lift stock.

THE LIFT STOCK

The appearance and ease of carving your model depends a great deal on the wood you use. The stock should be stable, easy to work with edge tools, take a finish well, and be pleasing to the eye. Although I have had good luck with both white pine and white cedar, given my choice, I would take basswood. Basswood has good color and nice, tight grain, and is a joy to work with. Commercially it is used for moldings, yardsticks, and pattern stock. Occasionally, a contrasting wood is desirable for the hull below the waterline. Honduras mahogany fits the bill nicely.

The first step in building your model is to plane the lift stock to the proper thickness, which must be equal to

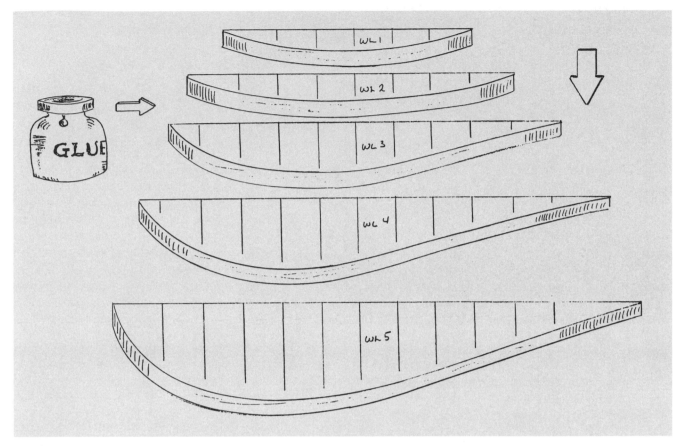

24-2: Cut out and label the lifts.

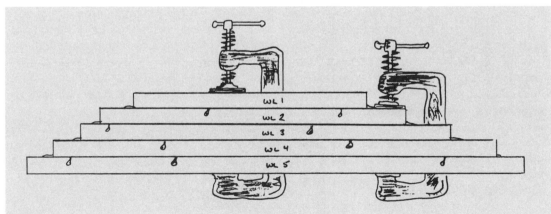

24-3: Spread glue and clamp the lifts in the proper order.

the distance between the parallel waterlines in the profile plan. Once you have planed the stock you can check the thickness by stacking up the pieces and holding them against the drawn waterlines on the profile plan. The lines between the pieces must align with the waterlines on the plan. The pieces can be a hair undersized, because the glue in the joints will make up the difference.

Lay each pattern on the lift stock in a way that uses the wood most economically while avoiding defects and blemishes, and trace around it with a pencil. Mark the station lines on the wood and number them. These lines will help to properly align the lifts while gluing and will be reference points for your station templates.

CUTTING AND GLUING THE LIFTS

Cut out the lifts, keeping outside the drawn line. This allows a little extra room to play with when you are gluing up the model. If necessary, plane straight the centerline side—the side that will be the back of the model—of each piece. Then, square down from the previously marked station lines onto the newly planed surface and mark with a pencil.

For gluing up the lifts, I use either yellow carpenter's glue, the type that comes ready-mixed in a plastic squeeze bottle, or plastic resin glue, which is a powder that is mixed with water. Carpenter's glue is somewhat

24-4: A glued-up block of lifts ready to be shaped.

The newly planed back side should be square with the uppermost lift.

CUTTING THE PROFILE

With the back of the model smooth and square, it is time to draw the profile of the hull, using the appropriate pattern, on the back of the block. If you will be adding a keel and a stem, use the rabbet line pattern. If, on the other hand, you plan to carve out the keel and stem from the glued-up block, use the full profile pattern. Match the pattern to the waterlines and the stations, and trace around it.

Now cut out the profile with a bandsaw or sabersaw.

A note of caution: The profile is marked on the back of the model. To simply freehand the unsupported model through a bandsaw with just one edge of one lift in contact with the saw table can be very dangerous. One slip, and the blade could bind, probably ruining the model and blade, and possibly causing injury to you. Why take chances? Fasten some temporary guides, or rails, to the block to keep it stable and level, or use a right-angle block. (See Figure 24-5.) If you are cutting with a sabersaw, leave plenty of wood outside the line, because the blade may twist and under cut the line. (Take note of the same precaution when cutting the sheer.)

Another method, perhaps the

easier to use because it is premixed, but it is thick and hence makes for tricky clamping. Plastic resin glue is thinner and produces nice, brown glue lines—good if you want defined waterlines, not so good if you don't.

Before gluing up the lifts, make a dry run to check your clamping procedure. Do you have enough clamps?

Lay down wax paper or a plastic sheet to keep glue off the bench. Spread glue evenly on all gluing surfaces, starting with the largest lift. (A notched plastic or home-made wooden spreader works well for this.) As each lift is glued, align it with its mate, using the marked station lines as guides. You can keep one lift aligned with another while the glue sets up with a couple of small brads, but be careful to locate the brads away from the profile line, where cutting tools will be used.

To ensure that the model has tight waterline joints, use as many clamps as necessary. As you are clamping the lifts, check to see that the centerline (the back of the model) is as flat and square as possible. The station lines you have drawn on each lift should all line up. Wipe off excess glue.

After the glue has set up, plane the back side of the model flat and smooth. Remember to index the station lines so you will be able to reestablish them on the back of the model after the planing is finished.

24-5: Rig up a jig to support the block when bandsawing the profile.

simplest and safest way of all, is to transfer the profile lines to the other side of the model with dividers, using the station lines as reference points. This allows the model to be sawn with the back (flat) side in contact with the table of the bandsaw. As always, watch out for fastenings, and cut outside of the line, especially along the sheer.

If you don't have power tools and there's no tool rental store nearby, you can cut out the profile shape with hand tools. With a hand-saw, make a series of cuts from the outside of the block to within ⅜ inch of the profile line. Keep the cuts about 2 inches apart, except along the stem, where the cuts should be closer together. Remove the wood between the cuts with a chisel.

SHAPING THE SHEER

The model is now ready for shaping with hand tools. Because the sheer-line will be worked on first, the model should be held in a vise in an upright position. The best way to do this is by screwing a wooden block to the backside of the model. This holding block has to be wide enough to take at least two screws and of a size and shape that will fit firmly into the vise either on the flat or on edge. Lastly, the block must be fastened to the model in a position that will allow full access to the sheerline area.

Using a spokeshave, work from each end toward the middle, "sneaking up" on the drawn sheerline. Check your work often with a square. Watch that unwanted lumps or hollows don't develop.

To check that the curve of the sheer is fair, bend a light slice of wood or piece of ⅛-inch plywood down onto the sheer. You have a fair sheer when there is no light visible between the bottom of the bent piece and the top of the sheer.

SHAPING THE HULL

The hull of the model is now ready for carving. Reposition the holding block so the keel is up and the sheer is down. You can rough out the model using a gouge, a block plane, a large chisel, or a spokeshave.

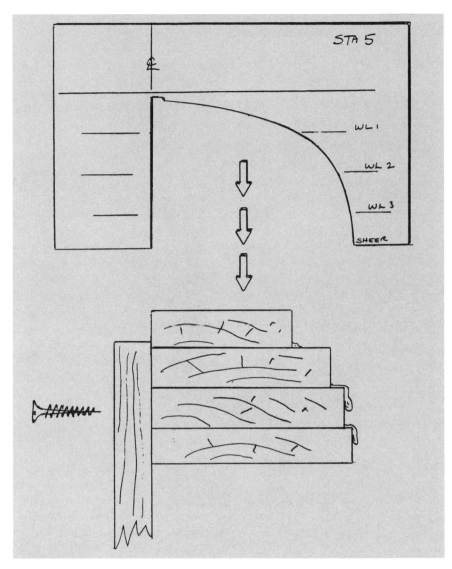

24-6: When shaping the half hull, the goal is to carve away the excess wood until the concave station templates fit the convex hull.

Knock off the square corners of the lifts, working from amidships toward the ends, following the grain of the wood. Stop carving when the lifts have almost been faired together and you are close to the glue lines. At this point, smooth the face of the transom and trace its proper shape with the transom pattern.

You can now begin the finish shaping of the hull. Work in a diagonal direction, across the lifts, from amidships toward the ends. Do concentrate on one section of the hull while ignoring the rest; work down the hull gradually; you will get a better feeling of your progress with a large field of reference.

A note on rasps: A half-round can be quite effective when hollowing out such areas as the flare forward; a flat rasp works well in developing tumblehome, if it exists, in the quarters in the area of the transom. A flat rasp is also useful in getting rid of unwanted lumps, but be wary of becoming overenthusiastic with the tool. Those deep grooves the tool produces can be devilishly difficult to sand out.

Use the station templates frequently to check your progress. Simply slide a template over the model at the corresponding station and make a mark where the model touches the template. This is a high point. Shave it off and try the template again. Check the model's shape often with your hand; your fingers can pick up subtle bumps or hollows that your eye will miss. When the centerline, sheer, waterlines, and bottom of the keel all line up at each station, you have arrived—almost!

If you are carving in the stem and keel, you will want to join and smooth their flat surfaces. A flat file works well for this task. You may also wish to fair the stem to a cutwater. Use the file circumspectly! At this point, it is very easy to take off too much. Check your progress with the profile pattern.

KEEL, STEM, AND RUDDER

If you are adding the keel assembly and stem separately, this is the time to work up the pieces. Using the patterns, lay out each piece onto the construction stock, matching color with the model as much as possible. Saw each piece

out, staying to the outside of the line, as before. Fit the inside edges to the model but leave the outside edges oversized. This will be trimmed after the assembly has been attached to the model.

Glue up and assemble the keel. "Five-minute" or "quick-set" glue works well here.

Give your keel assembly and stem a final fit to the hull. This is persnickety work, but it's well worth the effort. Glue the keel and the stem to the hull as the model lies flat on the bench. Blocks and wedges will help hold everything together while the glue sets. Don't forget to put a plastic sheet or wax paper on the bench.

After the glue has set, fair the keel and the stem to the hull, and

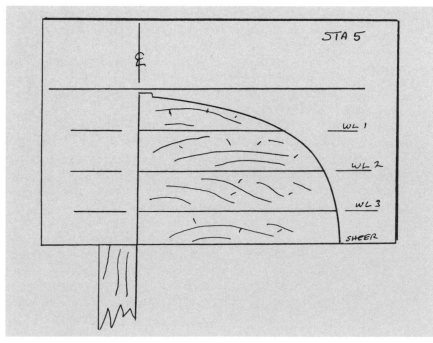

24-8: You have an accurate shape at a station when the template fits precisely and the waterlines marked on the template match the lift lines.

trim them to the final outside profile face. Then work the bevel to the half nosing into the stem.

If your model has a rudder, cut it out and shape it according to the pattern. The finished rudder can either be glued to the model now, or fastened later to the backboard with escutcheon pins.

FINISHING

Smooth the model with sandpaper, being careful not to round of corners that should be sharp, such as at the transom and the sheer. Crisp edges where appropriate provide much of the model's beauty. Give the model a final sanding with fine-grit paper.

Traditionally, the finish is a matter of taste or utility. A boatbuilder's working half model is oiled, painted flat white, or left unfinished. Other suggested finishes that are easy to apply and good looking are varnish or clear urethane.

Before applying the finish, dust the model with a tack rag. Apply a first coat to prime and seal the wood, then add at least three more finish coats. Rub down the final coat, after it has hardened, with a polishing compound. This gives the model a nice, uniform satin appearance and removes any brush marks or dust.

24-9: The final fit at Station 5.

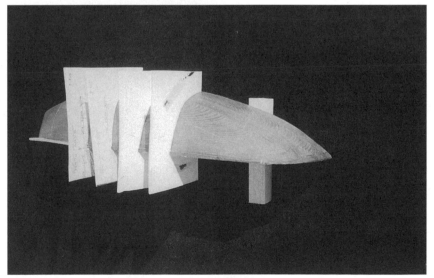

24-10: All of the templates fit.

APPENDIX A • GLOSSARY

Apex—The lowest point in a cut rabbet where the inside face of a plank would end. In profile, it lies between the rabbet and bearding line. Sometimes called the "Middle Line."

Apron—A structural backing piece fit behind the stem. Often wider than the stem and set to form the after part of the rabbet.

Athwartships—At right angles to the centerline plane of the hull.

Batten—A long, thin, flexible piece of wood, usually rectangular in shape and made of clear, straight-grained softwood. Used to create a smooth, fair line.

Backbone—The full assembly of all the components, including the stem, keel, and transom, that make up the center foundation of the hull.

Beam Mold—A pattern or template used for marking the shape (camber) of deckbeams.

Bed Logs (for centerboard case)—The rabbeted structural members of the centerboard case that run fore and aft next to the centerboard slot. The logs are fastened to the keel with screws or bolts. The rabbets are designed to accept the side panels of the trunk and face inward toward the slot.

Bedding Compound—A non-hardening putty that is used as a gasket between two pieces of wood to exclude water.

Bearding Line—The point where the inside face of the planking touches the outside face of the stem as it enters the rabbet.

Bevel—An angle cut into a piece of wood, usually to facilitate the joining of that piece of wood to another. A lapstrake plank is beveled on the outside upper edge to allow the lower edge of the next plank to overlap it for a watertight fit.

Bevel Gauge—A two-bladed tool used to capture angles.

Breasthook—A triangular structural member fit at the sheer immediately behind the stem. Fitted and fastened to the stem and the adjacent planking, the breasthook acts as a gusset in a truss to add great strength to the upper part of the stem.

Body Plan—The view on a set of lines or lofting portraying the athwartships view of the stations. Generally only one-half of the width of the stations is illustrated. The Body Plan normally offers a split view, one side illustrating the stations as they would appear if viewed from the bow, the other, as they would appear if viewed from the stern.

Bore—To drill a cylindrical hole.

Broadstrake—The second strake up from the keel, next to the garboard.

Bulkhead—A vertical partition in the interior of the boat.

Bung—A wooden plug used to cover a countersunk fastening.

Butt Block—A gusset-like block of wood used to join two parts of a strake together.

Buttock—A fore-and-aft slice or plane through the hull that runs parallel to the centerline plane.

Camber (or Crown)—A convex curve on a deck, cabintop, breasthook, or any other transverse member. Also the term used to describe an unwanted curve on a flat-planed bevel.

Carlin—Deck framing that runs fore and aft, forming the foundation for the inboard edge of the side deck; connected to, and supports, the stud beams.

Carvel—Planking fit edge to edge to produce a smooth hull.

Ceiling—Fore-and-aft planking laid on the inside of the frames; adds to structural strength and prevents debris from getting between frame members.

Centerboard—A pivoting, sliding keel made either of wood or metal.

Cheeks—Pieces affixed to the side of a structure to strengthen it.

Chine (or Chine Log)—A longitudinal member in a V-bottom hull running along the knuckle where the side and bottom legs of the frames are joined.

Clench Nail—A square-cut nail that is driven through a pre-drilled hole; the point of the nail is bent over to make a one-legged staple.

Clinch Ring—A round, dished washer with a hole in the center into which the tip of a metal rod can be inserted and peened over to create the head of a drift pin.

Clinker—See Lapstrake.

Counterbore—A cylindrical hole that is drilled to allow the head of a fastening to be sunk below the surface. Usually filled with a bung or putty.

Crook—A naturally grown branch or root of a tree in a shape suitable for a structural member, such as a knee, stem, deckbeam, or frame.

Cross Spall—A member used to hold together the two sides of a mold. Also the name for a temporary spreader running athwartships from sheer to sheer to hold the shape of a hull until permanent interior bracing is installed.

Deadrise—The angle the bottom of the boat makes with the horizontal plane at the keel.

Deadwood—Solid pieces of wood used as fillers in the backbone assembly.

Deckbeam—An athwartships structural component that not only supports the deck but also ties the hull together at the sheer. Deckbeams usually have camber and are made of either solid or laminated stock.

Diagonal—A diagonal slice drawn through the lines plan when lofting to check the fairness of the hull.

Diminishing Device—An architectural tool used to graphically divide up distances; often used for lining out the planking.

Dory Lap—A planking method similar to lapstrake, except it uses two complementary bevels in the laps rather than a single one.

Drift (or Drift Pin)—A homemade spike often used to blind-fasten heavy keel members together. Also used to edge-fasten rudders, centerboards, and transoms.

Edge-Set—The forcing sideways of a plank on the flat. Edge-set is undesirable when using a spiling batten, sometimes necessary when hanging a plank.

Expand—To draw out a part, such as a transom, to its full size and shape from a foreshortened view.

Fair—A smooth line, without any unnatural distortions, lumps, or hollows in it.

Flitch Sawn—Planks or timbers sawn through and through as two-sided slabs with bark on either side. Also known as live edge.

Floor (or Floor Timber)—A framing member roughly the same thickness as a frame running athwartships across the keel, fitted and fastened to the garboard strake and the keel. It is a key component that ties one side of the boat to the other.

Forefoot—The lower portion of a built-up stem that falls in the region between the stempiece and the keel.

Frame—The nautical equivalent of a stud in house construction. Sawn or steam-bent to shape, frames generally run perpendicular to the keel and the planks are fastened to them.

Garboard—The plank next to the keel.

Green Wood—Newly cut wood with a high moisture content.

Grid—A pattern of regularly spaced horizontal and vertical lines forming squares on a set of plans or a lofting board and used as a reference for locating points.

Gripe—See Forefoot.

Gudgeon—A fitting that takes a pintle fitted to the rudder, forming a hinge on which the rudder swings.

Half-Breadth—Distance measured out from the centerline.

Hanging Knee—A vertical knee, usually used to tie the underside of the end of a deckbeam to the hull.

(To) Hog—A distortion of the hull in which the forward and after ends droop lower than the middle section.

Hog Piece—Similar to a keel batten. Used on top of the keel to give better landing for the garboard plank.

Hood End—The forward end of the plank where it fits into the rabbet.

Horn (or Horn In)—To check the squareness of an athwartships member (thwart, frame, mold) by measuring from a point on the centerline to the outermost edges of the piece being checked—thus forming an isosceles triangle. If both legs of the triangle are the same, the piece is square to the centerline.

Inside of Plank—The shape of the hull minus the plank thickness.

Inwale—A longitudinal member fastened at the top inside face of the frames in an open boat. It generally serves the same purpose as a clamp in a decked boat.

Joining—The mating of one piece of wood to another.

Keel—The main longitudinal structural member of a hull.

Keelson (or Keel Batten)—A structural member fastened to the top of the keel for added strength. Wider than the keel, it also adds greater bearing surface for the planking.

Kerf—Groove or slice made by a cutting tool, such as a saw.

Kiln Dried—Wood that has been artificially dried in an oven to a specific moisture content.

Knee—A brace or bracket between two adjoining members.

Landing (or Lap)—The flat bevel planed into the edge of a plank to allow the next plank to lie flush against it.

Lapstrake—A system of planking where the lower edge of one strake overlaps the top edge of another.

Ledges (or Centerboard Case Posts)—The fore-and-aft vertical end pieces of the centerboard case.

Limber—Drain hole cut in the lower edge of a floor next to the keel.

Lining Off—Determining the layout of the planking on the hull.

Live Edge—See Flitch Sawn.

Load Waterline (or LWL)—The theoretical level at which the hull will float when carrying its designed weight.

Lodging Knee—A horizontal knee; used primarily to tie the side of a deckbeam to the hull.

Lofting—The full-size lay-down of the lines of a hull.

Long Lines—In lofting, drawn lines that run the length of the vessel; e.g., sheerline, buttocks, waterlines, diagonals, etc.

Loom—The portion of an oar between the handle and the blade.

Mast Partner—Extra framing added around an opening for the mast to provide strength.

Maststep—Piece used to anchor the heel (bottom end) of the mast.

Mold—Three-dimensional manifestation of the station curves drawn on the lofting.

Molded—See Sided.

Nib—A square cut made at the wedge or featheredge end of a piece of wood. Usually used on planking and on the ends of mechanical scarf joints.

Normal—In lofting, a line drawn square, or 90 degrees, to the tangent of a curve.

Outwale—The rubrail or longitudinal chafing strip on the outside sheer of the boat.

Plank—A longitudinal piece fastened to the outside of the frames to form part of the skin of a boat. A strake can be made up of one or more planks.

Poppet—A brace for supporting a boat during construction or storage.

Profile—The side view of the vessel as seen at a right angle to the keel or centerline.

Quartersawn—Lumber sawn so the grain runs at a right angle to the flat side of a board. Sometimes called edge- or vertical-grain lumber.

Rabbet—A cut or groove in a structural member to allow another piece to fit flush against it. An example would be the cut rabbet in the side of a stem into which the hood end of the strake is fit and fastened.

Rake—An angle or inclination (generally aft) from the vertical. Transoms on traditional small craft tend to be raked aft.

Ribbands—Temporary batten-like wooden straps bent around the molds to which the steamed frames are bent. The ribbands not only dictate the shape of the frames but also strengthen the setup and provide resistance to wracking.

Riser—A longitudinal member fastened to the inside of the frames to support the thwarts.

Rivet—A fastening consisting of a nail and a washer-like burr—also known as a rove or ring—over which the nipped-off end of the nail is peened.

Rocker—Fore-and-aft curvature of the keel.

Rove—See Burr.

Scantlings—Dimensions and sizes of all structural parts used in building a vessel.

Scarf—A beveled joint between two short pieces of wood to make one long one. A scarf joint in a keel member is generally fastened with bolts; that in planking is generally glued.

Scribe—To mark a piece of wood for fitting with either a compass, or a block of wood and a pencil. The word also refers to the scratching or etching of a line into a piece of wood with a sharp tool.

Shaftlog—The part of the backbone assembly through which the propeller shaft passes. Some shaftlogs are made of a single piece of wood with a hole bored all the way through; others are built up of two pieces, bolted together.

Sheer—The uppermost visible line of the hull in profile view, the outermost (usually) in the half-breadth view. The line of the sheer probably has the least to do with how well the boat performs and the most with how well it looks.

Shutter Plank—The final plank that is hung to close up the hull when planking from the keel up and the sheer down. It is usually fitted in an area with little shape and/or twist to minimize complications.

Sided and Molded—Two terms used to describe the thickness of a given part. The sided dimension of a part is a constant thickness throughout the part; i.e., the side-to-side thickness of a frame is the sided dimension. The molded dimension is the varying thickness of the piece as cut and is usually at right angles to the skin of the boat; i.e., the dimension of a frame measured from the skin of the hull inboard is the molded dimension.

Spall—See Cross Spall.

Spar—A round- or square-sectioned mast, boom, yard, or bowsprit for the support of the sails and rigging.

Spile—To make a pattern for an oddly shaped piece, such as a plank, by recording measurements onto another piece of expendable stock. These measurements are then transferred to the actual stock and connected by battens and drawn in pencil to provide the proper shape of the new piece.

Spiling Batten—A long, flexible batten made of light stock to record information when spiling a plank.

Springback—Any bent stock, either steamed or laminated, will retain "memory" and try to straighten out to some extent when released from its clamps. The amount the piece straightens is called springback.

Stanchion—A supporting post or pillar, such as a vertical brace under a thwart.

Stations—Cross-sectional slices of the hull made at regular intervals. Similar to slices in a loaf of bread.

Staving—In boat construction, the equivalent of wainscoting.

Stealer—A short plank used to fill in an area or straighten out a run of planks.

Stemband—Protective strip of metal (usually half-round or oval) fastened to the face of the stem.

Sternpost—The vertical, or nearly vertical, backbone member that supports the transom.

Sternsheets—The seat and benches in the after end of an open boat.

Stopwater—A softwood dowel placed in a drilled hole where the rabbet crosses an underwater backbone joint. Used to stop water from leaking by into the hull, hence the pithy name.

Strake—A continuous longitudinal run of hull planking. A strake can be either a single plank or more than one plank fastened end to end.

Stretcher—A foot brace, usually adjustable, for the rower.

Strongback—A frame or horse to support a boat while under construction.

Stud Beam—A short beam under a side deck.

Template—A pattern made of thin stock for any structural member.

Thwart—A transverse seat in a small boat. It not only provides a place to sit but also ties the boat together.

Trammel Points—Two discrete points, usually steel or brass, that can be positioned anywhere on a bar, usually wooden, making a tool that can be used in the same manner as a compass or a pair of dividers.

Transom—The transverse structure (usually flat) at the after end of the boat on which the planks land.

Trunnel—A homemade dowel-like fastening that is driven into a pre-drilled hole and wedged at either end.

Tumblehome—The narrowing or returning inward of the topsides as they approach the sheer.

Turnbutton—A small button or cleat for holding in place doors, panels, and floorboards.

Waterline—On a set of plans, it is a regular height of elevation above a base—similar to those found on a topographic map. In profile view, the waterlines are straight and parallel. In the half-breadth view, they are curved.

Appendix B • Sources

PLANS

Adirondack Museum
P.O. Box 99
Blue Mountain Lake, NY 12812–0099
518–352–7311
Adirondack small craft incl J. H. Rushton.

John G. Alden, Inc.
Donald G. Parrot
89 Commercial Wharf
Boston, MA 02110
617–227–9480; fax 617–523–5465
More than 1,000 original plans dating back to the early 1900s.

Atkin & Co.
Pat or John Atkin
P.O. Box 3005
Noroton, CT 06820
203-655-0886
More than 200 designs previously published in Motor Boating. *Sailing dinghies, houseboats, double enders, utilities.*

R. H. Baker Boats
29 Drift Rd.
Westport, MA 02790
508–636–3272
Traditional small craft.

George Buehler Yacht Design
P.O. Box 966
Freeland, WA 98249
360–331–5866
Long-range cruising designs to 102'.

Howard I. Chapelle
Chesapeake Bay Maritime Museum
P.O. Box 636
St. Michaels, MD 21663–0636
410–745–2916
Yet more Chapelle.

Pete Culler Plans
George B. Kelley
22 Lookout Ln.
Hyannis, MA 02601
508–775–2679
100 Pete Culler designs from 11' pram to 125' Tern schooner.

Duck Trap Woodworking
Walter Simmons
P.O. Box 88
Lincolnville Beach, ME 04849
207–789-5363; fax 207–789–5124
Traditional wooden small craft.

Selway Fisher Design
15 King St.
Melksham, Wilts, UK, SN12 6HB
tel./fax (0)122 570 5074
Canoes and daysailers to steam and electric launches.

Glen-L Marine Designs
9152 Rosecrans Ave.
Bellflower, CA 90707
562–630–6258
Sailboats, canoes, dinghies, workboats, 7' to 55'.

William H. Hand, Jr.
Hart Nautical Collections
M.I.T. Museum
265 Massachusetts Ave.
Cambridge, MA 02139
617–253–5942; fax 617–258–9107
Elegant classics.

L. Francis Herreschoff
LFH Plans—Elizabeth Vaughn
620 Galland St.
Petaluma, CA 95952
Vessels of L. F. Herreschoff.

N. G. Herreschoff
Hart Nautical Collections
M.I.T. Museum
265 Massachusetts Ave.
Cambridge, MA 02139
617–253–5942; fax 617–258–9107
Works of the old master.

Independence Seaport Museum
211 S. Columbus Blvd.
Philadelphia, PA 19106–1415
215–925–5439
Traditional small craft.

George Lawley and Son
Hart Nautical Collections
M.I.T. Museum
265 Massachusetts Ave.
Cambridge, MA 02139
617–253–5942; fax 617–258–9107
Designs from 1910 to 1940.

Maine Maritime Museum
243 Washington St.
Bath, ME 04530
207–443–1316
Traditional small craft from the coast of Maine.

The Mariners' Museum
100 Museum Drive
Newport News, VA 23606–3759
804–596–2222
Nearly 50,000 plans on file detail the construction of modern pleasure craft (including Hacker and all Chris-Craft), warships, junks, schooners, sloops, steamboats, and much more.

Mystic Seaport Museum, Inc.
Ships Plans Division
P.O. Box 6000
Mystic, CT 06355–0990
860–572–5360 ext. 5028
Traditional small craft from the Mystic Seaport collection. Also plans of Elco, Henry Devereaux, F. D. Lawley, William F. Crosby, and others.

Iain Oughtred
Altyre Stables
Forres, Moray, UK, IV36 0SH
(0)130 967 3121; fax (0)130 967 6865
Lapstrake rowing and sailing craft.

Harold H. Payson and Co.
Pleasant Beach Rd.
S. Thomaston, ME 04858
207–594–7587
Instant boats and dories, as well as Phil Bolger designs.

San Francisco Maritime National Historical Park
Historic Documents Dept.
Building E, Fort Mason
San Francisco, CA 94123
415–556–9874
Plans for traditional and historic Pacific Coast vessels.

Smithsonian Institution
Div. of Transportation
NMAH 5010/MRC 628
Washington, D.C. 20560
Plans from the published works of Howard I. Chapelle and Harry V. Sucher.

Weston Farmer Associates
Mark Farmer
18970 W. Azure Rd.
Wayzata, MN 55391
612–470–0238
23 Weston Farmer designs including Tahitiana.

Joel White Designs
Brooklin Boat Yard, Inc.
P.O. Box 143
Brooklin, ME 04616
207–359–2236; fax 207–359–8871
Classic small craft up to 74' cruising craft.

Charles W. Wittholz, N.A.
Mrs. Estelle A. Wittholz
100 Williamsburg Dr.
Silver Spring, MD 20901
301–593–7711
Trawler yachts to plywood catboats.

The WoodenBoat Store
P.O. Box 78
Brooklin, ME 04616
800–273–7447
Various classic and new designs: kayaks, canoes, shells, rowing and sailing small craft.

TOOLS

Conant Engineering
P.O. Box 498
Boothbay, ME 04537
207–633–3004
Planking clamps.

Cumberland General Store
#1 Highway 68
Crossville, TN 38555
800–334–4640; fax 931–456–1211
Blacksmithing tools, anvils, forges, bolt rod nuts (nuts w/ handle for making homemade clamps), and rivet sets.

Faering Design
P.O. Box 322
E. Middlebury, VT 05740
802–388–8692
Copper clench nails, Norwegian and English boat nails, roves, rivets, and riveting tools.

Garrett Wade Company, Inc.
161 Sixth Ave.
New York, NY 10013
800-221-2942
Hand tools of all sorts.

John Henry, Inc.
P.O. Box 7473
Spanish Fort, AL 36577
334–626–2288
Tool to convert planer for scarfing plywood.

Jamestown Distributors
P.O. Box 348
Jamestown, RI 02835
800–423–0030
Hand tools, marine supplies.

Lee Valley Tools Ltd.
1080 Morrison Dr.
Ottawa, ON, Canada K2H 8K7
or
12 E. River St.
Ogdensburg, NY 13669
800–871–8158; fax 800–513–7885
Lots of hand tools.

Lehmans Non-Electric Catalog
Lehman Hardware and Appliances Inc.
P.O. Box 41
Kidron, Ohio 44636
330–857–5757; fax 330–857–5785
Blacksmithing tools, lead melting pots and ladles, woodworking tools, and gas hot plates.

Lie-Nielsen Tool Works
P.O. Box 9
Warren, ME 04864–0009
888–751–2106 or 800–327–2520
fax 207–273–2657
Makers of traditional woodworking tools.

Professional Graphics
P.O. Box 1327
Auburn, ME 04211
207–783–9132; fax 207–777–3570
Ship curves, adjustable curves, spline weights (ducks), scale rules, mechanical pencils, et al.

Sears Power and Hand Tools
2740 W. 79th St.
Chicago, IL 60652
800–377–7414
Hand and power tools. The catalog is back.

Tools on Sale
Seven Corners Hardware Inc.
216 W. 7th
St. Paul, MN 55102
800–328–0457
Discount power tools.

Wag-Aero
P.O. Box 181
Lyon, WI 53148
800–558–6868; fax 414–763–7595
Pneumatic tools—air drill, air hammer and rivet set, bucking bars, and other oddities such as wire twisters, snake drill attachment, and industrial heat gun.

Woodcraft
P.O. Box 1686
Parkersburg, WV 26102–1686
800–225–1153
Unusual or hard-to-find hand tools (spare parts for wood planes), domestic and imported. Also glues, hardware, and a selection of power equipment.

SUPPLIES

Davey & Co. London Ltd.
1, Chelmsford Rd. Ind Est.
Great Dunmow, UK, CM6 1HD
(0)137 187 6361
Traditional marine hardware, red lead powder, white lead paste, and lanocoat waterproofer.

Defender Marine Supply NY, Inc.
P.O. Box 820
New Rochelle, NY 10801
800–628–8225
Dynel cloth and other marine supplies.

DuPont Preservation Shipyard
Mystic Seaport Museum
P.O. Box 6000
Mystic, CT 06355
860–572–5343 (5341)
Genuine, high-quality, imported tarred hemp oakum.

Fisheries Supply Co.
1900 N. Northlake Way
Seattle, WA 98103
800–426–6930
Paints, compounds, fasteners, abrasives, etc.

George Kirby Paints
153 Mt. Vernon St.
New Bedford, MA
617–997–9008
Custom and old-time marine paints.

Hamilton Marine
P.O. Box 227
Searsport, ME 04974
207–548–6302 or 800–639–2715
Fasteners, paints, glues, hardware, oakum, and other marine supplies.

Jamestown Distributors
P.O. Box 348
Jamestown, RI 02835
800–423–0030; fax 800-423-0542
Fasteners, paints, hardware, glues, and tools (including Fuller bits).

Maritime Wood Products Corp.
3361 S.E. Slater St.
Stuart, FL 34997
800–274–8325
Boatbuilding and repair materials.

McFeely's
P.O. Box 11169
Lynchburg, VA 24506–1169
800–443–7937; fax 800–847–7136
Square drive screws, et al.

Newman B. Gee
281 Hartland Rd.
St. Albans, ME 04971
207–938–2380
Hackmatack (a.k.a. tamarack, larch) knees.

Northwoods Canoe Co.
336 Range Rd.
Atkinson, ME 04426
888–534–2710; fax 207–564–3667
Canoe hardware, canoe tacks, clenching irons, and plans.

Pert Lowell Co., Inc.
Lane's End
Newbury, MA 01951
978–462–7409
Mast hoops, parrel beads, wood cleats, and custom bronze hardware.

Robbins Timber
Merrywood Rd.
Bedminster, Bristol, BS3 1DX, UK
(0)117 963 3136, fax (0)117 963 7927
WEST SYSTEM epoxy, lumber, and lots more.

Rostand RI, Inc.
P.O. Box 737
Chepachet, RI 02814
tel./fax 800–635–0063 or 401–949–4268
Specializes in 1930s and other difficult-to-find hardware.

Standard Fastening
800 Mt. Pleasant St.
New Bedford, MA 02745
800–678–8811; fax 508–995–3886
Fasteners, paints, hardware, glues, etc.

Strawberry Banke, Inc.
P.O. Box 300 BBM
Portsmouth, NH 03801
603–433–1100; fax 603–433–1129
Copper clench nails.

Traditional Marine Outfitters
58 Fore St.
Portland, ME 04101
207–773–7745
        or
P.O. Box 268
Annapolis Royal, NS, Canada B0S 1A0
902–532–2762
Traditional old-time hardware.

Tremont Nail Co.
P.O. Box 111
Wareham, MA 02571
508–295–0038 or 800–842–0560
Hot-galvanized boat nails

W. H. Keys Ltd.
Church Ln.
W. Bromwich
W. Midlands, UK, B71 1BN
(0)121 553 0206; fax (0)121 500 5820
Alfred Jeffery marine glue.

The Wooden Boat Shop
1007 N.E. Boat St.
Seattle, WA 98105
800–933–3600
Rove irons, clench nails, Hall & Rice rivets and roves, Irish ship sheathing felt, oakum, cotton, and caulking irons.

GLUES

Aircraft Spruce and Specialty Co.
225 Airport Cir.
Corona, CA 91720
909–372–9555 or 800–824–1930
Aerolite: two-part waterproof glue.

Dynochem UK Ltd.
Alyn Works
Denbigh Rd.
Mold, Flintshire, UK, CH7 1BF
(0)135 275 7657; fax (0)135 275 8914
Aerodux resorcinol glue.

Gorilla Glue
The Gorilla Group
P.O. Box 42532
Santa Barbara, CA 93140-2532
805–884–4065
Unique one-part waterproof glue.

Gougeon Brothers, Inc.
P.O. Box 908
Bay City, MI 48707
517–684–7286
WEST SYSTEM epoxy and supplies.

Industrial Formulators of Canada, Ltd.
3824 William St.
Burnaby, BC, Canada V5C 3H9
604–294–6315 or 800–778–0833
G2 epoxy (for gluing oily hardwoods) and Cold Cure.

Matrix Adhesive Systems
1501 Sherman Ave.
Pennsauken, NJ 08110
888–627–3769
        or
MAS Europe Ltd.
P.O. Box 90
Truro, Cornwall, UK, TR4 84E
(0)187 256 0675; fax (0)187 256 0188
Epoxy and supplies.

System Three Resins
P.O. Box 70436
Seattle, WA 98107
206–782–7976
Epoxy and supplies.

Wessex Resins and Adhesives Ltd.
Cupernham House
Cupernham Ln.
Romsey, Hants, UK, SO51 7LF
(0)179 452 1111; fax (0)179 451 7779
WEST SYSTEM epoxy and supplies.

APPENDIX C • TABLES

ENGLISH — METRIC CONVERSION TABLES

Fraction, Decimal, and Millimeter Equivalents
Conversion: 1 mm = .03937″   .001″ = .0254 mm

Fraction	Decimal	Millimeter	Fraction	Decimal	Millimeter
1/64	.015625	0.397	33/64	.515625	13.097
1/32	.03125	0.794	17/32	.53125	13.494
3/64	.046875	1.191	35/64	.546875	13.891
1/16	.0625	1.588	9/16	.5625	14.288
5/64	.078125	1.984	37/64	.578125	14.684
3/32	.09375	2.381	19/32	.59375	15.081
7/64	.109375	2.778	39/64	.609375	15.478
1/8	.125	3.175	5/8	.6250	15.875
9/64	.140625	3.572	41/64	.640625	16.272
5/32	.15625	3.969	21/32	.65625	16.669
11/64	.171875	4.366	43/64	.671875	17.066
3/16	.1875	4.763	11/16	.6875	17.463
13/64	.203125	5.159	45/64	.703125	17.859
7/32	.21875	5.556	23/32	.71875	18.256
15/64	.234375	5.953	47/64	.734375	18.653
1/4	.25	6.350	3/4	.75	19.050
17/64	.265625	6.747	49/64	.765625	19.447
9/32	.28125	7.144	25/32	.78125	19.844
19/64	.296875	7.541	51/64	.796875	20.241
5/16	.3125	7.938	13/16	.8125	20.638
21/64	.328125	8.334	53/64	.828125	21.034
11/32	.34375	8.731	27/32	.84375	21.431
23/64	.359375	9.128	55/64	.859375	21.828
3/8	.375	9.525	7/8	.875	22.225
25/64	.390625	9.922	57/64	.890625	22.622
13/32	.40625	10.319	29/32	.90625	23.019
27/64	.421875	10.716	59/64	.921875	23.416
7/16	.4375	11.113	15/16	.9375	23.813
29/64	.453125	11.509	61/64	.953125	24.209
15/32	.46875	11.906	31/32	.96875	24.606
31/64	.484375	12.303	63/64	.984375	25.003
1/2	.5	12.700	1	1.000	25.400

SOURCE: K. L. JACK INDUSTRIAL FASTENER CO., 145 WARREN AVE., PORTLAND, ME 04102

MILLIMETERS TO INCHES

mm	Inches	mm	Inches	mm	Inches	mm	Inches
.1	.0039	19	.7480	46	1.8110	73	2.8740
.2	.0079	20	.7874	47	1.8504	74	2.9134
.3	.0118	21	.8268	48	1.8898	75	2.9528
.4	.0158	22	.8661	49	1.9291	76	2.9921
.5	.0197	23	.9055	50	1.9685	77	3.0315
.6	.0236	24	.9449	51	2.0079	78	3.0709
.7	.0276	25	.9843	52	2.0472	79	3.1102
.8	.0315	26	1.0236	53	2.0866	80	3.1496
.9	.0354	27	1.0630	54	2.1260	81	3.1890
1	.0394	28	1.1024	55	2.1654	82	3.2283
2	.0787	29	1.1417	56	2.2047	83	3.2677
3	.1181	30	1.1811	57	2.2441	84	3.3071
4	.1575	31	1.2205	58	2.2835	85	3.3465
5	.1969	32	1.2598	59	2.3228	86	3.3858
6	.2362	33	1.2992	60	2.3622	87	3.4252
7	.2756	34	1.3386	61	2.4016	88	3.4646
8	.3150	35	1.3780	62	2.4409	89	3.5039
9	.3543	36	1.4173	63	2.4803	90	3.5433
10	.3937	37	1.4567	64	2.5197	91	3.5827
11	.4331	38	1.4961	65	2.5591	92	3.6220
12	.4724	39	1.5354	66	2.5984	93	3.6614
13	.5118	40	1.5748	67	2.6378	94	3.7008
14	.5512	41	1.6142	68	2.6772	95	3.7402
15	.5906	42	1.6535	69	2.7165	96	3.7795
16	.6299	43	1.6929	70	2.7559	97	3.8189
17	.6693	44	1.7323	71	2.7953	98	3.8583
18	.7087	45	1.7717	72	2.8346	99	3.8976
						100	3.9370

SOURCE: K. L. JACK INDUSTRIAL FASTENER CO., 145 WARREN AVE., PORTLAND, ME 04102

FLATHEAD SCREWS FOR PLANKING

Plank Thickness	Screw Length and Size
³⁄₈″	¾″ x No. 7
½″	1″ x No. 8
⅝″	1¼″ x No. 8 or 9
¾″	1½″ x No. 10
⅞″	1¾″ x No. 12
1″	2″ x No. 14
1³⁄₈″	2¼″ x No. 16
1¼″	2½″ x No. 18
1½″	3″ x No. 20

SOURCE: *SKENE'S ELEMENTS OF YACHT DESIGN*

SHANK CLEARANCE HOLE BORING RECOMMENDATIONS

Bit or Drill Sizes

Screw No.	Shank Clearance Holes	Pilot Holes Hard Wood	Soft Wood
7	22	39	51
8	18	35	48
9	14	33	45
10	10	31	43
12	2	25	38
14	D	14	32
16	I	10	29

SOURCE: K. L. JACK INDUSTRIAL FASTENER CO., 145 WARREN AVE., PORTLAND, ME 04102

RIVETS (US)

Size Nail	Burr to Rivet Fit			Size	Copper Burrs Hole I.D.	Approx. Count/Lb.
	Loose	Drive				
15	15	N/A		14	0.093	2050
14	14	N/A		13	0.106	1350
12	12	13		12	0.124	1240
11	12	13		10	0.138	750
10	9	10		9	0.146	580
9	8	9		8	0.166	465
8	7	8		7	0.176	380
6	5	6		6	0.206	184

COPPER COMMON NAILS

Penny	Gauge	Length	Shank Diameter	Head Diameter	Approx. Count/Lb.
2d	15	1″	0.072	$3/16$″	685
3d	14	$1\frac{1}{4}$″	0.083	$3/16$″	424
4d	12	$1\frac{1}{2}$″	0.109	$1/4$″	205
5d	12	$1\frac{3}{4}$″	0.109	$1/4$″	165
6d	11	2″	0.120	$9/32$″	133
8d	10	$2\frac{1}{2}$″	0.134	$5/16$″	86
10d	9	3″	0.148	$5/16$″	55
12d	9	$3\frac{1}{4}$″	0.148	$5/16$″	52
16d	8	$3\frac{1}{2}$″	0.165	$3/8$″	40
20d	6	4″	0.203	$7/16$″	23
40d	4	5″	0.238	$17/32$″	14

SOURCE: JAMESTOWN DISTRIBUTORS CATALOG

FASTENER ALLOYS

Nominal Composition of Corrosion Resistant Nail Materials

Copper	Silicon Bronze	304 Stainless	316 Stainless	Monel
Cu 99.92%	Cu 96.75%	Fe 71%	Fe 68.5%	Ni 67%
O2 .08%	Si 3.25%	Cr 19%	Cr 17.0%	Cu 31.6%
	Ni 10%	Ni 12.0%	Fe 1.4%	
		Mo 2.5%		

SOURCE: HAMILTON MARINE CATALOG

LIQUIDS

1 pint = 0.4732 liter
1 pint = 0.5000 quart
1 quart = 0.9464 liter
1 quart = 0.2500 gallon
1 US gallon = 3.785 liter
1 liter = 2.113 pints
1 liter = 1.057 quart
1 liter = 0.2642 U.S. gallon
1 imperial gallon = 1.2 U.S. gallon
1 U.S. gallon = .833 imperial gallon

WEIGHT

1 ounce = 28.35 grams
1 gram = 0.03527 ounce
1 pound = 16 ounces
1 pound = 453.6 grams
1 kilogram = 2.2046 pounds

APPENDIX D • BIBLIOGRAPHY

That's the thing about boatbuilding, you never know it all.
—John W. Brown, master shipwright

Perhaps that is why people build boats: each one is different from the last. The technique that may have worked so well previously might be a total washout on this job; the new adhesive you were so skeptical about could be just the thing that will save the day. On the other hand, a method your grandfather used might do the job twice as fast as you can with the new whiz-bang device you just spent $300 for. In this business you are always learning, always being challenged.

Of course, the best way to learn the traditional tricks of the trade is at the side of an old-timer. But old-timers are getting more and more difficult to find these days, or they may not be where you are, and besides, some old-timers are not as forthcoming with their patented tricks of the trade as one might hope.

And then there are the new guys on the block with their iconoclastic techniques and bubbling pots of glue. If you are looking for information on the higher qualities of hackmatack knees, these fellows might not be the ones to ask.

You can always throw caution to the winds and just "go for it." There is a certain virtue in making all your own errors, if you have the time and the money. But if you don't? That's where perusing the boatbuilding books comes in.

There is something to be said for getting the opinion of Bud McIntosh or John Gardner before jumping into a task you've never done before. And instead of grumbling about that blasted epoxy that didn't work the way you wanted it to, why not confer with the Gougeon Brothers? Lofting seem beyond the pale? Maybe a session with Allan Vaitses or Sam Rabl will convince you otherwise.

Is a book a substitute for practical experience or a face-to-face chat with that fabled old-timer? Of course not. But a good boatbuilding book will get you started in the right direction, provide inspiration to ask the right questions, and give you the courage to tackle the job. Maybe that's good enough.

The following is a but a sampler of some reference works that have proven valuable to me and others. Most are still in print. A few, such as Hervey Garrett Smith's *Boat Carpentry* or Allan Vaitses's *Lofting*, are like Brigadoon: They appear briefly, then vanish. All are chock-full of good information, tips, data, and lore; all are intended to obviate reinventing the wheel.

TRADITIONAL BOATBUILDING

Bingham, Fred P. *Boat Joinery and Cabinetmaking Simplified.* (Published in 1983 as *Practical Yacht Joinery.*) Camden, ME: International Marine, 1993. ISBN 0-07-87742-354-7.

An excellent how-to volume presented in two parts. The first deals with tools, both hand and electric, their use, techniques, handy jigs, and accessories. The second part deals with joinery—interior, cabin sole, galley, decks, spars, bulkheads, berths, patterns, and more. A boon to anyone finishing out a 'glass hull, with plenty of application for the traditionally built wooden boat as well.

Chapelle, Howard I. *Boatbuilding.* New York: W. W. Norton & Co., 1941, 1994. ISBN 0-393-03554-9.

Still considered the must-have "bible" for traditional boatbuilding, encyclopedic in scope, this volume covers nearly all facets of construction (at least up to 1940) from plans to painting. The volume documents the construction of flat-bottom, V-bottom, and round bottom (both carvel and lapstrake) hulls, as well as joinerwork, plumbing, sparmaking, finishing, and tools.

Dept. of the Navy. Wood: *A Manual for Its Use as a Shipbuilding Material.* 1957. Rev. ed., Kingston, MA: Teaparty Books, 1983. ISBN 0-9610602-0-4.

A collection of four volumes produced from 1945 to 1957 by the Department of the Navy, with the cooperation of the Forest Products Laboratory, Forest Service, and the Department of Agriculture, this work was originally intended as a reference manual for Navy shipwrights. Invaluable resource for understanding the characteristics of wood as an engineering material, wood preservation, causes of rot, lamination, repairs, steam-bending, scarfing, wood storage, why fastenings work (or fail), and much more.

Gardner, John. *The Dory Book.* 1978. Reprint, Mystic, CT: Mystic Seaport Museum, Inc., 1987. ISBN 0-913372-44-7.

The best (and perhaps only) book written on the dory. Combining John Gardner's clear writing style and Sam Manning's top-notch drawings, the book not only illustrates the unique building techniques used in these boats, but also provides a historical background, a clear explanation of lofting and lines, and complete plans for 23 boats.

Gardner, John. *Building Classic Small Craft.* Rev. ed. of vols. 1 & 2, Camden, ME: International Marine, 1997. ISBN 0-07-022864-7.

No one has had more influence on the revival of interest in classic boat construction than John Gardner, and it could be said that no book has inspired more builders than this one. This is a how-to volume with 20-plus designs that can be built right from this book. Containing plenty of construction details, a good appendix on boatbuilding methods, and a healthy dollop of historical background, this tome not only has plenty of information but also is a good read as well.

Gougeon Brothers. *The Gougeon Brothers on Boat Construction.* 1979. 4th ed., rev., Bay City, MI: Gougeon Brothers, Inc., 1985. ISBN 0-87812-166-8.

If you are new to working with epoxy, this is a good place to start. Plenty of techniques illustrated as well as problems to avoid. Also includes a good chapter on lofting and perhaps the best treatise on boatshop safety and health concerns in print. Well worth reading.

Leather, John. *Clinker Boatbuilding.* 1973. Reprint, London: Adlard Coles Nautical, 1996. ISBN 0-7136-3643-2.

For some reason little has been written on the subject of lapstrake (clinker) planking. Yet, this technique is light, rugged, and elegant, and therefore a planking style well worth considering. This clearly written classic takes you though the construction of a small sailing lapstrake boat from setup to spars, including oars, using English techniques.

Lowell, Royal. *Boatbuilding Down East.* 1977. Reprint, S. Portland, ME: Simonton Cove Publishing Co., 1994. ISBN 0-87742-088-2.

A book oft-overlooked by those not in the market for a lobster boat. This book takes you through the construction of a traditional wooden hulled powerboat in a progression that makes sense. Plenty of techniques and tricks of the trade are illustrated, pitfalls to be avoided are duly noted, and homemade tools and jigs demonstrated. This is good, rugged, no-frills boatbuilding.

McIntosh, David C. "Bud." *How to Build a Wooden Boat.* Brooklin, ME: WoodenBoat Publications, Inc., 1987. ISBN 0-937822-10-8.

This one takes you though the construction of a larger, ballast-keel hull, from soup to nuts. With Bud McIntosh's pithily descriptive text and Sam Manning's drawings you have the tools to lay a deck, cut a rabbet, fit a deckhouse, and more.

Rabl, S. S. *Boatbuilding in Your Own Backyard.* 1947. 2nd ed., Centreville, MD: Cornell Maritime Press, Inc., 1958. ISBN 0-87033-009-8.

Albeit a bit dated, this is a good, can-do introductory volume covering the nuts and bolts and beyond, including tool making, lofting, set-up, framing, planking, and patternmaking.

Smith, Hervey Garrett. *Boat Carpentry.* 1955. 2nd ed., rev., New York: Van Nostrand Rheinhold Co., 1965. ISBN 0-442-37784-3.

Lots of non-dogmatic tips on woods, tools and tool use, glues, fastenings, repairs, etc.

Planking & Fastening. Edited by Peter H. Spectre. Brooklin, ME: WoodenBoat Publications, Inc., 1996. ISBN 0-937822-41-8.

Gleaned from the pages of *WoodenBoat* magazine, this book contains techniques presented by various boatbuilders: planking, butt blocks, scarfing and plywood, fastenings—screws through clench nails—the last word on galvanic action, and a multiplicity of clamps.

Steward, Robert M. *Boatbuilding Manual.* 4th ed., Camden, ME: International Marine, 1994. ISBN 0-87742-379-2.

This hard-to-beat volume has been constantly updated over the years and is as fresh as it was when first published in 1970. It offers a thorough exploration and explanation of plans, tools, wood, fiberglass, fastenings, lofting, backbones, molds and setup, framing, planking, decks, and plenty more. Another must-have, as it takes up where Chapelle's *Boatbuilding* leaves off.

LOFTING

Rabl, S. S. *Ship and Aircraft Fairing and Development*. Centreville, MD: Cornell Maritime Press, Inc., 1992. ISBN 0-870330-96-9.

Although not the last word on lofting, Rabl's approach (first published in 1941) is definitely user friendly, light on turgid jargon and heavy on the easy to understand drawings. A good introduction that makes you feel as if maybe lofting isn't such a big deal after all. Also contains a tasteful lines plan for a Glenn Martin *China Clipper*.

Vaitses, Allan H. *Lofting*. Camden, ME: International Marine, 1980. ISBN 0-87742-113-7.

For many, lofting is a mystical art better left to high priests, yet it is an essential step in building a boat—unless one is resigned to using only kit boats and patterns. A tough subject to write about, and Vaites has done the best job to date.

REPAIR

Scarlett, John. *Wooden Boat Repair Manual*. Camden, ME: International Marine, 1981. ISBN 0-87742-143-9.

In many ways, building a boat is easier than repairing or restoring one. New construction is done in a systematic fashion. Repairs are done "out of order" and are definitely romance challenged. Scarlett introduces some fiendishly clever tips that restorers use in order to save a hull, be it replacing frames, planks, decks, or a stem.

Frame, Stem & Keel Repair. Edited by Peter H. Spectre. Brooklin, ME: WoodenBoat Publications, Inc., 1996. ISBN 0-937822-42-6.

Another compilation from the pages of *WoodenBoat*. Ingredients are as advertised, plus building a gaggle of steam boxes, what makes wood bend, laminating, keelbolts, and lots more.

HISTORY AND DESIGN

Bray, Maynard. *Mystic Seaport Museum Watercraft*. Mystic, CT: Mystic Seaport Museum, Inc., 1979. ISBN 0-913372-16-1.

Lines plans are great, but many times they leave out the details that can only be garnered from a photo of the real McCoy. In this fine catalog of Mystic Seaport Museum's extensive collection, you'll find photos accompanied by a brief historical sketch of each craft. Also included are 57 pages of plans.

Chapelle, Howard I. *American Small Sailing Craft*. New York: W. W. Norton & Co., Inc., 1951. ISBN 0-393-03143-8.

If you have been thinking that there are but a few traditional small craft designs to choose from, take a tour with Mr. Chapelle as he introduces you to scores of fascinating American small craft—including garveys, sailing dories, sharpies, Whitehalls, peapods, and skipjacks. Contains more than 100 plans and perspectives, many of which are available in building scale from the Smithsonian Institution at bargain rates.

Chapelle, Howard I. *Yacht Designing and Planning*. 1936. New York: W. W. Norton and Company, Inc., 1971. ISBN 0-393-03756-8.

While not every builder or boat owner wishes to create their own design, it is valuable to have an insight into what goes into developing one. This volume first introduces the reader to the use of drafting instruments, battens, and scale rules that are used to draw a set of plans and then clearly explains the meaning of the terms, lines, table of offsets and the various views on a set of plans. Without getting bogged down in theoretical calculations, Chapelle explains how displacement and center of gravity are derived, and offers rules of thumb on ballasting. In addition he explains the purpose and importance of various key components that go into the hull. To top it off, there is an appendix containing weights, capacities, which wood to use where, and more.

Skene, Norman L. *Skene's Elements of Yacht Design*. 1927. 8th ed., rev. and updated by Francis S. Kinney. New York: Dodd, Mead & Company, Inc., 1981. ISBN 0-396-06582-1.

A classic, brimming with tables, specifications, rules, calculations, and other useful data. Also includes an explanation of terms, selecting propellers, spars and rigging, tools required for designing, and ruminations on what makes a boat look good.